PRAISE FOR *SUPPLY CHAIN MANAGEMENT FOR HUMANITARIANS*

'This book is a huge leap forward in professionalizing the field. Practice of good supply chain management can only make delivering relief more effective. Kudos to the contributors and the editors for filling this need.'
Nezih Altay, Co-editor, *Journal of Humanitarian Logistics and Supply Chain Management*

'Written by expert authors in their field, this book offers a distinct perspective on how the problem-solving capacity of supply chain management principles can help humanitarian organizations and aid workers to operate under conditions that are much more complex, unpredictable and resource-demanding than we find in conventional "commercial" supply chains. This is a well-structured and comprehensive piece of work that guides the reader through well-designed and -executed solutions, supported by examples from various parts of the world. Cutting across topics such as supply chain strategy, procurement, warehousing, transportation, risk and sustainability, combined with generic skills of, eg, decision making and performance measurement, this book paves the way for the personal development of aid workers and their humanitarian organizations.'
Árni Halldórsson, Professor, Chalmers University of Technology, Sweden

'Nobody is more passionate or knowledgeable about humanitarian supply chain management than the HUMLOG team of Ira Haavisto, Gyöngyi Kovács and Karen Spens. They've assembled a great team of authors to guide you through the essentials of managing humanitarian supply chains – from the strategic view at 10,000 metres, to delivering aid where the rubber meets the road. They cover all of the latest topics,

including risk, sustainability, and the role of 3D printing. So, if you're interested in travelling the challenging but rewarding highway of humanitarian supply chains, this is the right place to start your journey.'
Stan Fawcett, John B Goddard Endowed Chair in Global SCM, and Director, Moyes Center for Supply Chain Excellence, Weber State University

Supply Chain Management For Humanitarians

Supply Chain Management For Humanitarians

Tools for practice

Edited by
Ira Haavisto
Gyöngyi Kovács
Karen Spens

KoganPage

First published in Great Britain and the United States in 2016 by Kogan Page Limited

2nd Floor, 45 Gee Street	1518 Walnut Street, Suite 900	4737/23 Ansari Road
London EC1V 3RS	Philadelphia PA 19102	Daryaganj
United Kingdom	USA	New Delhi 110002
www.koganpage.com		India

© Ira Haavisto, Gyöngyi Kovács, Karen Spens, 2016

The right of each commissioned author of this work to be identified as an author of this work has been asserted by him/her in accordance with the Copyright, Designs and Patents Act 1988.

ISBN   978 0 7494 7468 3
E-ISBN   978 0 7494 7469 0

British Library Cataloguing-in-Publication Data

A CIP record for this book is available from the British Library.

Library of Congress Cataloging-in-Publication Data

Names: Haavisto, Ira, author. | Kovacs, Gyongyi, 1977- author. | Spens, Karen M., 1963- author.
Title: Supply chain management for humanitarians : tools for practice /
    Ira Haavisto, Gyöngyi Kovács and Karen Spens.
Description: 1st Edition. | Philadelphia : Kogan Page, 2016. | Includes bibliographical references and index.
Identifiers: LCCN 2016022389 (print) | LCCN 2016029776 (ebook) | ISBN 9780749474683
    (alk. paper) | ISBN 9780749474690 (eISBN)
Subjects: LCSH: Business logistics. | Humanitarian assistance.
Classification: LCC HD38.5 .K683 2016 (print) | LCC HD38.5 (ebook) | DDC 361.2/50687--dc 3
LC record available at https://lccn.loc.gov/2016022389

Typeset by Graphicraft Limited, Hong Kong
Print production managed by Jellyfish
Printed and bound by CPI Group (UK) Ltd, Croydon, CR0 4YY

CONTENTS

PART THREE Supply chain strategy 77

PART FOUR Decision making in the supply chain 101

5.3   A procurement project in the Philippines 173

Jonas Stumpf (HELP Logistics – a programme of the Kuehne Foundation, Asia Office), Maximilian Foehse (HELP Logistics – a programme of the Kuehne Foundation, Asia Office) and Tom Godfrey (Save the Children, Asia Regional Office)

5.4   Partnerships and innovative procurement as enablers for sustainable development goals 182

Rolando M Tomasini, Head of Global Outreach at the United Nations Office for Project Services (UNOPS)

PART SIX Transportation, fleet management, delivery and distribution 189

6.1   Transport in humanitarian supply chains 191

Ruth Banomyong (Thammasat University, Thailand) and David B Grant (HUMLOG Institute, Finland and Hull University Business School, UK)

6.2   Humanitarian aid supply corridors: Europe–Iraq 209

*Anthony Beresford, Stephen Pettit and Ziad al Hashimi, Cardiff Business
School, Cardiff University, UK*

PART SEVEN Warehouse and inventory management 223

7.1   Warehousing in humanitarian logistics 225

*Alain Vaillancourt, Jönköping International Business School, Centre of
Logistics and Supply Chain Management, and HUMLOG Institute, Finland*

7.2   The ABC analysis 246

*Alain Vaillancourt, Jönköping International Business School, Centre of
Logistics and Supply Chain Management, and HUMLOG Institute, Finland*

PART EIGHT Information technology 257

PART NINE Sustainability, performance measurement, monitoring/evaluation and exit strategy 299

PART ONE
Logistics and supply chain management in the humanitarian context

Introduction   1.1

IRA HAAVISTO, GYÖNGYI KOVÁCS AND KAREN M SPENS

Humanitarian Logistics and Supply Chain Research Institute (HUMLOG Institute), Hanken School of Economics, Helsinki, Finland

Introduction

The need to focus on, and continuously improve, humanitarian logistics is tremendous. Natural disasters affect more and more people every year, which implies a continuous increase in the need for humanitarian aid – and for logistics and supply chain management to support the delivery of this aid. Furthermore, external trends such as climate change and urbanization are expected to increase the impacts of disasters in the future. Yet natural disasters are just a fraction of what impacts on humanity and society. We are surrounded by news of humanitarian crises around the world, where societies are demolished and people are hurt. According to the United Nations (UN), the biggest humanitarian crises that occurred during 2014 were the war in Syria, the escalated violence in Iraq, the ongoing violence in the Central African Republic, the ongoing and escalating violence in Sudan and South Sudan, ongoing conflicts in Afghanistan, and the Ebola outbreak in West Africa. None of these are captured under the umbrella of a natural disaster, yet all of these require a large-scale humanitarian response.

According to the UN OCHA report (2014), individuals estimated to be in need of humanitarian assistance rose from 82 million people in 2013 to 101 million in 2014. Some of the less sympathy-awaking humanitarian crises such as those in the Central African Republic and in Iraq were funded only up to 10 per cent of the estimated need, according to the same UN OCHA report. Not surprisingly, one of the elements in which logistics and supply chain management in the humanitarian context differs from business logistics is in operating under constrained supplies. Balcik and Beamon

(2008:102) summarize the characteristics of humanitarian supply chains as operating under the following conditions:

- unpredictability of demand in terms of timing, location, type and size;
- suddenly occurring demand in very large amounts and short lead times for a wide variety of supplies;
- high stakes associated with adequate and timely delivery;
- lack of resources (supply, people, technology, transportation capacity and money).

Even more to the point, Arminas (2005: 14) sums it up as 'purchasing and logistics for major disaster relief is like having the client from hell – you never know beforehand what they want, when they want it, how much they want and even where they want it sent'.

Apart from the disasters that hit the news, there are other, forgotten events, which have received less media attention: the Ludian earthquake that hit south-west China on 3 August 2014, with 230,000 people estimated to be affected; floods in the Balkans in May of the same year, with some 1.6 million people affected; and the ongoing and escalating food insecurity in the Sahel region in Africa, where the UN estimated that in 2014 over 20 million people were in need of humanitarian assistance, as compared to 11 million in 2013. Receiving much more media attention was the refugee crisis in the European Union (EU), which is thought to be only the tip of the iceberg. Globally, by the end of 2015, an estimated 60 million people had to leave their homes to live in internally displaced person (IDP) and refugee camps.

All these events are such that the societies themselves cannot care for those in need within their own borders. Thus, what triggers external humanitarian assistance, according to international law, is that a country in question calls for help. In practice, this means that international humanitarian organizations need an invitation to move in, or at least a mandate to operate.

Due to the complexity of disasters, the operational space of humanitarian aid workers has diminished. International aid workers are no longer guaranteed a safe and secure operating environment. This is due to the increase in humanitarian aid requests in the category of complex disaster. A complex disaster means several events occurring simultaneously or occurring in close sequence, which leads to humanitarian crises. Most of the humanitarian events on the African continent today can be classified as complex disaster. For example, they might have experienced simultaneously drought, a man-made conflict, and a cholera or measles outbreak. Many of these disasters even trigger one another in a cascade. This complexity in most humanitarian settings today can lead to extreme operating conditions for any humanitarian worker, which leads to high turnover of staff. This, in turn, can lead to inefficiencies, particularly regarding knowledge transfer and standard operating procedures.

Humanitarian organizations function in circumstances where they are both responding to an acute humanitarian need, eg in the aftermath of an earthquake or a battle; and simultaneously responding to a need to build back a society or at least maintain parts of societal functions in the form of, for example, continued schooling for children and maintaining a means of livelihood.

But how can a society and the families in the society maintain their means for living in the midst of a crisis? Man-made conflicts, in particular, tend to limit the mobility of both individuals and livestock. Limited mobility has been problematic in South Sudan, where the pastorals cannot move their cattle to the pastures they have used for centuries. Maintaining means of livelihood becomes even more complicated if families and individuals are on the move due to displacement from their homes. Thus, a large proportion of humanitarian activity is directed towards building up or striving to maintain the means of livelihood of affected populations. This can, however, be tricky, since the main goal of humanitarian efforts is to save lives, decrease suffering and aid the affected society to return to a status quo. Status quo is, by the humanitarian responders, often seen as the situation as it was before the crises started. This vision is sometimes not the same as the one of the people and the societies in need. A beneficiary or 'end user'[1] might have spent 20 years in a refugee camp (such as the refugee camp of Kakuma, where the third generation of refugee camp citizens have been born). During those 20 years, the surrounding world has moved on and the status quo is not the same any more. As stated by a humanitarian logistician at the Food and Agriculture Organization of the United Nations – 'No one wants buckets any more.'

Therefore, the humanitarian responders and the end user (beneficiary or right holder) are in a predicament where they need to figure out what the 'new' society could look like and how the humanitarian activities can best support this vision of a society. For humanitarian activities to take into consideration a long-term vision from the start of an operation, such as in response to an earthquake, a close relation with the aided community and an awareness of sustainability has been identified as a solution to linking long-term and short-term thinking in a humanitarian setting.

But can one request a humanitarian aid worker to keep in mind the aspect of 'linking relief, rehabilitation and development' (LRRD), such as the importance of procuring sustainable products, when people are dying and time is of the essence? Humanitarian workers themselves were asked to reflect on the debate over aid effectiveness in a book published on stories from humanitarians (Bergman, 2003). They were asked what they think of accusations that their work could potentially be doing more harm than good: for example, that end users might become dependent on aid; local markets might get distorted; and that aid might potentially prolong the conflict rather than contribute to the end of it. Humanitarian workers replied by saying, 'How can we not help? How can we stay away when such immense suffering is going on?'

Humanitarian organizations thus state that people come first – everything else, including sustainability, comes second. In an immediate humanitarian crisis, this is natural, but it can also lead to situations where humanitarian activity has done more bad than good. During aid efforts in Afghanistan, for example, most of the water supplied was handed out in small plastic bottles, thus, in the long run, it caused a major waste management problem with plots of potential agricultural land littered with empty water bottles. Is this sustainable? No. Is it natural that, as a humanitarian officer, one does not think about a potential waste problem in an immediate humanitarian crisis? Yes. What could be a solution to similar problems? An obvious response – and a word much used in supply chain management – is planning, or, in the humanitarian context, preparedness! If operations are planned well beforehand, they can be executed quickly at short notice without compromising long-term goals.

Currently, countries with reoccurring natural disasters are setting up systems of early warning as well as quick response units. In Thailand, a new tsunami early warning system has been set up nationwide. In Bangladesh, a complex structure of warning systems, evacuation routes and shelters has been set up, as well as preparedness integrated into the education system. Together, these efforts resulted in dramatically lowering the number of people killed in the cyclone season, from around 500,000 in 1970 during the Category 4 Bhola cyclone to under 5,000 during (also Category 4) cyclone Sidr in 2007 – compared with another similar-strength cyclone, Nargis, resulting in the estimated deaths of 150,000 people in neighbouring Myanmar in 2008 (Tatham, Spens and Oloruntoba, 2009).

Globally, humanitarian organizations have set up hubs where they pre-position stock, and prepare rosters to be able to mobilize people in the event of a disaster. Planning is therefore an essential part of all humanitarian activity. Unfortunately, humanitarian organizations criticize the funding structure they operate under, as a structure that does not support planning.

Donors, both institutional and private, are reluctant to support humanitarian activity in advance. This means that when an event such as an earthquake or tsunami hits, funds and supplies are donated – yet not beforehand, because of the fear that these funds will be used up by heavy administration. Unfortunately, this administration is exactly where the planning could occur. When a disaster hits, supplies and services are nevertheless rushed to the location – some well-planned, some less planned. There is an influx of people, supplies and services. But why are these supply chains of importance? Because the supply chain encompasses the processes and activities that lead to the end user getting what they need, when and where they need it. And humanitarian logistics is reported to amount to as much as 70 or even 80 per cent of the total cost of humanitarian efforts. Humanitarian organizations are consequently said to resemble logistics service providers.

The effect is that humanitarians and humanitarian organizations have started paying more and more attention to their supply chains and logistics activities. Anthony Lake, executive director at the United Nations Children's Emergency Fund (UNICEF), stated in an interview in 2012 that the greatest achievement of UNICEF was some of the high-impact, low-cost innovations that UNICEF has helped pioneer. He listed three factors: oral rehydration salts, greatly expanded vaccination campaigns, and developing supply chains to reach the most remote communities.

The essence of supply chains is to match supply and demand. But what happens with supply chains and, particularly, what can supply chain performance be, in a context where the demand is neither dictated by nor is the performance of the supply chain directly evaluated by the end users? What happens with supply chain performance in a context where the conditions are ever changing and harsh in almost every aspect one can think of? One where IT solutions are of no use since there is no electricity, or where the routes that were optimized for delivery cannot be taken since most bridges along the road are broken? Where supplies cannot be received since the harbour has been demolished? Where the distribution points, and thus, the end user, cannot be accessed because of armed soldiers?

The good news is that supply chain management is characterized by problem solving and trade-offs. Recent research even shows that although the humanitarian context is challenging, it is not completely riddled with uncertainty. Crises and disasters actually resemble one another quite a bit, at least from a supply chain perspective. The basic supplies and quantities needed to respond to a disaster remain much the same from disaster to disaster and, consequently, have become more standardized.

What is so special about humanitarian logistics?

In 2005 the Fritz Institute gathered a group of humanitarian logisticians to finally nail down a commonly accepted definition of humanitarian logistics. The outcome was to take the definition of logistics management as set out by the Council of Supply Chain Management Professionals and adapt it to the humanitarian context. The Fritz Institute states this as follows:

> Since the sector does not even agree on a common definition of logistics, this was the first step. After significant deliberation and discussion, humanitarian logistics was preliminarily defined as 'the process of planning, implementing and controlling the efficient, cost-effective flow and storage of goods and materials, as well as related information, from point of origin to point of consumption for the purpose of meeting the end beneficiary's requirements... When asked about the tasks that fall under the broad umbrella of humanitarian logistics, over 80 per cent of the respondents included the tasks of: preparedness, planning, procurement, transport, warehousing, tracking and tracing and customs clearance. (Thomas and Mizushima, 2005: 60)

As appears from both the definition and the approach to arriving at this definition, humanitarian logistics is nothing but logistics management, just in a different, specific context. Many of the same parameters, strategies, processes and tools that direct commercial supply chain management can also be used in the humanitarian context. There are even more similarities between a humanitarian supply chain and, for example, a temporary commercial supply chain functioning in a turbulent environment. Yet there is one factor that is very different between the commercial and the humanitarian sector – and this is the main goal of the overall operations. Whilst the commercial sector strives to make profit, or at least to continue existing as a company, the *raison d'être* of humanitarian organizations and their supply chains is to save lives and eliminate suffering. More specifically, the Organization for Economic Co-operation and Development (OECD) defines humanitarian aid as assistance 'designed to save lives, alleviate suffering and maintain and protect human dignity' (OECD, 2013). To be classified as humanitarian, aid should be consistent with the humanitarian principles of humanity, impartiality, neutrality and independence. Humanitarian aid includes disaster prevention and preparedness; the provision of shelter, food, water and sanitation, health services and other items of assistance for the benefit of affected people and to facilitate the return to normal lives and livelihoods; measures to promote and protect the safety, welfare and dignity of civilians. In a broader sense, humanitarian aid includes disaster relief but also elements of long-term programmes in a larger humanitarian setting. Perhaps the biggest distinguishing factor of humanitarian logistics and supply chain management is the aspect of uncertainty.

The humanitarian context could be considered one of the most uncertain environments in which any organization (commercial or not) operates. Apart from the uncertainties outlined in the introduction (as pertaining to the timing, location, volume and shape of demand as well as supply), other uncertainties relate to the existing market and availability of local resources. Market uncertainty can lead to relief operations being reactive rather than proactive, particularly on the demand side in the form of unpredictable need. In comparison, companies handle such uncertainties by improving the predictability of the customers' needs through better communication and advanced information flow, or they reduce response times by increasing the efficiency of their supply chain. For humanitarian organizations, it can be cumbersome to improve the predictability of needs – as in most cases the end users, their locations and their needs are unknown, and information sharing in the last mile of a humanitarian supply chain is rare. Supply chain efficiency is also hard to improve, as humanitarian organizations seldom have a pre-existing supply chain, instead they must reconstruct the relief supply chain each time a disaster occurs.

That said, the claim that humanitarian efforts will always be hindered by uncertainty has also been criticized. Jahre and Heigh (2008) argue that uncertainty only exists in rapid-onset disasters. The majority of disasters are, however, slow-onset ones that take a long time to develop, such as droughts (EM-DAT, 2013). Furthermore, the argument is that since most sudden-onset disasters (eg tsunamis, earthquakes and hurricanes) tend to occur in the same areas, their locations are not that unpredictable after all. As some areas are more disaster-prone than others, forecasting, planning and preparing for disasters that are typical in a region can increase the understanding of the needs, when and if they occur, as well as diminish their impact. However, in spite of the possibility of forecasting the needs and possible locations of future disasters, uncertainty factors remain in terms of size, exact locations and times of disasters. Therefore, supply chains cannot be completely pre-built to respond quickly to these disasters.

Trade-offs in humanitarian logistics

As in logistics and supply chain management overall, humanitarian logistics and supply chain management is an area that tackles various trade-offs. There are trade-offs in prioritization, between different performance measures, between strategic versus tactical versus operational objectives and activities, as well as between long- and short-term programmes and operations. The humanitarian context also brings along further trade-offs to consider. Expectations of humanitarian aid vary depending on whose perspective one takes. Society, as well as donors, often consider aid effectiveness in terms of the impact of aid on livelihoods and welfare. The economy, gross domestic product (GDP) and GDP growth have also been used as measures for aid effectiveness previously; however, while the humanitarian supply chain certainly supports society, measuring its impact in these terms is rather difficult. The expectation of beneficiaries, the recipients of aid, may differ somewhat from that of donors and society. Apart from receiving the aid they need in the first place, the primary focus of aid recipients is on being treated fairly and equitably.

Even within a humanitarian organization, expectations can differ. Typically, various activities are centred around 'programmes' and it is programme staff that set the parameters for what is being delivered and where. Often there is also a divide between 'supply' staff procuring goods and services and 'logistics' staff delivering it. Whilst all these groups of people should be working together, rarely is an extended 'supply chain' view taken within an organization.

Much of 'humanitarian logistics' focuses on the delivery of items and services to a defined port of entry or an implementing partner, and is separated from the actual activity of distributing these to end users. Humanitarian logistics, and humanitarian supply chains, do not exist in a vacuum, nor without the purpose of supporting society, end users and programmes. Therefore, also the cluster system of humanitarian organizations – whether UN agencies, non-governmental organizations (NGOs) or others – includes a 'Logistics Cluster' that supports all other thematic clusters, from water and sanitation to shelter, health, etc. Overall, the so-called 'cluster system' is a co-ordination mechanism that has been set up to bring together organizations working in the same thematic areas and align their operations globally and also in particular disaster areas.

'Humanitarian logistics' thus caters to a number of different expectations, and a number of different types of activities (see Figure 1.1.1). The humanitarian supply chain – now including also suppliers, logistics service

Figure 1.1.1 Various expectations of the humanitarian supply chain

Suppliers	Hum.org.		In the field
	Co-ord body: global cluster		Co-ord body: Local cluster and/or government

Society in the disaster area — Aid effectiveness

Supplier A → Global cluster lead → Cluster lead

Programme — Programme effectiveness

Supplier B → Hum.org.1 → Local chapter

... Hum.org.2 ...

Supplier X

Local supplier → Hum.org.n → Implementing partner

Beneficiary — Aid equity

Time and cost efficiency

Supply chain

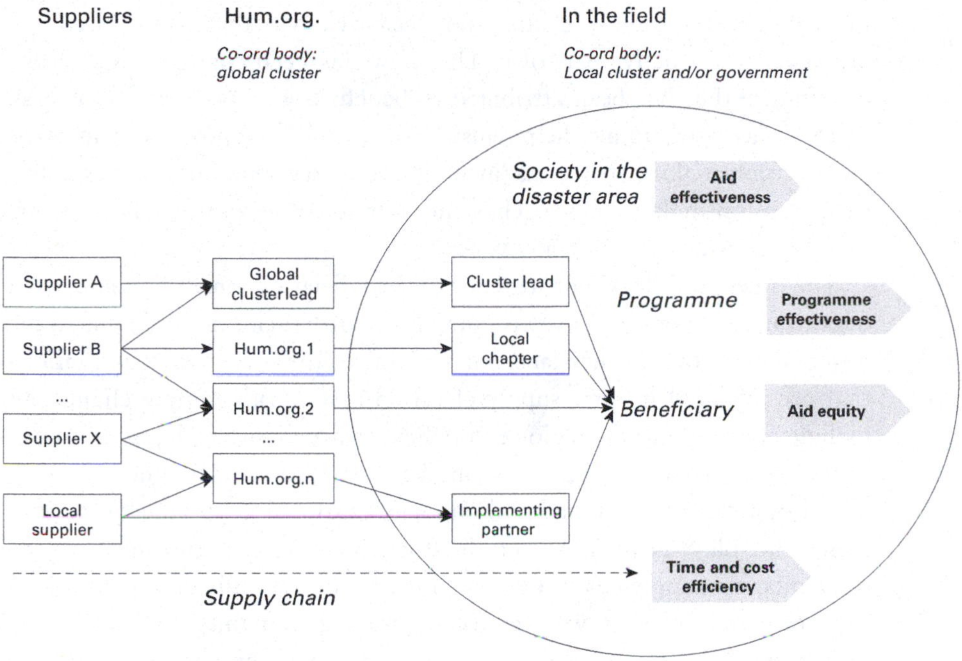

providers and implementing partners, among others – therefore needs to be designed around the operational principles of supply chain management such as effectiveness, efficiency, flexibility and dependability, also adding the objectives of fairness and equity.

Unfortunately, the trade-offs that humanitarian logisticians face and work with are not the same ones that donors would highlight or support. The old saying of 'one dollar spent on preparedness equals three in disaster response' still holds true, yet donors rarely support such a strategic view on humanitarian supply chains. Also, in-kind donations (ie materials and services donated instead of cash) still abound and, even if they have started to be solicited and matched with end-user needs, the problem of not paying for their actual delivery (ie any of the logistics costs that occur on the way) has not vanished. Logistics is still the main cost factor of humanitarian aid, partly because of such donor behaviour. Large humanitarian organizations have come together also to discuss logistics strategy, but many are lagging behind.

At the same time, extending beyond the supply chain, the humanitarian supply network includes a variety of organizations, both governmental and non-governmental organizations but also commercial entities such as suppliers and logistics service providers. When it comes to beneficiaries, as aid 'recipients', they and their needs were seen as the primary objective of humanitarian supply chains and networks, yet they were often not portrayed as an active part of it. This view has been changing, due to the importance that has been attributed to beneficiary empowerment, as cash and voucher programmes help reinstate the purchasing power of end users, and decision-making structures (including end-user committees) re-establish their decision-making power. Thus end users have become active members of the humanitarian supply network.

The question does not extend to beneficiaries only. Humanitarian organizations operate in a vastly complex environment, not only due to the different expectations they face, but also due to the variety of organizations that are involved in their supply chain. Humanitarian supply chains can include not only local and global suppliers (manufacturers, logistics service providers, other service providers), implementing partners and beneficiaries, but also, local, regional, national and supranational governmental entities come into play as donors, co-ordinators, providers or customers in the humanitarian supply chain. Local and international military organizations can come into play as well, either supporting humanitarian efforts, co-ordinating their efforts with these, or, in some cases, hindering such efforts – depending on the role they play in a particular context. To support material flows, a complex network of international logistics service providers – from customs clearance agents to various types of local logistics service providers – are needed. Financial flows may include a vast variety of donors, both those that supply funding and those that support a programme with in-kind donations. Broadening the perspective from supply chain members to stakeholders further widens the picture to include local communities, business communities and the media.

At the same time, it is rarely one single humanitarian organization and its supply chain that operates in a disaster area. Thus, co-ordination across organizations and programmes is key.

Co-ordination has often been criticized in the aftermath of a disaster. The media particularly questions why the co-ordination amongst the involved organizations has not improved over the years. In reality, the co-ordination amongst humanitarian organizations has increased immensely in the last 10 years. This is partly due to the setting up of the (UN) clusters, but also, organizations have come to realize that there is no value in working in silos. Duplication of efforts is not valuable to any of the members in the network. There is also an increase in joint logistics activities amongst the members of a humanitarian network, such as, for example, joint procurement. The most common form of co-ordination is in the area of information sharing, particularly in regard to needs assessment, infrastructural updates and security aspects. Other current forms of collaboration exist in consolidated transportation, shared warehouses or the establishment of inter-agency kits.

Strategic, tactical and operational levels

Although humanitarian organizations operate under the same conditions and the same environments, they can have completely different organizational structures. The International Red Cross and Red Crescent Movement, for example, is highly decentralist since it relies on local chapters that function relatively independently. Other organizations, such as those affiliated with the UN, can be highly centralized. Many organizations (UNICEF, Médecins Sans Frontières and the International Red Cross and Red Crescent Movement) incorporate a division between operational staff and so-called programme staff. Programme staff are responsible for programme planning and delivering programmes to end users. They are also contact points for external stakeholders such as donors, end users, local implementing partners, local governments, local authorities, military actors, and so forth. Operational, or supply chain, staff function as internal service providers to the programme and execute the main supply chain functions such as procurement, transportation and warehousing. The structure of most humanitarian organizations seems still to be fairly organic and adaptable to the environment, mostly because they are required to adapt. Sociocultural aspects, for example, are crucial to the successful delivery of aid, so the organizational structure needs to be decentralized enough to leave room for language and gender aspects to be customized into the services delivered. Logistics and supply chain management exists, however, on all levels in an organization, not only on the operational level. Decisions such as where to pre-position supplies and how to design the overall network are taken on a strategic and global level. On a regional level, decisions can be taken on resources (eg human resources, equipment) and strategic procurement (eg procurement from local or global supplier; procure less frequently in large quantities or more frequently in small quantities). Decisions in the field, on the other hand, can extend to the replenishment of stock (when to reorder, how much buffer stock to hold) and distribution (how often, from where and to where shall distribution occur; priorities of access, coverage or equity). In accordance with these structures in decision making, also the

Figure 1.1.2 Logistics functions in the organizational structure

Strategic	Logistics management headquarters
	Regional director
Tactical	Country director/Director of operations
	The field logistics co-ordinator The site logistics manager
Operational	The procurement manager The warehouse manager The transport manager

logistics functions in a humanitarian organization can be found on different levels (see Figure 1.1.2).

Thus, in spite of logistics often being considered only an operational activity, logistical decisions are taken also at headquarters and on regional/ zonal levels. More and more humanitarian organizations have realized that it is valuable to lift humanitarian logistics and supply chain management to a strategic level within the organization and that, since most decisions in any humanitarian organization would be concerned with logistics, the knowledge of logistics and supply chain managers should be valued and listened to.

Activities, phases and mandates

A pre-assumption that often defines the humanitarian logistics field is an understanding that humanitarian activity is separated into immediate relief and long-term development aid. In between these is a brief transition phase (from a few days to weeks) in which the actors involved shift from life-saving to development operations. This assumes that the immediate response is always temporary and that development aid is long term.

A major distinction is therefore often made between long-term development aid and short-term disaster relief, but this only points out the extremes.

The mandates of humanitarian organizations are set by theme (eg shelter versus water and sanitation), end-user groups (eg women, children) or even the divide between 'humanitarian' (ie disaster relief) and 'development' activities. These divides are not particularly helpful, as the earlier example of third generations born in refugee camps illustrates. Also, the variety of humanitarian programmes extends beyond such divides (see Table 1.1.1).

Table 1.1.1 A variety of humanitarian programmes

	(Immediate) Response Phase	Transition Phase	Recovery Phase
Short-Term Programme/ Funding	Short-term, life-saving supply chain (eg immediate food and water distribution)	Short-term, life-sustaining supply chain (eg vaccination campaign in refugee camp)	Short-term development supply chain (eg delivery of one-time service or product)
Long-Term Programme/ Funding	Long-term, life-saving/sustaining supply chain (eg building and operating a medical clinic to take care of the injured)	Long-term, life-sustaining supply chain (eg setting up and managing 'temporary' housing in refugee camp)	Long-term development supply chain (eg setting up an educational programme)

SOURCE: Modified from Haavisto, Kovács and Haavisto (2013)

Different frameworks and models exist to conceptualize the variety of disasters and also humanitarian activities.[2] All of them presuppose humanitarian operations being categorized into various phases. Most humanitarian organizations and funding bodies follow a similar division (for example, in funding applications), and some governments have specific regulations for the immediate response category, where customs clearance processes can be expedited for airlifted goods. However, many humanitarian organizations adopt a more circular, learning loop model that links these phases to one another.

One can further divide emergencies into the slow/rapid onset and man-made/natural disaster categories. An example of rapid-onset natural disasters is an earthquake, and slow-onset natural disasters can be famine, for instance. When viewing disaster statistics (EM-DAT, 2013), a similar categorization is used, but enhanced with a complex disaster category, where there might be a slow- or rapid-onset disaster simultaneous with an ongoing man-made conflict. Accessibility and security aspects make such environments among the most vulnerable, and humanitarian activity in complex disasters is challenging. Furthermore, environments with a looming, slow-onset disaster might be acutely hit by a rapid-onset disaster as well. On the one hand this situation poses challenges for addressing both disasters at the same time but, on the other, humanitarian supply chains are often already in place in such environments, leading to the scaling-up of these existing supply chains, not necessarily implementing completely new ones. One can further problematize the simple distinction between natural and man-made disasters from a peacekeeping and crisis management perspective. Nevertheless, a disaster taxonomy is very useful from a supply chain perspective, since it has led to a discussion of the applicability of humanitarian supply chain strategies such as lean and agile principles. For example, responsiveness and agility are key in short-term, life-saving disaster relief, whereas longer-term programmes are more plannable, and even lean principles can be applied to them. Thus, in conclusion, from a supply chain management (SCM) perspective, different programmes and phases can be managed with different SCM principles.

Concluding remarks

So, what is humanitarian logistics and supply chain management? Research in the field of humanitarian supply chain management has gained attention in recent years. The prominent fields of research are presented here and can be identified as:

- the different phases of disaster relief;
- processes and performance measurement in humanitarian logistics;
- co-ordination and collaboration among humanitarian organizations, with commercial partners, the military or in the humanitarian supply chain;
- specific functions and activities in the humanitarian supply chain;
- the agility and responsiveness of humanitarian supply chains;
- disaster management strategies;
- information flows in the humanitarian supply chain.

Challenges and success factors in humanitarian logistics have, however, been studied to some extent. Challenges have been identified as the lack of the following: exemptions from customs, clear mandates and legislation supporting national humanitarian organizations, and qualified in-country staff. Critical success factors in the context of humanitarian supply chains and logistics have been identified as: strategic planning, resource management, transport planning, capacity building, information management, technology utilization, human resource management, continuous improvement, supplier relations, and supply chain strategy. Further challenges in humanitarian logistics have been defined as: caps in NGO capacity, influx of humanitarian staff, lack of in-depth knowledge, funding bias towards short-term response, and lack of investment in technology and communication.

The area of humanitarian logistics is vast and complex. This book does not claim to be over-encompassing but, rather, it addresses a number of current concerns in the area. The book is structured in a way that moves from strategic concerns and decisions in the supply chain (Parts 2–4) to addressing logistics functions such as procurement, transportation, warehousing and logistics information systems (Parts 5–8) more in detail. In this, the book moves from strategic towards operational decisions. Adding flavour to these, each of the parts includes also at least one case study or example on the topic. Furthermore, the book concludes with a set of such cases (Part 9) that address the concerns of sustainability and performance measurement, but also the pressing topics of innovation, security and exit strategies. Contributors themselves come from various research environments as well as, importantly, different humanitarian organizations, and report on their own studies and problems. We hope their insights will help in managerial decision making in the area of humanitarian logistics and supply chain management, and contribute to the development of this field.

Notes

1 There are many names for the 'end users' of aid, varying from aid recipients, to victims, to beneficiaries, to 'right holders'. All of these come with different political connotations. As this book is taking a supply chain perspective, 'end user' will be the preferred term in the book if there is no reason to engage with any of the other connotations of the various terms.

2 There are quite a number of different disaster taxonomies to be found in the literature. Table 1.1.2 gives an overview of some of these:

Table 1.1.2 Disaster taxonomies

Disaster Taxonomy Literature	Scope of and Parameters in Taxonomy
Van Wassenhove (2006)	Relief versus development aid, slow versus rapid onset, natural versus man-made
Listou (2008)	Natural versus man-made from crisis management perspective
Altay and Green (2006)	Mitigation, immediate relief, recovery
Safran (2003)	Disaster relief cycle: planning, responding and recovery
Holguin-Veras *et al* (2012)	Adds scale to Van Wassenhove's disaster taxonomy
L'Hermitte *et al* (2013)	Disaster scale and socioeconomic, conflict, environmental, infrastructure and governmental situations

References

Altay, N and Green, W (2006) OR/MS research in disaster operations management, *European Journal of Operational Research*, 175 (1), pp 475–93

Arminas, D (2005) Supply lessons of tsunami aid, *Supply Management*, 10 (2), p 14

Balcik, B and Beamon, B M (2008) Facility location in humanitarian relief, *International Journal of Logistics: Research and applications*, 11 (2), pp 101–21

Bergman, C (ed) (2003) *Another Day in Paradise: International humanitarian workers tell their stories*, Orbis Books, Maryknoll, NY

EM-DAT (2013) [accessed April 2013] EM-DAT Emergency Events Database, *Université Catholique de Louvain, Louvain-La-Neuve: Centre for Research on the Epidemiology of Disasters (CRED)* [Online] www.emdat.be

Haavisto, I, Kovács, G and Haavisto, C (2013) Performance Objectives in Relief and Development Operations, EUROMA 2013 conference, Dublin, Ireland

Holguin-Veras, M *et al* (2012) On the unique features of post-disaster humanitarian logistics, *Journal of Operations Management*, 30 (7–8), pp 494–506

Jahre, M and Heigh, I (2008) Does the current constraints in funding promote failure in humanitarian supply chains?, *Supply Chain Forum – An International Journal*, 9 (2), pp 44–55

L'Hermitte *et al* (2013) A new disaster classification model based on humanitarian logistics implications for intervention, ANZAM Proceedings 2013

Listou, T (2008) Postponement and speculation in non-commercial supply chains, *Supply Chain Forum: An international journal*, 9 (2), pp 56–64

Organization for Economic Co-operation and Development (OECD) (2013) [accessed October 2013] DAC Glossary of Key Terms and Concepts [Online] http://www.oecd.org/dac/dacglossaryofkeytermsandconcepts.htm

Safran (2003) A strategic approach for disaster and emergency assistance, UN–ISDR Asian Meeting, 15–17 January 2003, Kobe, Japan

Tatham, P H, Spens, K M and Oloruntoba, R (2009) [accessed December 2015] Cyclones in Bangladesh: A case study of a whole country response to rapid onset disasters, *POMS conference 2009, paper 011–0029*, [Online] www.pomsmeetings.org/ConfPapers/011/011-0029.doc

Thomas, A and Mizushima, M (2005) Logistics training: necessity or luxury?, *Forced Migration Review*, 22, pp 60–61

Van Wassenhove, L N (2006) Blackett memorial lecture: humanitarian aid logistics – supply chain management in high gear, *Journal of the Operational Research Society*, 57 (5), pp 475–89

Acknowledgements

This book project could not have been achieved without the kind support of the Academy of Finland project 'Resilience in Disaster Relief and Development Supply Chains'.

Exploring logistics competences and capabilities in not-for-profit environments

The case of Médecins Sans Frontières

DIEGO VEGA

Neoma Business School and Cret-Log, France

The role of logistics as a source of competitive advantage for firms has been largely studied in the strategic management literature. This is supported by the idea that firms are a bundle of resources and, thus, firm-specific logistics resources and capabilities explain the differences in performance among firms in the same industry. A context in which logistics has recently achieved particular interest, due to its important contribution to the success of operations, is humanitarian relief. Over the past few years, the field of humanitarian logistics has witnessed great advances in both theory and practice. However, the logistics competences and capabilities needed to ensure the success of relief operations from an organizational perspective are seldom studied in academic literature. This chapter addresses this issue by studying the case of Doctors Without Borders, Médecins Sans Frontières (MSF), a medical humanitarian organization that is widely recognized by its logistics excellence. Based on a conceptual framework developed through an extensive academic literature review, semi-structured interviews and internal documentation were analysed, exploring the logistics competences and capabilities found at MSF. A set of capabilities were identified as important for the success of the operations, as well as a number of competences that result from the combination of such capabilities. Based on these results, it is suggested that for the case of MSF, logistics can be considered as both a core and a distinctive competence. Possible implications for the humanitarian community are drawn and further research with a wider sample of non-governmental organizations (NGOs) is encouraged.

Introduction

In the ever-growing body of knowledge of logistics and supply chain management, a lot has been written on the substantial role that logistics has in achieving sustained competitive advantage (Porter, 1980). Numerous authors argue that superior resources and skills contribute to sustained competitive advantage (eg Day and Wensley, 1988). Others suggest that firms must combine their resources and skills into core competences to achieve sustained competitive advantage (eg Prahalad and Hamel, 1990). For over 20 years, a considerable amount of research in logistics has been dedicated to the identification and definition of competences and capabilities, supporting the idea that firm-specific logistics resources and capabilities can explain the differences in performance among firms in the same industry (Olavarrieta and Ellinger, 1997). Recently, a context in which logistics has gained attention from both academia and practitioners is humanitarian relief, as almost 80 per cent of the activities undertaken are logistics-related (Van Wassenhove, 2006). However, studies on the organizational logistics competences and capabilities needed to ensure the success of humanitarian operations is almost non-existent, although humanitarian organizations compete for fund donors and emergency relief logistics is considered as a differentiator and a competitive tool in the 'crowded' humanitarian sector (Oloruntuba and Gray, 2006). This chapter addresses this point by exploring the organizational logistics competences and capabilities needed to ensure the success of humanitarian relief operations. The chapter is structured as follows. First, the most prominent works on logistics competences and capabilities are presented, as well as a short overview of the resource-based view (RBV), constituting a theoretical framework. The research design section then explains the methodological choices and the methods used to explore this phenomenon. The findings from the empirical study are presented, before concluding with a short discussion on the implication of such findings for both academia and practitioners.

Literature review

For over 20 years, a considerable amount of research in logistics has been dedicated to the identification and definition of competences or capabilities in order to support the idea that logistics can be considered as a source of sustained competitive advantage. However, findings show that research on this issue is far from being stable, as the terms 'logistics competences' and 'logistics capabilities' are used interchangeably in the literature (Morash, Dröge and Vickery, 1996). The following sections review, based on logistics and supply chain management (SCM) literature, the most prominent works on these two streams of research, logistics competences and logistics capabilities, and the relation of each of these two concepts with sustained competitive advantage.

Logistics competences and capabilities

One of the first works on logistics competence was conducted by the Global Logistics Research Team at Michigan State University (MSUGLRT). The research team proposed in 1995 a 'World Class Logistics Competency Model', based on a study on how some of the world's best-managed companies used logistics to achieve competitive superiority (MSUGLRT, 1995). In the model, each competency was conceptualized as being comprised of several functional capabilities, which in combination create a competency. The study reported some empirical evidence that world-class practices are correlated with better logistics performance. This first logistics competences framework was the basis for an important number of studies all over the world. Based on this framework, Stank and Lackey (1997) examined the relation between capabilities and competences and found integration and agility to be of great importance to logistics performance. Later on, Anderson, Jerman and Crum (1998) conducted a survey on the importance of quality management practices in the achievement of operational results and customer satisfaction with members of the American Society of Transportation and Logistics. Results show a causal relationship between quality management factors and logistics outcomes, specifically logistics operational performance and customer service. Daugherty, Stank and Ellinger (1998) confirmed the strong link between logistics capabilities and customer satisfaction from a study that examined the relation between buyers and sellers in a business to business (B2B) setting. Goldsby and Stank (2000) provided support to the relationship between the World Class Logistics Competency Model, and the implementation of environmentally responsible logistics practices. In Shang and Sun's (2004) work, the authors combined a resource-based view of the firm and logistics and supply chain management to classify organizations in the manufacturing industry in Taiwan, and confirmed that logistics can be regarded as a key strategic source for acquiring sustained competitive advantage. Shang and Marlow (2005) explored the relationship between performance and logistics capabilities and found that information-based capability plays an important role in the enhancement of the firms' performance and the facilitation of the firms' other capabilities. More recently, in Shang and Marlow's 2007 work, four logistics competences – namely integration and knowledge competence, customer-focused logistics competence, measurement competence and agility competence – were identified based on a survey of 1,200 manufacturing firms in Taiwan, confirming the MSU's framework.

Bowersox, Closs and Stank (1999) expanded the MSUGLRT (1995) study and proposed the 21st-Century Logistics Model with six supply chain competences – namely customer integration, internal integration, relationship integration, technology and planning integration, measurement integration and supplier integration – and the 'Supply Chain 2000 Framework', which identifies the competences essential to integrating supply chain logistics. The authors conducted a survey of 306 senior North American logistics executives in order to obtain information on the supply chain competences and performance metrics. Results confirmed that the companies possessing these key competences experienced operational and financial improvement. In an attempt to substantiate the academic relevance of Bowersox, Closs and Stank's (1999) work, Stank, Keller and Closs (2001) showed that superior logistics performance is a reward for high achievement on supply chain logistics integration competences and that customer integration is the most critical competency associated with improved performance. Many authors have applied this framework to international environments. Some of these works include Carranza, Maltz and Antun (2002), who used this framework to analyse the logistics strategy of Argentinian firms; Mollenkopf and Dapiran (1999, 2005) who used it to benchmark logistics capabilities and competences in Australia and New Zealand; and Closs and Mollenkopf (2004) who compare the data collected during the 21st-Century Logistics Model with data collected by Mollenkopf and Dapiran (1999) in Australia and New Zealand. Others studies emphasize either one specific logistics competence (eg Richey, Daugherty and Roath, 2007), in logistics competence as a whole (eg Bolumole, Frankel and Naslund, 2007; Peko and Ahmed, 2011) or in logistics competency building (eg Li and Lin, 2006). Surprisingly, no new models have been proposed or developed in recent years, mostly because studies apply either one of the frameworks presented above, or because they focus on a particular competence. Table 1.2.1 summarizes the most prominent works on this literature. Each logistics competence framework is presented, including the main reference, denoted by an asterisk (*), and the authors who carried out studies based on this framework. Subsequently, a list of the competences is presented as well as the capabilities that compose such competence.

Table 1.2.1 Logistics competence frameworks

Framework	Authors	Competences	Capabilities
World-Class Logistics Competency Model	MSUGLRT (1995)*; Anderson *et al* (1998); Goldsby and Stank (2000); Shang and Sun (2004); Shang and Marlow (2005, 2007)	Positioning	Strategy, supply chain, network, organization
		Integration	Supply chain unification, information technology, information sharing, connectivity, standardization, simplification, discipline
		Agility	Relevancy, flexibility, accommodation
		Measurement	Functional assessment, process assessment, benchmarking
	Stank and Lackey (1997)	Positioning	Costumer focus, organizational control, organizational implementation
		Integration	Connectivity, functional integration, information sharing, IT, supplier relations
		Agility	Operational flexibility, personnel flexibility
		Measurement	Activity-based costing, benchmarking, performance assessment

Table 1.2.1 *Continued*

Framework	Authors	Competences	Capabilities
21st-Century Logistics Model	Bowersox, Closs and Stank (1999)*; Mollenkopf and Dapiran (1999, 2005); Stank, Keller and Closs (2001); Carranza, Maltz and Antun (2002); Closs and Mollenkopf (2004)	Customer integration	Segmental focus, relevancy, responsiveness, flexibility
		Internal integration	Cross-functional unification, standardization, simplification, compliance, structural adaptation
		Relationship integration	Role specificity, guidelines, information sharing, gain/ risk sharing
		Technology and planning integration	Information management, internal communication, connectivity, collaborative forecasting and planning
		Measurement integration	Functional assessment, activity-based and total cost methodology, comprehensive metrics, financial impact
		Supplier integration	Strategic alignment, operational fusion, financial linkage, supplier management

A capability can be defined as 'complex bundles of individual skills, assets and accumulated knowledge exercised through organizational processes that enable firms to co-ordinate activities and make use of their resources' (Olavarrieta and Ellinger, 1997: 563). An important amount of research on strategic logistics is founded on the idea that logistics capabilities support different value disciplines (Snow and Hrebiniak, 1980). Morash, Dröge and Vickery (1996) present two main value disciplines, demand-oriented or customer-oriented and supply-oriented, and the different capabilities that compose these value disciplines. Based on a study on the perceived importance of strategic logistics capabilities for firm success, the actual implementation of such logistics capabilities, and measures of both firm performance and firm performance relative to competitors conducted in the US furniture industry, the authors found that delivery speed, reliability, responsiveness and low-cost distribution are the key logistics capabilities for sustained competitive advantage.

Later, Gilmour's (1999) work proposes a framework to evaluate supply chain processes based on a set of capabilities, namely process capabilities, technology capabilities and organization capabilities, which incorporate the extent of integration and the use of associated technologies in the supply chain processes of an organization, and the degree to which logistics is used as a key element of overall strategy formulation and implementation. The author performed a study on six Australian consumer product and automobile manufacturers, finding that for the automotive industry, the customer dialogue-driven supply chain capability results in a high differentiation on the market. As for the consumer product industry, integrated information systems capability and integrated performance measurement capability are the market differentiation facilitators. The framework provides a benchmark for measuring the match with the organization's logistics strategy and overall corporate strategy. Based on the MSUGLRT's (1995) study, Lynch, Keller and Ozmet (2000) divided logistics capabilities into two groups, ie value-added service capabilities and process capabilities, following the expert panel's beliefs that some are more important for achieving low costs, and others are more important for differentiation. The study, conducted in the North American (ie Canada, Mexico and the United States) retail grocery industry, showed a positive relationship between process capabilities and a cost leadership strategy, while value-added service capabilities have a positive impact in an organization's differentiation strategy. Later, Zhao, Dröge and Stank (2001) use MSU's framework to propose and test a model of the relationships among customer-focused capabilities and information-focused capabilities and firm performance. Based on senior logistics or supply chain executives in each North American-based manufacturing, wholesale/distributing and retail industry, a study confirmed that customer-focused capabilities are strongly related to firm performance. In 2004, Mentzer, Min and Bobbit categorized logistics capabilities based on the existing literature into four interfaces – namely demand management interface capabilities, supply management interface capabilities, information management capabilities and co-ordination capabilities – arguing that logistics capabilities demonstrate a firm's competitive advantage through the management of stakeholder goals. The authors also recognize the important role of logistics capabilities in boundary-spanning interfaces between internal functional areas and between the focal firm and the supply chain partners. Later, Esper, Fugate and Davis-Sramek (2007) reveal the most frequently discussed capabilities in the literature, including customer-focused capabilities, supply management capabilities, integration capabilities, measurement capabilities, and information exchange capabilities. Recent developments include the importance of logistics capability in the e-commerce market (Cho, Ozment and Sink, 2008), the contribution of capabilities to the logistics service providers' competitiveness in China (Liu *et al*, 2010), the identification of key logistics capabilities for international distribution centres (Lu and Yang, 2010), and the role of logistics capabilities as a source for competitive advantage in Swedish retail companies (Sandberg and Abrahamsson, 2011), among others. However, as it is the case for logistics competence, these recent studies do not include new insights but are rather confirmatory of previous literature. Table 1.2.2 summarizes the capabilities found in the literature (the capabilities are gathered by its focus or orientation, and no work is considered as main reference).

Further, in logistics and SCM literature, flexibility appears simultaneously as a competence (Fawcett, Cantalone and Smith, 1996) and a capability (Bowersox, Closs and Stank, 1999; MSUGLRT, 1995; Mentzer, Min and

Table 1.2.2 Logistics capabilities gathered by orientation

Authors	Orientation/Focus	Capabilities
Morash, Dröge and Vickery (1996)	Demand-oriented	Pre-sale customer service, post-sale customer service, delivery speed, delivery reliability, responsiveness to target markets
	Supply-oriented	Widespread distribution coverage, selective distribution coverage, low total-cost distribution
Gilmour (1999)	Process	Customer-driven supply chain, efficient logistics, demand-driven sales planning, lean manufacturing, supplier partnering, integrated supply chain management
	Information technology	Integrated information systems, advanced technology
	Organization	Integrated performance measurement, teamwork, aligned organization structure

Table 1.2.2 *Continued*

Authors	Orientation/Focus	Capabilities
Lynch, Keller and Ozmet (2000)	Process	
	Value-added service	
Zhao, Dröge and Stank (2001)	Customer-focused	Segmental focus, relevancy, responsiveness, flexibility
	Information-focused	Information sharing, IT
Mentzer, Min and Bobbit (2004)	Demand management interface	Flexibility, responsiveness
	Supply management interface	Total-cost minimization, efficient logistics processes
	Information management	IT, information sharing, connectivity

Bobbit, 2004), showing a lack of conceptualization of competences and capabilities in logistics literature. These and other discrepancies found in the literature make relevant the need for a deeper analysis on the definition of competences and capabilities.

Resource-based view

From a historical point of view, the RBV is the result of Edith Penrose's (1959) seminal work, where the author presents the key principles of the approach by considering that the firm's resource ownership is what determines its competitive advantage in comparison to others. The main postulates of the RBV of the firm are that firms are a collection or a bundle of resources (Penrose, 1959; Wernerfelt, 1984) and that its capacity to create sustainable competitive advantage depends on its capacity to implement strategies that exploit its internal strengths (Barney, 1991). Most works of this stream aim to link resources with competitive advantage and to analyse the conditions to ensure sustainability. However, during the evolution of this new theory of the firm, a parallel stream was developed based on the concept of distinctive competence (Selznick, 1957), to refer to those activities that a firm does better in comparison with its competitors.

The 1990s witnessed an important evolution in the field, mostly influenced by the works of Prahalad and Hamel (1990), Hamel and Heene (1994) and Sanchez and Heene (1997), setting the basis for competence-based management (CBM), a stream that postulates that competitive advantage is achieved through the development and use of its capacity to deploy resources. The strategic management literature offers an important number of definitions for both competence and capability concepts without achieving a consensus. For instance, Foss (1996: 1) defines competence as 'a typically idiosyncratic knowledge capital that allows its holder to perform activities – in particular, to solve problems – in certain ways, and typically do this more efficiently than others', while Sanchez and Heene (1997: 306) define it as 'an ability to sustain co-ordinated deployments of resources in ways that help that organization to achieve its goals'. Further, Hitt and Ireland (1986: 402) add the *distinctive* attribute to competence, defining it as 'a firm's ability to complete an action in a manner superior to that of its competitors or to apply a skill that competitors lack', and Prahalad and Hamel (1990: 82) rather choose the *core* attribute and define it as 'the combination of individual technologies and production skills that underlie a company's myriad product lines'.

From this overview, it is possible to say that the term 'distinctive competence' refers to activities that a firm performs better than its competitors, while 'critical' or 'core competence' encompasses technological and production skills or expertise that enables the firm to implement a strategy. However, none of the above definitions include the relation with a firm's capabilities, a term that has been shown to have direct relation with a firm's resources. A capability is defined as the capacity for a team of resources to perform some task or activity (Grant, 1991), or a firm's capacity to deploy resources (Amit and Schoemaker, 1993). These differ from core competences in the way that core competences, as presented earlier, emphasize technological and production expertise at specific points in the value chain, while capabilities are more broadly based, encompassing the entire value chain (Stalk, Evans and Shulman, 1992). Another difference between competence and capabilities relies on the fact that capabilities are the mechanisms and processes by which new competences are developed (Teece, Pisano and Shuen, 1997).

The above definitions make clear that most authors agree that capabilities refer to those skills, mechanisms, processes and knowledge that allow resources to be deployed and, when combined, create competences. When regarded from a corporate perspective, competence refers to those functional areas, critical activities or organizational processes that differentiate an organization from its competitors, and through which the strategy of the organization is implemented. Both competences and capabilities can be regarded as critical, the degree of which will depend on its uniqueness, scarcity and difficulty to imitate, and the amount of superior customer value that such competence or capability can provide (Day, 1994). Finally, these two can be either core or distinctive; 'core' refers to the central role of a firm's value-generating activities, while 'distinctiveness' implies that customers can distinguish a firm from its competitors.

Research design

In light of the existing literature and the discussion presented above, this chapter was designed to explore the logistics competences and capabilities needed to ensure the success of relief operations from an organizational perspective. Previous studies on this topic in for-profit environments have almost exclusively used quantitative methods, the survey being the preferred one (eg Morash, Dröge and Vickery, 1996; Stank and Lackey, 1997; Lynch, Keller and Ozmet, 2000; Closs and Mollenkopf, 2004). This confirms Ellram's (1996) observation that most empirical research in logistics that is based on quantitative methods is still valid. However, as pointed out by Halldorsson and Aastrup (2003), logistics as a discipline is experiencing a movement towards more qualitative methods. For instance, case study research has been used to investigate logistics competences and capabilities when exploration and in-depth analysis were targeted (eg Esper, Fugate and Davis-Sramek, 2007; Sandberg and Abrahamsson, 2011). This research was exploratory in nature and aimed to investigate an under-researched topic and, thus, the case study arose as a relevant research method given that 'it provides depth and insight into a little-known phenomenon' (Ellram, 1996: 97). Such is the case of logistics competences and capabilities for humanitarian relief.

As stated by Meredith *et al* (1989), in order to better understand the phenomenon the researcher should be as close as possible to the context in which such phenomenon occurs. Therefore, the perspective of the actors involved on humanitarian relief was chosen as the suitable type of information used for this chapter. Purposive sample procedures and multiple data collection techniques (Eisenhardt, 1989; Yin, 2009) were used in the case study of MSF undertaken in this chapter.

Data collection and analysis

The case study in this chapter is based on an international humanitarian organization that is known for its logistical excellence, and recognized for its 'pioneering humanitarian work on several continents' (The Nobel Foundation, 1999): Médecins Sans Frontières (MSF). The case study protocol and interview guide were built based on the previous literature review and the input from the head office of one of MSF's supply centres in Bordeaux, France. A total of 27 semi-structured interviews were conducted in two separate locations – MSF's headquarters in Paris and the Bordeaux supply centre – in a one-to-one setting following purposive sampling guidelines. The diversity of the sample was ensured through different dimensions, including job position (eg supply chain manager, production manager, procurement manager, transportation manager, purchasing manager, technical advisor, procurement officer, freight operator, warehouse operator, field logistics supervisor), tenure (6 months to 12 years), field experience (eg emergency response, development programme, armed conflict, natural disaster), gender and race. Each interview was audiotaped and lasted approximately 35–80 minutes, in which interviewees answered open-ended questions on the logistics competences and capabilities found at MSF. Interviewees were asked to bring up examples from their field experiences, searching for variety on the units of analysis possibly found in a single case study (Yin, 2009). The semi-structured interviews allowed new elements to be considered and further investigated, avoiding researcher biases (Eisenhardt, 1989). In addition to semi-structured interviews, internal documentation and direct observation, as well as other informal exchanges (eg meetings, discussions, e-mails, etc) were included as sources of information, ensuring data triangulation (Voss, Tsikriktsis and Frohlich, 2002).

Shortly after each interview, a process of selective transcription (Ochs, 1979) was conducted in order to eliminate the 'muddle in the middle' (Lapadat, 2000). The elements related to the context in which the interview took place were included in the process as field notes. Following Ellram's (1996) data analysis process, a first phase of 'open coding' was carried out in order to identify, conceptualize and develop the first categories of the results based on the insights from the literature review. Further, an 'axial coding' was performed to look for interactions between the results of the open coding. Finally, a 'selective coding' was completed for validation and further development of categories. The analysis of the data sources was conducted with the help of QDAS NVivo 8.

Research quality

The study followed Lincoln and Guba's (1985) concept of trustworthiness, aiming to respond to four criteria – namely credibility, transferability, dependability and confirmability. Credibility was ensured through a continuous check of the researcher's interpretations of the findings with the head office and members of the organization. The use of multiple sources of evidence, multiple informants and two different sites allowed the study to achieve a high level of transferability. Dependability was accomplished through the use of written protocols for data collection and analysis, and the use of the QDAS for storage and systematic coding of the data. Finally, confirmability was addressed through the examination and evaluation of the findings by several scholars in previous versions of this research.

Overview of the organization

MSF is an international medical humanitarian organization that, for over 40 years, has provided assistance to populations in distress, to victims of natural or man-made disasters and to victims of armed conflict. Today, MSF provides aid in nearly 60 countries to people whose survival is threatened by violence, negligence or catastrophe, primarily due to armed conflict, epidemics, malnutrition and exclusion from health care or natural disasters. MSF is composed of five operational centres (Amsterdam, Barcelona, Brussels, Geneva and Paris) and 19 sections (Australia, Austria, Belgium, Canada, Denmark, France, Germany, Greece, Holland, Hong Kong, Italy, Japan, Luxembourg, Norway, Spain, Sweden, Switzerland, the United Kingdom and the United States). In addition to this, MSF has two supply centres: MSF Supply (Belgium) and MSF Logistique (France), which offer logistical support to the different sections of the MSF movement and other NGOs such as Médecins Du Monde and the International Committee of the Red Cross.

Results

The primary objective of MSF is to respond to emergencies and to mitigate the suffering of populations at risk, through proper medical action reinforced by appropriate logistics (MSF, 2014a). However, this objective cannot be achieved without the help of other areas of expertise. The first findings of the case study revealed that in addition to logistics and medical know-how, the organization's experience in responding simultaneously to multiple emergencies was perceived as one of MSF's strengths. However, not surprisingly, logistics appeared as one of the pillars to achieve this capacity.

Logistics competency at MSF

During the 1980s, in response to an increasing demand from the teams in the field, and the need to master a highly efficient supply chain made up of a series of links, all of them crucial – purchasing, inventory, quality assurance and shipment – MSF set up a supply centre (MSFLog) whose *raison d'être* is to provide missions with high-quality supplies, whether for emergency situations or normal operations (MSF, 2014a). MSF's supply mission involves reliable and high-quality medical supplies (eg drugs and medical/surgical equipment), non-medical supplies (eg vehicles, water tanks and food) and transportation (timelines, insurance, etc). Over the past years, MSF has achieved what is considered by its members to be a logistics competency, gaining international recognition in this area, at the same level as that of their medical expertise. As stated by the warehouse operations manager:

> For MSF, logistics is the first point that will contribute to the success of a good response to an emergency... We could even deliver the material without having a medical team in the field and give this to other doctors different from MSF.

The importance of logistics at MSF is also attested by the growth of this activity over the years. From 2003 to 2014, MSFLog has almost doubled the number of delivered parcels from 131,259 in 2003 to 253,771 in 2014. This is the result of a strategic decision of expanding its warehousing capacity from 5,000 to 10,000 square metres, and to develop three decentralized warehouses (Dubai, Nairobi and Panama) to ensure the flow management from the different sections (MSF, 2010). This allows the organization to increase its medical and logistics stocks, improving MSF's capacity to respond to multiple crises, in different parts of the world at the same time.

For instance, during the emergency response to the 2010 Haiti earthquake, 17 planes chartered by MSF helped in the delivery of equipment for the implementation of an inflatable hospital on an athletic field of 7,000 square metres in the first six days after the crisis hit. At the end of the first month, the hospital consisted of 40 tents of which 13 were inflatable, including a triage room, an emergency room, an observation room, three operating rooms – including one reserved for osteosynthesis and clean surgeries, a sterilization section, a recovery room, an intensive care unit, several rooms of hospitalization, and a follow-up care and rehabilitation section. A specific burn treatment centre with its dedicated operating room was established in the third month of the intervention. In the words of the head of supply chain:

> We cannot be an emergency medical NGO with the level that we have without logistics... if we hadn't built this (MSFLog), we couldn't have responded to Haiti, it would be impossible!

Logistics for MSF is thus considered as the ultimate competence that allows the organization to respond to humanitarian crises at the point that, given this case, MSF is capable of supplying all the required material to assist the populations in any scenario without sending their own medical teams to the field. This is only possible through the deep understanding of the logistical processes and their transformation into capabilities and competences.

Between competences and capabilities

The MSF case study presents logistics as one of the pillars for the success of their operations, and is considered as essential for the medical activity. However, an important number of competences and capabilities are behind the notoriety of logistics.

Technical capabilities

Within logistics competency, technical capabilities are considered as important for the success of MSF's operations. This reputation is the result of a process of professionalization of different activities throughout the supply chain. These capabilities represent each *métier* that constitutes the logistics of MSF. These include purchasing and procurement, supplier management, stock management, transportation management, warehouse management, order processing, operational flexibility, delivery and information management, among others. An example of this is provided by a freight operator, who explains the crucial aspect of his work:

> In the commercial environment, at the end you've got very few people who are faced with the chartering of aircraft, because these are completely outsourced: the forwarder subcontracts to the broker, the broker takes care of it, and so on. We like to do it directly with the broker and as we have these capabilities at MSF Logistique, and as we want to be sure that things are going well, we want to be sure that the aircraft matches our criteria selection, we want to choose the departure airport on the basis of price, we make a big analysis, we want to know exactly where it is going to land, we want to know the crew... a lot

of things that we pay attention to for an operational choice, the choice of this
company or not, and so on. As it's not easy to find these capabilities outside,
we develop them here!

Throughout its history, MSF has expanded its logistics system with the
functions required to ensure good medical practice. Today, the organization
benefits from an important internal cohesion of logistics activities that go
even beyond the borders of the organization.

Integration competence

Logistics integration is crucial for the good unwinding of the operations.
As the quality manager at MSF Logistique stated:

> The competence of a system is always superior to the addition of individual
> competences, and [this] is especially true for MSF.

In order to ensure the delivery of the relief items requested by the teams
on the field, without errors and within a limited period of time, MSF relies
on a set of capabilities that combined create a successful integration.
It all begins with the identification of the need expressed by the teams of the
field. Good-quality information allows the purchasers and supply officers to
find the specific products that respond to those needs, while freight and
warehouse operators prepare what is necessary to smooth the transit between
the supplier and the field. This internal integration is explained through the
role that information plays within the organization. The order-processing
manager explains:

> It is mostly a co-ordination problem about how we communicate, how we
> will be able to understand that the information I have, if I keep it to myself, is
> useless, so it must be shared and shared quickly with maximum clarity, knowing
> that the other does not understand what he is told so one must be sure that the
> thing is understood and that the message went through.

In some cases, such integration goes beyond the organization limits and
reaches the suppliers, with whom the organization has built partnerships
that benefit the overall supply chain. The cold-chain referent explains:

> In a moment we had a lot of cold-chain disruptions, and I made a set of
> specifications for new packages that were very restrictive. I made a tender and
> all suppliers told me 'it's too restrictive, it is useless'. Eventually, we worked
> together with our long-time supplier, we developed new packaging and we went
> from €100,000 of product destroyed in 2008 to less than €200 in 2010.

MSF's operational structure enables downstream external integration (to some extent) with the organization's first customers, ie the teams on the field, while the relation with some of its suppliers enables upstream external integration.

Adaptability competence

For the year 2013, the operational portfolio was composed of 70 to 90 projects in 30 to 35 countries (MSF, 2014b). In some cases, a country's situation leads to constraints that make it difficult (or even impossible) to access and therefore to supply the teams. In other cases, it is the nature of the emergency and scale that can make it difficult to deliver. To deal with all factors, the organization has developed a strong capacity to adapt to different contexts, types of emergency and requested volumes that generate very different logistic choices. The stock manager explains:

> For the Indian tsunami, it was several countries that were affected, in several areas. For Haiti, we had to intervene and the focus was mainly on the capital city at the beginning. It was much easier to manage than responding in several countries (Indonesia, Sri Lanka, etc) but it was very complicated. In fact [for the tsunami] we delivered, but we didn't know the exact needs. In Haiti, I think it was much more measured. Now, in Kurdistan it was rather the extent... there were mountains filled with people, it was huge in terms of needs and the response was great in volume. Items sent from MSF Logistique: plastic, blankets... sometimes by plane; there was only one type of product, while in Haiti there were 500 or 600 different products per shipment. It was not at all the same logistics and it could not be apprehended in the same way.

Upstream, the supply of products from the supplier can also result in constraints to which MSF's logistics must constantly adapt. Product quality is the first criterion for the choice of a supplier, while delivery time is very important. In addition to this, the weight in the relationship with the supplier is not on MSF's side although MSF is an international organization recognized worldwide, and so the logistics must be able to perform its activity by adapting to the constraints imposed by its suppliers. This competence appears thus as multidimensional, with a first fixed dimension that is the humanitarian context to which MSF has adapted, a second dynamic dimension related to the constraints of countries in terms of clearance times and even access, a third dynamic dimension linked to the complexity of the field, a fourth dynamic dimension as a result of medical claims, and finally, a dynamic dimension upstream with the suppliers. In the words of the head of supply chain:

Logistics is like the top of a mountain. One side has all that is operational (programme definition, medical choices, etc) and the other side has the entire industrial world with whom we are in contact, the commercial reality... Normally, these two worlds do not know each other, and we [logistics] act as a buffer between the requests from MSF and the reality of implementation.

To deal with these two 'worlds', MSF's logistics relies on its technical capabilities that complement other organizational capabilities.

Responsiveness competence

Since its creation, MSF has been present in most of the greatest humanitarian crises in history, bringing assistance to affected populations. Emergency response, precisely to natural disasters, has been from the beginning at the core of MSF's work. What Rony Brauman, former president of MSF, considers as 'culture' or 'know-how' of the emergency, is what is seen as the responsiveness competence within the organization, an ability to respond quickly to any type of humanitarian crisis around the world, deploying different types of resources (physical and human) belonging to different professions (medical, logistics, water and sanitation, nutrition, construction, etc), by its own means, and without having too much impact on the course of the various programmes and projects. From high-media-coverage natural disasters to silent crises, from armed conflict to nutritional crises, MSF has shown that even with very limited access it is able to act and achieve its goal: to provide medical assistance to populations whose life or health is threatened. This capacity is achieved thanks to the responsiveness of the logistics system, which appears as the most important logistics competence within the organization. The procurement manager explains:

If there is an emergency and no one has in stock what it takes – it can be 48 hours or the next day – you have to manage to find a supplier that will be able to deliver in 24 hours. We did a lot of that for Haiti, because the freight department reserved entire aircrafts, 'full charters' who were leaving. For example, it was Monday and we had a 'full' that was leaving on Thursday, so it had to be charged on Wednesday. Here, on some missing items that we did not have in stock, we tried to negotiate with the supplier so that the products were charged on the plane, one way or another. So here it depends a lot on the supplier's responsiveness, because if the same supplier makes us wait a half day... For the procurement, [the media coverage] helped us a lot, because many providers were engaged, saying 'we want to do something for Haiti!'... I saw a manager of a big pharmaceutical company putting products in his car and taking them to DHL on Friday night.

Currently, MSF supply centres are able to respond to emergencies in 24 hours, and less than four weeks to regular field orders. Such lead times can be considered 'short' within the constraints of the respective context. This responsiveness competence is due mainly to the capacity developed by the organization to prioritize emergencies.

Discussion and implications

At the end of this research, probably the most important result is that the success of humanitarian relief operations is achieved through the organization's capacity to manage its logistical processes through the development of logistics capabilities and competences. This statement may not be revelatory, as most academic literature on humanitarian logistics puts forth the importance of logistics in humanitarian relief operations, but it constitutes a first attempt to show the link between logistics and the success of humanitarian operations through capabilities and competences, based on empirical data. The importance given to logistics at Médecins Sans Frontières, considered as a pillar for the success of their operations, let us think that from an organizational perspective logistics for humanitarian relief can be considered as a strategic function through which the overall strategy of an organization can be drawn. For humanitarian organizations, and for the humanitarian community at large, the evidence of logistics as the foundation of humanitarian operations' success represents an opportunity for the development of this activity towards a source for strategy. The MSF case study shows that logistics has the potential to be a strategic tool for the achievement of the organization's goals, as is the case for many firms in the commercial sector. If logistics is integrated in the overall strategy of humanitarian organizations, this activity could represent a cornerstone for interorganizational humanitarian co-ordination, reducing the effort of international NGOs when responding to emergencies and allowing a much more efficient resource allocation to provide better support to continuous aid operations and silent emergencies.

The case study results also presented a number of logistics competences and capabilities, among which responsiveness, adaptability and integration, as well as technical competences such as purchasing, procurement and transportation, were identified as the most important competences and capabilities for the organization. These results represent a small but substantial contribution towards an organizational logistics competence and capability model for humanitarian relief, a subject that is seldom found in academic literature. Moreover, the findings from the MSF case study provide a contribution to both logistics and SCM literature. The study of a context such as humanitarian relief provides insights that partially confirm the capabilities and competences found in most logistics competency models, but expands the knowledge on this topic to include competences and capabilities that are required in highly volatile environments and that can be used in industry. Further research on this topic is strongly encouraged through the replication of this study in other NGOs with similar characteristics (size, scope and logistics), in order to refine the results and improve the logistics competence and capability model.

References

Amit, R and Schoemaker, P J H (1993) Strategic assets and organizational rent, *Strategic Management Journal*, **14**, pp 33–46

Anderson, R D, Jerman, R E and Crum, M R (1998) Quality management influences on logistics performance, *Transportation Research Part E: Logistics and Transportation Review*, **34** (2), pp 137–48

Barney, J B (1991) Firm resources and sustained competitive advantage, *Journal of Management*, **17** (1), pp 99–120

Bolumole, Y A, Frankel, R and Naslund, D (2007) Developing a theoretical framework for logistics outsourcing, *Transportation Journal*, **46** (2), pp 35–54

Bowersox, D J, Closs, D J and Stank, T P (1999) *21st Century Logistics: Making supply chain integration a reality*, Council of Logistics Management, Oak Brook, IL

Carranza, O, Maltz, A and Antun, J P (2002) Linking logistics to strategy in Argentina, *International Journal of Physical Distribution & Logistics Management*, **32** (6), pp 480–96

Cho, J J-K, Ozment, J and Sink, H (2008) Logistics capability, logistics outsourcing and firm performance in an e-commerce market, *International Journal of Physical Distribution & Logistics Management*, **38** (5), pp 336–59

Closs, D J and Mollenkopf, D A (2004) A global supply chain framework, *Industrial Marketing Management*, **33**, pp 37–44

Daugherty, P J, Stank, T P and Ellinger, A E (1998) Leveraging logistics/distribution capabilities: the effect of logistics service on market share, *Journal of Business Logistics*, **19** (2), pp 35–51

Day, G S (1994) The capabilities of market–driven organizations, *Journal of Marketing*, **58**, pp 37–52

Day, G S and Wensley, R (1988) Assessing advantage: a framework for diagnosing competitive superiority, *Journal of Marketing*, **52**, pp 1–20

Eisenhardt, K M (1989) Building theories from case study research, *Academy of Management Review*, **14** (4), pp 532–50

Ellram, L M (1996) The use of the case study method in logistics research, *Journal of Business Logistics*, **17** (2), pp 93–138

Esper, T L, Fugate, B S and Davis-Sramek, B (2007) Logistics learning capability: sustaining the competitive advantage gained through logistics leverage, *Journal of Business Logistics*, **28** (2), pp 57–81

Fawcett, S E, Cantalone, R and Smith, S R (1996) An investigation on the impact of flexibility on global reach and firm performance, *Journal of Business Logistics*, **17** (2), pp 167–96

Foss, N J (1996) Introduction: the emerging competence perspective, in *Towards a Competence Theory of the Firm*, ed N J Foss and C Knudsen, pp 1–12, Routledge, New York

Gilmour, P (1999) A strategic audit framework to improve supply chain performance, *Journal of Business & Industrial Marketing*, **14** (5/6), pp 355–63

Goldsby, T J and Stank, T P (2000) World class logistics performance and environmentally responsible logistics practices, *Journal of Business Logistics*, **21** (2), pp 187–208

Grant, R M (1991) The resource-based theory of competitive advantage: implications for strategy formulation, *California Management Review*, Spring, pp 114–46

Halldorsson, A and Aastrup, J (2003) Quality criteria for qualitative inquiries in logistics, *European Journal of Operational Research*, **144**, pp 321–32

Hamel, G and Heene, A (1994) *Competence-Based Competition*, The Strategic Management Series, John Wiley & Sons, New York

Hitt, M A and Ireland, R D (1986) Relationships among corporate level distinctive competencies, diversification strategy, corporate structure and performance, *Journal of Management Studies*, **23** (4), pp 401–16

Lapadat, J C (2000) Problematizing transcription: purpose, paradigm and quality, *Research Methodology*, **3** (3), pp 203–19

Li, P-C and Lin, B-W (2006) Building global logistics competence with Chinese OEM Suppliers, *Technology in Society*, **28**, pp 333–48

Lincoln, Y S and Guba, E G (1985) *Naturalistic Inquiry*, Sage Publications, Newbury Park, CA

Liu, X, Grant, D B, McKinnon, A C and Feng, Y (2010) An empirical examination of the contribution of capabilities to the competitiveness of logistics service providers: a perspective from China, *International Journal of Physical Distribution & Logistics Management*, **40** (10), pp 847–66

Lu, C-S and Yang, C-C (2010) Logistics service capabilities and firm performance of international distribution center operators, *The Service Industries Journal*, **30** (2), pp 281–98

Lynch, D F, Keller, S B and Ozmet, J (2000) The effect of logistics capabilities and strategy on firm performance, *Journal of Business Logistics*, **22** (2), pp 47–67

Mentzer, J T, Min, S and Bobbit, L M (2004) Toward a unified theory of logistics, *International Journal of Physical Distribution & Logistics Management*, 34 (8), pp 606–27

Meredith, J, Raturi, A, Gyampah, K and Kaplan, B (1989) Alternative research paradigms in operations, *Journal of Operations Management*, 8 (4), pp 297–326

Mollenkopf, D A and Dapiran, G P (1999) Best Practice Logistics: How well do Australian/New Zealand firms perform?, Proceedings of the Council of Logistics Management Annual Conference, Toronto, Canada

Mollenkopf, D A and Dapiran, G P (2005) The importance of developing logistics competencies: a study of Australian and New Zealand firms, *International Journal of Logistics*, 8 (1), pp 1–14

Morash, E A, Dröge, C and Vickery, S K (1996) Strategic logistics capabilities for competitive advantage and firm success, *Journal of Business Logistics*, 17 (1), pp 1–22

MSF (2010) [accessed 29 April 2016] Rapport d'Activités 2010, *Médecins Sans Frontières* [Online] http://www.msf.fr/sites/www.msf.fr/files/msf_activity_report_2010_french_final_2.pdf

MSF (2014a) *Gestion harmonieuse des ressources humaines de l'administration et de la logistique*, Médecins Sans Frontières, Paris

MSF (2014b) [accessed 29 April 2016] Rapport d'Activité 2013–2014, *Médecins Sans Frontières* [Online] http://www.msf.fr/sites/www.msf.fr/files/rapac2013-2014.pdf

MSUGLRT (1995) *World Class Logistics: The challenge of managing continuous change*, Council of Logistics Management, Oak Brook, IL

Ochs, E (1979) Transcription as theory, in *Developmental Pragmatics*, ed E Ochs and B B Schiefflin, pp 43–72, Academic, New York

Olavarrieta, S and Ellinger, A E (1997) Resource-based theory and strategic logistics research, *International Journal of Physical Distribution & Logistics Management*, 27 (9/10), pp 559–87

Oloruntuba, R and Gray, R (2006) Humanitarian aid: an agile supply chain?, *Supply Chain Management: An international journal*, 11 (2), pp 115–20

Peko, G and Ahmed, M D (2011) Leveraging logistics core competence for competitive advantage in commodity markets: a New Zealand case study, *New Zealand Journal of Applied Business Research*, 9 (1), pp 11–24

Penrose, E (1959) *The Theory of the Growth of the Firm*, Blackwell, Oxford

Porter, M E (1980) *Competitive Strategy: Techniques for analyzing industries and competitors*, The Free Press, New York

Prahalad, C K and Hamel, G (1990) The core competence of the corporation, *Harvard Business Review*, 68 (3), pp 79–91

Richey, R G, Daugherty, P J and Roath, A S (2007) Firm technological readiness and complementarity: capabilities impacting logistics service competency and performance, *Journal of Business Logistics*, 28 (1), pp 195–228

Sanchez, R and Heene, A (1997) Reinventing strategic management: new theory and practice for competence-based competition, *European Management Journal*, **15** (3), pp 303–17

Sandberg, E and Abrahamsson, M (2011) Logistics capabilities for sustainable competitive advantage, *International Journal of Logistics Research and Applications*, **14** (1), pp 61–75

Selznick, P (1957) *Leadership in Administration*, Harper, New York

Shang, K-C and Marlow, P B (2005) Logistics capability and performance in Taiwan's major manufacturing firms, *Transportation Research Part E: Logistics and Transportation Review*, **41** (3), pp 217–34

Shang, K-C and Marlow, P B (2007) The effects of logistics competency on performance, *Journal of International Logistics and Trade*, **5** (2), pp 45–66

Shang, K-C and Sun, L-F (2004) Taxonomy in logistics management: a resource-based perspective, *International Journal of Management*, **21** (2), pp 149–65

Snow, C C and Hrebiniak, L G (1980) Strategy, distinctive competence, and organizational performance, *Administrative Science Quarterly*, **25**, pp 317–36

Stalk, G, Evans, P and Shulman, L E (1992) Competing on capabilities: the new rules of corporate strategy, *Harvard Business Review*, March–April, pp 57–157

Stank, T P and Lackey, C W J (1997) Enhancing performance through logistical capabilities in Mexican *maquiladora* firms, *Journal of Business Logistics*, **18** (1), pp 91–123

Stank, T P, Keller, S B and Closs, D J (2001) Performance benefits of supply chain logistical integration, *Transportation Journal*, Winter/Spring, pp 32–46

Teece, D J, Pisano, G and Shuen, A (1997) Dynamic capabilities and strategic management, *Strategic Management Journal*, **18** (7), pp 509–33

The Nobel Foundation (1999) [accessed 29 April 2016] The Nobel Peace Prize 1999, *Nobelprize.org*, Nobel Media AB 2014 [Online] http://www.nobelprize.org/nobel_prizes/peace/laureates/1999/

Van Wassenhove, L N (2006) Humanitarian aid logistics: supply chain management in high gear, *Journal of the Operational Research Society*, **57**, pp 475–89

Voss, C, Tsikriktsis, N and Frohlich, M (2002) Case research in operations management, *International Journal of Operations and Production Management*, **22** (2), pp 195–219

Wernerfelt, B (1984) A resource-based view of the firm, *Strategic Management Journal*, **5**, pp 171–80

Yin, R K (2009) *Case Study Research: Design and methods*, 4th edn, Sage Publications, Thousand Oaks, CA

Zhao, M, Dröge, C and Stank, T P (2001) The effect of logistics capabilities on firm performance: customer-focused versus information-focused capabilities, *Journal of Business Logistics*, **22** (2), pp 91–107

Acknowledgements

The author would like to acknowledge Médecins Sans Frontières (the French NGO that accepted and supported this research work), and Professors Nathalie Fabbe-Costes and Marianne Jahre for their comments on previous versions of this research.

PART TWO
Setting up a supply chain network

Setting up a humanitarian supply network

2.1

GRAHAM HEASLIP

HUMLOG Institute, Finland and Galway Mayo Institute of Technology, Ireland

GYÖNGYI KOVÁCS

HUMLOG Institute, Hanken School of Economics, Helsinki, Finland

Introduction

A first, strategic question is how to design the humanitarian supply chain, and how to set up its network. Many facets of network design are of importance to humanitarian supply chains, from facility location to relationship governance. The humanitarian context brings one aspect to network design questions that is different from others: the focus on collaboration. Whilst commercial supply chains would quickly run into antitrust regulations, humanitarian organizations are encouraged if not required to collaborate on many fronts, not least in questions of logistics and supply chain management. Thus, network design is not a matter of individual humanitarian organizations only but often one that is co-ordinated across several of them. Not surprisingly, much emphasis is placed on collaborative efforts, whether on the establishment of the Logistics Cluster, the operation of common services or the use of common enterprise resource planning (ERP) systems to joint facility location. Efforts are either run jointly, harmonized across organizations and programmes, or offered as services to one another (see the case study in Chapter 2.2). For example, various humanitarian organizations have started to offer warehousing (depot, hub), transportation (air or land) or procurement services to other humanitarian organizations.

Yet whilst much attention has been paid to collaboration across humanitarian organizations, the typical questions of supply chain collaboration also apply. Establishing long-term relationships with global suppliers is challenged by the trend towards the use of local and regional materials and suppliers, which, apart from being more culturally appropriate, also contributes to the building of local capacity, community resilience and local economic growth. 'As local as possible, as international as necessary' is the new mantra of the aid community (UNSG, 2016: A/70/XX). 'Core Responsibility Four' in the same report proposes a few other points as well that will impact on humanitarian supply network design: the reinforcement of existing national and local systems instead of setting up separate aid supply chains; the focus on anticipation and preparedness, factoring in new risks due to, for example, climate change; and a link between development and humanitarian activities. As for the last, the point is not any longer to deliver aid but to 'end need'. This sets a new agenda for how to set up humanitarian supply networks. It requires both the potential of scaling-up existing systems and structures (see, for example, the case on the nutrition supply chain in Kenya in Chapter 2.3) when needed, but also, that there is a long-term vision of ending need, and a sustainable approach to supply chain design (Haavisto and Kovács, 2014). Let's go through the implications of each of these.

Local versus global considerations in humanitarian supply chains

'Think global, act local' has been used in various settings before. The humanitarian one is no exception. (Minimum) standards and interoperability are global questions, but actual materials, modules and interpretations can be very local as long as these requirements are met. Local solutions bring many advantages also from the supply chain perspective: incorporating local implementing partners, suppliers and, also, end users not only contributes to local capacity building but improves the local appropriateness of product and service deliveries, and incorporates local (technical) know-how into the supply chain as well as being able to increase both supply chain efficiency and effectiveness (Matopoulos, Kovács and Hayes, 2014).

From a network design perspective, however, setting up global support systems with local interoperability may also represent a challenge. For a long time, network design had focused on the establishment of regional hubs or depot systems, and the very question of facility location with respect to these. Many of them were established in good collaborative fashion in a way that should serve many humanitarian organizations, including many types of organizations (eg the United Nations Humanitarian Response Depot (UNHRD) network), others for specific organizations, or specific groups of organizations. Common to these was the effort to decentralize operations globally (Gatignon *et al*, 2010) – though decoupling more regional warehousing and inventory management in a way that would speed up deliveries in various regions whilst not necessarily decentralizing other functions such as procurement.

Facility location in the humanitarian context follows the same considerations of the locations of supply and (forecasted) demand nodes as well as transportation rates, and the total costs of all facilities, as in any other context (Balcik and Beamon, 2008). There are a few other considerations that are specific to the humanitarian context beyond the ones in typical optimization models, such as:

- maximizing the outreach of a facility also across borders;

- increasing the speed and flexibility of deliveries;

- enabling intermodal solutions, while:

- considering the disaster proneness, political and economic stability, security, as well as ease of support operations (such as customs clearance) in the particular location.

Other solutions to network design even consider facilities in non-fixed locations such as the sea-basing of hospitals and warehouses (Tatham, Kovács and Vaillancourt, 2016), as well as mobile warehouses on the road, giving a new meaning to 'moving stock' or 'inventory in transit'. The latter has been used for the service of populations on the move, ie to be able to reach vast refugee movements.

Importantly, however, any facility with pre-positioned items stores stock that is usable across regions, and is for push supply chains, ie the first days after a disaster. Pre-positioning is a commonly used concept of speculation in humanitarian supply chains, though humanitarian supply chains do simultaneously also use postponement strategies in the use of blanket stock.

The potential use of the latter is challenged, though, by accountability requirements to donors alongside the implementation of rather rigid ERP systems, leading to a trade-off between flexibility, time and cost-efficiency on the one hand, and accountability and compliance on the other.

Returning to the mantra of 'as local as possible', however, it is not global but local and national pre-positioning that becomes central. Strengthening local preparedness, and scaling it up with global support if needed, emphasizes the interoperability of humanitarian organizations not just with one another but with their local counterparts. This may lead to a reconsideration of current facility locations and the needs for such facilities, as well as the items they hold, with respect to pre-positioned inventories in various countries they have served so far. Also, different logistical functions may gain or lose in emphasis in this process.

Anticipating, and preparing for, new risks

Every country has its disaster profile and thereby a possibility to learn from past disaster patterns. Also, many disasters are reoccurring in nature – even earthquakes have their cycles, pandemics their patterns as well as seasons – and natural and political crises have a way to trigger one another. Specific maps exist for certain types of concerns, from a focus on hydro-meteorological events, to risk maps that focus on terrorism. But whilst much has been learned from past events and trends, other developments are currently altering these patterns and deserve closer attention. What is more, global events may have local impacts far away from their actual occurrence, either as they trigger migration patterns or through supply chain disruptions.

Over the past decades, changes in climate, geopolitics, and global and local economies have contributed to a change in threat scenarios alongside actual disaster risks, patterns and impacts – whether these be in terms of conflicts, transnational crime, extreme weather events, pandemics or migration. For example, the current refugee crisis in the European Union (EU) can be traced back not only to the existing geopolitical crises and wars, but also to resource scarcity and climate variability, which, according to Kelley *et al* (2015), are key causes of the Syrian crisis. Amongst others, the UN Security Council and US Department of Defense have called climate change a 'threat multiplier' due to its potential to aggravate many of the security challenges, from infectious disease to terrorism. Concurrently, geopolitical changes in the Ukraine and also particularly in Syria impact on global power relations. However, notwithstanding existing research on triggers and impacts of extreme events, the incident evolution of extreme events, ie the ways in which such extreme events develop and evolve across sectors and countries, remain little understood (Hassel *et al*, 2015).

Thus, not only are humanitarian supply chains increasingly concerned with climate change, extreme weather events, geopolitical crises and migration patterns, but also, with efforts of early warning, preparedness and mitigation anywhere in the world (see Figure 2.1.1). As the same UNSG (2016) report stated, countries need to prepare for climate change-induced cross-border migration.

What does this mean for humanitarian supply networks? Not only do they need to be operational in a way that enables them to follow refugee flows, but also they need to be able to be anticipatory and proactive. This stresses the need for common appeals processes, and a common understanding of the factors that will change the operational environment. There is a strong need for also linking not only disaster patterns to logistical decisions but climate science to the changes in strategic supply chain decisions – not just one of pre-positioning but of the question when to start scaling up, and mobilizing. Order cycles are but one aspect stressing the need for anticipation, scaling up the manufacturing of specific items (eg of specific drugs for pandemic outbreaks) requires even more time and effort.

Figure 2.1.1 Local repercussions of global events

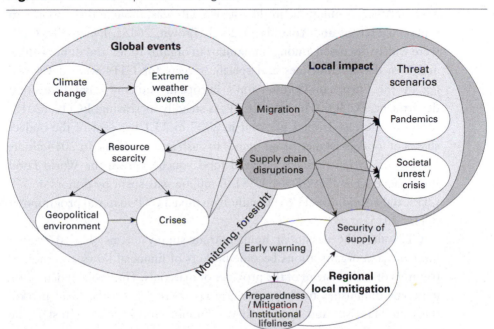

Cash transfer programmes changing the logic of humanitarian supply chains

Humanitarian supply chains have in the past been primarily concerned with the delivery of products and services. To date, the gradual introduction and acceptance of cash transfer programmes (CTPs) is radically altering supply chain design (Heaslip, Kovács and Haavisto, 2015). CTPs include a variety of financial instruments that can take different transfer modalities (cash, or vouchers, as opposed to the transfer modality of in-kind donations, ie materials) and transfer mechanisms for beneficiaries to access these modalities (from direct cash, to credit card systems, and even new mobile cash systems). CTPs are not novel per se; they have been used in development aid, including as micro-financing, for poverty alleviation (eg food vouchers), and as an integral part of various social programmes (Banerjee and He, 2007; Davies and Davey, 2008; Birdsall *et al*, 2010). What is new is their use in the immediate response phase of disaster relief, including in the very early stages of natural or man-made sudden-onset emergencies.

The origins of CTPs notwithstanding, in disaster relief, they have been gradually introduced, from experimentation with CTPs in hurricane Mitch in 1998 (IFRC, 2012) to more systematic discussions by 2010 (WFP, 2010), and during this time period, also the formation of communities of practice such as the Cash Learning Partnership (CaLP) that has since developed a 'Cash Atlas'. A milestone in the use of CTPs was, though, the response to typhoons Haiyan and Yolanda in 2013 (Brown, 2015). Eventually, CTPs were widely discussed among humanitarian organizations and donors alike, and even donor guidelines and specific targets for CTPs were developed (eg by the European Commission's European Aid and Civil Protection department, ECHO). The use of CTPs is steadily increasing; ECHO (2013) shows an increase from 2 per cent in 2007 to 23.1 per cent of the budget shares of food assistance programmes to cash and vouchers. In 2014 alone, 1.9 million Syrian refugees received food vouchers from the World Food Programme. Overall, in 2014, US\$113 million was spent by donors on full CTPs, and an additional US\$96 million on mixed CTP-material programmes (GHA, 2015).

CTPs alter the design of humanitarian supply chains (HSCs) in that humanitarian organizations become brokers of financial flows and the distributors of cash, instead of the provider of materials. Their role in delivering materials diminishes to those that are not available on the local market (Heaslip, Haavisto and Kovács, 2016). Simultaneously, CTPs reinstate the purchasing power of beneficiaries, by which beneficiaries become active members of the HSC. This implies a significant change in supply chain strategy and also network design, moving from following a push principle to a pull one as more information from needs assessments becomes available. CTPs enable a pull strategy to be implemented earlier, if not from the beginning. Through this, arguably, they can meet the actual needs of beneficiaries quicker and more accurately (Heaslip, Haavisto and Kovács, 2016).

Overall, CTPs include a variety of financial instruments. ECHO talks of conditional versus unconditional cash transfers as compared to vouchers (ECHO, 2013), while Brown (2015) also adds loan mechanisms (conditional grants, micro-finance) to the list of CTPs. In terms of transfer mechanism, CTPs vary from direct cash to transfers to bank accounts to different types of credit card and supplier card and voucher systems. Different conditions need to apply before any of these transfer modalities and mechanisms can be selected; most importantly, items need to be available on a market, be affordable and accessible. Furthermore, from the perspective of aid effectiveness, aid needs to reach the most vulnerable and, from the perspective of donors, regardless of the modality (in-kind, cash or voucher), the accountability of such flows need to be assured.

The long list of conditions under which CTP can be applied implies a fluctuating mix in the modality (in-kind, cash or voucher) of aid. Market conditions notwithstanding, disasters, whether natural or man-made, typically impact negatively on transport and communications infrastructure, even electricity supply and, thereby, the use of banking systems. Yet operating banking systems are a prerequisite for many CTP transfer mechanisms. CTPs highlight the importance not only of the security of the financial sector but also a reliance on energy security to support the financial sector overall. Interestingly, cashless societies are particularly vulnerable to any impact to their energy security from the perspective of their banking systems. In other words, not only do CTPs alter humanitarian supply network design but, also, they expose humanitarian supply networks to new vulnerabilities alongside the possibilities that they bring.

Concluding remarks

What does network design, and setting up a network, mean for humanitarian organizations? Even in the most traditional of network optimization questions, that of facility location, their considerations extend beyond the cost trade-offs that optimization techniques focus on. In the humanitarian context, chosen locations need to have vast outreach but minimize disaster proneness, offer intermodality, but also political stability. What is more, however, the ideal of strengthening local and national structures and scale-up instead of setting-up own networks challenges extant networks. Humanitarian supply networks need to be altered to increase their interoperability with local structures and implementing partners, and to support them in scaling up in emergencies.

At the same time, preparedness and the anticipation of risks is key. And yet at the same time, preparedness is not necessarily a question of pre-positioning but one of, again, supporting existing structures, and in fact reducing the holding of items, using, wherever possible, CTPs instead. This requires not only a change in focus from materials to services and financial flows but, also, the incorporation of entirely new supply chain members for the distribution of aid. From a network optimization perspective, it is an entirely new ball game.

References

Balcik, B and Beamon, B M (2008) Facility location in humanitarian relief, *International Journal of Logistics: Research and applications*, **11** (2), pp 101–21

Banerjee, A V and He, R (2007) *Making Aid Work*, MIT press, Cambridge, pp 91–97

Birdsall, N, Savedoff, W D, Mahgoub, A and Vyborny, K (2010) *Cash on Delivery: A new approach to foreign aid*, CGD Books

Brown, M (2015) Are cash transfers the 'new normal' in the Philippines? Challenges and opportunities from typhoon Haiyan, *Humanitarian Exchange Magazine*, **63**

Davies, S and Davey, J (2008) A regional multiplier approach to estimating the impact of cash transfers on the market: the case of cash transfers in rural Malawi, *Development Policy Review*, **26** (1), pp 91–111

ECHO (2013) Cash and vouchers: increasing efficiency and effectiveness across all sectors, *Thematic Policy Document No.3*, Dec 2013

Gatignon, Aline, Van Wassenhove, Luk N and Charles, Aurélie (2010) The Yogyakarta earthquake: humanitarian relief through IFRC's decentralized supply chain, *International Journal of Production Economics*, **126** (1), pp 102–10

Global Humanitarian Assistance (2015) [accessed 30 September 2015] Global Humanitarian Assistance Report 2015 [Online] http://www.globalhumanitarianassistance.org/wp-content/uploads/2015/06/GHA-Report-2015_-Interactive_Online.pdf

Haavisto, Ira and Kovács, Gyöngyi (2014) Perspectives on sustainability in humanitarian supply chains, *Disaster Prevention and Management*, **23** (5) pp 610–31

Hassel, H, Cedergren, A, Svegrup, L and Johansson, J (2015) Developing a framework for characterising cascading failures in past events to inform emergency response decisions, in *Safety and Reliability: Methodology and applications*, ed T Nowalkowski, M Młyńczak, A Jodejko-Pietruczuk and S Werbińska-Wojciechowska, Boca Raton, CRC Press, pp 33–42

Heaslip, G, Haavisto, I and Kovács, G (2016) Cash as a form of relief, in *Advances in Managing Humanitarian Operations*, ed C Zobel, N Altay and M Haselkorn, Springer

Heaslip, G, Kovács, G and Haavisto, I (2015) Supply chain innovation: lessons from humanitarian supply chains, in *Research in the Decision Sciences for Global Supply Chain Network Innovations*, ed J Stentoft, A Paulraj and G Vastag, Pearson Press, Australia, pp 9–26

IFRC (2012) [accessed 8 April 2014] International Federation of Red Cross and Red Crescent Societies, Annual Report [Online] http://www.ifrc.org/Global/Photos/Secretariat/201401/1259900-IFRC%20Annual%20Report%202012-EN_LR.pdf

Kelley, C P, Mohtadi, S, Cane, M A, Seager, R and Kushnir, Y (2015) Climate change in the Fertile Crescent and implications of the recent Syrian drought, *Proceedings of the National Academy of Sciences*, **112** (11), 3241–46

Matopoulos, Aristides, Kovács, Gyöngyi and Hayes, Odran (2014) Examining the use of local resources and procurement practices in humanitarian supply chains: an empirical examination of large scale house reconstruction projects, *Decision Sciences*, **45** (4), pp 621–46

Tatham, Peter, Kovács, Gyöngyi and Vaillancourt, Alain (2016) Evaluating the applicability of sea-basing to support the preparation for, and response to, rapid onset disasters, *IEEE Transactions on Engineering Management*, **63** (1), 67–77

UNSG (2016) [accessed 14 February 2016] One Humanity: Shared Responsibility, *Report of the United Nations Secretary-General for the World Humanitarian Summit*, advanced unedited draft A/70/XX [Online] https://www.worldhumanitariansummit.org/bitcache/5861a3b8dc0a6e280cf0da2f0fae9c6167bd0122?vid=569103&disposition=inline&op=view

World Food Programme (WFP) (2010) [accessed 30 September 2015] Revolution: From Food Aid to Food Assistance [Online] https://www.wfp.org/content/revolution-food-aid-food-assistance-innovations-overcoming-hunger

Service triad case study 2.2

GRAHAM HEASLIP

HUMLOG Institute, Finland and Galway Mayo Institute of
Technology, Ireland

- This case study examines the interaction between a buyer, a service provider and an end customer in a humanitarian environment.

- A key characteristic of service triads is that services are directly delivered by the service provider to the end customer on behalf of the buyer.

- The service provider's performance is determinative for end-customer satisfaction, and the buyer cannot directly control this performance other than through contracts and monitoring activities.

How to manage services in a business-to-business (B2B) setting is becoming important as increasing competition forces organizations to work more closely with external partners in the supply chain (Tate *et al*, 2010; Van Iwaarden and Van der Valk, 2013). An example of such collaboration is the service triad, in which purchased services are directly delivered by service providers to customers (Van Iwaarden and Van der Valk, 2013).

The perspective of humanitarian logistics (HL) as a service has been rare in management studies (Heaslip, 2013; Kovács, 2014). Delivery of the service (food, shelter, water) only happens under extraordinary conditions (Altay and Green, 2006; Heaslip, 2013; Matopoulos, Kovács and Hayes, 2014). Furthermore, most customers do not pay for the service (Oloruntoba and Gray, 2009; Kovács, 2014), as such, the service triad is a fleeting structure rather than an enduring one – but no less important for that. A trend in this context is that international humanitarian organizations (IHOs) have started to develop services that they offer each other (Kovács and Spens, 2011; Heaslip, 2013; Kovács, 2014), yet research on this topic is virtually non-existent (Heaslip, 2013). Interestingly, most of the services IHOs offer to each other fall under the realm of logistics (Van Wassenhove, 2006); for example, the World Food Programme (WFP) offers customs clearance, transportation and warehousing services through the Logistics Cluster to other organizations (WFP, 2013). For many IHOs the way to sustainable competitive advantage may not lie in changes in the product, promotion or pricing strategies of the organization, but rather in improving customer service within HL, ancillary services such as logistics and distribution (Oloruntoba and Gray, 2009; Kovács, 2014), customs clearance, procurement and servitization (Heaslip, 2013).

There are two unique features to service triads. First, there is direct contact between service provider and end customer (Li and Choi, 2009; Van der Valk, Wynstra and Axelsson, 2009; Van der Valk and Van Iwaarden, 2011). Hence, the service provider's performance is determinative for end-customer satisfaction, and the buyer cannot directly control this performance other than through contracts and monitoring activities (for example, through contracts and/or service level agreements). Second, while there is a contract between end customer and buyer, and between buyer and service provider, there is no contract, however, between the service provider and end customer.

Table 2.2.1 provides an overview of the humanitarian logistics service triad actors in a B2B service triad. The buying organization is highly dependent on the service provider for its business performance. The buying organization for this research is a donor organization, specifically, an international government. The donor purchases products and services to allow an individual end user to perform a job or task on its behalf. Donors are intrinsically interested in the results of humanitarian programmes, and set the constraints of these programmes (Jahre and Heigh, 2008; Majewski, Navangul and Heigh, 2010).

As in third-party logistics, there are various possibilities for these relationships. Material flows can originate from donors if they are suppliers at the same time, and go through IHOs to implementing partners (IPs), or just be administered by IHOs to reach IPs. Financial flows from donors can target IHOs, IPs or both – though the most typical situation would foresee a financial transaction from donor to IHO to IP, which is why the situation is sometimes described as consisting of sequential principal–agent relationships (Lundin, 2011) and not triads. Then again, also in third-party logistics

Table 2.2.1 Humanitarian service triad actors

Commercial Triad Actors	Humanitarian Triad Actors	Function	Authors
Buyer organization	Donors (including governments, institutional, private)	Provides funding for IHOs to procure staff, relief goods, and transport them to disaster sites and/or implementing partners for relief distribution The donor not only provides funding but may also provide supplies such as clothing, food or cooking oil – here the donor acts like a supplier, except that the donor does not get paid	Heaslip, 2013; Holguín-Veras *et al.*, 2013; Majewski, Navangul and Heigh, 2010; Oloruntoba and Gray, 2009; Jahre and Heigh, 2008; Van Wassenhove, 2006; Kovács and Spens, 2009
Service provider	IHOs (UN agencies, non-government organizations)	Act as delivery partners in particular programmes or through clusters Provide services such as: information consultancy; procurement; customs clearance; warehousing; distribution; inventory management; fleet service; postponement; training	Kovács, 2014; Heaslip, 2013; Jahre and Jensen, 2010; Oloruntoba and Gray, 2009
End customer	Implementing partner	Have relationship with buyer organization; these are specific organizations, with specific functions (such as water, shelter etc)	Kovács, 2014; Jahre and Jensen, 2010

(Bask, 2001), it is the sum of the flows (material, information, finance and title flows) that determines the triad.

The provision of services by IHOs has now turned into a conscious and explicit strategy with services becoming the main differentiating factor in a totally integrated products and service offering (Heaslip, 2013; Kovács, 2014). As this research is focused on B2B services it rules out the possibility of beneficiaries being part of the service triad, instead the implementing partner is considered the end customer. As noted by Kovács (2014: 280):

> The role of implementing partners also deserves more attention. Largely neglected in research, it is often not the big international NGOs (BINGOs) or aid agencies that conduct the last-mile distribution but their implementing partners on the ground.

In this chapter, we first provide a case history. The discussion is based on data that we obtained through data triangulations (ie data collected at different times at multiple locations from multiple participants). The case studied involved the service triad of Irish Aid (donor/buyer organization) – UNWFP (IHO/service provider) – Concern Worldwide (Ireland) (implementing partner/ end customer).

The buyer organization

Irish Aid (IA) has been in the top 20 of government contributions to humanitarian aid of the past decade (GHA, 2011). In 2014, the Irish Government spent €85 million on Ireland's aid programme, making it the seventh most generous humanitarian donor in the world (Humanitarian Assistance Policy, 2015). IA does not itself deliver aid on the ground in emergencies, it uses its various implementing partners to deliver aid on its behalf.

The service provider

UNWFP procures, manages, stores and transports emergency supplies on behalf of the humanitarian community; UNWFP through its affiliate the United Nations Humanitarian Response Depot (UNHRD) pre-positions inventory in six locations worldwide – Panama, Ghana, Dubai, Subang, Las Palmas and Brindisi. The WFP was selected for this case because the WFP is the lead agency of the Logistics Cluster, and has therefore developed numerous 'common services' for other agencies and organizations in the cluster.

The end customer

Concern Worldwide are dedicated to tackling poverty and suffering in the world's poorest countries. They work in partnership with the very poorest people in these countries, directly enabling them to improve their lives. Concern Worldwide operate as an implementing partner for IA, delivering aid on their behalf.

In the humanitarian service triad, as in third-party logistics, the actual material, financial, information and title flows determine the triad, regardless of the contractual set-up. In any case, financial flows originate from donors, hence they are the principal in the humanitarian service triad, whereas the UN agency or IHO as service provider, and the IP will conduct agent-like behaviour. The IP is mainly interested in the desired outcome of the service encounter and possibly in the process that brings about that outcome. Eisenhardt (1989) proposes that a contractual contract is more likely to lead any agent to behave in the interests of the principal. Based on this, we propose the following:

> *Proposition 1: Within the service triad, the contract applying to the donor–IP dyad is contractual based.*

Zsidisin and Ellram (2003) point out that the buyer (here donor) will primarily be interested in pricing, compliance and performance information as a means to reduce risk and monitor supplier behaviour. Van der Valk and Van Iwaarden (2011) posit that cost reduction may be an important buyer objective, while quality is likely an end-customer objective. Building on Tate *et al* (2010) we propose the following:

> *Proposition 2: Within the service triad, the contract applying to the donor–UN agency/IHO dyad is contractual based.*

Findings

Proposition 1

For proposition 1, similar to Eisenhardt (1989: 60) – who suggested, 'When the principal has information to verify agent behaviour, the agent is more likely to behave in the interest of the principal' – our research finds that end customers will opt for outcome-based contracts. Our findings are comparable to Neely (1999: 220) who found that people focus on the issues that are measured and rewarded within an organization, and it 'is likely that the agent will behave in its own interest by complying with the objectives that are more easily measured and thus are used to evaluate its performance'. In the contract between IA and Concern Worldwide the contract is based on measurable outcomes such as cost, timeliness and issue resolution. IA observed: 'As we got more experience in the area [humanitarian sector] we required more information regarding what outcomes needed to be included in our contracts. Part of this was to adhere to transparency and accounting procedures.' It should be noted, however, that certain aspects of the contract such as beneficiary satisfaction was not considered.

These findings show that if contracts are not designed carefully, opportunistic behaviour may occur in the unmeasured areas, so that the spirit of the contract may be lost. For example, IA had to continuously modify its measures, or its IP would act in their own self-interest and try to 'game' the system. IA remarked: 'There have been situations in the past where agencies have tried to take advantage and act in their self-interest and not in Irish Aid's interest, even though we would be purchasing the goods.' This finding is similar to those reported by Tate *et al* (2010) when investigating the purchasing of marketing services in a triadic relationship.

In this outcome-based contract, criteria had to be modified to take into account all possible deviations from the intent of the contract. The IP focused on what was measured, rather than performing to the behaviour that they clearly knew that IA was interested in. These findings show that if contracts are not designed carefully, opportunistic behaviour may occur in the unmeasured areas and the spirit of the contract may be lost – which leaves the buyer facing the risk of reputational degradation. It is thus highly important that appropriate measures are identified. Similar to Tate *et al* (2010) this research found that even if the IP possess the 'right' skills, they may still fail to use them if information asymmetry allows such actions and if there are cost savings involved. Similarly, buyers seek information to help make better choices. IA commented: 'It is important for our customers to tell us what services they would like... We have frank conversations with our customers so that we can understand their position.'

New insights were obtained regarding the presence of behavioural-based outcomes in the buyer/end-customer relationship. Our research suggests that a hybrid (mixed) contract exists. The hybrid approach has the benefit of providing detailed performance data regarding behaviour elements, such as processes for accessing funding, as well as outcome-based criteria such as cost, timeliness and issue resolution. While behaviour monitoring may be perceived by the end customer to be obtrusive, the presence of a behavioural contract appears to help prevent the end customer from displaying reactant behaviour. IA commented: 'We have very good relationships with UNWFP and Concern Worldwide and in some cases personal friendships, which facilitates more of the soft skills when negotiating contracts; we try to co-create with our implementing partners.' The presence of behavioural contracts reduces the possibility of misalignment of contracts. This finding suggests that in the cases studied, behavioural governance outweighs contractual governance.

To avoid opportunistic behaviour, incentive capability was adopted in the contract design. Contracts were subsequently designed so that the actions with the highest pay-off to the end customer are also the actions that are most appropriate from the donor's point of view.

Proposition 2

Proposition 2 stated that the contract applying to the buyer/service-provider dyad is outcome-based. In line with Tate *et al* (2010) we observe that the way in which the service is perceived governs much of the contractual behaviour related to services. The end-customer's preference for outcome-based contracts with the buyer is not necessarily reflected in the service provider–buyer contract. IA has a three-year contract with UNWFP, which is a hybrid contract consisting of outcome-based measurable outcomes, such as cost, timeliness and issue resolution and behavioural outcomes. Underlying the contract is a service level agreement, which includes arrangements for the service delivery process. It seems that the donor prefers to focus on aspects such as measurability of performance in determining their contracts, and to specify a behaviour-based contract rather than to transfer their end-customer's requirements to UNWFP. While the behaviour monitoring may be perceived by the service provider to be meddlesome, the presence of a behavioural contract looks like an aid in preventing the service provider from displaying opportunism behaviour. Contrary to earlier research by Van der Valk and Van Iwaarden (2011), this research determines that the preferred contract between the buyer and the service provider is a hybrid-based contract.

Eisenhardt (1989) observed that the right type of contract varies with the length of relationship. While this may be true, we did not find support for this in the practices among the case studies. For example, prior to UNWFP involvement, IA used behaviour-based contracts with its service providers within long-term relationships. Later, when UNWFP became involved, IA modified its contracting approach to improve measurable performance, and developed a mix of behaviour-based and outcome-based contracts. IA remarked: 'We learnt so much from our previous involvement in humanitarian aid. With UNWFP we think we have struck the right balance of accountable measurements.'

A major characteristic of humanitarian contexts is the lack of information available to humanitarian logisticians. The major difficulty is that the quality of service provision is difficult to assess; whereas the service provider may know product quality, the buyer often does not. This asymmetry of information between service providers and buyers creates problems for their market provision. UNWFP remarked: 'We try to build relationships with our customers, to build trust and maintain a connection and jointly overcome any unexpected problems.'

A hybrid approach reduces the conflict between IA and UNWFP by allowing both to incorporate their goals. From a logistics perspective, the hybrid approach also has the benefit of providing detailed performance data regarding the behaviour-based elements, while retaining UNWFP's preferred outcome focus. For IA, the hybrid approach allows the positive relationship with the service provider while still achieving the desired results. Since the hybrid contractual arrangement includes both behaviour- and outcome-oriented elements, the agent will be more likely to behave in the interests of the principal. This is similar to Eisenhardt's (1989: 60) observation that: 'When the contract between the principal and agent is outcome-based, the agent is more likely to behave in the interests of the principal'. By standardizing co-ordination with UNWFP, IA is able to obtain a good overview of the service provider's activities, learn from them, and make appropriate investments in their capabilities.

For practitioners, our findings suggest that it is highly important that behavioural outcomes are established between buyer and service provider, and buyer and end customer, as it appears to guide the service provider and end customer towards desired behaviour. Aligning all three parties in the triad by means of the right type of contract is beneficial not only for the buyer, but certainly also for the end customer and the service provider. This research suggests that co-operation between the principal and two agents can improve performance through sharing of information, knowledge and improved co-ordination. However, this alignment seems to be more easily achieved through behavioural contracts rather than legal arrangements:

- The case study highlights the importance of both relational and contractual contracts between the buyer, service provider and end customer.

- The alignment of the three parties in the service triad is more easily achieved through hybrid contracts rather than legal arrangements focusing on outcomes only.

- An increased understanding of managing services and their service providers in the triadic context of outsourced service delivery adds to the body of knowledge in supply management.

- The service triad clearly is a special situation, since contracts and service production do not occur on one and the same link, but across multiple links in the triad.

References

Altay, N and Green, W G (2006) OR/MS research in disaster operations management, *European Journal of Operational Research*, 175 (1), pp 475–93

Bask, A (2001) Relationships among TPL providers and members of supply chains – a strategic perspective, *Journal of Business & Industrial Marketing*, 16 (6), pp 470–86

Eisenhardt, K M (1989) Agency theory: an assessment and review, *Academy of Management Review*, 14 (1), pp 57–74

Heaslip, G (2013) Services operations management and humanitarian logistics, *Journal of Humanitarian Logistics and Supply Chain Management*, 3 (1), pp 37–51

Holguín-Veras, J, Pérez, N, Jaller, M, Van Wassenhove, L N and Aros-Vera, F (2013) On the appropriate objective function for post-disaster humanitarian logistics models, *Journal of Operations Management*, 31, pp 262–80

Humanitarian Assistance Policy (2015) [accessed 29 April 2015] Ireland's Humanitarian Assistance Policy, *Irish Aid, Department of Foreign Affairs and Trade* [Online] https://www.irishaid.ie/media/irishaid/allwebsitemedia/20newsand publications/publicationpdfsenglish/Humanitarian-Assistance-Policy-2015.pdf

Jahre, M and Heigh, I (2008) Does the current constraints in funding promote failure in humanitarian supply chains? *Supply Chain Forum: An international journal*, 9 (2), pp 44–54

Jahre, M and Jensen, L M (2010) Coordination in humanitarian logistics through clusters, *International Journal of Physical Distribution and Logistics Management*, 40 (8/9), pp 657–74

Kovács, G (2014) Where next? The future of humanitarian logistics, in *Humanitarian Logistics: Meeting the challenge of preparing for and responding to disasters*, ed M Christopher and P Tatham, 2nd edn, Kogan Page, London, pp 275–85

Kovács, G and Spens, K M (2009) Identifying challenges in humanitarian logistics, *International Journal of Physical Distribution and Logistics Management*, 39 (6), pp 506–28

Kovács, G and Spens, K M (2011) Trends and developments in humanitarian logistics – a gap analysis, *International Journal of Physical Distribution and Logistics Management*, 41 (1), pp 32–45

Li, M and Choi, T Y (2009) Triads in services outsourcing: bridge, bridge decay and bridge transfer, *Journal of Supply Chain Management*, 45, pp 27–39

Lundin, S (2011) [accessed 27 March 2015] Den icke-statliga organisationens agerande inom utvecklingsbiståndskedjan ur ett samarbets- och maktperspektiv, *Masters thesis* [Online] http://hdl.handle.net/10138/27941

Majewski, B, Navangul, K A and Heigh, I (2010) A peek into the future of humanitarian logistics: forewarned is forearmed, *Supply Chain Forum: An international journal*, **11** (3), pp 4–18

Matopoulos, A, Kovacs, G and Hayes, O (2014) Local resources and procurement practices in humanitarian supply chains: an empirical examination of large scale house reconstruction projects, *Decision Sciences*, **45** (4), pp 621–46

Neely, A (1999) The performance measurement revolution: why now and what next?, *International Journal of Operations & Production Management*, **19** (2), pp 205–28

Oloruntoba, R and Gray, R (2009) Customer service in emergency relief chains, *International Journal of Physical Distribution & Logistics Management*, **39** (6), pp 486–505

Tate, W, Ellram, L, Bals, L, Hartmann, E and van der Valk, W (2010) An agency theory perspective on the purchase of marketing services, *Industrial Marketing Management*, **39** (5), pp 806–19

Van der Valk, W and Van Iwaarden, J (2011) Monitoring in service triads consisting of buyers, subcontractors and end customers, *Journal of Purchasing & Supply Management*, **17**, pp 198–206

Van der Valk, W, Wynstra, F and Axelsson, B (2009) Effective buyer–supplier interaction patterns in ongoing service exchange, *International Journal of Operations & Production Management*, **29** (8), pp 807–33

Van Iwaarden, J and Van der Valk, W (2013) Controlling outsourced service delivery: managing service quality in business service triads, *Total Quality Management and Business Excellence*, **24**, pp 9–10

Van Wassenhove, L N (2006) Humanitarian aid logistics: supply chain management in high gear, *Journal of the Operations Research Society*, **57**, pp 475–89

Zsidisin, G A and Ellram, L M (2003) An agency theory investigation of supply risk management, *Journal of Supply Chain Management*, **39** (3), pp 15–27

Setting up a supply chain network in the Kenyan nutrition sector

2.3

TUNCA TABAKLAR

HUMLOG Institute, Hanken School of Economics, Helsinki, Finland

OLIVIA AGUTU

UNICEF Kenya, Nairobi, Kenya

Introduction

This case study is about the Kenyan nutrition supply chain, focusing on procurement of nutrition commodities for treatment of severe acute malnutrition (ready-to-use therapeutic foods, therapeutic milk and ReSoMal), trade-off decisions in the procurement activities, collaboration in the nutrition supply chain, sustainability and performance from a UNICEF Kenya perspective. This is followed by overall concluding remarks with recommendation for complexities and procurement decisions in the supply chain. The case study is based on data collected through semi-structured and group interviews in early 2014 in Kenya with a research team from Humanitarian Logistics and Supply Chain Research (HUMLOG) Institute, with the collaboration of UNICEF Kenya Nutrition Section. Data collection is part of the project 'Nutrition Surge Capacity' under the Academy of Finland project 'Resilience in Disaster Relief and Development Supply Chains'.

In the nutrition supply chain UNICEF Kenya acts as a main procurement agency, procuring therapeutic nutrition commodities on behalf of the Government of Kenya (GoK) as well as providing procurement services to the GoK and other humanitarian organizations in the supply chain.

The United Nations Children's Emergency Fund (UNICEF) has a central procurement unit, Supply Division, at its headquarters in Copenhagen and it is the major purchaser of ready-to-use therapeutic food (RUTF). RUTF is delivered to 57 seven countries; however, there is higher demand in some countries – Kenya, Ethiopia, Somalia, Niger, Pakistan, Nigeria, the Democratic Republic of Congo, Yemen, Sudan and Chad (Komrska *et al*, 2013).

Trade-offs in procurement decisions in setting up a supply chain network

Local procurement versus global procurement

Nutrition commodities are procured globally by the Supply Division at UNICEF headquarters in Copenhagen. There is a Kenya-based producer INSTA, which also produces RUTF, but the purchase order is done through the Supply Division in Copenhagen. Commodities procured globally are shipped through Mombasa port, and are exempted from import taxes as there is an operation agreement between the government and UNICEF Kenya; this decreases the advantage of local procurement over global procurement in terms of efficiency of delivery. Commodities procured locally do not incur any freight costs, thus increasing savings and lowering the cost of treatment for acute malnutrition, in addition to providing opportunity in the growth of the local economy.

Quality versus efficiency

UNICEF prioritizes quality over efficiency of delivery in procurement decisions, as the nutrition commodities are important in that they affect human health and should therefore be of good quality. UNICEF has over 10 global suppliers. UNICEF's Supply Division has a long-term agreement (LTA) with Nutriset and INSTA for procuring RUTF. Nutriset is a nutrition commodity producer located in France; INSTA is a local producer. Considering the global operations of UNICEF, the central procurement and global procurement activities do not affect the efficiency negatively.

Central versus decentralized procurement

Although INSTA is a local producer of RUTF, the purchase orders are done through the Supply Division from Copenhagen. According to the Kenyan Red Cross, central procurement is more cost-effective and economically more rational because they can purchase higher volumes of products at reasonable prices through UNICEF Kenya. Central procurement also helps to overcome duplication of efforts.

Kenyan nutrition supply chain

The nutrition supply chain in Kenya aims to enhance access and utilization of high-impact nutrition services that are responsive in times of shocks and stress for the most vulnerable children under the age of five years. UNICEF is the technical lead for nutrition in Kenya, providing technical and funding support to the government for quality implementation of the nutrition programme in Kenya. UNICEF supports the nutrition supply chain through procurement, warehousing and distribution of nutrition supplies to the counties for use by health facilities in treatment of acute malnutrition. UNICEF also offers procurement services to government and other human-itarian organizations. The UN agency is supporting the government in key areas such as co-ordination, policy development at national level, and programme implementation at county and community level, as well as pro-curement of nutrition commodities. They are also helping to support the government's implementation of national policies to address malnutrition. All of this work is done in collaboration with other governmental ministries, such as agriculture and education.

The government, on the other hand, has invested by ensuring that there is existing infrastructure, ie the health facilities and staffing (health workers) for implementation of the nutrition programme, and that the partners only support where there are gaps existing in the system.

The World Food Programme (WFP), on the other hand, has a role in supporting the government in treating moderate acute malnutrition through provision of supplementary feeding-programme supplies. Through a World Bank loan to GoK, UNICEF-procured ready-to-use supplementary food (RUSF) was handed over to WFP for distribution in treatment of moderate acute malnutrition in the health facilities; however, this was a one-off activity, as UNICEF does not routinely procure on behalf of WFP. Both UNICEF and WFP complement the work of the government, based on each agency's comparative advantage.

UNICEF supports the government to scale up nutrition interventions in 23 vulnerable counties located in the Arid and Semi-Arid Lands (ASALs) and with the highest-ranking child deprivation indexes, two refugee camps and urban informal settlements in Nairobi and Kisumu. Although the other parts of the country are provided with nutrition services to some extent, the situation in those places are not as acute as the ASAL areas. Thus, the nutrition sector is prioritizing the ASAL areas.

The basic nutrition commodities flowing in the chain are therapeutic milk, ReSoMal, ready-to-use therapeutic food (RUTF) for treatment of severe acute malnutrition and ready-to-use supplementary food (RUSF) for treatment of moderate acute malnutrition. While RUTF and RUSF (see Figure 2.3.1) are for home treatment, the therapeutic milk is for in-facility treatment.

Figure 2.3.1 Ready-to-use nutrition commodities (RUTF and RUSF)

The supply chain involves many diverse actors: donors, UN agencies, non-government organizations (NGOs), chapters and government bodies. The Kenyan nutrition supply chain is managed by the Ministry of Health (MoH) with additional funding support from key donors and partners, including USAID Food for Peace, the Department for International Development (DFID), UNICEF, the World Bank and the European Commission's Humanitarian Aid and Civil Protection (ECHO) department. The nutrition programme is integrated within the existing government health system and in times of disaster (eg drought) additional support is provided by members of the supply chain for scale-up of response in order to meet the surges in demand. Collaboration and linkages with other sectors such as agriculture, water and education is critical for enhancing nutrition-sensitive interventions for better nutrition outcomes.

During the surges in demand as a result of drought, NGOs specializing in emergency and UNICEF apply for additional funding from donors such as DFID and ECHO for nutrition intervention.

Figure 2.3.2 Isiolo District Hospital, Isiolo County

Procurement activities

At the time of the data collection (early 2014), the World Bank provided a loan to the GoK for nutrition supplies for the treatment of acute malnutrition in children under the age of five, with UNICEF as the approved procurement agent.

The procurement plan has two parts. The first part involves demand forecasting by the nutrition section; the second part, the UNICEF Kenya nutrition section, involves the supply section in developing the supply plan based on the forecast.

In forecasting, the UNICEF Kenya nutrition section calculates the annual needs of the target population with the stakeholders in the nutrition sector. For this, the supply section and the nutrition section work together to plan the quantities to order for the planned destinations, which is called the 'annual supply and distribution plan' for all the supplies, as well as the nutrition supplies. The plan also consists of information on the source of procurement, the mode of shipment, the target arrival date, the final destination and the delivery time to the final recipient. Sales orders are raised by the nutrition section and processed by the supply section in co-ordination with the supply division once the funds for procurement are available. The commodities are mostly shipped by sea via Mombasa and are stored in a transit warehouse managed by Kühne+Nagel in Mombasa.

The demand forecast is done once a year, and adjustments can be made based on the situation, which is monitored continuously by the nutrition sector. All the information gathered through the channels provides early warnings as to evidence of the worsening of food security and the nutrition situation. If the situation worsens, additional funding is sought from the donors for procurement of additional nutrition commodities, in case there are gaps.

Figure 2.3.3 UNICEF warehouse in Nairobi (operated by Kühne+Nagel)

UNICEF Kenya is collaborating with logistics service provider (LSP) Kühne+Nagel to outsource their inventory in Nairobi and all the nutrition commodities are stored in a warehouse operated by Kühne+Nagel (Figure 2.3.3). UNICEF has an agreement with Kühne+Nagel and they automatically update the inventory level that they have in the warehouse. Therefore, UNICEF is always informed of the stock levels in the warehouse.

Collaboration in the nutrition supply chain

Co-ordination and co-operation are considered the antecedents of achieving collaboration in the supply chain. The Kenyan nutrition supply chain is under the leadership of the MoH. The supply chain consists of primary and supporting members providing services during regular times and in times of disaster. The supply chain increases its capacity in order to meet the demand of emergency nutrition situations in times of drought. The nutrition supply chain has many complexities due to the criticality of the commodities, volatile market conditions and diverse members. The supply chain includes the MoH (leadership), partners (NGOs at national and county level), UN agencies (UNICEF and WFP) and county governments.

Implementing the nutrition programmes is understood by the members of the supply chain to be a collaborative process. All members of the supply chain know who is doing what and where, and in which period of time – in order to avoid duplications and overlaps. During the regular monthly co-ordination meetings – the Nutrition Technical Forum (NTF) – issues related to nutrition are raised under the leadership of the MoH.

Information on when to activate scaling up or scaling down, and information on the data related to the nutrition situation, are discussed and shared among the partners at these meetings. During emergencies, the frequency of the co-ordination meetings is increased in order to monitor the situation closely; these meetings could be held even on a daily basis during emergencies.

Through collaboration, members can share their assets with the partners in a supply chain or hand over the activities to another member, as observed in the Kenyan nutrition supply chain. For example, the MoH is using the Kenya Red Cross Society warehouse in Lodwar, Turkana county.

Sustainability and performance in the nutrition supply chain

There are diverse views on sustainability from the participants in the nutrition sector in Kenya. At the time of the data collection (early 2014), Kenya was transitioning from a centralized system to a devolved system of governance in the form of 47 newly created county governments expected to take up substantial roles, including planning, resource mobilization and service delivery. Devolution of health care to the counties provides an enabling environment for supporting the provision of equitable, affordable and quality health and related services at the highest attainable standards. Sustainable investments in nutrition varies by county and is dependent on various factors, including funding.

Views related to sustainability focus on the capacity of the system to respond during emergencies. Kenyan nutrition services are integrated within the existing health system and during emergencies the services are scaled up within the existing system as opposed to the setting up of parallel services by NGOs. The humanitarian actors in Kenya through the existing government-led co-ordination mechanism have been able to learn from past experiences in emergency response and have built on good practices to enhance sustainability. The nutrition sector's preparedness and response plan is reviewed and updated on a regular basis. Moreover, UNICEF Kenya is trying to ensure that the government has the capacity and adequate funds to provide quality integrated nutrition services to respond to the needs of the most deprived communities.

From the community point of view, capacity building is key to sustainability. Thus, organizations are training communities in agriculture in order to enhance household food security, increase household income and potentially contribute to improvement in child nutrition.

Sustainability can be seen as one of the components of performance in supply chain management. There are many ways to measure the success of the nutrition programme. From the supply chain perspective, it differs according to the organizations and sections. From the supply section side, success is often based on the delivery time of the nutrition commodities or on stock-levels at the facilities. From the nutrition section point of view, it is related to the number of children treated, and the sustainability and efficiency of an operation. Another indicator of performance is cost-effectiveness; this can be determined by comparing the cost of similar operations in other countries to those taking place in Kenya, and by examining the quality of commodities. Other indicators for programme success include service continuity, death rates and the number of beneficiaries who have recovered.

Concluding remarks

In this case study, we elaborate on procurement activities, collaboration, sustainability and performance in the Kenyan nutrition supply chain.

The important hints from the case study for procurement decisions and supply chain complexities in setting up a supply chain network are as follows:

- Local procurement and global procurement have their own advantages. Procuring locally is effective, reduces the lead times and increases savings, while global procurement organizations manage higher volumes of commodities and often supply higher-quality products.

- UNICEF Kenya is the procurement agency in the nutrition supply chain, and UNICEF has a central procurement policy. The central procurement policy provides advantages to the partner humanitarian organizations' cost-effectiveness and having higher volumes of nutrition commodities at relatively lower prices.

- Funding is the main facilitator not only for the procurement activities and service continuation but also for sustainability in the Kenyan nutrition supply chain. Continuous funding can also decrease the staff turnover and contribute to human resource, which is one of the most important resources in the supply chain.

- A vibrant co-ordination mechanism with clarity on which partner is doing what, where and when is key to overcoming the duplication of efforts; the co-ordination forums are key to supply chain understanding and collaboration.

- In the Kenyan nutrition supply chain it is helpful to collaborate and share knowledge, information and risk, as getting reliable data regarding the nutrition situation in the supply chain is important in order to get the funding for procurement activities and service continuation. Furthermore, collaboration contributes to overcoming complexities caused by volatility and uncertainty in dynamic environments.

- Nutrition supply chain integration into a government-led supply chain system through collaboration and co-ordination is critical to overcome complexities in a supply chain.

- Strong information systems with good monitoring mechanisms are key to ensuring continuous availability of data on the situation, which is critical in informing the demand forecasting, procurement and fund-raising efforts for the supply chain.

Reference

Komrska, J, Kopczak, L R and Swaminathan, J M (2013) When supply chains save lives, *Supply Chain Management Review*, **17** (1), pp 42–49

Acknowledgements

The author, Tunca Tabaklar, would like to thank all the participants and UNICEF Kenya for their contribution and thank the Academy of Finland for their kind support through the 'Resilience in Disaster Relief and Development Supply Chains' project.

PART THREE
Supply chain strategy

Supply chain strategy

3.1

IRA HAAVISTO

HUMLOG Institute

GRAHAM HEASLIP

HUMLOG Institute and Galway Mayo Institute of Technology

PAUL D LARSON

University of Manitoba, Canada

Introduction

The classical approach to strategy is that strategy aligns organizational 'strengths' (competences and resources) with the environment (opportunities and threats) (Mintzberg and Lampel, 1999). Strategy can be viewed as a pattern or stream of decisions to make in order to be able, as an organization, to align with internal structures and processes as well as the environment. When supply chain performance or performance objectives are defined and articulated, they can become company or organizational strategy. Although the articulation of a supply chain strategy is claimed to be important for successful supply chain performance, empirical research shows that supply chain strategy is seldom articulated in any company (Harrison and New 1999: 27). Perez-Franco (2010) came to similar conclusions in his research where only 2 out of 20 case companies explicitly had a stated supply chain strategy.

A stated supply chain strategy can be crucial as a supply chain by definition has several actors involved and a statement of strategy can align the activities and understandings between those actors. Supply chain strategy can be defined to be 'the set of guiding principles, driving forces and ingrained attitudes that help to communicate goals, plans and policies to all employees that are reinforced through conscious and subconscious behaviour at all levels of the supply chain' (Harrison and van Hoek, 2002: 103). In this chapter we discuss different supply chain strategies and present them from the humanitarian perspective.

Supply chain strategies

As a result of today's turbulent business environment, companies face potentially significant losses because of unexpected events that render traditional strategies and rules less applicable than before. In this sense, new supply chain strategies and different approaches to supply chain management have emerged. What might a supply chain strategy look like when it is articulated? Perez-Franco (2010) came to the conclusion in his research that even though the supply chain strategy was articulated by a company, the policy and practices were not necessarily aligned with the strategy. He claims in his research that the articulation of the strategy is imperative for the strategy to 'flicker down' to a tactical and operative level in the company.

To get a better understanding of what the performance objective or the supply chain strategy can be, Table 3.1.1 identifies common themes such as responsiveness and efficiency, cost reduction and service improvement. Supply chain performance is often defined as effectiveness and efficiency, but can as well be understood as quality, productivity, quality of work life, innovation and profitability/budgetability.

What does it mean to have an efficient or responsive supply chain? Prior to the global financial crisis of 2008–09 many supply chains restructured to utilize lean philosophies but increased their level of vulnerability to severe disruptions. The global crisis highlighted the vulnerabilities of supply chains' cost minimization strategies (Datta and Christopher, 2011). Lean philosophies emphasize the elimination of 'waste' in a supply chain or a process. Waste here meaning, for example, excess time or warehousing cost. However, lean philosophy or strategy has been criticized for, although being cost-efficient for the focal organization, putting pressure on suppliers

Table 3.1.1 Examples of performance objective and strategy themes

Supply Chain Performance Objective and Strategy Themes	Authors
Efficiency	Chase, Aquilano and Jacobs (2001); Russell and Taylor (2003)
Flexibility	Russell and Taylor (2003)
Cost reduction, service improvement	Ballou (2004)
Responsiveness	Chase, Aquilano and Jacobs (2001)
Integration	Heizer and Render (2008)
Quality, productivity, innovation, profitability	Sink (1986)

SOURCE: Haavisto and Goentzel (2015)

to keep high stock levels and depending on a stable demand. Thus, it is not capable of coping with quick changes. When flexibility is needed, researchers (Oloruntoba and Gray, 2006) suggest that an agile strategy is most fitting. An agile strategy again is not striving for cost-efficiency but rather responsiveness. Humanitarian supply chains have been called the most agile supply chains as they have the capacity to flex according to changing geographical locations, fluctuations in quantities of demand and even unpredictability in time of demand. Kovács and Tatham (2009) have suggested that during preparation for emergencies humanitarian supply chains could adapt a lean strategy, while in the heat of emergency relief adopting an agile strategy.

The agile strategy is based on another concept called postponement. From the terms of supply chain strategy, postponement means postponing decisions/activities in the supply chain until information about the demand is known. If a strategy of postponement is implemented in a humanitarian supply chain it could, for example, mean the provision of cash-based assistance where the end user and thus the determiner of the demand takes decisions. The opposite to postponement is the strategy of speculation, which in a humanitarian context could include, for example, pre-positioning of stock.

Table 3.1.2 Strategic elements, collaboration and performance

Strategic Element	Collaboration	Performance
Resource deployment	Complementarity*	Cost; service; utilization
Risk management	Risk pooling	Cost; service; sustainability
Local capacity	Relationship building	Cost; service; sustainability
Lean/agile logistics	Information sharing	Cost; service; utilization; sustainability
Accountability/transparency	Compatibility**	Sustainability

*Complementarity refers to relative capabilities (eg transportation and warehousing capacity, number and expertise of personnel, supplies, information sharing, communication technology, presence within a nation or region, etc) of potential collaborators.

**Compatibility among potential collaborators includes their views on the importance of principles such as humanity, neutrality, transparency and independence. Comparing organizational missions could yield insight into compatibility (Larson, 2012).

Table 3.1.2 outlines some connections between various elements of supply chain strategy and the themes of collaboration and performance. In terms of collaboration, resource deployment is largely a matter of identifying and exploiting complementary capabilities for reduced cost and/or improved service. A worthy goal is to maximize collective utilization of scarce resources. In addition to cost and service, risk management and local capacity development use techniques such as risk pooling and relationship building to address supply chain sustainability. To support lean or agile logistics strategies, information sharing is a crucial aspect of collaboration. Given their focus on continuous improvement and waste reduction, lean strategies can have a favourable impact on cost, customer service, (capacity) utilization and sustainability. Finally, collaboration in matters of accountability and transparency relies on compatibility of organizations – and can enhance financial continuity and operational sustainability.

Humanitarian supply chain and performance

Supply chain strategy or humanitarian organizational core strategy has not been covered much in humanitarian logistics research (Abidi and Klumpp, 2013). The lack of performance measurement in humanitarian organizations has been recognized by both Davidson (2006) and Blecken (2010). In Blecken's (2010) findings, only 20 per cent of humanitarian organizations measure their performance consistently. The challenges for measuring the supply chain performance in a humanitarian setting have been identified in a literature review by Abidi and Klumpp (2013) as: difficulty of obtaining accurate data, limited information technology, chaotic environment, lack of motivation, potential negative media exposure, human resource issues,

Table 3.1.3 Humanitarian supply chain performance

Suggested Humanitarian Supply Chain Performance Measure from Academia
Output
Flexibility
Efficiency (resources)
Cost
Service level (customer/beneficiary/donor)
Accuracy
Financial control and efficiency
Process adherence
Time (eg donation-to-delivery)
Coverage, equity
Utilization
Innovation and learning

SOURCE: Modified from Haavisto (2014)

general reluctance, conflict between long-term versus short-term goals, and lack of internal recognition of the importance of supply chain management.

Performance measurements for the humanitarian sector have been developed (Table 3.1.3) where most frameworks are based on the balanced scorecard introduced by Kaplan and Norton (1992). The balanced scorecard can be seen as unfit for the humanitarian sector due to the rigidness of the framework and the complexity of the humanitarian context. (The four dimensions of the original balanced scorecard – customer, financial, internal process, learning/growth – can make the framework rigid. However, it is possible to adapt the balanced scorecard to the humanitarian context, by creating context-specific dimensions, such as beneficiary, donor, budget, accountability/transparency, etc.) Common to most studies on performance measurement in the humanitarian context is the notion of efficiency. Similar findings can be seen in Table 3.1.3, where studies on performance measurement acknowledge efficiency and often take a cost or time perspective (Davidson, 2006; Beamon and Balcik, 2008; Blecken *et al*, 2009; van der Laan, de Brito and Vergunst, 2009; de Leeuw and Fransoo, 2009; Schulz and Heigh, 2009; Heaslip, Sharif and Althonayan, 2012).

If supply chain performance were to be defined in terms of how it is measured in the humanitarian sector, the most common meaning would be financial performance (Beamon, 1999) and time- and volume-related performance (Gleason and Barnum, 1982), with indicators such as lead time and fill rate.

While performance could mean the final output and the impact on the society or the environment of the supply chain, this holistic perspective is not much considered in performance measurement of humanitarian supply chains (Haavisto and Kovács, 2012). Performance in humanitarian settings has been suggested to be measured as the output, resources and flexibility (Beamon and Balcik, 2008) or as customer service, financial control and process adherence (Schulz and Heigh, 2009). While Blecken et al (2009) argued that in relief supply chains donation-to-delivery time, the output and resources should be measured, Beamon and Balcik (2008) take into consideration the output along with population coverage or order fulfilment rate. More specifically, the actual measurements are suggested to be: order fulfilment cycle time, supply chain adaptability, coverage rate, order fulfilment rate, on-time delivery, cost efficiency, resource efficacy and system utilization rate (Beamon and Balcik, 2008; Blecken et al, 2009).

Performance metrics should ideally be aligned with the organization's goals and strategy and push the supply chains towards the right goals, pursuing the idea that the performance that is being measured actually improves. Furthermore, a learning perspective would be emphasized when measuring performance, with more attention paid to expanding skills and the implementation and use of humanitarian supply chain performance measurement as key for improving performance. The learning loop is, according to Caplice and Sheffi (1994), one of the main goals for measuring the performance. Organizations such as Oxfam, the Red Cross and IRC, amongst others, have realized that measuring their supply chain performance is not only a necessity for the donor, but if the measurements are analysed useably they lead to internal development. Furthermore, large donors such as USAid, European Development Fund and the United Nations (UN) request humanitarian organizations to report on their performance through a monitoring and evaluation (M&E) process. However, the reporting can take up resources in the organization, and humanitarian organizations claim that heavy reporting requirements can counteract requirements for efficiency.

Discussion – alignment of strategy

Supply chain strategy in the commercial sector is often linked to efficiency. However, both in the humanitarian and in the commercial sector a supply chain strategy is rarely articulated. A stated supply chain strategy could enhance the common understanding of the processes and activities in a supply chain amongst its various actors.

Figure 3.1.1 Alignment of supply chain performance

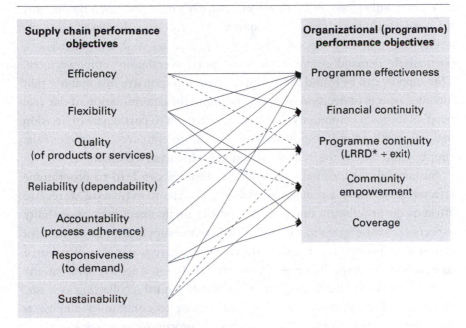

SOURCE: Haavisto and Goentzel (2015)
* LRRD = Linking Relief, Rehabilitation and Development

In pursuing a method to detect an alignment or misalignment, Figure 3.1.1 portrays how different examples of operational performance objectives support examples of organizational and programme goals. The arrows in Figure 3.1.1 indicate direct alignments (harmonization and support), and the dotted lines show indirect support. An exercise such as the one shown in Figure 3.1.1 demonstrates that when efficiency is defined as cost or time efficiency, it can directly support programme effectiveness and financial continuity. Flexibility can directly support programme effectiveness, community empowerment and coverage. Flexible supply chains can be viewed as supporting community empowerment; if the supply chain is decentralized and adaptable to change, it can take local requirements into consideration and empower the local population. It also supports coverage, since in an adaptable supply chain, changes in modes of transportation, distribution points and timetables can be made to direct resources more easily to beneficiaries' locations and to improve access to the services and supplies.

The quality of supplies or services can directly support programme effectiveness and continuity, since a high-quality supply or service (eg durable construction material or professional teachers) enhances the longevity of the programme's outcome and could hasten the ability to turn over the programme to the local community. The aspect of accountability, here used as process adherence and control in a supply chain, can directly support financial continuity, since it is a requirement by donors; however, accountability can indirectly support all other objectives as well. Responsiveness, particularly demand responsiveness, supports community empowerment. This support can be found if the supply chain is responsive in a manner that includes aspects of decision postponement and the determination of the 'real need' of the local community and its empowerment to participate in decision making. Furthermore, responsiveness can lead to enhanced coverage if the supply chain targets the 'real' need and not a forecasted demand.

Sustainability as a final supply chain objective can lead to programme effectiveness, while an unsustainable supply chain may have a reverse effect on the programme outcome. A supply chain that neglects sustainability aspects can cause harm to the context where the supply chain operates. An example of this was identified in Afghanistan, where water was distributed to beneficiaries in small bottles (Haavisto, 2014) – in a society without any disposal system this led to a new problem of empty bottles collecting as waste. Sustainable supply chains can also lead directly to community empowerment through, for example, local, small-scale procurement activities.

References

Abidi, H and Klumpp, M (2013) Performance measurement in humanitarian logistics: a literature review, in *Proceedings of the Nordic Logistics Research Network (NOFOMA)*, June 2013, Gothenburg

Ballou, R H (2004) *Business Logistics/Supply Chain Management*, 5th edn, Pearson Education, New Jersey

Beamon, B M (1999) Measuring supply chain performance, *International Journal of Operations & Production Management*, 19 (3), pp 275–92

Beamon, B M and Balcik, B (2008) Performance measurement in humanitarian relief chains, *International Journal of Public Performance Sector Management*, 21 (1), pp 4–25

Blecken, A (2010) Supply chain process modelling for humanitarian organizations, *International Journal of Physical Distribution & Logistics Management*, 40 (8/9), pp 675–92

Blecken, A, Hellingrath, B, Dangelmaier, W and Schulz, S F (2009) A humanitarian supply chain process reference model, *International Journal of Services Technology and Management*, 12 (4), pp 391–413

Caplice, C and Sheffi, Y (1994) A review and evaluation of logistics metrics, *International Journal of Logistics Management*, 5 (2), pp 11–28

Chase, R B, Aquilano, N J and Jacobs, F R (2001) *Operations Management for Competitive Advantage*, Irwin/McGraw-Hill, Boston

Datta, P P and Christopher, M G (2011) Information sharing and coordination mechanisms for managing uncertainty in supply chains: a simulation study, *International Journal of Production Research*, **49** (3), pp 765–803

Davidson, A L (2006) Key Performance Indicators in Humanitarian Logistics, Master's Thesis, Massachusetts Institute of Technology Boston, MA

de Leeuw, S and Fransoo, J (2009) Drivers of close supply chain collaboration: one size fits all?, *International Journal of Operations & Production Management*, **29** (7) pp 720–39

Gleason, J M and Barnum, D T (1986) Toward valid measures of public sector productivity: performance measures, *Urban Transit, Management Science*, **28** (4), pp 518–47

Haavisto, Ira (2014) Performance in humanitarian supply chains, *Economics and Society*, **275** (publication of the Hanken School of Economics)

Haavisto, I and Goentzel, J (2015) Measuring humanitarian supply chain performance in a multi-goal context, *Journal of Humanitarian Logistics and Supply Chain Management*, **5** (3), pp 300–24

Haavisto, I and Kovács, G (2012) Measuring sustainability in humanitarian operations, in *Proceedings of the Joint EUROMA/P&OM World Conference 2012*, Amsterdam

Harrison, A and New, C (1999) The role of coherent supply chain strategy and performance management in achieving competitive advantage: an international survey, *Journal of the Operational Research Society*, **53**, pp 263–71

Harrison, A and van Hoek, R (2002) *Logistics Management and Strategy*, 1st edn, Pearson Education Limited, Essex

Heaslip, G, Sharif, A M and Althonayan A (2012) Employing a systems-based perspective to the identification of inter-relationships within humanitarian logistics, *International Journal of Production Economics*, **139** (2), pp 377–92

Heizer, J H and Render, B (2008) *Operations Management*, 1st edn, Pearson Education, India

Kaplan, R S and Norton, D P (1992) The balanced scorecard – measures that drive performance, *Harvard Business Review*, **70** (1), pp 71–79

Kovács, G and Tatham, P (2009) Humanitarian logistics performance in the light of gender, *International Journal of Productivity and Performance Management*, **58** (2), pp 174–87

Larson, P D (2012) 'Strategic partners and strange bedfellows: relationship building in the relief supply chain' Chapter 1 in *Relief Supply Chain Management for Disasters: Humanitarian aid and emergency logistics*, eds G Kovács and K Spens, pp 1–15, IGI Global, Hershey, PA

Mintzberg, H and Lampel, J (1999) Reflecting on the strategy process, *Sloan Management Review*, **40** (3), Spring, pp 21–30

Oloruntoba, R and Gray, R (2006) Humanitarian aid: an agile supply chain?
Supply Chain Management: An international journal, **11** (2), pp 115–20

Perez-Franco, R (2010) A Methodology to Capture, Evaluate and Reformulate
a Firm's Supply Chain Strategy as a Conceptual System, thesis publication,
Massachusetts Institute of Technology Engineering Systems Division,
Cambridge, MA

Russell, R S and Taylor, B W (2003) *Operations Management*, 4th edn, Prentice
Hall, New Jersey

Schulz, S F and Heigh, I (2009) Logistics performance management in action
within a humanitarian organization, *Management Research News*, **32** (11),
pp 1038–49

Sink, P E (1986) Performance and productivity measurement: the art of developing
creative score boards, *Industrial Engineer*, **1**, pp 86–90

Van der Laan, E A, de Brito, M P and Vergunst, D (2009) Performance measurement
in humanitarian supply chains, *International Journal of Risk Assessment and
Management*, **13** (1), pp 22–45

Case study   3.2

Partnerships – supply chain strategy

GRAHAM HEASLIP

HUMLOG Institute and Galway Mayo Institute of Technology

- In general, humanitarian relief organizations have focused on 'getting the job done' and have put little effort into performance measurement, especially partnership performance.
- Addressing the evaluation of each partnership increases the understanding of civil–military partnerships and institutional learning of the different actors.
- The greatest factor to affect the success of the partnerships was the personal capabilities and 'soft skills' – the common sense and communications skills – of deployed personnel.
- In civil–military partnerships both military and civilian actors frequently lack clear objectives.

Even though military forces make a difference in humanitarian logistics through their relatively ready funding, trained manpower and appropriate equipment, sensitivities remain. Practical realities on the ground necessitate various forms of civil–military co-operation, co-ordination and collaboration for humanitarian operations (Whiting, 2009). It is argued, therefore, that the military forces of many countries are not only well prepared to conduct operations in the field of combat, but are also important in the generically similar circumstances found in the aftermath of a disaster or an emergency (Kovács and Tatham, 2009; Heaslip, Sharif and Althonayan, 2012). In particular, many military forces are, as a result of their ability to move quickly with appropriate equipment and trained manpower, ideally suited to offer assistance in the logistic arena (Heaslip and Barber, 2014).

This case study presents examples of partnerships between a military actor and humanitarian agencies.

Although it seems that there could be a fundamental philosophical difference in the rationale for the collaboration of humanitarian organizations and military forces, the United Nations Security Council (UNSC) has used global military forces to create a protective environment for humanitarian operations, for example, UN Security Council Resolution (UNSCR) 794 for Somalia, UNSCR 1199 for Kosovo, UNSCR 1497 for Liberia and UNSCR 1778 for Chad. Therefore, the doctrines of intended deployments in the past have been quite distinctive but over the last decade many military doctrines have included humanitarian doctrinal aspects (Rietjens, Voordijk and De Boer, 2007; Heaslip and Barber, 2014).

Case history Kosovo

UNSCR 1244 provided for the deployment in Kosovo of international civil and security presences under UN auspices. The text of the resolution suggested four pillars for the UN Mission in Kosovo (UNMIK):

- Pillar I: humanitarian affairs, under the direction of the UN High Commissioner for Refugees (UNHCR).
- Pillar II: civil administration, led by UNMIK.
- Pillar III: democratization and reconstruction, under the auspices of the Organization for Security and Co-operation in Europe (OSCE).
- Pillar IV: economic development, led by the European Union (EU).

This case study focuses on humanitarian–military partnerships between humanitarian actors and military forces, specifically the Irish Infantry Group, 32nd Infantry Group (deployed from March to October 2007). The military company operated as part of the Multinational Task Force (Centre). The Irish company's area of responsibility (AOR) covered 190 square kilometres and it carried out its mission through vigorous and regular patrols in their Mowag armored personnel carriers (APCs). The eastern part of the AOR is mountainous and dotted with Albanian villages while the western part consists of smaller hills and contains a Serb enclave. There are two villages in the AOR with mixed populations, Janjevo and Robovce. The Irish Defence Forces participated in the Multinational Task Force (Centre) along with troops from the Czech Republic, Finland, Latvia and Sweden, which covers an area including Pristina, Kosovo's capital city.

Case history Chad

Since 21 February 2008, the Irish Defence Forces troop contribution commenced to the UN mandated, EU-led peacekeeping mission to Chad and the Central African Republic (CAR). Initially the force was EU led (known as EUFOR Chad/CAR) the force changed over to UN command on 15 March 2009 and became known as MINURCAT (United Nations Mission in the Central African Republic and Chad). The Initial Entry EU Force consisted of Special Forces troops from Austria, Belgium, France, Ireland and Sweden. This EU mission was mandated under UNSCR 1778 on 25 September 2007 (UNSC, 2007), to operate in eastern Chad and work in conjunction with the civilian UN mission in the region. The military force was authorized to protect refugees, internally displaced persons (IDPs) and International Humanitarian Organization (IHO) personnel in danger. The mission of the force was to create a safe and secure environment whereby humanitarian aid could be delivered safely and the local population could go about their daily lives safely too.

This case study focuses on humanitarian–military partnerships between humanitarian actors and the Irish Infantry Battalion, 99th Infantry Battalion (deployed from May to September 2009). As part of the Irish contingent this battalion operated in Goz Beida in south-east Chad, to establish and maintain a secure environment in their area of operations (AOO). MINURCAT HQ is based in the Chadian capital, N'Djamena, and through the Humanitarian Relief Co-ordination Centre (based at MINURCAT HQ) supports requests either directly or indirectly carried out by the CIMIC cell of the 99th Infantry Battalion.

Outcome

This section begins by addressing the practice of civil–military partnerships based on the analysis of partnerships in two cases (Kosovo and Chad). The case studies showed that by addressing the evaluation of each partnership this increased the understanding of civil–military partnerships and institutional learning of the different actors.

The case studies identified numerous factors that could influence the performance of civil–military partnerships. For example, size, mandate, capacity and levels of professionalism of the humanitarian actors all affect the partnership. In addition there are great differences between local, national and international humanitarian organizations. The greatest factor to affect the success of the partnerships was the personal capabilities and 'soft skills' – common sense and communications skills – of deployed personnel (both military and non-military). Kovács, Tatham and Larson (2012) previously highlighted the gap between skills and humanitarian logistics performance. For example, as all military officers in both case studies were of the same nationality and underwent the same military, logistics, operations and management training and education programmes, the common approach created equality in addressing the needs of the local population in a small area, both quantitatively and qualitatively. It created an atmosphere of transparency in which humanitarian organizations knew what to expect and what not to expect of a military force, and therefore led to successful partnerships.

Similar to previous studies (Arshinder and Deshmukh, 2008; Co and Barro, 2009) this research found that early senior management engagement, commitment to medium-term collaboration, organizational fit, an adequate socialization period, clear programme objectives and deliverables ensured that partnership projects started off on the right foot and had a high probability of success. Interestingly, working out differences in culture (de Leeuw and Fransoo, 2009), ensuring resource alignment (Goffin, Lemke and Szwejczewski, 2006; Sarkis, Talluri and Gunasekaran, 2007; Oh and Rhee, 2008) and relevance of assistance (Kovács, Tatham and Larson, 2012) ensured smooth partnership implementation.

The language proficiency of all participants, particularly the standard of English, was a determinant in the success of the partnership, particularly in the initial partnership formation phase. As the military force conversed in English, the use of another language required translators and thus some information or nuances were 'lost in translation'. The literature would concur (Kampstra, Ashayeri and Gattorna, 2006; Heaslip and Barber, 2014) that the use of different 'language' and terminology obscures understanding of common objectives between the actors. This issue presented itself when humanitarian organizations and the military used different names and definitions for transportation modes, supplies and the composition of worker teams.

Similar to the importance of supplier and customer involvement in partnerships (Vereecke and Muylle, 2006; Wasti, Kozan and Kuman, 2006), the involvement and participation of the local population was a key factor in the success of the partnerships, as was the use of local standards (Rietjens, Voordijk and De Boer, 2007), such as construction standards. Those partnerships that paid little attention to the involvement of the local population resulted in decreased sustainability, a lack of cohesion with social structures, a lack of ownership and mismatches between the assistance activities and the actual needs. Furthermore, partnership activities were selected and prioritized based on the capacity of the military force or humanitarian organization, rather than the needs of the local beneficiaries. Of these, partnerships in which humanitarian organizations were involved often led to better performance due to their expertise and knowledge, and long-term focus. The approach of many humanitarian organizations was process-oriented in these partnerships, while the military approach was often result-oriented.

In partnerships where there was an absence of a written contract it was never perceived as a problem, contrary to the literature (Teng and Das, 2008; Pettit and Beresford, 2009). Written contracts were initiated when the military made a financial contribution that had to be accounted for with the military's Department of Foreign Affairs or if the military was engaging with a local government organization. At times, joint contingency planning between the military and humanitarian organizations helped reduce lead times and avoid reliance on expensive transport options (eg airlifting) or last-minute sourcing. Through this partnership agreement the development of alternative plans ensured the mobilization of the right range of relief items. For those involved in partnerships that originated through a verbal agreement both humanitarian organizations and the military contingent mentioned several drawbacks to the prospect of having a written contract:

- The situation was often too uncertain to rely on a contract.
- The military could not guarantee to be involved in humanitarian activities for a specified period. If the situation changed they could have been forced to focus on other activities.
- The risk of legal claims was an important drawback.

By contrast, in later partnerships, particularly in the Chad case study, Civil Military Co-operation (CIMIC) officers argued that through formalizing a relationship (eg Memorandum of Understanding (MoU), Letter of Intent or Terms of Reference) – as would be the norm in a commercial setting (Beamon and Balcik, 2008; Carols, Humphries and Wilding, 2009) – the continuity, or rather the lack of it, can be addressed rather than the more frequently used ad hoc approach. Since most military units rotate once every four or six months, and the personnel of humanitarian organizations come and go, it is very difficult to build a sustainable relationship between a military force and a humanitarian organization (Heaslip, Sharif and

Althonayan, 2012). Drawing up a MoU can facilitate the transfer from one rotation or person to another and the partnership will become less person-bonded and ad hoc. This diminishes loss of scarce resources and waste of effort. It is not uncommon that organizations in assessing each other's capabilities contact one another regularly, simply because they are unaware of former co-operation activities or attempts (Rietjens, Voordijk and De Boer, 2007; Kovács and Tatham, 2009; Akhtar, Marr and Garnevska, 2012). The most important criterion used by the humanitarian organizations in the selection of an appropriate partner was the extent of means and capabilities of an organization (ie, complementary resources). Manpower, machines and technical assistance were preferred. For the military, personal fit compatible strategies and objectives, and reliability, were the preferred capabilities. Both humanitarian and military actors in the Chad case agreed that a MoU could increase clarity and transparency and could address several issues, such as construction standards that could otherwise lead to problems, for example legal claims, in later stages of the co-operation process.

Even before activities started it was important to consider termination of the partnership, including the requirements of the final users (local population and humanitarian organizations). These varied from paying teachers, paying for classroom interiors in the case of schools, to a maintenance plan in the construction of waterworks. Normally there was no specific committee put into place to prepare the implementation of the partnership, as in joint ventures between business organizations (Johnston and Kristal, 2008). The main reason for this was that both the military and the humanitarian partners wanted to maintain their independence. The short time frame of the partnerships, which varied from a few days to several months, also contributed to this.

As a partnership drew to an end the tasks and responsibilities were usually transferred to the humanitarian or local actors. If assistance activities were for the direct benefit of the local population, normally all tasks and responsibilities were transferred to them. These often included the maintenance of houses and community centres. In a few cases the military remained responsible after the partnership was ended, for example the military in Kosovo remained responsible for de-mining graves and possible booby traps of remains, logistic support such as transport of the remains, and guarding the (opened) gravesites.

The cost-effectiveness of the partnerships showed considerable differences. In some the military had a clear comparative advantage and was the only actor who could carry out the activities. This included the distribution activities in co-operation with the International Organization for Migration (IOM), which required large transport capacity. However, in several other partnerships the capacity of the military was favoured over local contractors or local villagers when these actors could have fulfilled a large share of the activities. Additionally, employing local villagers and local construction companies would stimulate the local economy (Pettit and Beresford, 2005; Chandes and Pache, 2010; Tatham and Kovács, 2010).

An examination of the partnerships found that the willingness of the military and humanitarian organizations had a major role in developing the trust in the partnership. Similar to literature on commercial partnerships (Fynes, De Búrca and Voss, 2005) and humanitarian literature (Tatham and Kovács, 2010) high levels of trust in partnerships had a positive impact on humanitarian operations performance and organization performance of the partners. After selecting a partner, a verbal agreement or MoU was made between the military and the humanitarian organization. Often this agreement was based on trust. An agreement, written or verbal, normally included the details of the implementation (such as initial planning). It also dealt with the activities of each actor in the partnership, for example which actor would transport the construction materials. Tatham and Kovács (2010) noted that a learning and educational period helps build mutual appreciation and understanding. The research validates this concept as successful partnerships invested considerable time ensuring the adequate and timely allocation of dedicated resources to the partnership. As well, the partnership consciously avoided an undue resource and expertise dependency by the humanitarian organization on the resources of the military partner. To ensure the observed partnerships delivered valued services to beneficiaries, emphasis was placed on the need for the humanitarian organization to articulate its requirement and assess its own absorptive capacity as early on in the partnership as possible.

As far as strategic partnerships are concerned, to guide the two parties in their partnership path, a checklist is proposed (see Table 3.2.1). The research demonstrated that for a successful partnership emphasis should be placed on well-motivated partnerships that are driven by pre-identified objectives and linked to the core competencies and values of the partnering organization. To achieve the desired level of credibility, the research stresses that it is important that partnerships commit resources for a medium- to a long-term period. The importance of partnering with the 'best' humanitarian organization and devoting enough time to the preparation phase cannot be stressed enough.

Table 3.2.1 Proposed co-operation checklist

Activity	Purpose
<ul><li>Design a medium- to long-term strategic initiative</li><li>Ensure organizational fit</li><li>Select 'best' cause-specific humanitarian organization</li><li>Early organizational buy-in</li><li>Remain focused: design initiatives that leverage your core competencies and respond to identified needs of the humanitarian organization</li><li>Confirm relevance of assistance offered</li><li>Establish deliverables and monitoring processes</li><li>Work on organizational 'understanding'. Take time out to learn about the operations, culture, working style, practices and jargon of the humanitarian organization</li><li>Resource alignment. Request the humanitarian organization to dedicate resources to the co-operation</li><li>Request the humanitarian organization to articulate needs during the design and implementation of the co-operation activity</li><li>Gauge absorptive capacity of the humanitarian organization</li></ul>	<ul><li>To ensure credibility among military personnel, don't engage in strategic initiatives for the 'wrong' reasons</li><li>Don't allow too much time to elapse between the launch and the actual implementation of the co-operation activity</li><li>Don't under-resource the co-operation activity</li><li>Avoid frequent changes in the liaison team composition</li><li>Avoid creating undue resource/ expertise dependency</li></ul>

Military and humanitarian partnerships have the potential to operate as effective co-ordination mechanisms. In structured partnerships, the military partner has the means to match the specific needs of the assisted organization. If well managed, these types of partnerships ensure that services, goods and assets provided meet the prerequisite, accessibility, usability and simultaneity constraints criteria (flow and fit dependency) of the assisted humanitarian organization as defined by the partnership theory. As such, their contribution improves the performance of the assisted organization as the right thing is provided to the right place at the right time. Below are some lessons learnt:

- The cases identified numerous factors that could influence the performance of civil–military partnerships. For example, size, mandate, capacity and levels of professionalism of the humanitarian actors all affect the partnership.

- Early senior management engagement, commitment to medium-term collaboration, organizational fit, an adequate socialization period, clear programme objectives and deliverables ensured that partnership projects started off on the right foot and had a high probability of success.

- Ensuring resource alignment and relevance of assistance ensured smooth partnership implementation.

- The language proficiency of all participants, particularly the standard of English, was a determinant in the success of the partnership, particularly in the initial partnership formation phase.

- The involvement and participation of the local population was a key factor in the success of the partnerships, as was the use of local standards.

References

Akhtar, P, Marr, N E and Garnevska, E V (2012) Coordination in humanitarian relief chains: chain coordinators, *Journal of Humanitarian Logistics and Supply Chain Management*, **2** (1), pp 85–103

Arshinder, K A and Deshmukh, S G (2008) Supply chain coordination: perspectives, empirical studies and research directions, *International Journal of Production Economics*, **115** (2), pp 316–35

Beamon, B M and Balcik, B (2008) Performance measurement in humanitarian relief chains, *International Journal of Public Performance Sector Management*, **21** (1), pp 4–25

Carlos, M, Humphries, A and Wilding, R (2009) A comparison of inter- and intra-organizational relationships: two case studies from UK food and drink industry, *International Journal of Physical Distribution & Logistics Management*, **39** (9), pp 762–84

Chandes, J and Pache, G (2010) Investigating humanitarian logistics issues: from operations management to strategic action, *Journal of Manufacturing Technology Management*, **21** (3), pp 320–40

Co, H C and Barro, F (2009) Stakeholder theory and dynamics in supply chain collaboration, *International Journal of Operations & Production Management*, **29** (6), pp 591–611 de Leeuw, S and Fransoo, J (2009) Drivers of close supply chain collaboration: one size fits all? *International Journal of Operations & Production Management*, **29** (7), pp 720–39

Fynes, B, De Búrca, S and Voss, C (2005) Supply chain relationship quality, the competitive environment and performance, *International Journal of Production Research*, **43** (16), pp 3303–20

Goffin, K, Lemke, F and Szwejczewski, M (2006) An exploratory study of 'close' supplier–manufacturer relationships, *Journal of Operations Management*, **24** (2), pp 189–209

Heaslip, G and Barber, E (2014) Using the military in disaster relief: systemising challenges and opportunities, *Journal of Humanitarian Logistics and Supply Chain Management*, **4** (1), pp 60–81

Heaslip, G, Sharif, A M and Althonayan, A (2012) Employing a systems-based perspective to the identification of inter-relationships within humanitarian logistics, *International Journal of Production Economics*, **139** (2), pp 377–92

Johnston, D A and Kristal, M M (2008) The climate for co-operation: buyer–supplier beliefs and behaviour, *International Journal of Operations & Production Management*, **28** (9), pp 875–98

Kampstra, R P, Ashayeri, J and Gattorna, J (2006) Realities of supply chain collaboration, *International Journal of Logistics Management*, **17** (3), pp 312–30

Kennerley, M and Neely, A (2003) Measuring performance in a changing business environment, *International Journal of Operations & Production Management*, **23** (2), pp 213–29

Kovács, G and Tatham, P (2009) Responding to disruptions in the supply network – from dormant to action, *Journal of Business Logistics*, **30** (2), pp 215–29

Kovács, G, Tatham, P and Larson, P (2012) What skills are needed to be a humanitarian logistician? *Journal of Business Logistics*, **33** (3), pp 245–58

Oh, J and Rhee, S K (2008) The influence of supplier capabilities and technology uncertainty on manufacturer–supplier collaboration, *International Journal of Operations & Production Management*, **28** (6), p 28

Pettit, S and Beresford, A (2005) Emergency relief logistics: an evaluation of military, non-military and composite response models, *International Journal of Logistics: Research and applications*, **8** (4), pp 313–31

Pettit, S and Beresford, A (2009) Critical success factors in the context of humanitarian aid supply chains, *International Journal of Physical Distribution & Logistics Management*, **39** (6), pp 450–68

Rietjens, S J H, Voordijk, G and De Boer, S J (2007) Co-ordinating humanitarian operations in peace support missions, *Disaster Prevention and Management*, **16**, pp 56–69

Sarkis, J, Talluri, S and Gunasekaran, A (2007) A strategic model for agile virtual enterprise partner selection, *International Journal of Operations & Production Management*, **27** (11) pp 1213–34

Tatham, P H and Kovács, G (2010) The application of 'swift trust' to humanitarian logistics, *International Journal of Production Economics*, **126** (1), pp 35–45

Teng, B and Das, T K (2008) Governance structure choice in strategic alliances: the roles of alliance objectives, alliance management experience, and international partners, *Management Decision*, **46** (5), pp 725–42

UNSC (2007) [accessed 29 April 2016] United Nations Security Resolution 1778, Chad the Central African Republic and the Sub Region, *United Nations Security Council* [Online] http://www.un.org/en/ga/search/view_doc.asp?symbol=S/RES/1778(2007)

Vereecke, A and Muylle, S (2006) Performance improvement through supply chain collaboration in Europe, *International Journal of Operations & Production Management*, **26** (11), pp 1176–93

Wasti, S N, Kozan, M K and Kuman, A (2006) Buyer–supplier relationships in the Turkish automotive industry, *International Journal of Operations & Production Management*, **26** (9), pp 947–70

Whiting, M (2009) Chapter 7: Enhanced civil military cooperation in humanitarian supply chains, in *Dynamic Supply Chain Management*, ed J Gattorna, pp 107–22, Gower Publishing, Surrey

PART FOUR
Decision making in the supply chain

Decision making in humanitarian logistics 4.1

MINCHUL SOHN

HUMLOG Institute, Finland

EIJA SUSANNA MERILÄINEN

HUMLOG Institute, Finland

DAVID B GRANT

HUMLOG Institute, Finland and Hull University Business School, UK

Introduction

The primary objective of humanitarian aid is to prevent and alleviate human suffering during humanitarian crises. Logistics and supply chain management provide the backbone for such humanitarian interventions that deliver various relief items and services, mitigate future disasters, and/or respond from non-affected regions to disaster-stricken areas. Thus, effective humanitarian supply chains enable aid organizations to provide adequate materials and services in these crises. Supply chain and logistics decisions are highly important for the success of humanitarian missions, and all organizations involved in humanitarian activities require an understanding of them to fit with their own organizational goals.

Successful humanitarian logistics management requires the integration of multiple objectives. Further, humanitarian organizations must make trade-offs between these widely differing objectives to ensure a result that maximizes the overall positive impact of humanitarian aid in challenging resource-deprived environments. These objectives are usually disproportionate. In changing environments organizations must carefully consider trade-off decisions in order to achieve the appropriate humanitarian goals.

The aim of this chapter is to highlight the importance of both cost-effective and context-specific supply chain decision making and suggest decision-making criteria to support the different objectives and phases found in humanitarian operations. The chapter's objective is to assist humanitarian organizations in designing and operating their humanitarian-aid supply chain effectively and efficiently.

Some considerations related to cost-effective performance in commercial supply chain management – eg cost reduction or capital adequacy, efficient resource allocation and service improvement – are surely relevant to humanitarian interventions (Kovács and Spens, 2007). However, humanitarian supply chain management requires particular attention to context-specific decisions in an event management perspective, ie a one-time, temporary occurrence that has a fixed duration and differs from routine planning processes (Bourlakis and Grant, 2005). Context, as a concept, provides a ground for analysing humanitarian crises in relation to 'current developments and preoccupations, and with respect to their variation from place to place' (Alexander, 1997). Thus, the primary aim of this chapter, therefore, is to assist international humanitarian logistics managers in identifying the context-specific decisions they will need to make under a variety of circumstances, to help ensure better impact of humanitarian intervention over time.

The chapter opens with a brief introduction to cost-effectiveness considerations in a commercial supply chain context; it then next underlines key linkages between commercial logistics/supply chain management and humanitarian logistics strategies before considering contextual specifics in humanitarian logistics situations, which are illustrated by two case examples. It then presents a decision-making model for humanitarian events that combines the key elements of commercial and humanitarian logistics; this is followed by some concluding remarks.

Cost-effective decision criteria in logistics and supply chain management

The fundamental basis for supply chain design is the development of strategic supply chain objectives that encompass efficiency and effectiveness. For example, if a goal to achieve differentiation in the market is through offering fast, reliable deliveries (ie making a trade-off between cost versus delivery and reliability), management would likely choose trucking over rail. If low cost, however, is the primary objective, management might choose the cheaper, but slower, rail transport mode to deliver products to customers. Such efficiencies are often regarded as something that only belongs to the private sector. However, humanitarian organizations are constantly required to reduce relevant costs such as overheads and to improve impact of their action. A large part of performance evaluation concerns efficiencies of operational aspects together with aid effectiveness to recipients. Both government and donors increasingly pressure humanitarian organizations to be cost-efficient while also ensuring greater accountability and operational transparency. Thus, humanitarian organizations are increasingly required to engineer opportunities for significant benefits through balancing efficient and effective supply chain management.

In the following, based on Ballou's (2007) suggestions, we propose that logistics and supply chain management must consider three cost-effective decision criteria: 1) cost reduction; 2) capital adequacy; and 3) service improvement. These three objectives broadly concern the trade-off decisions between efficiency and effectiveness that may not be achieved simultaneously but are required to be balanced in order to yield a competitive advantage.

Cost reduction

Organizations strive to realize supply chain efficiency through potential cost savings in their supply and distribution network. Supply chain costs occur in every supply chain and logistics activity, including inventory management, facilities/warehousing and transportation, information systems, and/or various personnel expenses related to providing assistance of goods and services. Cost reductions can include both direct costs (eg facilities/warehousing, transportation) and indirect costs (eg inventory carrying costs, obsolescence of items). However, despite potential functional disjunctions in each of the above activities, organizations need to consider total supply chain costs. A longitudinal assessment of costs and investment opportunities will also help enable appropriate overall cost reductions, eg investment in better information systems, forecasting capacity and inventory management. Moreover, costs often occur at the interface between supply chain actors and are also created when goods and services are outsourced. Typically, a humanitarian organization will have a network-like supply chain with multiple stakeholders, including suppliers, customers, implementing partners as well as government and donor organizations. The management of these network interfaces is critical for supply chain cost reduction. Such relational aspects require as much careful consideration as the structural supply chain design. Cost reductions in humanitarian supply chains should help lead to better use of financial/in-kind resources from donors, and any budget savings from such cost reductions should help make more resources available for organizations to utilize for future preparedness activities.

Capital adequacy

Capital adequacy is about having sufficient capital resources in an organization and its supply chain in order to achieve the organization's objectives while also maximizing its return on investment and reducing related operating costs. Here, capital means the amount of cash, inventory or fixed assets an organization has to undertake operations. While inventory is a current asset that should be included in turnover in a fiscal year, obsolete or unsaleable inventory becomes locked in and acts as a fixed asset – but has little value since it likely cannot be sold or disposed of adequately. The more capital that is tied up in non-productive assets, the less capital resources are available for other purposes.

The amount of capital that business organizations have, or have access to, is constrained by the organization's profitability (ie self-generated capital) or its external sources of capital funding such as shareholders or financial institutions. Again, considerations of trade-offs are required as an over-investment in inventory might preclude investing in new warehouse handling equipment or vehicles. Hence, it is important to maintain an adequate level of capital without compromising the level of service quality in operations. Proper capital management will be positively related to cost reduction and, as noted above, optimal management of inventories and labour is crucial. However, it is important to note that a reduction of an organization's capital often influences other actors in the supply chain and such effects can be detrimental. For example, lowering inventory levels will increase order cycle and can cause pressures and conflicts with, and between, suppliers. Thus organizations need to consider capital management simultaneously with supply chain reinforcement, such as supplier development.

Service improvement

In response to humanitarian crises, it is important for supply chains to be resilient, to respond rapidly to uncertain demands, and to adequately adapt to the consequential phase of disaster recovery. Through such capabilities humanitarian supply chains can provide better aid, better save human lives and mitigate further damages to society – the prime objectives that surpass the cost constraints. As a guideline for humanitarian aid quality, the internationally recognized Sphere project specifies the minimum levels of standards required for life-saving humanitarian responses (Sphere Project, 2011). This may not be, however, so simple as a guideline – as instructions are not given on how to achieve the standards (Gostelow, 1999). In commercial supply chains, service improvements can directly link to profit generation, creating a mutually reinforcing value chain cycle. Satisfied customers will continually support companies who successfully meet their needs (Grant, 2012).

Humanitarian supply chains do not have such a closed-loop cycle as the commercial one. It is unlikely to gain constant feedback from the recipients of the aid service in terms of service standards. Also, the recipient of final aid in the form of goods or services may not be the one who pays for it, and they may not need such aid again. Hence, it is difficult to convert humanitarian service improvements into organizational financial sustainability. In many cases, humanitarian organizations may need to demonstrate the outcome of service improvement to donors instead, in order to secure more funding. Further, the concept of 'customer' has various meanings in humanitarian supply chains. It may signify the end-user beneficiaries of humanitarian aid, but it can also mean supply chain partners, or even donors. Thus, service improvement can be different depending on the definition of the 'customer' (Heaslip, 2013).

Table 4.1.1 presents a summary of the three cost-effective supply chain decision criteria and their related characteristics. Whilst these three criteria are the fundamental elements of any supply chain design and operation, humanitarian supply chains must consider specific contextual decision criteria and challenges, which will be elaborated in the following sections.

Table 4.1.1 Cost-effective supply chain decision criteria

Cost-Effective Decision Criteria	Description	Areas to Address
Cost reduction	To minimize the cost in supply and distribution activities	Facility location Transportation mode
Capital adequacy	To minimize the investment in the supply chain system while maximizing the return on the investment	Inventory level Distribution centre or direct shipping Ownership of warehouse
Service improvement	To provide better assistance and resilient capacity	'Customer' satisfaction

Contextual specifics in humanitarian supply chains

In the previous section the cost-effective decision criteria – cost reduction, capital reduction and service improvement – were discussed. However, for humanitarian organizations it is important to obtain value for money, ie as much efficient and effective aid as possible without wasting valuable resources, since the primary objective of humanitarian logistics is to alleviate human suffering. Effectiveness of the aid becomes a crucial factor – and a hard one to balance under disaster circumstances. Although we have briefly discussed some of the key tenets of humanitarian aid, it is also important to understand the specific contextual elements of humanitarian settings. Such elements can have strong implications when making decisions for a humanitarian supply chain or for disaster logistics preparedness, and must be considered in tandem with the three basic cost-effective supply chain decision criteria already examined. Three structural components are presented, namely environment, internal and external, which comprise the humanitarian contextual specifics, as shown in Table 4.1.2.

Table 4.1.2 Humanitarian context-specific decision criteria

Contextual Specifics	Description	Decision Criteria
Environmental structure	Nature of disasters and circumstances pre-impact of unfolding disasters	Nature and characteristics of disaster Speed of disaster onset Scale of disaster Geographical conditions Assistance accessibility Population density
Internal structure	Objectives, purposes and desires within organizations that are drawn upon as the means of an organization's action	Organizational objectives Organizational priority Long-term sustainability engagement Resource transfer modality
External structure	Independent forces and demanding circumstances that limit or determine an organization's action	Result of (rapid) needs assessment Identified needs Culture, religion Political complexity, fragility, security

Environmental structure – the nature of disasters

Environmental structures signify the nature and characteristics of disasters in relation to the circumstances, including environmental and geographical challenges. Equally, as in a response to the onset of disasters, humanitarian logistics managers are required to examine the environmental structures and potential impacts of a disaster-prone area even before the disaster. Natural or man-made hazards evolve into disasters at different speeds. Some crises are foreseeable and can be prepared for, whereas others have a rapid onset. The speed of the onset impacts the time to prepare for humanitarian operations. In terms of natural disasters, earthquakes have the most rapid onset. Despite that some scientists possibly can provide warnings of an impending earthquake, the time may not be enough for an adequate preparation. Cyclones and floods come rapidly in a short period of time, although they can be predicted or speculated in advance to some extent due to weather forecasting and regional seasonality. On the other side of the spectrum, droughts are relatively slow disasters and are often combined with food insecurity and poverty that requires consequent food assistance.

In humanitarian logistics, such lead times really matter as time delays will negatively affect the loss of life. In the case of rapid-onset disasters, the International Federation of Red Cross and Red Crescent Societies (IFRC) would, for example, need to develop emergency response units (ERUs) to be deployed within the first few hours and the deployment to the destination would usually be completed within the first 12 hours at a minimum.

The urgency of humanitarian relief provision is also related to the geographical conditions and accessibility of the aid. When roads are impassable or infrastructure is destroyed, organizations need to consider using helicopters and aircraft to deliver emergency items and workforces to cut-off communities in the inaccessible places of the affected area. With lesser urgency, organizations may have other alternatives such as small boats or barges in order to access isolated area in case of flood.

Also, it is essential for humanitarian logistics managers to consider the scale and impact of disasters. Unlike large-scale disasters that affect a substantial number of people, small-scale disaster events may not have extensive logistics preparedness and support available. These events affect a relatively limited number of people usually in sparsely populated areas. Thus, small-scale disasters are understood as less intense threats and rarely trigger prominent emergency attention, despite the potential devastation created locally. Remote locations of villages with small populations have made pre-positioning of emergency items unviable. Pre-positioned emergency resources for disasters with low frequency would be too costly for local authorities to maintain. Instead, it requires strategic decisions to be made in order to design a supply chain that would source and deliver directly from suppliers at very short notice, although this practice would cost more than maintaining pre-positioned stocks. Therefore, it is important to manage the relationships with suppliers as well as the distribution of items in the emergency situation.

Internal structures – the means of an organization's action

Internal structures are the objectives, purposes, knowledge and desires within organizations that are drawn upon as the means of an organization's action in a particular context. An organization's strategic goals and objectives detail the overall actions or approaches they carry out, including supply chain design. It is important to note that humanitarian organizations can have different mandates, missions and values of aid from each other. For instance, aid objectives of organizations intervening in an area to assist a large-scale earthquake or abrupt extreme weather events will be different from those of organizations that serve more long-term disaster-risk reduction that would strengthen the resilient capacity of a civil protection mechanism. The latter is a public service that aims to ensure activities and interventions for major disasters and emergency situations to protect the civil population. The supply chain set-up of these organizations with their different objectives will be largely varied.

Even under a single organization, various different objectives may coexist in the form of different projects and programmes. In other words, aid objectives could extend to both development and humanitarian concerns. For example, an organization with child-focused community nutrition programmes could also have a dedicated budget and strategy to respond to abrupt seasonal floods or severe drought. In doing this the organization is able to improve the quality of life of the children through food assistance intervention and, at the same time, be confident in their ability to provide first-hand disaster response and management.

While the main aid objective of the programme concerns a relatively longer-term development, there can be different organizational activities considering an organization's humanitarian mission and/or efforts to facilitate disaster risk-reduction practices. The humanitarian objectives embedded in development programmes like the above can be vice versa; eg developmental approaches embedded in humanitarian interventions. The degree of emphasis upon which efforts they would make will differ for individual organizations. However, decisions related to supply chain and logistics management will largely be distinguishable depending on organizational emphasis of either efforts, as the underlying logistics preparedness between immediate response and disaster risk reduction may divide the potential sources and utilization of resources.

Therefore, it is important for humanitarian organizations to identify their overall organizational objective, together with the objectives and implications of each programme within the organization. By doing this, organizations help ensure that programme objectives are not contradictory and narrow expertise confined in sectoral silos, and that individual supply chains can be complemented so that organizations can find the way to supplement different capacities to reduce risk vulnerabilities.

CASE EXAMPLE Techo

Techo is a non-governmental organization working in 19 countries in Latin America and the Caribbean. Their story started in 1997 in Chile with young people passionate about reducing poverty and the mission of the organization is to work without rest in the precarious settlements to reduce the poverty (Techo, nd).

While Chile can be considered a financially wealthy country in the Latin American context, the income distribution is highly unequal. The people living in the impoverished neighbourhoods, *campamentos*, earn very little and barely afford to have a roof over their heads. The neoliberal reforms performed by the former dictator Pinochet and his 'Chicago boys' – economists educated by Milton Friedman and his neoliberal fellows at the University of Chicago – in the 1970s and onwards are considered to have accentuated the income divide, poverty and political marginalization.

Chile is today, in many respects, the country of extremes. In just a few hundred kilometres, the roaring ocean in the west turns to the sharp-toothed Andes Mountains in the east. From the yellow-tinted desert of Atacama in the north the narrow country stretches over 4,000 kilometres to the chilly Patagonia in the south.

But it is not just the geography that is dramatically extreme, as geography and demographics of poverty and inequality are connected. For example, in Valparaíso, a coastal city known for its hills, vibrant culture scene as well as its industrial port, the income levels go down as one rises up on a hill. Maintained roads turn into narrower paths, the water no longer runs in pipes but is delivered in containers, the sturdy houses turn into makeshift structures and access to good education becomes less likely. In Chile, these impoverished neighbourhoods are often referred to as *tomas* or *campamentos*.

The name 'Techo' refers to 'roof' in Spanish and the symbol of the organization is a silhouette of a house. Through building teams of volunteers who collaborate with the impoverished neighbourhoods, Techo tries to reduce the poverty – especially through building houses, providing roofs. Ideally, there would be no campamentos of shaky living conditions left in Chile.

However, when a disaster strikes – as they often do in a seismic country with earthquakes, tsunamis, forest fires and mudslides – Techo aids the impacted communities by building temporary buildings, or *mediaguas* (prefabricated wooden-panelled houses) with volunteer forces. The people most affected by the disasters are those who were the most vulnerable prior to the disaster. Self-employed people living in shaky housing and having their social contacts focused in their neighbourhoods can lose everything in a disaster: their job, their family, their home. The result of disaster relief aid from Techo may then be a contribution to building temporary housing, to campamentos to relieve immediate suffering.

While giving shelter in the short term, these mediaguas contribute to the makeshift nature of the campamentos, instead of drilling deeper to the roots of inequality or poverty. Some Chileans call this, with irony, the 'temporary permanent solution'. This highlights how, for a humanitarian organization, it may be hard to balance between the long-term goals – and answering to the short-term suffering.

What to take away:

- An organization in the humanitarian sphere needs to know its objectives in order to be effective.

- But even if an organization knows its objectives, disasters put its supply chain constantly into making trade-offs to alleviate human suffering.

- Disasters are complex phenomena that affect the most vulnerable (eg from the point of view of the current economic system) the hardest.

- The ways for the organizations to support local communities depend not only on the organization, but on each disaster and the impacted community.

Further, humanitarian supply chains should aim to consider the operational continuity of services provided during the aid assistance. By making strategic decisions that are more engaged with, and considerate of, the issues of disaster risk reduction (DRR) and linking relief, rehabilitation and development (LRRD), organizations would help the humanitarian supply chain foster further development through the strengthening of local partners, market, and the state civil protection system. For example, an organization that practises 'do no harm' principles and is concerned with issues related to DRR and LRRD would prepare an exit strategy when planning their response to a humanitarian disaster, in order to phase out, or consider phasing out, intervened humanitarian support where non-humanitarian actors (such as state or development actors) are able to fulfil the needs of the population. It is particularly the case when temporary intervention has been made during a disaster response. In such cases, the effort and aid that a humanitarian organization provides to an area is duplicated and paralleled by other aid organizations, or by the government structure of the afflicted area. Due to this it is appropriate to design supply chains in collaboration with government structure to support the national and regional ownership of the aid work from the beginning of the intervention. Careful consideration of the economic and political impact of aid on local environments should also be considered. Such an approach would strengthen the local civil protection system and help maintain emergency capacity for a potentially large-scale disruption in the future.

An example can be suggested of important implications of considering operational continuity of aid on humanitarian supply chain management. The European Commission's Humanitarian Aid and Civil Protection (ECHO) department noted that there were important shifts in the late 1990s from traditional in-kind commodity food aid to a diverse set of food assistance tools, such as cash and vouchers, in order to tackle both the transient and chronic causes for food insecurity. This shift has had implications for logistical concerns and operations. Cash and vouchers are quick to deliver, cost-effective and provide people in need with greater choice by letting them buy goods to meet their own specific needs. Advantages include empowerment of the beneficiaries and supporting the local economies by distributing economic benefit beyond the direct beneficiaries.

However, it requires deliberate preparation for humanitarian supply chain design when shifting the modality. It is a prerequisite to analyse the capacity of in-country partners to implement cash and voucher systems, and to consider the time necessary to increase this capacity if needed. The management of a cash and voucher system requires different types of skills and capacity of aid organization. Managing in-kind transfers dealing with transportation, distribution and delivery of aid commodities will demand different expertise than carrying out market analysis and boundary activities between local suppliers and beneficiaries.

External structures

External structures are the independent forces and demanding circumstances that surround the aid organizations. These circumstances exist independently from the organization and have important implications for organizational action since they may constrain the organization but also provide possibilities and basis for potential actions. External structures, what we conceptualize here, are not something physical or tangible. These structures are arrangements, conditions or configurations that would be operationalized by the organization that will limit or determine possible actions. When designing and managing humanitarian supply chains, these external structures are by no means essential. The primary element of external structure for humanitarian supply chains would be the outcome of a needs assessment of an affected population, conducted by the organization or others.

One situational analysis by the IFRC, done in the early stage of an emergency appeal following the devastation caused by a cyclone, Nargis, in Myanmar, describes the massive impact of disasters during the first few days:

> Communities across the mid-south of Myanmar are reeling after a massive storm – tropical cyclone Nargis – devastated vast populated areas. The scale of destruction and loss is massive: casualty figures are still rising with reported numbers at the time of this appeal launch: 22,000 dead, 41,000 missing and millions affected. The Category 4 cyclone struck west-south-west of Yangon city, Friday 2 May 2008. Winds exceeded 190 kilometres per hour and the storm ripped through the delta city (estimated population 6 million) for more than 10 hours until Saturday noon on 3 May. Homes were flattened, more sturdy structures damaged, trees uprooted and power lines downed. State officials, along with Myanmar Red Cross Society, were first on the scene to help some of the shattered communities in terms of basics, such as water and temporary shelter. Debris blocked many roads and telecommunications were badly hit. (IFRC, 2008)

The outcome of need assessments as above will be the primary basis for planning the supply chain, although with the outcome it will not be sufficient enough considering the complexity of the situation and evolvement. IFRC (2008) points out such evolving complexity in the aftermath of the cyclone as follows:

> While the disaster is clearly massive, its true extent and detail are still emerging in a fragmented snapshot of assessments, reports and anecdotes. This is one of the significant challenges of the operation in this early phase. (IFRC, 2008)

When aid organizations enter a disaster setting, they may have had very little pre-warning about where the disaster was about to unfold. While large humanitarian organizations might have local wings or activities in many disaster-prone countries, the intervening organizations that are mobilized in the disaster zone carry their own organizational culture that is often different from that of the region they are entering. This is a result of both individual cultural make-ups of the aid workers, as well as the organization as a whole.

As the purpose of disaster relief aid is to support people in their survival, it is of vital importance to understand how people view their life and its survival, especially as disaster relief is concerned with disasters that affect whole communities. Demand identification based on numerical values of individual needs must consider the cultural and contextual aspects that the individuals cannot be isolated from. Commercial supply chains take care of their 'customer relations' and a customer orientation is important for continuing purchases and repeat business (Grant, 2012). For a non-government organization (NGO) coming to provide aid following a disaster, it is important to ask whether that NGO really knows what it is that adds value to the lives of the people they are helping, especially in the long term.

CASE EXAMPLE   International Federation of Red Cross and Red Crescent Societies (IFRC)

The International Federation of Red Cross and Red Crescent Societies (IFRC) was founded in 1919 after the First World War. Today IFRC is the world's largest humanitarian organization with 190 national member societies. It carries out relief operations to assist victims of disasters, and combines this with development work to strengthen the capacities of its member national societies (IFRC, nd). According to ALNAP's most recent 2015 report 'The State of the Humanitarian System', 61 per cent of humanitarian donor funding flowed to the UN and 8 per cent to the Red Cross/Red Crescent. Together they receive 69 per cent of donor funding – so what the UN and RC/RC Movement do and say has weight in the humanitarian sector.

Humanitarian supply chains do not answer to customer demands, but to humanitarian needs. Some refer to the affected as 'beneficiaries', but essentially they are humans under dire circumstances. The locals are best aware of what their actual needs are and hence working together with the local people – both the affected as well as local organizations – is important. According to ALNAP's 2015 report, aid recipients feel that they are not involved enough in the aid efforts.

IFRC works in a multitude of cultural contexts, with its aid workers likewise multicultural. In order to effectively aid the disaster-affected populations, there needs to be intercultural collaboration. But how to take the cultures and the local community into account? The question of how to see the culture is essentially about whether to see the trees apart from the forest, or whether to zoom out in order to see the forest without the individual trees. Further, whether to provide aid for individuals with a certain cultural background, or whether to support the whole community with a different culture.

The view on culture has changed within the IFRC over time. The title of an IFRC 2004 report was 'World Disasters Report 2004: From risk to resilience – helping communities cope with crisis'. The idea behind the report was that local impacted communities are resilient and that resilience should be supported. In this report the community as a whole was the one served by an external aid-supply chain.

The introduction to the 2004 report states: 'Evidence suggests that everyday threats to livelihoods are a greater concern to most poor communities than "one-off" disasters. Meanwhile, local consensus and co-operation are as important in protecting communities as concrete walls. The report argues that a more developmental approach to creating disaster resilience is needed, which puts communities in charge of defining their needs and crafting the right solutions.' The same message has been echoed by various researchers.

However, 10 years later the IFRC's World Disaster Report (2014) focused on culture and risk and discusses whether the idea of a community is actually just a myth. Instead of community, the report describes the culture as a background logic within which the people aided by the organization operate.

While the difference may seem semantic, it is important because in a disaster situation NGOs are making some decisions in the name of the beneficiaries, with a limited understanding about how the people themselves want their lives to unfold. In the 'conventional' supply chain, where customer demand shapes the supply, these questions are not as vital, but humanitarian supply chains act in the name of the good of the beneficiaries, supplying their needs. When they are acting in the name of the beneficiaries, they need to do their best to understand the actual needs.

What to take away:

- Disasters are hazards evolving in social and natural settings – they do not happen in a vacuum and they are all different and require a tuned response.

- Both the people affected and the ones helping the affected come from their own respective cultures with their respective ways of doing things and their respective infrastructure for doing so ('the external structures').

- Nature also shapes how a hazard turns into a disaster – and it also shapes the cultures.

- While conceptualizing culture and understanding it under rapidly developing disaster conditions is hard, it is vital to think about 'who' the community is, even if no clear answer would exist.

Together with identified needs and cultural context, other important elements should be also considered. There are some areas with political complexity or where state government would not easily allow international humanitarian assistance. In such areas, challenges related to aid ownership can be often observed. For example, the government of the affected area will not allow an external organization to be in control of the aid intervention. In such a context, supply chain decisions – eg estimating the lead time, channelling the relief commodities, and implementation of storing and delivery – can be hugely affected. Related to political complexity, security is another issue to be considered. The apparent operational changes of Médecins Sans Frontières (MSF), also known as Doctors without Borders, is a good example of how an organization copes with a high level of insecurity.

While the crisis in Syria was deepening in 2013, for example, MSF had reduced the amount of their direct delivery of medical activities due to unsafe operating conditions. Instead, MSF continued to support the local medical networks with medicines and medical materials – hence changing the composition of their supply chain activities. This highlights the fact that MSF tried to effectively support the health care of Syrians, while choosing their supply chain strategy under the dire disaster conditions (MSF, 2015).

Illustration of the facility location decisions

During the preparation phase, supply chain decisions made around facility location and the physical structure of the supply chain – eg pre-positioning, warehouses, distribution centres – are very important (Balcik and Beamon, 2008; Gatignon, Van Wassenhove and Charles, 2010). Many organizations, recognizing that such decisions have large implications for other supply chain activities, place considerable emphasis on facility location and product flow. Figure 4.1.1 presents the basic elements that must be considered and traded off against each other when making a decision on facility location.

After the role of facility is decided in a pre-planned scheme, the subsequent decisions are all made in a trade-off framework that considers total cost and impact of service. The framework is not a linear decision, rather all elements are interconnected. For example, consider an organization with a limited budget to set up logistics facilities. The number of facilities will influence the location of each one as well as the size. If the organization has

Figure 4.1.1 Basic facility location elements of trade-offs decision

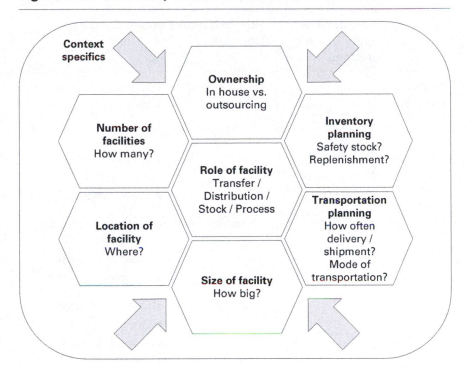

multiple, but smaller facilities, the last-mile delivery capacity of the organization will increase because facilities can be located nearer to the areas in need. Smaller stores will, however, require more frequent replenishment of stock and this must be factored in to a transportation plan that will provide rapid and secure delivery of aid goods and services. This will also mean a higher transportation cost. If frequent transportation of stock is not possible, this will have an impact on inventory planning, with inventory in turn an important consideration in decisions related to number, location and/or size of facility.

As illustrated in Table 4.1.3, cost-effective decision criteria for facility location are closely interconnected and also need to accompany humanitarian context-specific decisions. For example, a government's long-term commitment to utilize facilities as a mitigation resource for future disasters would affect cost-effective decision approaches. On the other hand, political complexity and insecure circumstance would not allow such long-term infrastructure commitment into the facility, but the facility would only be used to maintain emergency supplies flowing into the country.

Table 4.1.3 Decision criteria for facility location problem

	Cost-Effective Supply Chain Decisions	Humanitarian Context-Specifics Decisions	
Facility Location	• Total cost? • Economy of scale? • Capital investment? Ownership? • Time constraints? • Safe storage? • Last-mile delivery?	Environmental structure	• Abrupt outbreak? • Recurring? Seasonal? • Transportation accessibility? • Population accessibility? • Time, complexity?
		Internal structure	• Temporary? Disaster risk reduction? • Potential future use? • Functional change?
		External structure	• Cluster? Sharing? • Government plan? • Political complexity? • Security?

A comprehensive decision-making model

In the course of delivering humanitarian aid, humanitarian logistics and supply chains may confront multifaceted challenges and changes under conditions of great uncertainty and/or urgency. In addition, multiple and interrelated factors of development – ie causes of poverty, fragility, security and vulnerability – may require that organizations adapt their goal and adjust the ways in which they pursue their objectives.

Humanitarian supply chains primarily provide disaster relief in the field but also they support and strengthen national response capacity, promote partnerships with local actors and utilize existing market structures to the benefit of ongoing development efforts. The varied and changing operational environments found in humanitarian crisis situations require distinct management perspectives and humanitarian supply chain designs.

The comprehensive decision-making model for humanitarian supply chains shown in Figure 4.1.2 identifies three structures of humanitarian

Figure 4.1.2 Comprehensive decision-making model for humanitarian supply chain

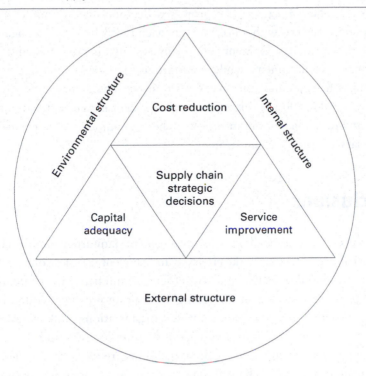

context specifics that surround the core objectives of cost-effective supply chain strategic decisions. Two objectives, cost and capital reduction, place relatively larger weight towards achieving a cost-efficient supply chain. Operational and financial performance could be the principal focus of such objectives. This is an obvious trend in the humanitarian sector with more demand from donors to be cost-efficient. Also, competition between humanitarian organizations accelerates the trend to make better and wider performance with less cost and investment. The third objective, service improvement, places emphasis on aid effectiveness of the humanitarian supply chain. Unlike common belief, different orientation of supply chain objectives does not signify that they are opposing goals. However, trade-offs decisions will always have to be made when determining the balanced objectives for the right supply chain.

The humanitarian context-specific structures are again divided into environment, external and internal structures, where the inputs from each structure are integrated, analysed and interpreted simultaneously and combined with three objectives of supply chain strategic decisions. These structures are not static. The structures should go through a structuration process that creates and reproduces each structure, reflecting the dynamic network of organizations and their practices. The proposed decision-making model would provide supply chains with a holistic approach that would better engage an ongoing process of development and redefine the manner of interaction with the changing environment, while maintaining the core strategic issues of balancing efficiency and effectiveness in supply chain management. The model is useful for disaster/emergency management managers from humanitarian and development organizations, where a comprehensive perspective is necessary for supply chain strategy.

Conclusions

High expectations as well as pressures on humanitarian supply chains require that organizations make effective and efficient use of resources. Both governments and donors demand cost-efficiency and better use of financial/in-kind resources, while also increasingly requiring greater accountability. In order to achieve this, it is important that organizations think comprehensively when making decisions about humanitarian logistics and the supply chain. Three cost-effective supply chain decisions are fundamental elements for humanitarian supply chain design. Moreover, an organization should consider contextual specifics for particular humanitarian interventions and suggest a comprehensive decision-making model for humanitarian logistics and supply chain, incorporating these structural components: environmental, internal and external structures. This model should be useful for humanitarian logistics managers to consider, together with cost and performance criteria, comprehensive and holistic approaches that will reflect the duality of relief and development embedded in humanitarian aid interventions.

References

Alexander, D (1997) The study of natural disasters, 1977–97: some reflections on a changing field of knowledge, *Disasters*, 21 (4), pp 284–304

ALNAP (2015) *The State of the Humanitarian System*, ALNAP Study, ALNAP/ODI, London

Balcik, B and Beamon, B M (2008) Facility location in humanitarian relief, *International Journal of Logistics Research and Applications*, 11 (2), pp 101–21

Ballou, R H (2007) *Business Logistics/Supply Chain Management*, 5th edn, Pearson Education, Harlow UK

Bourlakis, M and Grant, D B (2005) Logistics and supply chain issues in event management: the case of the 2004 Athens Olympic Games, Proceedings of the 10th Annual Logistics Research Network (LRN) Conference, University of Plymouth, September, pp 77–82

Gatignon, A, Van Wassenhove, L N and Charles, A (2010) The Yogyakarta earthquake: humanitarian relief through IFRC's decentralized supply chain, *International Journal of Production Economics*, **126** (1), pp 102–10

Gostelow, L (1999) The sphere project: the implications of making humanitarian principles and codes work, *Disasters*, **23** (4), pp 316–25

Grant, D B (2012) *Logistics Management*, Pearson Education, Harlow UK

Heaslip, G (2013) Service operations management and humanitarian logistics, *International Journal of Humanitarian Logistics and Supply Chain Management*, **3** (1), pp 37–51

IFRC (nd) [accessed 30 May 2016] IFRC – Our Vision and Mission [Online] http://www.ifrc.org/en/who-we-are/vision-and-mission/

IFRC (2004) *International Federation of Red Cross and Red Crescent Societies: World Disasters Report 2004 – From risk to resilience – helping communities cope with crisis*, International Federation of Red Cross and Red Crescent Societies, Geneva, Switzerland

IFRC (2008) [accessed 30 November 2015] International Federation of Red Cross, Emergency Appeal 6 May [Online] http://www.ifrc.org/docs/appeals/08/ MDRMM002EA.pdf

IFRC (2014) *International Federation of Red Cross and Red Crescent Societies: World Disasters Report 2014 – Focus on culture and risk*, International Federation of Red Cross and Red Crescent Societies, Geneva, Switzerland

Kovács, G and Spens, K M (2007) Humanitarian logistics in disaster relief operations, *International Journal of Physical Distribution & Logistics Management*, **37** (2), pp 99–114

MSF (2015) [accessed 1 October 2015] Syria: An Unnacceptable Humanitarian Failure, *Médecins Sans Frontières* [Online] http://www.doctorswithoutborders. org/article/syria-unacceptable-humanitarian-failure

Sphere Project (2011) [accessed 1 October 2015] Sphere Handbook: Humanitarian Charter and Minimum Standards in Disaster Response, 2011 [Online] http://www.sphereproject.org/

Techo (nd) [accessed 30 May 2016] Misión/Visión – ValoresMission/Vision – Values/Juntos por un Mundo sin Pobreza [Online] http://www.techo.org/techo/ mision-vision-valores/

Forecasts, financing and acceleration of humanitarian logistics

4.2

From supply chain to value chain

JANOT MENDLER DE SUAREZ, PABLO SUAREZ, ERIN COUGHLAN DE PEREZ AND DAK MARTIN DOLEAGBENU

Red Cross Red Crescent Climate Centre, Netherlands

We cannot continue business as usual.
We have to change; we have to adapt.

AMER DAOUDI, DIRECTOR, WORLD FOOD
PROGRAMME LOGISTICS DIVISION, 2009

The early warning–early action gap

As climate change increases uncertainties and extreme events, making full use of available scientific information to improve decisions and action before a disaster occurs becomes increasingly urgent (IPCC, 2012). Yet there is an operational gap in humanitarian logistics: much is known about how to do things better, yet scarcely implemented. Kovács and Spens (2011) highlight four challenges confronting humanitarian supply chains: unpredictability of demand (timing, location, type, size), surge of demand (large quantities but short lead times), the high stakes of adequate and timely delivery, and an overall lack of resources.

Given the up-until-the-disaster-strikes uncertainty of demand, and the event-driven supply chains, how can humanitarian logisticians overcome the co-ordination problems of orchestrating disaster-preparedness activities across a complex networked system with greater agility (eg Christopher and Tatham 2011)? Climate forecasters who provide weather predictions, disaster managers and people at risk need to build common ground in order to formulate smart forecast-based decisions – as well as simple decision-based forecasts (Suarez, 2009). While it would be desirable to accelerate supply chains by shifting from acting in response to an observed disaster to acting in response to a forecast with a high probability of leading to disaster, the humanitarian sector faces many barriers to the effective use of forecasts.

Modelling is a simplification of the parameters and key variables that interact within a given system, which can be used to simulate the outcomes of interactions within the system to reveal future conditions; eg to anticipate the necessary humanitarian response in case of disaster. Supply chain modelling emphasis is on deterministic real-time triggers based on observed needs; because the logistical supply chain is not triggered until a need arises, in actuality often necessary items and assistance are supplied too late (Braman *et al*, 2013). To be actionable, weather forecasts generally require some translation in order to first identify the geographic region for which the forecast applies, then to choose a threshold of likely intensity at which action would be warranted to prepare for impending disaster, and finally to define the time frame within which such preparatory action would be feasible, before the disaster strikes. Thus to be actionable, weather forecasting requires the translation of complex hydrometeorological data into a localized impact probability, upon which a decision can be taken as to what preparedness action is advisable (eg Pagano, Hartmann and Sorooshian, 2002). In order to understand what the impact of increased rainfall will be on the ground, rainfall data needs to be fed into a hydrological model to understand how that water will flow on the ground. This means, for example, integrating a multitude of hydrological factors that together determine the rate and volume of runoff into water bodies that can lead to flooding.

Given that rainfall data is generally collected by national meteorological services and water data is generally collected by national hydrological services, unless there are established modes of co-operation, the integration of the meteorological and hydrological data required to produce actionable disaster forecasting may be difficult. For example, in Togo, the primary function of weather forecasting is to enable the national airport to service aviation, so the meteorological service is under the Ministry of Transport, while the hydrology service is under the ministry charged with water, sanitation and village hydraulics. Hence such structural, institutional or political barriers (Rayner, Lach and Ingram, 2005; Demeritt *et al*, 2010; Demeritt *et al*, 2013), including aversion to acting in vain given the inherent uncertainty of using probabilities (Coughlan de Perez, van Aalst *et al*, 2015), further impede the use of forecast information. Without a clear mandate to act on a forecast, neither humanitarian organizations nor stakeholders at risk are likely to have confidence in deciding what action is 'worth' taking (eg Hillbruner and Moloney 2012). Early warning systems rarely trigger systematic action based on increased likelihood that a hazard will occur, and there are very few funding mechanisms for operationalizing action on such early warnings (Coughlan de Perez, van den Hurk *el al*, 2015; Kellett and Caravani, 2013; Jahre and Heigh, 2008). To close this gap, the Red Cross Red Crescent Climate Centre and partners have developed the concept of forecast-based financing (FbF).

Forecast-based financing

FbF was conceived as a means to improve the ability of humanitarian actors to reduce the risks of disasters *before they strike* as well as to strengthen the resilience of vulnerable communities to withstand likely continuing exposure to extreme events and adapt to a changing climate. FbF works by determining various thresholds of risk, based on hydrometeorological forecasting and scientific data. Once a threshold is reached it triggers specific, predesignated actions, which are then carried out – before a disaster strikes.

FbF can make supply chains smarter through the use of forecast information to inform a new approach to standard operating procedures for disaster risk reduction and response. The German Federal Foreign Ministry and Ministry for Economic Co-operation and Development, with the German Red Cross and partners, are providing pioneering support for FbF pilot projects in developing countries.

Uncertainty as to the timing and sufficiency of financing is at the root of many delays and inefficiencies in disaster management. Funding difficulties stemming from demand unpredictability, and when disasters trigger a sudden surge in the need for financing, also contribute to systematic failure to consider longer-term opportunity costs in disaster preparedness and response. The humanitarian sector, while cognizant of the pitfalls of acting in vain,

Figure 4.2.1 Taking preparedness action triggered by a forecast can reduce the number of people affected by an extreme event and reduce the losses they suffer, with a consequent reduction in disaster response needs and cost

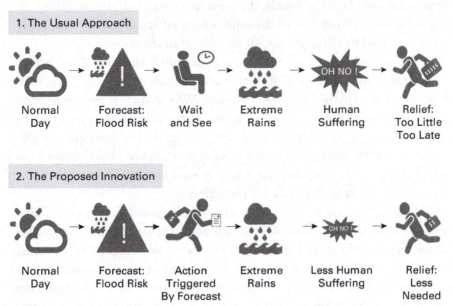

NOTE: The usual approach in response to science-based forecasts of likely but not certain extreme events is to not trigger humanitarian action until the need to act is deemed absolutely necessary. The proposed innovation consists of establishing pre-agreed, pre-funded triggers for preparedness action based on probabilistic forecasts, thus reducing suffering and/or making expenditures more productive.

must also tackle the problem of financing as a 'just in time' factor in disaster management. Figure 4.2.1 illustrates the business-as-usual scenario, whereby money necessary to respond simply doesn't flow until the disaster happens, and people suffer needlessly from the impacts of predictable weather extremes. The result is that people suffer from impacts that could have been prevented, had the means been available to take preparatory action at the moment that known disaster risk began to go up.

What remains to be known is where and when such action will need to be mobilized, how many times, or at what scale for any particular forecast. Acting on a forecast means there is some level of probability that the extreme event may not materialize, and acting in vain can lead to the perception of bad decision making, wasted effort and squandered resources. Given the probabilistic nature of forecasts, there is a need for a probabilistic framework for decision making to trigger forecast-specific preparedness action. For example, determining what actions are worth taking two days in advance of a flood is to some extent related to how far in advance of a disaster the forecast has skill, and perhaps more importantly, whether it can withstand the probability of acting 'in vain' associated with this particular forecast. In other words, if people are only comfortable taking an action 'in vain' 20 per cent of the time, a forecast would not be actionable if it would lead to acting in vain 40 per cent of the time.

There are additional trade-offs in ascertaining thresholds for action versus inaction. For example, if there is a high probability of flooding with low impact, should the Red Cross mobilize? What if there is low probability with high impact potential? What are the potential liabilities of acting in vain versus failing to act if a disaster strikes? Answering these questions in advance enables actors across the operational supply chain network to weigh the risks (and appetite for acting in vain versus not acting), and to ascertain the acceptable thresholds for action.

Taking early action based on an early warning means there is a fixed time window until the event occurs, at which point the standard response continues. In order to take full advantage of the window of opportunity opened by a forecast, the humanitarian organization must be ready to mobilize from the moment the forecast is received. This means that if the financing necessary to, for example, fuel up the fleet, ramp up the chain of communications or mobilize volunteers, is not immediately available, then the window of opportunity may close without being fully utilized.

Togo's FbF pilot project

In the West African nation of Togo, a robust commmunity-based early warning system has been established with technical and financial support from the German Red Cross through its ongoing Climate Change Adaptation project. The Togo Red Cross system consists of warnings transmitted by mobile phone from upstream to downstream communities, based on water level observations of river poles installed with German support within the flood plain. To enable easy visual observation of flood-risk levels, these river poles are painted with a colour code equating water level to three levels of risk. Togo Red Cross has worked with each community with a river pole to determine the green–yellow–red colour code levels according to the community. Green indicates low-level flooding for which minimal action is needed; yellow the water level at which they have decided that certain agreed flood preparedness activities should be undertaken; and red, the highest level, indicates the point at which the community must decide and mobilize to evacuate. This system enables the Togo Red Cross to support communities in taking preparatory actions with a few hours' lead time when river levels upstream indicate imminent flooding downstream.

In 2012 the Red Cross Red Crescent Climate Centre proposed to build on Togo's operational community-based early warning system, to introduce the use of scientific forecasting that offers the possibility of predicting flood risk on the order of days instead of hours in advance. Togo Red Cross is interested in hydrometeorological flood forecasting as a means to give communities more lead time in which to prepare for imminent flooding. To ensure timely action within the window for action opened by a forecast, the German Red Cross provided seed funding to establish a dedicated preparedness fund. The creation of this dedicated fund aims to ensure prompt action, whereby a specific flood-risk forecast simultaneously triggers the mobilization of Togo Red Cross to take action, and the release of predetermined financing necessary to carry out the specific pre-planned flood-risk reduction actions.

The experience of Togo Red Cross in operating a forecast-based financing mechanism offers a practical example of the complex orchestration required when using probabilistic real-time information to trigger pre-planned, pre-disaster, forecast-specific actions. The focus of this project was to strengthen the existing community-based early warning flood system with the emphasis on using scientific information to reduce disaster risk and avoid likely losses. We highlight this aspect as complementary to preparedness for the traditional supply of items necessary to cope with the disaster conditions. Hazard risk information is shared horizontally across an unusual network of partners, and then vertically upstream and downstream within the Red Cross network of operations. This level of synchronized action is rare within the humanitarian sector.

The unusual partner is a hydroelectric dam. Togo Red Cross initially explored co-operating with the bi-national Nangbeto dam authority (also serving Benin) for flood alerts and in 2013 began receiving advance warning whenever the retention reservoir approached levels that might require the dam to make a release. The Climate Centre expanded collaboration with the dam authority, leading to the co-creation of an innovative hydrological flood-risk modelling and scenario simulation system to estimate the probabilities of flooding in specific downstream communities, based on observed and forecast rainfall upstream. Simultaneously, with German Red Cross support, Togo Red Cross staff and volunteers developed an initial set of new standard operating procedures (SOPs) for flood-risk reduction in the downstream communities. The SOPs specify what action should be taken by whom at what probability and magnitude of forecast. Because the forecast also triggers the release of funds necessary to carry out the SOPs, time delays in accessing financing needed to mobilize are eliminated. Hence FbF accelerates and fine-tunes an agile just-in-time risk-reduction and disaster-preparedness supply chain.

The new SOPs aim to prevent avoidable losses, for example the procurement of resealable plastic bags allows families to protect vital household documents and so is considered a priority in vulnerable communities. These plastic bags avoid losses by delivering 'protection of value', because children's birth certificates, for example, required for school registration, have a high replacement cost, which is avoided. The plastic bags thus protect a value that can also be monetized, further enabling analysis of the social and financial cost to benefit ratio of expenditure by the Red Cross on procurement and distribution of bags compared to the avoided losses, calculated in terms of uninterrupted schooling, days away from work to replace documents, as well as the fees to reissue lost documents. The pre-purchase and targeted distribution of water purification tablets is triggered by elevated flood risk in specific downstream communities, accelerating the supply chain to deliver targeted prevention *before* flooding that typically leads to the outbreak of cholera – whereas observed cholera cases formerly triggered this response.

To address the lack of hydrometeorological data needed to support expansion of the FbF early warning system, Togo Red Cross also partnered with the Togo national meteorological and hydrological services. With support from the World Bank and the Togo Ministry of Environment, by 2016 over 1,000 Red Cross volunteers were trained to collect data on daily river levels and rainfall, setting a global precedent for engaging humanitarian volunteers at the community level in collecting data for national weather and water technical services. This innovation in information flows adds value to enhanced modelling developed with the dam and the Climate Centre, drawing on additional technical partners. This new hydrometeorological modelling of upstream and downstream flows through the Nangbeto dam is laying the scientific foundations for the development of a national early warning–early action system.

Further, with support from German Red Cross, a local team of young digital designers was engaged to develop an automated online SMS data entry system, which is also making the new 'scientifically crowdsourced' data freely accessible (eg to the national services, dam operators, researchers). The hydrometeorological modelling and flood-risk forecasting system is being technically enhanced with support from the Global Facility for Disaster

Reduction and Recovery, effectively enabling Togo Red Cross to build a 'citizen science' platform that engages people as sensors making and transmitting data on rainfall and river levels, and as beneficiaries (Michelucci, 2013) who can take action based on the new flood-risk predictions. In a classic 'win-win' the dam authority expects the modelling collaboration to also realize increased efficiencies in hydropower production.

The participatory SOP planning process enabled the same communication and logistics chain to be utilized for other loss aversion and preventive health SOPs triggered by the same flooding forecast. This added value through efficiency (for example, the resealable bags mentioned previously were used to distribute water purification tablets). Informational radio spots about flood preparedness already developed by Togo Red Cross are now programmed according to specific forecasts, with the addition of new pre-recorded spots and live reporting, including interviews with local disaster management volunteers on preparedness activities they are taking in flood-risk areas in real time. Through the release of predetermined funds necessary to fulfil contractual obligations negotiated with radio stations, as well as other short-term actions necessary to reduce the risk of a likely disaster before the event actually occurs, Togo Red Cross expects FbF to improve outcomes as well as performance efficiency. All of these pilot interventions have a durable value, since even if flooding fails to happen within the predicted time frame, the risk-reduction measures remain in place, and over time the repetition of the conveyed flood-risk management information reinforces a culture of preparedness.

In order to understand whether and how the new SOPs are effective, household surveys will be conducted following the flood season, including control communities that have similar weather conditions but have not received direct flood-risk information or preparedness interventions. The ability to monitor and evaluate at the household level enables Togo Red Cross to establish a new level of data-driven performance analysis to inform decision making in the next planning cycle. Creating this feedback loop for data-driven learning from results adds transformative value to the FbF supply chain through continuous improvement, which will undoubtedly provide fertile ground for future research.

Full value proposition

It is difficult to predict specifically when, where, how frequently and how hard disasters may strike, with the long lead times required for planning and budgeting what will be needed to prepare for disasters. Furthermore, practical and financial constraints make it difficult to maintain a state of preparedness in all the places that might be subject to a disaster within any given period. It is, however, increasingly possible to anticipate, given a defined level of disaster risk, what could be done in a specific location within a specific time frame. FbF offers a way for humanitarian outcomes to be improved, by tailoring locality and risk-specific actions ahead of time, which are only initiated when a forecast is issued that corresponds to a predetermined threshold for action. By funding short-term actions to reduce the risk of an expected disaster, before the extreme event actually happens, forecast-based financing delivers targeted, timely funding that accelerates disaster management logistical supply chains. By making the availability of financing more agile, multiple SOPs can be more efficiently budgeted and programmed. As FbF scales up, the dedicated preparedness fund will pool risk management financing, smoothing demand unpredictability and surge, while ensuring adequate and timely delivery unimpeded by a lack of resources.

Thomas and Mizushima (2005) define the supply chain as: 'The process of planning, implementing and controlling the efficient, cost-effective flow and storage of goods and materials as well as related information, from the point of origin to the point of consumption for the purpose of meeting the end beneficiary's requirements.' FbF offers a way of making supply chains smarter by accelerating and allowing for innovation within the supply chain, which results in better outcomes for beneficiary communities.

Assessing these outcomes will require ways to measure system performance in a context of incommensurable variables (such as money/resources versus lives saved versus trust lost), which means that there may be no optimal solution. Beamon and Balcik (2008) discuss three types of performance metrics in humanitarian supply chain systems:

- *Output performance metrics*: where the purpose is effectiveness, eg reduced death and suffering thanks to shorter response time.

- *Resource performance metrics*: where the purpose is efficiency, eg more people helped per unit spent by reducing relief delivery costs.

- *Flexibility performance metrics*: where the purpose is to improve ability to respond to a changing environment, eg by accommodating fluctuations in type of demand.

Lopez *et al* (forthcoming) offer a mathematical framework outlining the range of values at which FbF outperforms the alternative of waiting until the disaster strikes to take action. For any given set of parameters (capturing the costs of action and inaction and the probability of acting in vain versus

Figure 4.2.2 Forecast-based Financing (FbF)

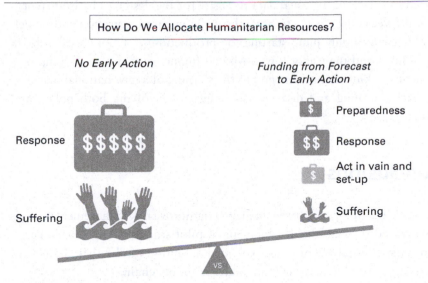

NOTE: FbF for disaster preparedness is worth embracing when the usual choice of 'no early action' is outperformed by FbF in terms of output, resource or flexibility performance metrics.

failing to act), there are a range of forecasts for which forecast-based actions offer better results in terms of output performance and resource performance (see Figure 4.2.2).

In 'Saving Lives, Preventing Suffering and Building Resilience: The UK Government's Humanitarian Policy', the first policy goal is to 'strengthen anticipation and early action'. FbF can help, especially since skilful hydro-meteorological forecasting systems are an emerging technology for the humanitarian sector. Defining anticipatory governance as 'a new approach to manage the uncertainties embedded on an innovation trajectory with participatory foresight', Ozdemir, Faraj and Knoppers (2011) acknowledge the social construction of technology design and innovation. The Togo Red Cross collaboration with Nangbeto dam, and an array of technical partners unusual to the humanitarian sector, illustrates this process. Despite the significant resource and technical and logistical constraints of a very poor country, the need to manage climate uncertainty is catalyzing operational innovation, with implications beyond the immediate aims of saving lives and avoiding disaster losses. Developing innovative ways to bridge structural gaps in hydrological and meteorological data collection is enabling the foundations of a robust future data-driven early warning system, to be built hand in hand with the new young generation of computer and software expertise and Red Cross volunteers in vulnerable communities. Innovation driven by a lack of the usual data requisite for the design of hydrometeorological forecasting has led to breakthroughs in data integration and modelling that is not only jump-starting the production of actionable flood-risk predictions and the use of forecast-based financing, it is also opening new ways of working that are integral to the shaping of a new national platform for early warning and disaster-risk reduction involving both public and private actors.

Conclusions

The structure of forecast-based financing to improve risk management systems has evolved through the development of pilot studies. Coughlan de Perez, Van Aalst *et al* (2015) offer an expanded definition of FbF that aligns with a smart, agile value-creating humanitarian supply chain:

> When a forecast states that an agreed-upon *probability* threshold is exceeded for a *hazard* of a designated *magnitude*, then an *action* with an associated *cost* must be taken that has a desired *effect* and is carried out by a designated *organization*.

Forecasts offer opportunities for establishing more agile-networked value chains, which build on smarter information-infused standard operating procedures (SOPs) to accelerate humanitarian logistics at different time scales; for example, initiating preparedness actions with two to five days' lead time for tropical cyclones, three to ten days for flooding in large river basins, and weeks to months for seasonal forecasts based on El Niño. Forecast-based financing (FbF) was initially piloted in Togo and Uganda, and is being expanded to projects in Bangladesh, Mozambique and Peru – with plans to develop projects in several more countries.

We have the opportunity to rethink logistical supply chains in the precious time window before a disaster, a window that is opened or expanded by a forecast. For the future, there are huge opportunities for continual improvement in managing extreme events: if people and organizations are equipped conceptually and materially to anticipate risks that would otherwise lead to disaster, these risks can be reduced, avoided or transferred. The value proposition holds even more future potential in leveraging climate extremes – for example through diversion of floodwater, to build resilience (ie storage as a buffer against subsequent drought risk) and support productive activities (such as agriculture or fish farming) that promote prosperity and well-being.

References

Beamon, B M and Balcik, B (2008) Performance measurement in humanitarian relief chains, *International Journal of Public Sector Management*, 21 (1), pp 4–25

Braman, L, van Aalst, M, Suarez, P, Mason, S, Tall, A and Ait-Chellouche, Y (2013) Climate forecasts in disaster management: Red Cross flood operations in West Africa, 2008, *Disasters*, 37 (1), pp 144–64

Christopher, M and Tatham, P (eds) (2011) *Humanitarian Logistics: Meeting the challenge of preparing for and responding to disasters*, Kogan Page, London

Coughlan de Perez, E, van Aalst, M, Deva, C, van den Hurk, B, Jongman, B, Klose, T, Linnerooth-Bayer, J and Suarez, P (2015) Managing the risk of extreme events in a changing climate: trends and opportunities in the disaster-related funding landscape The Hague: Red Cross Red Crescent Climate Centre, Working Paper Series No 7, commissioned as an input paper for the United Nations Office for Disaster Risk Reduction (UNISDR), Global Assessment Report on Disaster Risk Reduction 2015

Coughlan de Perez, E, van den Hurk, B, van Aalst, M, Jongman, B, Klose, T and Suarez, P (2015) Forecast-based financing: an approach for catalyzing humanitarian action based on extreme weather and climate forecasts, *Natural Hazards and Earth System Science*, 15 (4), pp 895–904

Demeritt, D, Nobert, S, Cloke, H and Pappenberger, F (2010) Challenges in communicating and using ensembles in operational flood forecasting, *Meteorological Applications*, 17, pp 209–22

Demeritt, D, Nobert, S, Cloke, H and Pappenberger, F (2013) The European flood alert system and the communication, perception and use of ensemble predictions for operational flood risk management, *Hydrological Processes HEPS Special Issue*, 27, pp 147–57

Hillbruner, C and Moloney, G (2012) When early warning is not enough – lessons learned from the 2011 Somalia Famine, *Global Food Security*, special issue on the Somalia Famine of 2011–12, 1 (1), pp 1–28

IPCC – Intergovernmental Panel on Climate Change (2012) [accessed 25 April 2016] Special Report on Managing the Risks of Extreme Events and Disasters to Advance Climate Change Adaptation [Online] http://ipcc-wg2.gov/SREX

Jahre, M and Heigh, I (2008) Does the current constraints in funding promote failure in humanitarian supply chains?, *Supply Chain Forum*, 9 (2), pp 44–55

Kellet, J and Caravani, A (2013) [accessed 25 April 2016] Financing Disaster Risk Reduction: A 20 year story of international aid, *GFDRR Global Facility for Disaster Risk Reduction* [Online] https://www.odi.org/sites/odi.org.uk/files/odi-assets/publications-opinion-files/8574.pdf

Kovács, G and Spens, K (2011) Humanitarian logistics and supply chain management: the start of a new journal, *Journal of Humanitarian Logistics and Supply Chain Management*, 1 (1), pp 5–14

Lopez, A, Coughlan de Perez, E, Suarez, P, van den Hurk, B and van Aalst, M (forthcoming) Bridging forecast verification and humanitarian decisions: a valuation approach for setting up action-oriented early warning systems, *Bulletin of the American Meteorological Society*

Michelucci, P (ed) (2013) *Handbook of Human Computation*, Springer, New York

Ozdemir, V, Faraj, S A and Knoppers, B M (2011) Steering vaccinomics innovations with anticipatory governance and participatory foresight, *OMICS*, **15** (9), pp 637–46

Pagano, T C, Hartmann, H C and Sorooshian, S (2002) Factors affecting seasonal forecast use in Arizona water management: a case study of the 1997–8 El Nino, *Journal of Climate Research*, **21** (3), pp 259–69

Rayner, S, Lach, D and Ingram, H (2005) Weather forecasts are for wimps: why water resource managers do not use climate forecasts, *Climactic Change*, **69**, pp 197–227

Suarez, P (2009) *Linking Climate Knowledge and Decisions: Humanitarian challenges*, Boston University, Frederick S Pardee Center for the Study of the Longer-Range Future, Boston

Thomas, A and Mizushima, M (2005) Logistics training: necessity or luxury?, *Forced Migration Review*, **22**, pp 60–61

Acknowledgements

The authors would like to honour the pioneering support of the German Federal Ministry for Economic Cooperation and Development and the German Red Cross in funding FbF. We are indebted to the German Red Cross for both technical and financial support for FbF in the context of the ongoing Adaptation to Climate Change project in Togo, and to the Togo Red Cross Society and Joachim Schröder for the diligence in learning by doing, and generosity in sharing the methodologies developed and, perhaps most importantly, the ways in which challenges have been met, some of which this chapter seeks to illuminate. Icons for Figures 4.2.1 and 4.2.2 were created with design support from Jamie Murphey. Additional research support was provided by the Norwegian Research Council, through the project 'Humanitarian Policy and Practice in a Changing Climate'.

The findings and conclusions detailed in this case study are those of the authors alone and do not necessarily reflect the views of the Red Cross Red Crescent Climate Centre, the IFRC or its National Societies.

PART FIVE
Procurement

Procurement in humanitarian supply chains

5.1

ALA PAZIRANDEH

University of Gothenburg, Sweden

Procurement, or purchasing, is the process of obtaining resources required but not owned by an organization, and embraces all decisions related to gaining access to resources, capabilities and knowledge of external actors. It contains *all activities associated with identification and specification of needs, identification of decision criteria, initial screening of preferred suppliers, selecting suppliers and monitoring performance* (see Van Weele, 2010; Kakouris, Polychronopoulos and Binioris, 2006).

Procurement in the humanitarian sector is a support function to both permanent or long-term development projects and temporary disaster relief operations. In both situations a large portion of the costs and added value are associated with the procurement function. Research conducted in the commercial sector suggests that ensuring effective procurement can contribute to better returns: 'up to 4 per cent of sales value or 30 per cent to profitability' (Thompson, 1996: 6). In disaster relief operations, up to 65 per cent of the costs have been connected to procurement (Schultz and Søreide, 2008).

Additionally, the way supplies and services are procured (eg the selected supplier, duration of relationships with suppliers, or batch sizes) directly impacts efficiency and effectiveness of humanitarian operation; eg how transport, storage and deliveries are set up, co-ordination among organizations, and relationships with other involved actors.

In this chapter, I first briefly introduce procurement in the humanitarian sector, some sector unique challenges related to procurement and a discussion of the procurement process in light of such challenges, and then present a general overview of procurement strategies that could be transferred to the sector. This is followed by a deeper discussion of co-operative procurement, which has attracted much focus in the sector.

An overview of procurement in the humanitarian sector

Within the humanitarian sector, the procurement decision starts when organizations interact with the commercial market to purchase various aid items or logistics services required for delivering aid to beneficiaries. In some organizations, procurement has been centralized to headquarters and in other cases it is more decentralized, meaning that local country offices have the authority to carry out needs-based procurement (often up to certain financial limits).

Procurement in the humanitarian sector is mostly carried out in a traditional manner. Due to, for example, funding uncertainties and the unpredictability of beneficiary needs, long-term agreements with suppliers are not widely accepted (Balcik *et al*, 2010). Establishing supplier relationships is further complicated by strict procurement rules and regulations meant to ensure transparency, fair competition and best-value-for-money purchases – similar to those found within public procurement (Erridge and McIlroy, 2002). Consequently, the sector has historically emphasized independent and competitive practices as opposed to co-ordination and relationship building. For instance, humanitarian organizations, instead of binding themselves to pre-disaster purchase commitments, have relied on pre-positioned stock and spot purchases, in which demand is purchased on a short amount of time or on the spot and for immediate delivery (Kovács and Spens, 2011; Balcik *et al*, 2010).

Recent calls for increased sector efficiency and effectiveness are, however, transforming procurement practices. To avoid duplications of efforts and increase efficiency, the rhetoric in the sector is moving towards innovation, co-ordination and alignment among organizations (Kovács and Spens, 2011; Gustavsson, 2003). For instance, although organizations within the sector are legally independent entities with sometimes widely different mandates, there are many items and services purchased commonly across them, and in general, there are small-quantity orders of many different stock-keeping units in the sector (Herlin and Pazirandeh, 2015). As a result, the sector has seen pooling initiatives, or informal collaborative forms among two or more organizations, which will be discussed later in this chapter.

There are several procurement situations in which humanitarian organizations have to compete with each other, other sectors, or multinational commercial companies for the same product or service, for which demand can then be comparably negligible. In terms of context-specific demand (eg specific medication), suppliers might not always find it attractive to invest, or demand is not always transparent, which historically has resulted in scarcity of some supplies (Herlin and Pazirandeh, 2012; UNICEF, 2009). Consequently, organizations have become increasingly aware of the need to diversify their supply base in order to avoid the risks associated with a limited supplier base (Pelchant, 2004).

In general, procurement decisions are subject to the higher-level organizational strategy and structure that commonly results in an overarching procurement strategy. For instance, if a given organization has a general strategy to cut costs, the focus of procurement also shifts to lower costs by, for example, selecting the lowest offer and maintaining short-term contracts. The context of the procurement shifting between different phases of disaster relief (eg preparedness, response or reconstruction) or development can also change the overall strategy of procurement.

The choice between the general procurement strategies can have long-term consequences on the organization's purchase situation; eg opting for larger or smaller supplier-base size by strategizing for single versus multiple sourcing. For example, developing long-term partnerships with one or a few suppliers can result in benefits stemmed from closer interactions, developed understanding, specified experience gained, and so on. However, in a concentrated market such a strategy can have adverse results, and diversifying the supplier base is critical to mitigate the risks of single sourcing.

Another example is the choice between local or global sourcing. Local sourcing has advantages such as shorter distances, supporting the development of local markets, reducing negative consequences of natural environments in relation to transport (Coulter, Walker and Hodges, 2007) and advantages related to the local culture and knowledge. A study on Uganda and Ethiopia showed that local procurement could contribute to an estimated saving of 25–30 per cent of the total import cost, but had poorer quality (Coulter, Walker and Hodges, 2007). However, local suppliers may not have the adequate supplies in quality and quantity (Balcik and Beamon, 2008) and also for quality-sensitive products such as health-related products, there is a debate whether local sourcing should be encouraged.

Before discussing the procurement process in the humanitarian sector, first some sector-specific challenges of procurement are reviewed in the next section.

Main challenges of procurement in humanitarian supply chains

Whether dealing with longer-term development projects, or with disaster relief situations, two recurring issues when procuring in humanitarian supply chains are the lack of a clear view of demand and funding uncertainties (Balcik *et al*, 2010). As a result, some buyers in the sector have relied on dormant supplier relationships for spot purchases (Kovács and Spens, 2011; Balcik *et al*, 2010).

While procurement in the humanitarian sector is not specifically subject to public procurement regulations, the public and the not-for-profit nature of the products and services delivered, and of the funds donated, subjects it to many of the same values, such as accountability, equity, probity and transparency (see Erridge and Nondi, 1994). Procurement strategies in the humanitarian sector are thus restricted by similar rules and regulations, which has resulted in tenders and competitive bidding becoming common practice, as opposed to the potentially more beneficial practices of co-ordination and relationship building. This has resulted in short-term contracts usually being awarded based on the lowest price, a similar practice to that observed in public organizations (Erridge and Nondi, 1994). Such regulations also limit buyers' leverage towards their supplier base.

In addition to these general characteristics, there are specific differences between procurement for disaster relief operations and for development operations. Some general differences between the two operations are related to higher predictability of demand in development programmes and thus easier forecasting and supplier-relationship developments.

In summary, the main challenges of procurement within humanitarian supply chains can be classified as those related to the limited funding and resources, high-demand uncertainty, system restrictions and limited knowledge by purchasers (based on UNICEF data, 2010; also found in several studies such as Jahre and Heigh, 2008).

The procurement process and the humanitarian sector

The procurement process commonly starts with assessment of need, followed by market analysis and selection of possible suppliers, negotiation and contracting with the selected supplier, development of ordering procedures, expedition, follow-up and evaluation of suppliers (see Van Weele, 2010). In different sectors, companies or situations the procurement process can look different. For example, while negotiation is often considered an important part of procurement, in some situations, if suppliers are selected directly from a tender process, contracts may be signed without negotiations. In another example, in the case of spot purchase, ordering is oftentimes combined with contracting in a one-time communication. The same diversity of process can be seen in the humanitarian sector, depending on the organizational strategy, structure, common practices and regulations.

In the first stage of the procurement process, the needs and requirements of final users (ie internal, external or beneficiaries) are to be identified, based on the technicality, quality and quantity required (Van Weele, 2010). Different characteristics of the local community and their geographical location have to be taken into account, eg the climate and its impact on expiry dates and potency, the local population's diet, lifestyle, norms and traditions, the needs related to the type of disaster, the possibility of related subsequent disasters, and the immediate and potential diseases related to the situation. For instance, we can recall the inappropriate clothing sent to populations of past disasters, the pre-packed meat food sent to the vegetarian survivors of the Nepal earthquake, or the unforeseen diarrhoea outbreak following the Haitian disaster due to lack of clean water. Additionally, when assessing needs and determining its specification, one should always consider alternative products that might be found with a lower price tag, or more suited to the situation.

Needs assessment is one of the most challenging parts of humanitarian operations. Lack of a clear understanding of demand has resulted in a push strategy in the past, in which supplies or in-kind donations are delivered to last-mile users without a clear picture of need. A specific challenge related to this stage is how and where to gather information. While in some disaster situations, contact with the local offices of organizations and an actual presence in the field is the best way to gather information, during recent years the humanitarian logistics sector as a whole has also accumulated and made available significant amounts of data via emergency-item catalogues and web interfaces. Some humanitarian organizations even pre-specify products or pre-qualify suppliers ahead of time.

Interwoven with needs assessment, the buying entity is required to understand and learn about the supplier market and options available; tools such as requests for information (RFI) and request for quotations (RFQ) can be used to gather market information (Van Weele, 2010). In the humanitarian context, especially related to disaster relief operations, in-kind donations and pre-positioned stocks are additional sources of supplies.

When selecting suppliers, different strategies – ranging from competitive bidding or tendering, to spot purchasing, to the purchase of stock from existing suppliers – can be practised by procurers. As noted, tenders are the most common practice in the humanitarian sector to select suppliers. Within such practice, suppliers are invited to submit bids for an often strictly pre-specified service or product. The submissions are then evaluated, either manually or, as seen in recent years, using electronic platforms. An alternative approach is to practise performance-based contracting, which allows companies to submit a tender based solely on a given performance outcome – eg tons delivered to given locations – and disregards the method and channel of delivery. While there is added risks and costs associated with this method, there is more freedom of operation, resulting in possible efficiency gains.

Additionally, questions regarding power and leverage are raised in the supplier selection and negotiation stage, ie who drives the negotiation and what are the different safeguards needed? Strategies such as group procurement (eg procurement consortiums or co-operative procurement), future contracts, increasing transparency and amount of information shared are examples of practices that have resulted in higher procurement leverage for buyers (Pazirandeh, 2014). The impact of these strategies on different relational and transactional aspects of procurement need to be accounted for, eg how it impacts the relationship, demand share or information asymmetry. Studies have suggested that a negative impact on relational aspects can outweigh the potential positive impacts of increased volumes (Pazirandeh and Herlin, 2014).

In the next stage of the procurement process, contracts are signed with selected suppliers for different durations of time and with different levels of specificity. Trust and previous experience with the suppliers, common practice of the organization, and the criticality of the product or service impact both aspects of time and specificity. Lack of specification and over-specifying contracts can cause problems. An example of the former is a lack of clear specification concerning packaging, which can cause storage problems in distribution centres. On the other hand, over-specification adds administrative costs and can harm the relationship.

Finally, the buying organization must be competent when controlling and monitoring orders and delivery, and be able to evaluate, and even develop, partner suppliers (Van Weele, 2010). Based on the contract, ordering routines are either developed, or one-time orders are placed. Depending on aspects such as the 'criticality of the purchase', orders are expedited using prior (eg following up the order before the delivery date) or firefighting (ie checking later or no deliveries from suppliers) follow-ups. Within the commercial sector it is common to record a supplier's delivery data, which can later be used to help evaluate supplier performances, evaluate any delivery issues encountered, help select new suppliers, or even be included in annual supplier reviews. Given the high levels of uncertainty found within the humanitarian sector, however, and in spot procurement specifically, less weight is given to this stage of the procurement process.

Procurement strategies and factors impacting their choice

In this chapter, we use the term procurement strategies as patterns of strategic decisions about different stages of the procurement process (Terpend, Krause and Dooley, 2011), for example, decision on quantity purchased, number of suppliers, supplier selection strategies, or supplier relationship management strategies, to name just a few.

Overall, different, but often overlapping, objectives can be identified for procurement (see Table 5.1.1 for a list of objectives and some example procurement strategies for each objective). The same strategies can be used

Table 5.1.1 Procurement objectives and related procurement strategies

Overall Procurement Objective	Example of Procurement Strategies
Minimize cost	Spend management; streamlining administration; pooling demand; co-operative procurement
Exploit purchase power	Coercive strategies
Minimize supply vulnerability	Pooling demand or co-operative procurement; formalization; socialization; diversification
Mitigate risk of opportunism	Information-sharing strategies; procurement intermediaries; outsource of procurement; formalization; socialization
Improve supplier relations	Increased information sharing; longer-term relationships; socialization; supplier development strategies
Improve supplier-base size	Multiple sourcing versus single sourcing
Improve supply-market choice	Global procurement versus local procurement

SOURCE: From Pazirandeh (2014: 14)

for different objectives. For example, to reduce cost the buyer is suggested to streamline, and thus minimize administrative and logistics cost, pooling demand, practising e-procurement or reverse auction. While many of the strategies listed in Table 5.1.1 are well known, we will review some of the less common ones below.

Co-operative procurement (Turner *et al*, 2000) and pooling demand (Caniëls and Gelderman, 2005) are possible strategies to minimize cost and supply vulnerability. In pooling demand, different needs from across the organization – which are not necessarily the same type of product or service – are gathered and presented to the same supplier to increase negotiation leverage. Co-operative procurement, on the other hand, is the horizontal co-operation between organizations when they 'pool' their procurement functions (Bakker, Walker and Harland, 2006). The effectiveness and efficiency gains from such co-operation has popularized the strategy in a number of industries, including in the humanitarian sector. Efficiency is often gained through economies of scale, reduced transaction costs, better development of products or services, and access to markets and technologies, among others. Effectiveness, on the other hand, is gained through accumulation of knowledge, resources or capabilities (Bakker, Walker and Harland, 2006). We will discuss co-operative procurement, which has received notable attention in the humanitarian sector, in more detail later in this chapter.

Coercive strategies motivate compliance through reward and punishment (Kähkönen and Virolainen, 2011; Gelderman, Semeijn and Zoete, 2008), and are most suited when the supplier is highly dependent on the business (Gelderman, Semeijn and Zoete, 2008). In such a situation, the suppliers can be pushed into accepting only limited returns and to deliver quality and prices that are more favourable for the buyer (Cox, 2001). In the softest form, recommendations on, for example, quality or price, are given to the suppliers without further explanation. Other examples include promised rewards in case of compliance, threat of punishment (for example, by discontinuing the relationship) or legal measures based on the contract.

In formalization strategies the transactional relationship is explicated through, for example, contracts. Formalization can help organizations to control costs and quality, and structure their supply chains (Li *et al*, 2010). This strategy can result in high risk due to the higher commitment associated with formalization (Turner *et al*, 2000: 19). Additionally, due to limitations in foreseeing all possible outcomes and the human factors involved, contracts are suggested to be, most often, 'incomplete' forms (Williamson,1985), and require complementary strategies and regulations. Examples of formalization can include both detailed contracts with safeguards and penalty clauses and soft contracts with less details.

Socialization can be an alternative or complement to formalization. In socialization strategies, partners increase their relational bonds and develop mutually accepted norms and practices, or co-operative norms, through informal socializing. For example, soft contracts can replace the control gained from formalization with such developed co-operative norms. Socialization is, in general, suggested to be important for successful supply chain relationships (Petersen *et al*, 2008).

Diversification is common practice when a buyer organization has limited purchase options in terms of product type or suppliers. In such locked-in relations, where the buyer does not find alternative suppliers to switch to, the supplier can use its position to force the buyer into a co-operative relationship and thereby reduce its own exchange uncertainties. Traditionally, buyers would consider backward integration, in which the buyer develops the need previously purchased within its own premises (Kraljic, 1983; Williamson, 1985). The buyer can, however, possibly improve this situation by diversifying its supplier base or finding alternative supply or demand options.

Use of procurement intermediaries or functional outsource of procurement is the strategy in which a third-party agent is contracted to carry out either the whole purchase process or parts of it. This strategy is common, for example, among firms that find the purchase of advanced information technology systems complicated, and are often faced with complex and infrequent procurement situations due to market changes (Flowers, 2004). In the absence of internal expertise, buying organizations can use external capabilities of consultants during the procurement process. The third party can also be contracted to carry out only part of the purchase process. Different forms of this strategy are prevalent in the humanitarian sector, which have resulted in development of specialized procurement groups.

The amount of information shared by either partner in an exchange can have important consequences for the business (eg transaction cost economics theory (TCE) in Williamson, 1985; or RDT in Pfeffer and Salancik, 1978). Buyers need as much information as possible about the exchange, the demand, available suppliers, and the specific supplier whom with they are negotiating, or will negotiate. Gaining such market- or transaction-specific information requires considerable time and financial investments (Williamson, 1985), but can contribute to a better business deal. On the other hand, in an effort to maximize their own returns suppliers will try to capitalize on the buyer's misinformation by keeping cost information (and other sensitive information) private. Suppliers can use the lack of information of the buyer to gain 'industry standard pricing' and earn higher margins (Cox *et al*, 2002). However, higher level of information sharing by both partners can develop higher mutual trust and commitment in longer periods.

Many different factors can affect the choice of procurement strategies, such as the product, the industry, the market or power relations. The level of each partner's dependence on the other can indicate the level of influence, or power, that each partner has on the other (Batt, 2003). Based on, for example, social positions and market characteristics, some organizations have more power than others (Pfeffer and Salancik, 1978). Power is context-related, and multifaceted, making it difficult to have a complete view of all factors that give rise to more or less power.

Pazirandeh and Norrman (2014) combine the different sources of procurement power mentioned in the literature into five groups: 1) substitutability, 2) the level of interconnection in relations, 3) asymmetry of information, 4) demand share, and 5) reputation. Pazirandeh and Herlin (2014) find that restrictions due to procurement regulations such as public procurement or corporate strategy can also limit buyer power. Table 5.1.2 summarizes these 'sources of power', including some example factors identified for each source. The combination of these power sources gives rise to different levels of procurement power.

Table 5.1.2 Typical sources of procurement power

Sources of Power	Example Factors
Substitutability	Availability of product; number of suppliers available; entry barriers/market regulations; availability of demand substitutes
Interconnection	Importance of partner in the exchange decision; duration of relationship (history); perceived importance of the exchange by partners; partner switching cost; mutual trust and commitment
Information asymmetry	Awareness of the demand; control over information/ position in the communication flow; knowledge of the supply market; knowledge on the exchange; transparency of information
Demand share	Competition/number of buyers available; volume or value exchanged compared to total volume or value in the market
Reputation	Legitimacy; size; brand; financial status (cost/price structure); technology sophistication; expertise, resources and know-how; logistics situation
Procurement regulations	Laws and regulations for purchase; corporate strategy and mandate

SOURCE: Modified from Pazirandeh (2014: 22)

Procurement power should be understood within a network context and not merely in a dyadic relationship. In other words, procurement power is the combination of the perceived level of sources of power, relative to all potential suppliers (Pazirandeh and Norrman, 2014). Figure 5.1.1 is a simplified depiction of the possible procurement power positions that buyers can have, dependent on the size of the demand and supply markets. So, for example, in this figure, if a procurement organization is placed in the bottom-left corner, where price and quality levels are regulated by market forces, suppliers will have limited opportunities to increase power (eg buyer incompetence) (Cox, 2001). But, moving to the bottom-right corner, due to the limited number of buyers a buying organization can leverage suppliers' performance on quality and cost, and maintain only marginal returns for the supplier. In the central interdependence position both partners have resources that require them to work closely together. Finally, within the supplier dominance position, the buying organization is expected to be a mere receiver of price and quality. There are possible procurement strategies that can help an organization in this position to move to more favourable ones, which were previously explored in my PhD dissertation (Pazirandeh, 2014) and which we will revisit further below.

Figure 5.1.1 A simplified depiction of possible procurement powers depending on the supply-and-demand market size

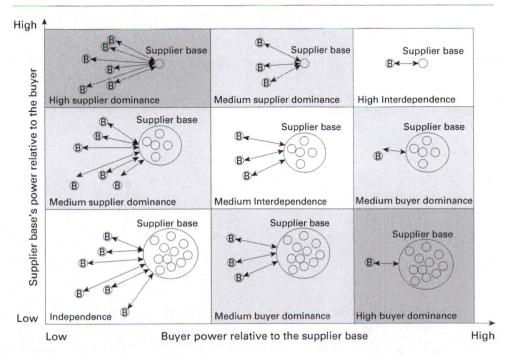

SOURCE: From Pazirandeh (2014: 20)

Procurement strategies for a better procurement power

'Withdrawal' is a group of procurement strategies in which the less-powerful partner renounces either all or part of its motivational bounds from the relationship (Emerson, 1962). Complete termination of the contract, outsourcing of the procurement function (or parts of the procurement process) or refraining from sharing information are examples of procurement strategies that fall within the 'withdrawal' group. Shift of business focus or backward integration are examples of complete withdrawal of the relationship, which can replace a terminated contract (Kraljic, 1983).

The replacement of the withdrawn supply channel can determine changes in the procurement power. For instance, in a locked-in relationship where procurement power is extremely low, most withdrawal strategies can contribute to a better power position since the level of dependency is reduced (see Figure 5.1.2). P1a in Figure 5.1.2 shows a withdrawal strategy where the buyer reduces its link with the supplier by, for instance, developing the need in-house. Outsourcing of procurement to a third party, since the contracted intermediary is commonly pooling demand from multiple buyers and is often a specialized unit, can improve procurement power to a higher extent (see P1b in Figure 5.1.2).

In a real-time example, in procurement of vaccines low supplier interest in some region-specific demand has led to low supply availability, and thus

Figure 5.1.2 Illustration of two possible withdrawal strategies by a buyer (B1)

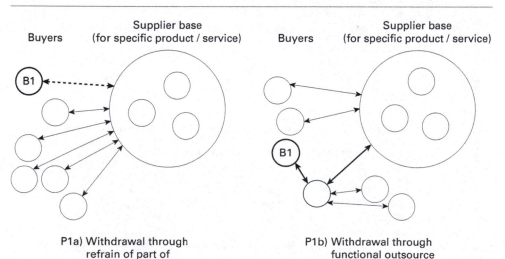

P1a) Withdrawal through refrain of part of relationship bond

P1b) Withdrawal through functional outsource of purchasing

low procurement power by the buyers. The government of Zambia, among other countries within a similar situation, have tackled the problem by outsourcing their procurement process to a third party, that is, to the United Nations Children's Emergency Fund (UNICEF). They hoped to take advantage of economies of scale and hence better prices from the outsource. Such withdrawal was mostly favourable for them, since UNICEF has developed expertise in vaccine procurement from one side, and also takes advantage of higher volumes pooled from multiple countries. However, one drawback of this strategy is the increased dependence of the buyer – in this case Zambia's government on the intermediary UNICEF.

A second strategy is to add more suppliers (ie new links) to the network of existing relations, ie 'network expansion'. This strategy would extend the procurement power from the original network to the extended one, and hence contribute to a better procurement position. Supporting new and smaller suppliers, or developing local suppliers (in general diversification) are examples of network expansion (see Figure 5.1.3). For example, by bending patent regulations for new market entrants or giving technical support to them, the World Health Organization (WHO) has managed to increase the number of possible suppliers and thus the buyer organization's procurement leverage. If these suppliers are developed within local emerging markets, most often they become highly dependent on the business from, for example, United Nations (UN) agencies, and thus the buyer, in this case the UN agency, gains strong relationship ties with these suppliers (see P2b in Figure 5.1.3).

The third strategy is 'status improvement', in which the procurement power is improved by improving the motivational investments in a relationship (Emerson, 1962: 38). Improving organizational expertise, investing in IT or logistics capabilities, or funding mechanisms within the humanitarian sector are examples of this strategy (P3 in Figure 5.1.3). In the vaccine procurement example given previously, tapping into funding mechanisms such as that of GAVI – the vaccine alliance formed by a global public–private health partnership – has stabilized the financial status of buyers such as Zambia, and has contributed to better supplier incentives.

'Socialization' and 'formalization' can also be practised to safeguard low procurement power. Through socialization, the developed norms within a relationship act as protective measures and can improve the purchase situation (see P5 in Figure 5.1.4). In formalization strategies, legal obligations are used to safeguard the lack of power and its associated uncertainties (see P6 in Figure 5.1.4). An example of formalization is when a procuring organization is buying from an unfamiliar supplier market, and thus signs

Figure 5.1.3 Illustration of two possible network expansion strategies and status improvement by a buyer (B1)

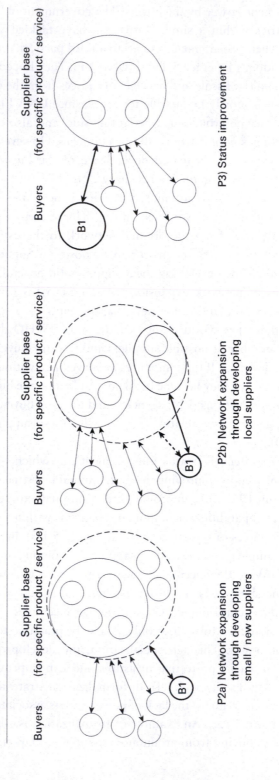

Figure 5.1.4 Illustration of socialization and formalization strategies by a buyer (B1)

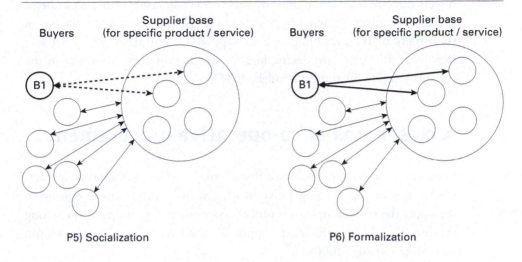

P5) Socialization   P6) Formalization

highly detailed contracts due to low trust of suppliers. In such a situation of low trust, the buyer can also increase trust through socialization (eg suggestions from Petersen *et al*, 2008) by, for example, sharing more information (see Cox *et al*, 2002) or engaging in long-term relationships (see suggestions from Casciaro and Piskorski, 2005; Kraljic, 1983).

Finally, 'coalition formation' (see Figure 5.1.5) can also increase procurement power (see Bastl, Johnson and Choi, 2013; Emerson, 1962). Co-operative procurement (eg Turner *et al*, 2000) is a clear example of this idea, which

Figure 5.1.5 Illustration of coalition formation strategies by a buyer (B1)

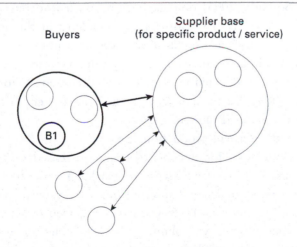

we will discuss in more detail in the next section. While the coalition of buyers directly attempts to improve their power situation with this strategy, it can have adverse impact by, for example, becoming an entry barrier in the supply market, resulting in high supply concentration (eg Nollet and Beaulieu, 2005), or introducing high co-ordination costs and risks in the consortium (Herlin and Pazirandeh, 2015).

A closer look at co-operative procurement

Different terms are used to discuss this strategy, such as procurement synergy, pooled procurement, co-operative procurement or procurement consortia. We apply the term co-operative procurement, meaning co-operation among the buyers, which is the most commonly used term in the public sector, according to Essig (2000).

Usually buyers enter these forms of co-operation when they experience low purchasing power, and when demand uncertainty has resulted in a fragmented industry. The most-mentioned drivers of co-operative procurement are decreasing administrative and labour costs; getting better terms, conditions and prices due to better leverage; increasing access to markets; building networks to bundle resources and capabilities; and reducing supply uncertainty (eg Bakker, Walker and Harland, 2006; Nollet and Beaulieu, 2003; Essig, 2000). The practice has gained popularity in the airline industry and the public sector, among other industries that need to increase bargaining power (see Bakker, Walker and Harland, 2006; Nollet and Beaulieu, 2005).

Some studies have recognized three distinct forms of co-operative procurement, namely collaborative forms, use of third-party organizations (Nollet and Beaulieu, 2005) or piggybacking on a lead buyer's contract (Schotanus *et al*, 2011). The case represented later in this chapter is a collaborative form. Different stages of the procurement process – including specification, bidding, negotiation, contract management and supplier evaluation – are consolidated in co-operative procurement forms (Nollet and Beaulieu, 2003). The main benefits of the strategy stem from standardization of specifications (Pedersen, 1996).

Suppliers with sufficient production capacity can also benefit from co-operative procurement, for instance through increased order volumes, continuous business, increased access to market information (Scheuing, 1998), better visibility of demand and thus improved capacity planning and communication with buyers. However, benefits gained may not outweigh the risks. A concentration of volume is, for example, not beneficial for smaller suppliers with limited production capacity and can drive them out of the market. In addition, some suppliers that already have a good individual relationship with a buyer may resist the new practice due to the fear of losing the leverage gained through previously developed relationships (Pazirandeh and Herlin, 2014). New, relatively short-term contracts often reduce buyer loyalty. Co-operative procurement is also reported to decrease suppliers' operating margins, which can subsequently bring down the quality of service. Furthermore, some suppliers may fear that their trade secrets are more likely to leak out to competitors. If the levels of standardization and co-ordination between members in the co-operative procurement group are low, suppliers can also not achieve economies of scale.

Two of the main risks of the strategy for buyers are increased co-ordination costs, and the practice of raising unfair competition, or acting as an entry barrier for smaller suppliers (eg Herlin and Pazirandeh, 2015; Nollet and Beaulieu, 2005). The practice can lead to market domination by a few big suppliers with high production capacity and asset specificity. As a result, the buyer may become locked in, shifting the power back to suppliers at the end of the contract period (Caldwell *et al*, 2005).

There is also a risk of goal incompatibility between members in the co-operation (Nollet and Beaulieu, 2005) and since the group is usually formed by competing members it might become a forum to gain information (Hendrick, 1996). So, co-operative procurement might be more suitable in co-operative structures (Nollet and Beaulieu, 2005).

Herlin and Pazirandeh (2015) suggest that co-operative purchasing is at high risk of failure when co-ordination and control among consortium members is low, partly due to the little potential to gain relational rents. Trust has been suggested to be one of the modes of control in interorganizational relationships, ensuring that members are not acting selfishly. But, as organizational objectives differ and performance ambiguity is common, organizations might formalize control in an effort to formalize trust eg by establishing joint policies, dispute resolution procedures or exit clauses (Dekker, 2004). The meaning and process of co-ordination between involved buyers will be further discussed in the next section.

Co-ordination for successful co-operative purchasing

Co-ordination occurs when multiple organizations that strive towards the same goal align their tasks. At the very least, through co-ordination organizations seek to avoid duplications, and at most, they are part of a highly institutionalized system governed by uniform standards (Calvert, 1995). In practice, co-ordination boils down to division of labour, resource allocation, information sharing and mediation of conflicting priorities (see Grandori and Soda, 1995), and it involves both careful planning of activities and joint decision making.

There is always a cost in co-ordination, which is dependent on the transaction structure and the interaction process (Artz and Brush, 2000). Co-ordination costs can be grouped in four categories: resource sharing, decision style, level of control, and risk and reward sharing. High resource sharing is associated with low physical flow costs, but high risk costs. Centralized decision making decreases co-ordination costs, but increases the risk of opportunism by the partner in control. It is also more difficult to reach consensus in decentralized decision making. The cost of co-ordination also increases with the level of control (Xu and Beamon, 2006). When the level of control is low (and informal) co-ordination costs are lower, but the risk is high. Finally, power symmetry fosters fair risk and reward allocation, which decreases risk costs. However, risk costs are higher if one or more of the involved partners gains less from the joint action and thus decides to exploit the co-operation at the expense of others (Xu and Beamon, 2006).

In theory, unlimited numbers of partners can co-ordinate their activities. But, in practice, the larger the group gets, the more costly and less effective co-operation tends to get. Different expectations, different missions and target groups, divergent legal mandates, turf protection and competition for the same resources surface as barriers to effective co-ordination (Jennings and Ewalt, 1998). Organizations often have different stakes and different preferred outcomes:

> If players have different expectations about when and by whom co-operation is expected, and about when, how and by whom punishment or reward is to be carried out, they are likely to end up punishing one another for actions intended to be appropriately co-operative. (Calvert, 1995: 242–43)

Issues of implementation are often addressed at lower organizational levels and in relation to clients, but policy, turf and organizational survival issues are more difficult to solve (Peters 1998). Co-ordination leadership has been considered a potential key to this, but does not guarantee success. In general, in order to overcome problems and achieve successful co-ordination, communication is critical. A prerequisite for good co-ordination is that members of the group explicitly share their suggestions, preferences and intentions (Herlin and Pazirandeh, 2015). Depending on the authority of the member and how centralized or decentralized the group is, these individual statements may or may not influence group decision making in the end (Calvert, 1995).

Concluding remarks

Procurement is an important function in humanitarian operations, affecting both other supply chain management decisions and set-ups, and accounting for a large portion of the total cost of operations. Decisions regarding how to procure (eg long-term relationships or spot purchase) and where to procure from (eg local or regional sources or close-to-product suppliers) will impact the distribution channels, relationship with forwarder, set-up of shipping and logistics, and all associated costs and risks. Thus, professionals are required to make procurement decisions with great care, knowing the options available, the factors important for different strategies, and their possible consequences.

Procurement within humanitarian operations is subject to specific limitations of the sector, which can include high uncertainties, lack of demand transparency and, for specific sectors or specific products or services, the possible lack of supplies and alternatives. These limitations alter as, for example, the urgency of deliveries changes from the response phase to recovery and preparedness, and also across different actors. Oftentimes, procurement practices by humanitarian actors resemble public procurement in terms of strict regulations and the need for transparency and probity. But, procurement practices in this sector also share many of the same concepts and principles as the commercial sector, which can broadly guide practitioners.

In this chapter, an overall view of procurement within humanitarian operations and a toolbox of possible procurement strategies was given, and co-operative procurement as a growing popular strategy in the sector was further elaborated.

In practice, the consequence of the procurement strategy on many different aspects should be accounted for. A changed market or relationship dynamic can possibly eliminate the expected benefits of, or the need for, practising a specific strategy. For instance, in the practice of co-operative procurement, merely increasing purchase volumes will not increase overall procurement leverage if, for example, buyer–supplier relationships are hurt in the negotiation process. Often different strategies can be combined to get a more favourable output (eg combining co-operative procurement with multiple sourcing or supplier partnerships). The connection between such mixed strategies and the outcome should be studied.

References

Artz, K W and Brush, T H (2000) Asset specificity, uncertainty and relational norms: an examination of coordination costs in collaborative strategic alliances, *Journal of Economic Behavior & Organization*, **41** (4), pp 337–362

Bakker, E, Walker, H and Harland, C (2006) Organizing for collaborative procurement: an initial conceptual framework, in *Advancing Public Procurement: Practices, Innovation and knowledge-sharing*, ed K Thai and G Piga, Academic Press, Boca Raton, pp 14–44

Balcik, B and Beamon, B M (2008) Facility location in humanitarian relief, *International Journal of Logistics Research and Applications*, **11** (2), pp 101–21

Balcik, B, Beamon, B M, Krejci, C C, Muramatsu, K M and Ramirez, M (2010) Coordination in humanitarian relief chains: practices, challenges and opportunities, *International Journal of Production Economics*, **126** (1), pp 22–34

Bastl, M, Johnson, M and Choi, T Y (2013) Who's seeking whom? Coalition behavior of a weaker player in buyer–supplier relationships, *Journal of Supply Chain Management*, **49** (1), 8–28

Batt, P J (2003) Building trust between growers and market agents, *An International Journal of Supply Chain Management*, **8** (1), pp 65–78

Caldwell, N, Walker, H, Harland, C, Knight, L, Zheng, J and Wakeley, T (2005) Promoting competitive markets: the role of public procurement, *Journal of Purchasing and Supply Management*, **11** (5–6), pp 242–51

Calvert, R (1995) The rational choice theory of social institutions: cooperation, coordination, and communication, in *Modern Political Economy*, ed J S Banks and E A Hanushek, Cambridge University Press, Cambridge, UK, pp 216–68

Caniëls, M C and Gelderman, C J (2005) Purchasing strategies in the Kraljic matrix: a power and dependence perspective, *Journal of Purchasing and Supply Management*, **11** (2–3), pp 141–55

Casciaro, T and Piskorski, M J (2005) Power imbalance, mutual dependence, and constraint absorption: a closer look at resource dependence theory, *Administrative Science Quarterly*, **50**, pp 167–99

Coulter, J, Walker, D J and Hodges, R (2007) Local and regional procurement of food aid in Africa: impact and policy issues, *Journal of Humanitarian Assistance*, **13**, pp 1–28

Cox, A (2001) Understanding buyer and supplier power: a framework for procurement and supply competence, *Journal of Supply Chain Management*, **37** (2), pp 8–15

Cox, A, Ireland, P, Lonsdale, C, Sanderson, J and Watson, G (2002) *Supply Chains, Markets and Power: Mapping buyers and suppliers power regimes*, Routledge, New York

Dekker, H C (2004) Control of inter-organizational relationships: evidence on appropriation concerns and coordination requirements, *Accounting, Organizations and Society*, **29** (1), pp 27–49

Emerson, R M (1962) Power-dependence relations, *American Sociological Review*, **27** (1), pp 31–41

Erridge, A and McIlroy, J (2002) Public procurement and supply management strategies, *Public Policy and Administration*, **17** (1), pp 52–71

Erridge, A and Nondi, R (1994) Public procurement, competition and partnership, *European Journal of Purchasing & Supply Management*, **1** (3), pp 169–79

Essig, M (2000) Purchasing consortia as symbiotic relationships: developing the concept of 'consortium sourcing', *European Journal of Purchasing & Supply Management*, **6** (1), pp 13–22

Flowers, S (2004) Contingent capabilities and the procurement of complex product systems, *International Journal of Innovation Management*, **8** (01), pp 1–20

Gelderman, C J, Semeijn, J and Zoete, R D (2008) The use of coercive influence strategies by dominant suppliers, *Journal of Purchasing and Supply Management*, **14** (4), pp 220–29

Grandori, A and Soda, G (1995) Inter-firm networks: antecedents, mechanisms and forms, *Organization Studies*, **16** (2), pp 183–214

Gustavsson, L (2003) Humanitarian logistics: context and challenges, *Forced Migration Review*, **18**, pp 6–8

Hendrick, T E (1996) *Purchasing consortiums: horizontal alliances among firms buying common goods and services: what? who? why? how?* Center for Advanced Purchasing Studies, Tempe AZ

Herlin, H and Pazirandeh, A (2012) Nonprofit organizations shaping the market of supplies, *International Journal of Production Economics*, **139** (2), pp 411–21

Herlin, H and Pazirandeh, A (2015) Avoiding the pitfalls of cooperative purchasing through control and coordination: insights from a humanitarian context, *International Journal of Procurement Management*, **8** (3), pp 303–25

Jahre, M and Heigh, I (2008) Does the current constraints in funding promote failure in humanitarian supply chains?, *Supply Chain Forum: An international journal*, **9** (2), pp 44–54

Jennings, E T and Ewalt, J A G (1998) Interorganizational coordination, administrative consolidation, and policy performance, *Public Administration Review*, **58** (5), pp 417–28 http://doi.org/10.2307/977551

Kähkönen, A-K and Virolainen, V M (2011) Sources of structural power in the context of value nets, *Journal of Purchasing and Supply Management*, **17** (2), pp 109–20

Kakouris, A P Polychronopoulos, G and Binioris, S (2006) Outsourcing decisions and the purchasing process: a systems-oriented approach, *Marketing Intelligence & Planning*, **24** (7), pp 708–729

Kovács, G and Spens, K M (2011) The Journal of Humanitarian Logistics and Supply Chain Management: first reflections, *Journal of Humanitarian Logistics and Supply Chain Management*, **1** (2), pp 108–13

Kraljic, P (1983) Purchasing must become supply management, *Harvard Business Review*, **61** (5), pp 109–17

Li, G, Yang, H, Sun, L, Ji, P and Feng, L (2010) The evolutionary complexity of complex adaptive supply networks: a simulation and case study, *International Journal of Production Economics*, **124** (2), pp 310–30

Nollet, J and Beaulieu, M (2003) The development of group purchasing: an empirical study in the healthcare sector, *Journal of Purchasing and Supply Management*, **9** (1), pp 3–10

Nollet, J and Beaulieu, M (2005) Should an organisation join a purchasing group? *Supply Chain Management: An international journal*, **10** (1), pp 11–17

Pazirandeh, A (2014) Purchasing Power and Purchasing Strategies: Insights from the humanitarian sector, Doctoral dissertation, Lund University

Pazirandeh, A and Herlin, H (2014) Unfruitful cooperative purchasing, *Journal of Humanitarian Logistics and Supply Chain Management*, **4** (1), pp 24–42

Pazirandeh, A and Norrman, A (2014) An interrelation model of power and purchasing strategies: a study of vaccine purchase for developing countries, *Journal of Purchasing and Supply Management*, **20** (1), pp 41–53

Pedersen, J (1996) Product standardization: playing to win, *Vivo*, **14** (6), pp 15–20

Pelchant, M C (2004) Enterprising Asian NPOs: Social entrepreneurship in Taiwan, Conference of Asian Foundations and Organizations, Taiwan

Peters, B G (1998) Managing horizontal government: the politics of co-ordination, *Public administration*, **76** (2), pp 295–311

Petersen, K J, Handfield, R B, Lawson, B and Cousins, P D (2008) Buyer dependency and relational capital formation: the mediating effects of socialization processes and supplier integration, *Journal of Supply Chain Management*, **44** (4), pp 53–65

Pfeffer, J and Salancik, G R (1978) *The External Control of Organizations: A resource dependence perspective*, Harper & Row, New York

Scheuing, E E (1998) *Value-Added Purchasing: Partnering for world-class performance*, vol 13, Thomson Crisp Learning

Schotanus, F, Bakker, E, Walker, H and Essig, M (2011) Development of purchasing groups during their life cycle: from infancy to maturity, *Public Administration Review*, **71** (2), pp 265–75

Schultz, J and Søreide, T (2008) Corruption in emergency procurement, *Disasters*, **32** (4), pp 516–36

Terpend, R, Krause, D R and Dooley, K J (2011) Managing buyer–supplier relationships: empirical patterns of strategy formulation in industrial purchasing, *Journal of Supply Chain Management*, **47** (1), pp 73–94

Thompson, M (1996) Effective purchasing strategy: the untapped source of competitiveness, *Supply Chain Management: An international journal*, **1** (3), pp 6–8

Turner, G B, LeMay, S A, Hartley, M and Wood, C M (2000) Interdependence and cooperation in industrial buyer–supplier relationships, *Journal of Marketing Theory and Practice*, **8** (1), pp 16–24

UNICEF (2009) [accessed January 2011] Supply Annual Report, *UNICEF Supply Division, Copenhagen* [Online] http://www.unicef.org/supply/

Van Weele, A J (2010) *Purchasing and Supply Chain Management: Analysis, strategy, planning and practice*, Cengage Learning, Andover

Williamson, O E (1985) *The Economic Institutions of Capitalism: Firms, markets, relational contracting*, Free Press, New York

Xu, L and Beamon, B M (2006) Supply chain coordination and cooperation mechanisms: an attribute-based approach, *Journal of Supply Chain Management*, **42** (1), pp 4–12

Joint tender for freight-forwarding services

5.2

Promises and pitfalls[1]

ALA PAZIRANDEH

University of Gothenburg, Sweden

HEIDI HERLIN

HUMLOG Institute, Finland

In 2010, a group of humanitarian agencies decided to aggregate their freight-forwarding demands and jointly tender for possible providers.[2] The hope was to gain better negotiation leverage in front of the forwarders, be more competitive, and to reduce the intensity of individual tendering processes. The process did not go as expected: it took much longer than originally anticipated, some agencies dropped out midway and the remaining group did not gain the negotiation leverage it was hoping for.

This case is a representation of the events from 2010 to 2011 in this joint tender, which eventually led to the unexpected outcomes. It is based on the observations of individuals at the humanitarian agencies and at the forwarders and aims to further elaborate on: 1) the complexities of joint tenders (ie co-operative procurement), and 2) how it can impact buyer's procurement power.

The case highlights the following trade-offs in the practice of co-operative procurement:

- Larger number of members in co-operative procurement increases the aggregated volumes but makes co-ordination between members much more complex.

- Inter-agency co-ordination in terms of communication, fair sharing of risks and rewards, management of expectations and requirements, and division of labour is essential for successful co-operative procurement.

- Procurement consortiums face a trade-off between routines and norms developed through trust and formalized control mechanisms.

- Increased volumes alone do not necessarily increase procurement power.

Initiation of the joint tender

One common need among humanitarian agencies is shipping, which is why a number of humanitarian agencies decided to consolidate their procurement of global freight-forwarding services with a joint tender in 2010. In 1998, two of the agencies had co-operated in a joint tender. The success of that practice attracted more players and, by 2010, they decided to include more agencies with the hope of increasing benefits. The joint tender would potentially increase the purchase leverage of the agencies. The general feeling before the tender was that:

> If we're all using potentially the same freight forwarders... then we might as well just do it together. (Interviewed manager, February 2013)

Over the years the freight forwarders had shown an increasing interest to partner with the humanitarian agencies. This interest is partly due to the added legitimacy that they can gain from engagement in the socially responsible operations, especially by partnering with some of the agencies with strong 'brand' names. The joint tender was expected to increase this interest even more and to provide additional incentive for the forwarders to perform well:

> We're quite prestigious, and so forwarders want to have a relationship with us, and given that we team up, they're more eager to deliver. (White manager, February 2013)

Profiles of involved agencies

All humanitarian agencies that were involved in the tender have country offices with more operational functions, and more strategic/tactical functions managed from their headquarters (HQs). For all agencies the country offices work independently under the overall organization strategy and policies. In the joint tender the HQs were consolidating their international freight-forwarding needs. Table 5.2.1 shows the procurement profile of these agencies.

Table 5.2.1 Procurement of the involved buyers

Org.	Average Annual Demand (USD)	Main Source of Demand	Department Responsible for Freight
Blue	100 m	Org. operations and clients	Shipping
Green	5–10 m	Support to country offices	Procurement
Red	Data not available	Emergencies	Procurement
White	10 m	Support to country offices	Procurement
Violet	50,000 TEUs*	Emergencies	Shipping

* 20-foot equivalent unit
SOURCE: Modified from Pazirandeh and Herlin (2014) and Herlin and Pazirandeh (2015)

All agencies except for 'Violet' fully outsourced their freight-forwarding needs and selected the forwarder through a tender process and for long-term agreements of five years (usually in a two- or three-year initial contract, with possibility of extension). The tendering process is resource intensive and both agencies and forwarders appear to prefer long-term agreements. For all agencies except for Violet, freight funding comes from a share of the general donations received by the organization; such funding, however, is not budgeted in advance and is allocated per shipment. In contrast to the other agencies, Violet does not have any core funding and instead finances its freight purely from voluntary emergency donations.

Profile of freight forwarders for the humanitarian agencies

At the time of the tender, there were 5–10 global forwarders and some smaller regional ones in the market for humanitarian agencies. In general, demand from agencies is volatile, often based per operation/emergency, while contracts are based on historical projections with no set figures on the volume. These environmental conditions are well understood by the forwarders.

In the past, agencies 'Blue' and 'White' had long-term contractual relationships with two or three of the forwarders, whereas 'Green', 'Red' and some other smaller agencies have been piggybacking on, specifically, Blue's long-term agreements. Blue and Violet have comparatively large volumes among the agencies. Violet purchases both commodities and freight at spot markets. Since commodities are generally purchased from the spot market, depending on the market price, freight is also either purchased on the spot or handled in FOB (free on board) or CFR (cost and freight) contracts. In attempts to address their large and fragmented supplier base, today, Violet works with around 18–27 shortlisted forwarders, which they contact upon demand. For Violet, the main barrier towards having longer-term agreements is the low frequency of orders, which are bound to emergencies and funding.

Table 5.2.2 shows the background information of the winning forwarders and their historical relationships with the humanitarian agencies. Some forwarders who placed bids in the tender were not selected due to a comparatively weak geographical presence in certain areas. There was also one forwarder omitted from the selection process due to a technical error at the time of submission.

Table 5.2.2 Profiles of the involved forwarders

Forwarder	Average Annual Aid Transaction (USD)	Dept Responsible for Aid
Alfa	3,000 TEUs; $15 million (sea freight)	Special unit
Beta	Data not available	Special unit
Gamma	$30 million	In other units
Delta	15,000 TEUs, 10,000-ton airfreight; $170 million	Special unit

SOURCE: Modified from Pazirandeh and Herlin (2014) and Herlin and Pazirandeh (2015)

Historically, all forwarders except for 'Alfa' have been working with at least one of the agencies. Alfa has only had smaller contracts with either local offices of the agencies or on a 'per shipment' basis. 'Beta' has had long-term agreements of over 15 years with Blue, on which Green has been piggybacking. They have also been working with Violet in some local regions. 'Gamma' has had contracts with Blue and Red, and 'Delta' with all the agencies, with the longest being with Blue (over 25 years).

Reactions and expectations among the agencies

Individuals at Blue initiated the new joint tender in late 2009, based on the interest communicated by other agencies. The aim was to pool volumes and include the new interested partners, especially Violet, with their significant volumes. There was also a political push within the sector and from the top to '*stop wasting resources and duplicating things*' (White manager, February 2013) and to start working more jointly. Expectations from the joint tender were different among management and operations, but also individuals within and among different agencies. The main expectation by most was to obtain better rates. Other expectations from the initiative were to gain leverage from the synergy, each other's knowledge, resources, get better geographical coverage and service from the suppliers, attract more suppliers, and reduce the efforts spent on tenders. On one of the initial tender documents the goal is stated as:

> To combine the buying power, and thereby obtain the best possible market position and solutions.

According to a manager from Violet, while they knew their requirements differed widely, they were interested in the project and committed to '*see how it goes*'. The manager thought that smaller agencies with less volume had more to gain from the tender, though, and thus their motivation was much higher. The smaller agencies were all hoping for better rates. The two bigger agencies were mostly hoping to increase their number of partners and to reduce their dependence on the freight forwarders.

Blue's freight volume and experience, in comparison to the other partners, drove the expectation among the other agencies for Blue to lead the process. There was also an internal desire at Blue to lead the process due to some special requirements they had on parts of the cargo.

Within Violet, there were different reactions to the joint tender. The parts of the organization that were working with more stable cargo (eg blankets from pre-positioned warehouses) were interested in the initiative, while the parts dealing with fluctuating cargo (both unknown order amounts and unspecified sourcing locations and cargo destinations) were resistant to the idea. The main issue was whether the rates achieved from long-term agreements could be justified compared to the fluctuating ones that Violet achieved on the spot market. The Violet manager, however, thought that buying on the spot market pushed most of the risk to the beneficiaries, and that switching to long-term agreements would ensure more consistency of supply.

Reactions and expectations among the freight forwarders

The forwarders had heard about the joint tender through their ongoing relationships with the agencies. They were all initially interested in the idea, since it meant one tender instead of several. They had specific hopes from the tender, but also concerns regarding its consequences and execution:

> It potentially saves the issue of having to do multiple tenders from both sides
> of the table, because tenders are never easy, or they are a long process. So that's
> one aspect of it. (Gamma manager, February 2013)

Knowing about the interest of other agencies than Blue, most forwarders were hoping for an uptake in their business. They hoped to gain access to other agencies that they had not done previous business with. They also saw the joint tender as an opportunity to gain know-how. One of the interviewed freight-forwarding managers said that the joint tender: 'seemed like a wise and smart idea giving [humanitarian agencies] more power; but also giving us more leverage in front of the carriers. It was also beneficial in terms of geographical coverage.'

The tender process

In 2010, the agencies were approached through a higher-level procurement group and, after preliminary interest, the new, more extensive joint tender process started. Originally, a total of eight agencies were listed, from which the five listed in Table 5.2.1 took part in the tender process, and only four used the results.

In the beginning, representatives from the agencies met to decide on the modalities of the co-operation, development of solutions to requirements, and to draft a call for an expression of interest (EOI) from the forwarders. However, participation was at different levels. Of the three agencies that dropped out prior to the tender, one never attended any of the meetings since they had extremely low volumes and could not justify their commitment. Another of these three agencies sent in their bids too late in the process and decided to stay outside, with the option to piggyback on the results. The last of the three realized that the timing of this tender came after the end of their current contracts, which would leave a gap in their transport services and so necessitated their withdrawal.

Between two and three meetings were initially held by the tender project team to discuss details regarding volumes, division of responsibility among member agencies, the time line of the tender, definition of geographical regions, as well as contract requirements needed to finalize the request for proposals (RFP). Blue led the discussions and their contracts were used as the foundation for new contracts, including, for example, the division of regions. The tender was carried out in two sections, one for airfreight and one for sea freight.

Representation in the consortium was at varying levels from different agencies (there were high-level logistics managers, procurement, finance and operational clerks). There were one or multiple representatives from each agency. Smaller agencies mostly fully trusted the capabilities and decisions of the bigger agencies, especially if they had generic cargo that was not bound to specific requirements (White manager, February 2013). All individuals thought that all agencies got the opportunity to express their views and requirements: 'Blue would inform the team of the time plan, what they had envisioned, and the information and resources required from us' (White manager, February 2013).

Agencies had specific requirements and differed in procurement practice. Blue's shipping standards were used in most cases since the team thought it covered most other agencies' requirements. The Violet manager, however, thought that even the requirements and needs of the agencies with very small volumes were taken into account. For instance:

> Sometimes they ship goats... particular food supplements and things that are somewhat out of the ordinary and perhaps also request particular shipping amounts... so that's what they of course stipulated in the tender documents to ensure that was covered. (Violet manager, 2013)

To increase transparency of the tendering process, the freight-forwarder selection and freight costs, and to improve financial management, an electronic tendering tool was used. The tender started with a pre-qualification round, where the involved agencies jointly shortlisted the freight forwarders who had submitted an EOI. Pre-qualification was done based on technical qualifications, especially in terms of geographical coverage, capacity, experience and know-how. No monetary quotes were submitted in this round.

The shortlisted forwarders were invited by e-mail to submit their proposals within a closed forum within three months. Before submissions the shortlisted forwarders were invited to a full-day question-and-answer seminar. Submissions were evaluated from technical and commercial aspects, with a weight of 65 per cent and 35 per cent given to each respectively. While sea-freight forwarders were evaluated based on their capacity and coverage at the destination points, airfreight forwarders were evaluated based on their handling and coverage capacity at the point of origin. Submissions were collected and evaluated using the electronic tool.

Turbulence before the finish line

During the last phase of the tender process (ie before and during contracting and negotiations), staff rotation impacted most individuals involved in the process among the agencies. Only one individual remained at the same position, while others were relocated to either different positions, had moved to other agencies or had left the member agencies. Consequently, the forwarders received the results in April–May instead of the planned December.

Upon receipt of the rates from forwarders, and before final selection, Violet representatives saw the obstacles to be too big for their organization. Compared to their normal procedures, the 30-page contract with several different rates seemed too difficult to justify internally at the organization. Additionally, the person in charge of the project was subject to job rotation and had only two days to transfer all projects (including the joint tender) to their successor. This led to a slow withdrawal of Violet from the joint tender: 'people just sensed that we weren't involved any more' (Violet manager, February 2013).

Four forwarders were awarded for sea freight and two for airfreight. For Blue this was an increase from the previous two forwarders they had.

Although tendered jointly, contracts were signed independently between agencies and freight forwarders. Original tender documents note that the five agencies involved would jointly tender and should respect the joint evaluation. However, the document did not specify how the resulting evaluation was to be used by the different agencies, and different individuals understood it differently. While the forwarders expected that the individual agencies would sign independent contracts, the extent of difference in terms and conditions was not clear. All forwarders were under the perception that the results would be used in a more aligned manner:

> No one anticipated the amount of deviation in terms and conditions among the agencies from the tender documents. (Gamma manager, February 2013)

Some of the freight forwarders were also surprised by the fact that winning the tender did not grant them automatic contracts with all the involved agencies: 'We had to chase ourselves the individual agencies for getting something that we had already been appointed to do' (Beta manager, February 2013).

For some agencies, winning the tender meant only that forwarders were invited to a new round of bidding and negotiations: 'So in terms of securing the volume, you had only secured it in as far as you had a ticket to the negotiation table' (Alfa manager, February 2013).

In other words, what had started as a joint tender, ended in quite a complicated and fragmented process from the forwarders' point of view:

> When we won part of the tender, we only got the agreements with Blue, then we had to go to other agencies and ask if they were willing to sign a contract too.
> (Beta manager, February 2013)

Blue and Red were the only agencies that followed the outlined tendering procedures entirely and stuck to the stated contract terms, with some minor differences. For these agencies, forwarders were selected in parallel to deliver in different regions. The contracts were non-exclusive and valid for five years (two initial years and a possible three-year extension).

The remaining agencies realized quite suddenly that they had different contractual terms that required further negotiation with forwarders. One reason behind agencies signing different contracts was that each contract must get the approval from that agency's legal authority. The main contractual differences are related to payment terms, geographical requirements and thus forwarder allocation, as well as liability terms.

For some forwarders the contractual deviations meant that they could not fulfil the requirements of all the agencies, even though they had been appointed as winners of the joint tender: 'Organization Green had their own geographical division, and White implied complete liability to the freight forwarder, which we could not insure' (Alfa manager, February 2013).

The differences in geographical division for Green related to the fact that the organization had widely different freight origins compared to agencies with pre-positioned stock in warehouses. This was realized quite late in the process, as illustrated by the following comment by the manager: 'when it came down to the actual award... it just looked a little scattered for our taste'.

Green and White organized a secondary bidding with the chosen forwarders upon each request in order to try to achieve even lower rates. They generally use different payment terms than Blue. While Blue pays according to price at the time of invoice, Green and White lock in the price at the time of the order placement. This is partly due to the different funding mechanisms. In case of Green, funds are allocated and fixed at order placement, and thus the price must be clear at this point.

Another major contractual difference that surfaced during the last stages of the tender process related to liability. After the tender was completed, the legal departments of some agencies saw the standard shipping liability terms, which had not been questioned in the past, as a 'major risk exposure' (Green manager, February 2013) that was unacceptable and required that freight forwarders would assume full liability in case of, for example, lost cargo and thus: 'completely broke down the contract into bits and pieces only fitting their needs and requirements' (Delta manager, February 2013).

This created a dispute with the forwarders, who thought that this new term was not in line with the RFP document, and prolonged the contract discussions for months. According to the Delta manager, some agencies even deviated from the transport convention accepted and practised in the sector, 'which none of the freight forwarders thought they would'. Forwarders who had based their proposals on the tender documents, and initially announced volumes, perceived the tender outcome to be rather unfair:

> The terms and conditions that the other parties were starting to look for
> were completely different to what we bid for in the tender. (Gamma manager,
> February 2013)

The manager from Delta also noted that this was commercially unjust, as handling and mark-up fees had been calculated under 'false assumptions'. It is worth mentioning that at the time of this study (February 2013) some agencies were still negotiating terms with the forwarders.

Conclusions

The initiative failed to meet its objectives mainly due to the fact that buying agencies were not sufficiently co-ordinated. There was a lack of inter-agency communication before entering into the tender and a false belief about shared expectations and process overlaps. In addition, the process was delayed due to staff turnover and organizational politics. The lack of formal control was also highlighted as an issue, along with bureaucracy, turf protection and risk-averse attitudes. Since the term- and requirement-differences between the involved agencies were not problematized and planned for during the specification phase, in the end the contracts became fragmented rather than collective.

In future applications of such co-operative procurement practices (eg joint agency tenders), the following points should be taken into account:

- Inter-agency co-ordination is vital for the success of co-operative procurement, eg joint tenders.

- In the absence of established routines and sufficient inter-agency trust, there is a need for formalized control systems.

- Requirements, expectations and commitment of members needs to be clarified and planned for in the initial phase of such inter-agency efforts.

- It is essential to plan for frequency and channels of member communications during the procurement process.

- The organizational politics and regulations of the individual members in a consortium can be obstacles in inter-agency co-ordination and co-operation.

Notes

1 The case has been previously used in two academic articles: Pazirandeh and Herlin (2014) and Herlin and Pazirandeh (2015).

2 Due to confidentiality agreement, all cases and representatives are anonymized.

References

Herlin, H and Pazirandeh, A (2015) Avoiding the pitfalls of cooperative purchasing through control and coordination: insights from a humanitarian context, *International Journal of Procurement Management*, 8 (3), pp 303–25

Pazirandeh, A and Herlin, H (2014) Unfruitful cooperative purchasing: a case of humanitarian purchasing power, *Journal of Humanitarian Logistics and Supply Chain Management*, 4 (1), 24–42

A procurement project in the Philippines 5.3

JONAS STUMPF

HELP Logistics – a programme of the Kuehne Foundation, Asia Office

MAXIMILIAN FOEHSE

HELP Logistics – a programme of the Kuehne Foundation, Asia Office

TOM GODFREY

Save the Children, Asia Regional Office

Introduction

The Philippines is widely known to be one of the most disaster-prone countries in the world. When typhoon Haiyan hit the central part of the country in November 2013, it caused widespread destruction and left millions of people in dire need of humanitarian assistance. Delivering aid to the affected population turned out to be a major logistics and supply chain challenge for responding actors such as local government, United Nations (UN) agencies and non-governmental organizations (NGOs). The challenges were faced at all process steps along the supply chain, starting from assessment and procurement up to warehousing and transportation.

Having learnt from typhoon Haiyan, the NGO Save the Children decided to prepare better for future disasters in the Philippines and launched its

Supply Chain Efficiency Project (SCEP) in June 2014 in joint collaboration with the HELP Logistics AG (the programme of the Kuehne Foundation). The aim of the SCEP was to conduct detailed research to help Save the Children to build more efficient, responsive and agile supply chains. During a follow-up project of the SCEP in April and May 2015, opportunities were explored to further streamline Save the Children's procurement processes and special focus was drawn to the capability of delivering end users' needs of the highest quality in agreed time frames, whilst providing donors with value for their money.

Methodology of the procurement project

During the project, the following trade-offs were encountered:

- Value for money is a subjective measure, and requires more information than simple price comparisons.

- There is always a trade-off between efficiency and optimality in the procurement of items.

- In the humanitarian sector, value for money is not always the most important factor when the need for speed is taken into account, hence it is difficult to propagate the value added of saving costs in procurement.

The project went through three stages: spend analysis, establishing a price capturing mechanism and development of improvement recommendations.

First, a comprehensive *spend analysis* revealed that from January 2014 until April 2015, over 80 per cent of total expenditures (US $15.5 million) in all regions could be allocated to seven categories: construction materials (22 per cent), miscellaneous (16 per cent), books and education materials (15 per cent), water and sanitation (WASH) equipment (12 per cent), IT equipment (6 per cent), shelter and nutrition, and food (each 4 per cent).

Second, a long-term *price capturing mechanism* was designed to keep track of product price developments. Based on the spend analysis, the following 11 items with high spend and high purchase frequency were incorporated in the price-capturing mechanism: hygiene kits, plastic sheets, corrugated galvanized iron (CGI) sheets, cement, household kits, student kits (elementary), student kits (high school), teacher kits, temporary learning space (TLS) tents, jerry cans and concrete hollow blocks (CHB). The price-capturing mechanism provides Save the Children with a sophisticated tool that strengthens its position in supplier negotiations. Additionally it ensures value for money, can be used in internal reporting and provides a new key performance indicator (KPI) 'procurement cost efficiency'.

The price-capturing mechanism was demonstrating the potential for cost savings on the 11 key items. Especially plastic sheets as well as jerry cans were identified as 'quick wins'.

With the knowledge of Save the Children's procurement processes, the spend analysis and the price-capturing mechanism respectively, the HELP Logistics AG provided comprehensive *recommendations* for Save the Children on how to improve their existing procurement operations (see Figure 5.3.1):

- Changes in the procurement tracker (purchasing tracking system) used by Save the Children were suggested to improve overall visibility and information management.

- A new, standardized quality evaluation process for procurement items, with two quality measures, was proposed. This would ensure the procurement of products of a defined quality as well as support Save the Children employees in making objective decisions.

- A closer collaboration with suppliers was proposed to develop cost-reduction opportunities. More than 100 potential suppliers were identified, expanding Save the Children's existing supplier database in the Philippines. During the project, half of the suppliers were contacted informally and 20 per cent of the received responses contained cheaper offers for plastic sheets and cement, compared to the latest price paid by Save the Children. In this context the price-capturing mechanism provides the necessary basis to conduct effective supplier negotiations and ensure competitive prices.

- The introduction of regular supplier summits was suggested, offering a great opportunity to raise suppliers' awareness for working with NGOs and developing cost-saving strategies together.

- Buying items in a kit from two or more suppliers was discussed and recommended for certain low- and medium-volume purchases in order to achieve better prices.

- The elimination of intermediaries (merchandise businesses) was recommended for plastic sheets and jerry cans. Furthermore, a strategy on how to source kits from manufacturers instead of intermediaries was provided.

Figure 5.3.1 Recommendations on how to improve Save the Children's supply chain performance

Information management	• **Cleanse and validate** existing data of the procurement tracker in order to allow fast and effective analyses in the future and create visibility over spend data • **Maintain and extend** price-capturing mechanism
Standardized quality evaluation	• Design and implementation of a uniform and harmonized process that will ensure procurement of products of defined quality • To keep it simple, two quality measures are recommended: **one KO and one quality indicator**
Supplier negotiation and collaboration	• Research shows that supplier negotiations are significantly more successful for buyers who have **detailed cost information** (information contained in the price-capturing mechanism) • The more information the tool contains, the more **power** that Save the Children International (SCI) will gain in supplier negotiations
Supplier summits	• Supplier summits pose a great opportunity not only to raise awareness for working with NGOs, but also to **develop cost-reduction opportunities** together with the suppliers
Splitting kits	• Buying items of kits from different suppliers can be attractive especially for low- to medium-volume purchases since **prices for kits could be reduced** dramatically
Buying from the source	• Plastic sheets and jerry cans are single items that could be **supplied directly from manufacturers** to achieve better prices

Furthermore, the foundation for improved NGO procurement collaboration was laid by approaching 15 other humanitarian organizations in the Philippines and encouraging them to share information between organizations more actively. The resonance was very positive with four organizations that have already responded and welcomed the initiative. Within three weeks, two of them shared valuable information that helped to reveal savings potential for plastic sheets (21 per cent) and jerry cans (23 per cent). In the long run, this collaboration will certainly have cost-saving impact and help to improve the NGO's supply chain efficiency.

The approach and methodologies of the spend analysis and the price-capturing mechanism are further detailed below.

Spend analysis

A comprehensive spend analysis provides the necessary basis for establishing better, faster and more confident buying decisions. A systematic analysis of the expenditures allows leveraging buying power, reducing costs and providing better oversight of suppliers. Technically, a spend analysis is a process of systematically collecting, cleansing, classifying and analysing historical purchasing data from all sources within an organization.

Once data is collected, cleansed and categorized, actionable analysis provides an overview of how much an organization is spending with different suppliers. A detailed view on the items that an organization is buying from different suppliers can be established and helps to estimate savings potential in different categories. Top commodities can be identified and strategic sourcing opportunities can be developed through opportunities for spend reduction. In this context, the spend analysis uncovers cost disadvantages and prioritizes 'quick wins', hence immediately supporting decision making.

Usually, the core driver to perform a spend analysis is profitability. Although relief organizations do not yield profit as commercial businesses do, they still try to improve their spend performance and efficiency in order to reach more end users and maintain accountability towards their stakeholders, especially donors.

Figure 5.3.2 shows a general framework for conducting spend analyses. First, data is extracted and gathered from internal sources. These sources can be business management software such as enterprise resource planning (ERP), product-lifecycle management/product data management (PLM/PDM), e-procurement systems or paper systems. Second, data has to be standardized, cleansed and classified to ensure that it is accurate, error-free and meaningful. Data enrichment with related information of the organization (eg vendor or item enrichment) is the last step of creating visibility. Last but not least, descriptive analytics reporting can be conducted through advanced data analytics. Based on the findings of descriptive analytics, opportunities can be identified and measures to improve procurement performance can be implemented. This step can include spend volume aggregation, supplier rationalization, strategic sourcing and inventory optimization.

Figure 5.3.2 Spending analysis

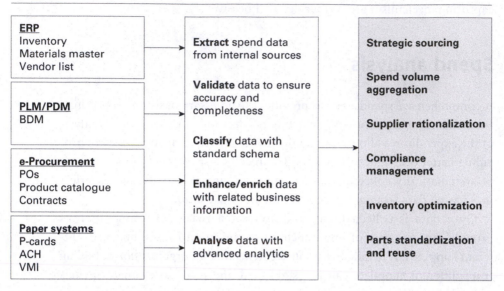

SOURCE: PWC (2012); Berger (2011)

Spend visibility is both an enabler and a gatekeeper for an integrated procurement framework and should be the focal point for all further steps. It builds the basis for defining an advanced sourcing strategy, which could contain supply chain redesign, supply base optimization, cost analysis, volume consolidation and rationalization of product specifications (PWC, 2012; Berger, 2011). Spend analyses in businesses are often visualized in 'spend cubes', referring to the three dimensions of the cube (suppliers, corporate business units and category of item) (Pandit and Marmanis, 2008).

Price-capturing mechanism

Built upon the basis laid by the spend analysis, the price-capturing mechanism uses the outcomes to set up a tool in regard to pricing information.

To meet the first and most important criterion, usability, the price-capturing mechanism was designed as a Microsoft Excel file (due to the ubiquity of Excel within the global workplace). The Excel worksheet consists of product worksheets and a dashboard, which is placed on the first sheet.

To get a meaningful result, it is necessary to provide as much relevant information as possible in the product worksheets. The price-capturing mechanism takes into account the following data (see Figure 5.3.3): date

Figure 5.3.3 Basis for price-capturing mechanism

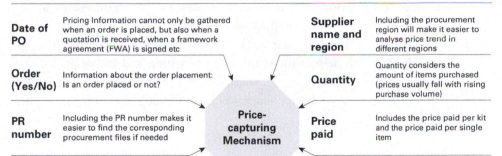

Date of PO	Pricing Information cannot only be gathered when an order is placed, but also when a quotation is received, when a framework agreement (FWA) is signed etc
Order (Yes/No)	Information about the order placement: Is an order placed or not?
PR number	Including the PR number makes it easier to find the corresponding procurement files if needed
Process type	The process type gives information about the type of procurement process and indicates if more than one quotation is received
Supplier name and region	Including the procurement region will make it easier to analyse price trend in different regions
Quantity	Quantity considers the amount of items purchased (prices usually fall with rising purchase volume)
Price paid	Includes the price paid per kit and the price paid per single item
Benchmark price	When evaluating the performance of a quote it is important to compare it against an appropriate benchmark

Price-capturing Mechanism

of purchasing order (PO), order (yes/no), purchasing request (PR) number, process (type of procurement process), supplier name, supplier region, quantity, total price of kit and prices of single items. Simultaneously, the benchmark price per item and the benchmark price per kit are calculated and displayed at a dashboard that summarizes the most important information. It automatically collects and updates data from the product worksheet. In particular, the latest order of an item or kit and the unit price paid (respectively the price per kilogramme for plastic sheets) are displayed. Last but not least, the dashboard illustrates the theoretical cost efficiency and the theoretical cost-reduction potential per kit and per item by relating the unit price paid to the benchmark price.

It is important to remember that the benchmark price does not include any quality indicators yet, hence it might compare prices of items of different qualities in kits. This means that a low cost-efficiency does not necessarily mean that Save the Children does not get value for money. In contrast, a high cost-efficiency does not necessarily mean high value for money since the accuracy of the benchmark price depends on the amount of information given in the sheets (the more information, the more accurate the benchmark price gets). The theoretical cost-efficiency rather provides a quick overview of where cost-reduction potentials might be found and where spend performance could be increased. Yet, until there are standardized quality management processes in place, and reliable measures for the quality of single items available, the user cannot rely on the dashboard alone but will have to take the product worksheets into consideration when making decisions.

To sum up, and in regard to the objective (to evaluate prices of relief items), the price-capturing mechanism provides a powerful tool that illustrates whether Save the Children gets competitive prices when purchasing commodities. Even though the benchmark prices and cost efficiencies in the dashboard cannot yet be used alone to indicate value for money, used in combination with the detailed single-item pricing information given in the worksheets it will help in the evaluation of existing and future prices, and so support decision making. Furthermore, the price-capturing mechanism can easily be used to strengthen Save the Children's position in supplier negotiations.

Summary

The overall objective of the project was to examine whether Save the Children receives competitive prices in the Philippines and to give recommendations on how Save the Children can improve its procurement operations in the Philippines. The spend analysis unveiled that over 80 per cent of total spend in all regions (2014) can be allocated to seven main categories: construction materials, miscellaneous, education materials, WASH equipment, IT, shelter and food. The newly developed long-term price-capturing mechanism was applied to 11 high-spend and high-frequency items and keeps track of their product price developments. The application of both methods revealed potential cost reductions for several of the 11 items. Based on the findings, different recommendations were developed such as proposing to set up a new quality evaluation process, to extend Save the Children's supplier base, to establish a joint procurement hub, or to buy items in a kit from two or more suppliers.

In summary, several of the identified key items or kits showed cost-savings potential, which became visible through the price-capturing mechanism. The question of whether Save the Children gets 'value for money' cannot be answered easily since value is a highly subjective measure; it comes down to the question of whether one is willing to pay for higher quality even though standard quality would be good enough. Credit is due to Save the Children for establishing framework agreements for key categories through the tendering process in order to help achieve value for money.

When maintained on a regular basis, and especially when combined with suitable quality measures, which require new standardized quality evaluation processes, the price-capturing mechanism provides Save the Children with a sophisticated tool that strengthens its position in supplier negotiations, ensures value for money and can be used in internal reporting as well as provide a new KPI.

In case of future applications of spend analysis followed by a price-capturing mechanism, the following points should be taken into account:

- Be aware of inaccurate/incomplete data. It is very unlikely to receive a 100 per cent complete set of data; often you need to work with what you get.

- Consolidation and validation of the final set of data claims a substantial amount of time.

- Incongruent naming conventions cause the need for standardization, cleansing and classification to ensure that the data is accurate, error-free and meaningful.

References

Roland Berger (2011) [accessed 29 April 2015] Purchasing Excellence Study, Purchasing Trends and Benchmarks 2011, *Roland Berger Strategy Consultants* [Online] https://www.rolandberger.com/media/pdf/Roland_Berger_Purchasing_Excellence_E_20111201.pdf

Pandit, K and Marmanis, H (2008) *Spend Analysis: The window into strategic sourcing*, Ross Publishing, Fort Lauderdale, FL, pp 3–22

PWC (2012) [accessed 29 April 2016] 2012 Americas School of Mines, Spend Analysis and the Supply Chain, *PricewaterhouseCoopers LLP* [Online] https://www.pwc.com/gx/en/mining/school-of-mines/2012/pwc-spend-analysis-within-the-supply-chain.pdf

Partnerships and innovative procurement as enablers for sustainable development goals

5.4

ROLANDO M TOMASINI

Head of Global Outreach at the United Nations Office for Project Services (UNOPS)

International organizations, especially in development, are endowed with the responsibility to allocate funds in an accountable and transparent manner to meet the objectives agreed with their donors and partners. This may involve contracting logistics services for the delivery of aid to beneficiaries, eg the most suitable type of blankets or sheltering, but also for services such as engineering and construction companies to build bridges, schools, hospitals and affordable housing solutions. In order to guarantee a transparent and accountable process, these allocations are done in compliance with internationally recognized public procurement policies and best practices. However, over recent decades it has become quite clear to both private and public organizations that traditional procurement is faced with some limitations when it seeks to best address the needs of populations in complex settings and projects. This is particularly true in development and sustainability where social, economic and environmental issues are hard to isolate and reduce to single sets of independent requirements.

Traditional procurement focuses on finding the best solutions to a specific and well-defined need. Such procurement is based on substantial technical or functional specifications, and demands suppliers to limit their response on those requirements.[1] The requirements become a prerequisite for suppliers to submit a tender, and the award criteria is limited to the specifications that are communicated to the supplier. This is all done with a well-defined boundary between the supplier and contractor during the needs definition and formulation of specification phases of the procurement process. The boundary ensures a fair and transparent selection process, though often at the expense of innovation or more efficient and sustainable solutions. In recent years, we have seen several efforts to evolve traditional procurement into new forms of solicitations and awards for public goods and services, with a greater emphasis on open yet regulated dialogue.

Several countries and organizations have defined and implemented their own guidelines for competitive dialogue and the promotion of public–private partnerships, leading to new consultation methods that enable a more interactive conversation around the definition of the need. For example, in 2004, the European Commission introduced competitive dialogue for complex projects after accepting the limitations of their previous directives in this area.[2] They defined competitive dialogue as a procurement system that consists of several rounds of discussion between the principal and potential suppliers, during which all aspects of the tender are considered (including technical specifications and price levels), assisted by the authorities with the aim to develop one or more suitable alternatives capable of meeting the requirements for tendering. Countries such as France and the United Kingdom followed soon after,[3] introducing the same mechanism into their legislation for public tendering.[4] The fruits of these instruments have been valuable in the definition of several complex projects, enabling multi-stakeholder consultations leading to innovation, the ability to respond to new trends in technology and regulation around social and environmental performance, and contributing to the perennial quest for cost savings, value for money and efficiency.

While partnerships are nothing new, and in fact, are longer standing than competitive dialogue, their use and role in policy has also seen an interesting evolution. They have become a central topic in public procurement policy as their use is transferred from the private sector to public institutions.[5] Historically, partnerships between the public and private sector were primarily a financial tool to fund infrastructure projects through concessions, different modes of ownerships and revenue-sharing models. Estimates point to over US $394 billion of funding on infrastructure public–private partnerships globally from 2005 to 2010.[6] Over the past decade we have also seen the evolution of partnerships as more service-led contracts in which the 'scope is extended from the delivery of a product into the operation and maintenance phase of that product and is driven by the client requirements',[7] creating more complex requirements and selection processes than those supported by traditional procurement.

Development agenda paradigm shift

Acknowledging the rising complexity and increasing magnitude of the development agenda, international organizations under the leadership of the United Nations (UN) Secretariat and member states have shifted their focus on how to complement development funds with private development aid. The new ambition for the Sustainable Development Goals goes beyond corporate philanthropy and corporate social responsibility initiatives, into a closer collaboration with the private sector on longer-term projects and solutions to development and social issues.[8] In July 2015 the heads of governments and high representatives of international organizations met in Addis Ababa to reinforce their commitment to address the challenge of financing progress towards the end of poverty. More explicitly, they had a strong focus on inclusive socioeconomic growth through greater collaboration with the private sector as a source of funding, but also as a partner in defining new models for solving the problems identified at the heart of the Sustainable Development Goals in the post-2015 agenda. Towards this, the members of the Addis Ababa conference agreed, among many other points, to 'develop policies, and where appropriate, strengthen regulatory frameworks to better align private sector incentives with public goals'.[9]

In practice, this type of engagement with the private sector represents a paradigm shift towards stronger and more inclusive supplier relations that will work towards development goals in the post-2015 agenda. For this to work efficiently we must rethink our traditional solicitation methods (ie expression of interest, request for information, request for proposal, etc) and the type of regulatory engagement (eg purchase order, contract, long-term agreement, memorandum of understanding) so they become facilitators of the relationships rather than entry points. Traditionally, a supplier relationship is built upon successful outcomes from a solicitation mode and formalized by a regulatory agreement (ie contract). In this paradigm shift, however, the supplier relations are built from the *acknowledgement* of the need rather than from the *definition* of the need. This new paradigm presents both the need and the opportunity to engage with suppliers in a dialogue about how to define the specifications, how to find the best solution for them, and what is the most sustainable form of collaboration. All this while adhering to public-procurement principles and finding a balance between value for money, value for the beneficiaries and value to the organizations. Doing this should not be at the expense of blurring the lines in the supplier relationship, nor compromise the need for transparency and equal access that define public procurement. In fact, this paradigm shift reinforces the need to have well-defined boundaries for exchange, such as those acknowledged by international and public bodies through the adoption of best practices from competitive dialogues, and partnership directives and procedures.

Partnerships risks

Partnerships are not without risks, as noted by the many scholars who have compared traditional procurement and partnerships. Ross and Yan advise that the choice between using traditional procurement or a partnership 'depends on a number of factors including the likelihood that changes will be necessary, the productivity of non-contractible efforts exerted by the private partners, and the bargaining power vis-à-vis private parties'.[10] Hoppe and Schmitz would also argue that the choice depends on 'information gathering cost, the effort cost, and the degree to which the effort is contractible'.[11] Combined, all these points about the use of procurement versus the use of partnerships illustrate the need for both approaches to coexist in harmony, providing both the organization and the suppliers with vehicles to address problems with innovative solutions from different engagement modalities. Traditional procurement can be very effective to contract clearly defined needs from existing solutions and suppliers, while partnerships may be used, as defined by the UN Secretariat, as 'a voluntary and collaborative agreement or arrangement between one or more parts of the United Nations system and the Business Sector, in which all participants agree to work together to achieve a common purpose or undertake a specific task and to share risks, responsibilities, resources, and benefits'.[12]

Ross and Yan also conclude that while partnerships may provide suppliers with incentives for cost-reduction and innovation, they may also lead to lengthy engagements with little room for negotiation.[13] Renegotiation is inherent in partnership as needs evolve, and the partners' relationship shapes the roles and interests of the parties. In fact, the World Bank Institute confirms that out of over 1,000 partnerships signed in Latin America, renegotiation was performed in 30 per cent of the cases.[14] Renegotiation implies to some extent that partnership agreements, just like service-led contracts, are incomplete over the long run. To this extent, Grimsey and Lewis highlight the importance of getting the incentive structure right for the agreements.[15] When addressing sustainability and developmental issues we could argue this is increasingly more important given the long-term nature of the investments required, and the importance of the roles and motivation of each party, ie what the role and benefit is for a public organization versus that of their private partner over the long run.

Partnerships and dialogues can also raise tensions around transparency and confidentiality, as the parties share their ideas and resources through the partnering process.[16] Darwin *et al* argue that the exclusive nature of partnership may encourage corruption among the selected members.[17] All these arguments reiterate again the need for well-defined policies for private sector engagement. Following the UN Secretariat Guidelines for Private Sector Engagement, several agencies have worked in recent years on developing the relevant policies and processes to implement partnerships while remaining aligned to the public procurement principles, where transparency and non-exclusivity are paramount, and their financial rules and regulations. Lessons learned, as described by many of these agencies during the 15-year anniversary of the UN Global Compact,[18] highlight that drafting the policies and procedures is only a portion of the task. The rest involves explaining and aligning your potential private sector partners to the policies and strategy to avoid confusions and conflicts of interest about the use of traditional procurement and partnerships.

On the flip side of all these risks, the benefits for partnerships have been well documented. Erridge and Greer reiterate that closer supplier relations reduce transaction cost and increase efficiency as trust is built, and information flow is structured and regulated.[19] Keeping communication open yet regulated, as in competitive dialogue, helps guarantee that neither party becomes over-dependent on the other, while transparency and visibility help ensure that partnerships remain open for competition and innovation. Finally, as partnerships begin to show their benefits and become recognized by the public beneficiaries, social capital builds up and both parties are more inclined to contribute resources from their networks, such as engaging new partners or accessing funding and know-how from their client and supplier base.

Conclusion

Having experienced similar procurement roles in the private sector and my experience with policy at international organizations, I can attest that the focus on supplier relations and a structured but open dialogue with suppliers is valuable to identify competitive and innovative solutions for the sustainability agenda that most industries and sectors can no longer afford to ignore. Solutions for tomorrow's problems demand a closer and more interactive dialogue with different players who will contribute to more sustainable and comprehensive approaches to reach our goals. This dialogue may lead us into multiple forms of commercial and non-commercial engagement. It is our duty, as suggested by the members of the Addis Ababa conference, to make sure that the framework for this type of collaboration with the different sector is solid and efficient, while preserving the very objectives that define our public institutions.

Notes

1 Uttam, K and Lann Ross, C (2015) Competitive dialogue procedure for sustainable procurement, *Journal of Cleaner Production*, **86**, pp 403–16

2 See http://ec.europa.eu/internal_market/publicprocurement/docs/explan-notes/classic-dir-dialogue_fr.pdf

3 See https://www.gov.uk/government/uploads/system/uploads/attachment_data/file/225317/02_competitive_dialogue_procedure.pdf

4 Annexe au décret no 2006-975 du 1er août 2006 portant code des marchés publics (Code des Marches Publiques 2006, 2015)

5 Erridge, A and Greer, J (2002) Partnerships and public procurement: building social capital through supplier relations, *Public Administration*, **80** (3), pp 503–22

6 Infrastructure Journal Project Database [Online] http://www1.ijonline.com [accessed 25 July 2011]

7 Alderman, N, Ivory, C, McLoughlin, I and Vaughan, R (2005) Sense-making as process within complex service-led contracts, *International Journal of Project Management*, **23** (5), pp 380–85

8 See https://sustainabledevelopment.un.org/topics/sustainabledevelopmentgoals

9 Article 35 of the Addis Ababa Action Agenda of the Third International Conference on Financing for Development

10 Ross, T and Yan, J (2015) Comparing public–private partnerships and traditional procurement: efficiency vs. flexibility, *Journal of Comparative Policy Analysis: Research and practice*, **17** (5) pp 448–66

11 Hoppe, E and Schmitz, P (2013) Public–private partnerships versus traditional procurement: innovation incentives and information gathering, *RAND Journal of Economics*, **44** (1), pp 56–74

12 Definition from Guidelines on Cooperation between the United Nations and the Business Sector

13 Ross, T and Yan, J (2015) Comparing public–private partnerships and traditional procurement: efficiency vs. flexibility, *Journal of Comparative Policy Analysis: Research and practice*, **17** (5) pp 448–66

14 Gausch, J L (2004) *Granting and Renegotiating Infrastructure Concessions: Doing it right*, World Bank Institute, Washington DC

15 Grimsey, D and Lewis, M K (2004) *Public Private Partnerships*, Edward Elgar, Cheltenham

16 Hoezen, M, Van Rutten, J, Voordijk, H and Dewulf, G (2010) Towards better customized service-led contracts through the competitive dialogue procedure, *Construction Management and Economics*, **28**, pp 1177–86

17 Darwin, J, Duberley, J and Johnson, P (2000) Contracting in ten English local authorities: preferences and practices, *International Journal of Public Sector Management*, **13**, 1, pp 38–57

18 See www.Globalcompact.org

19 Erridge, A and Greer, J (2002) Partnerships and public procurement: building social capital through supplier relations, *Public Administration*, **80** (3), pp 503–22

PART SIX
Transportation, fleet management, delivery and distribution

Transport in humanitarian supply chains

6.1

RUTH BANOMYONG

Thammasat University, Thailand

DAVID B GRANT

HUMLOG Institute, Finland and Hull University Business School, UK

Introduction

Efficient and effective transportation is critical to the success of both commercial and humanitarian operations. From a supply perspective, transportation infrastructure and the capability of various transport modes are often the most critical issues that need to be considered in humanitarian supply chain management (SCM). It is therefore necessary to understand transportation issues when considering the design of the humanitarian supply chains.

This chapter provides an overview of the transportation function and its importance to humanitarian supply chains. The purpose of this chapter is to examine the role of transportation modes in humanitarian supply chains, and to understand what issues need to be considered when making transport-related decisions in humanitarian situations. A transport decision-making model for humanitarian aid is presented as a reference framework in assessing transportation issues in the development of humanitarian supply chains.

The role of transport in humanitarian SCM

There are six different modes of transport:

- road transport, for example in trucks or van;
- rail transport, for example on dedicated freight trains;
- inland waterway transport, for example on river barges, tows or canal boats;
- ocean or sea shipping, for example on container ships or crude oil super-tankers;
- air transport, for example in dedicated air cargo freighters or as belly-hold cargo in passenger airlines;
- pipeline transport for oil, other liquids and slurries (Grant, 2012).

However, pipeline transport is likely non-existent in the case of humanitarian supply chains and therefore will not be discussed further in this chapter. Further, the transport of goods to enable humanitarian aid may also use multiple transport modes; this is known as door-to-door multimodal transport and usually involves a container or other fixed storage unit being transferred from one mode to another, for example road to rail, during its journey to the affected area.

One important aim of a humanitarian supply chain is to establish a transport network for aid that is tailored to fit a particular crisis. A developed or ad hoc transport network for aid can be considered as a conduit running from a donor country's port of origin all the way to warehouses or distribution centres (DCs) in or near the affected areas. The network will often pass across an ocean, arriving at a discharge port in the destination country or a country near to the destination. It may also pass through warehouses or DCs and be served by rail, road, air and even barge. The main job of the humanitarian supply chain is to get this transport network up and running quickly, to establish it as robust as circumstances dictate in order that supply interruptions do not occur and, while satisfying these objectives, keep the costs of operating the transport network to a minimum.

Ocean transport

The principal leg of such a transport network is generally sea transport. It is appropriate therefore to consider ocean freight first. The main choice within ocean freight is between vessel chartering or sending goods via an existing scheduled liner service. There are advantages and disadvantages to both approaches.

A chartered ship can either be hired for the humanitarian organization's sole use or it can be hired on behalf of a number of humanitarian organizations. There are many types of charter, the most common of which are the voyage charter, the time charter or the bareboat/demise charter. In a voyage charter, a ship is hired for a particular voyage. The precise nature and volume of cargo is set out in the charter-party, as is the port of loading and discharge, the lay-time and demurrage terms. Under the conditions of a time charter a vessel is hired for a specified period of time regardless of location. This allows the charterer greater flexibility in the choice of loading/discharging ports and in terms of freedom to respond to changes in circumstances. The bareboat/demise charter is different from the other forms of charter in that the charterer operates the ship as if the humanitarian organization owns it. The bareboat charter generally means that the ship has been hired for long-term use. This could have advantages if a particular crisis is likely to persist for many months or even years.

The advantage of chartering a ship, irrespective of the form of charter, is that it provides an opportunity to consolidate cargo either for different locations or for one final destination. This improves efficiency and can dramatically reduce overall costs of the sea leg. However, the charterer is then responsible for all ancillary costs and, if the port of destination is congested, then not only will the goods not reach the affected area fast enough but the costs will increase as well.

Liner shipping is generally more expensive than chartering. It involves the hiring of space on a vessel that is already on a specified trade route. The most obvious advantage is that small/medium volumes of goods can be handled as it is not necessary to fill an entire ship. However, the most suitable ship, with regard to time and trade route, may not have sufficient space for the goods to be transported. Also, there simply may not be a suitable ship at the desired time going to the required destination. Insurance can also be very high, or even impossible to obtain, if aid goods are passing through a danger zone, which in the case of a humanitarian crisis, vessels frequently do.

The main aim when distributing goods after the transport network has been established is to minimize costs. The reason for this is obvious: whatever is saved on the cost of transportation can be spent on vital aid and supplies. The decision as to whether to charter a ship or to place cargo on a liner ship is therefore generally determined primarily by costs.

When the World Food Programme (WFP) reviewed liner shipping costs, they estimated that transporting aid on liners typically costs between 2 and 21 times as much as shipping aid on ships chartered by the WFP. Consequently, in order to keep expensive liner shipments to the minimum, WFP has intensified their efforts to consolidate consignments into larger quantities more suitable for charter vessel carriage.

As ocean transport is generally slow, there can be a significant delay between the occurrence of the crisis and the receipt of the aid by those in need. The overall average time for aid goods shipment between supplier and recipient is four months. Therefore, other faster modes of transport must be adopted in the early stages of a humanitarian crisis.

The WFP adopts many different methods when transporting aid in order to reach an area of crisis very quickly. According to Myat (1995) the WFP chartered approximately 200 to 250 ships annually, implying that WFP has 40 to 50 ships – or about half a million tonnes of aid – either loading, discharging or sailing at any given time. This enables WFP to divert ships to areas where the need is greatest. WFP also 'borrows' aid goods from neighbouring countries or from their own stocks that are situated in strife-prone or disaster-prone areas. Another rapid response method is the use of air transport. This will be discussed in a later section.

An important factor to consider in ocean transport and logistics supply is unitization. Aid involves various types of commodities. Each of these commodities needs to be stored aboard sea vessels in different ways. For aid goods shipment on a liner vessel, different freight rates will apply for different cargo types.

As an example, the cheapest way to transport grain is in bulk as this utilizes all available ship space and minimizes costly handling. If the destination port does not have bulk handling equipment, then the grain will need to be further packed into 50-kilogramme sacks at the port of origin, absorbing valuable time and money (Jennings, Beresford and Banomyong, 2000). As stated earlier, any overspending on delivery ultimately reduces the amount of aid available to affected areas.

Land transport

Land transport is needed in virtually all humanitarian situations. This is due to the fact that disaster areas are very rarely conveniently situated at a point of entry, in the form of an airport or seaport. There are, however, two main scenarios where land transport plays a large role in the distribution of aid. According to Jennings, Beresford and Banomyong (2000) those scenarios are: 1) when aid goods are purchased from a nearby or neighbouring country; 2) when aid goods must travel through neighbouring countries as the recipient country is landlocked.

The main transport mode used when distributing goods overland is by road, or alternatively, road in combination with rail. Inland waterways transport can also be used to gain access to some landlocked countries. The respective advantages and disadvantages of road and rail for aid distribution are discussed below.

Road transport has many qualities: it is flexible, versatile, relatively inexpensive over short distances and the required infrastructure is usually available in most countries. Road transport's main advantage over rail is its ability to provide a service from door to door, it can also transport almost anything anywhere and at any time (Fawcett, McLeish and Ogden, 1992; Grant, 2012).

Road transport's versatility also stems from its ability to transport commodities that have special needs, for example refrigerated or chemical products. A further advantage is found in the frequent prevalence of local operators. This makes it relatively simple for an aid agency to mobilize and organize a fleet of trucks, and to deploy them where the need arises. Alternatively, the aid agency can bring in its own trucks and/or drivers where local capacity is insufficient.

However, road transport also has a number of disadvantages. Trucks are susceptible to drastic changes in weather conditions when the available infrastructure is not of a suitable quality. This is a major problem in many countries where roads are not paved and, for a number of weeks or even months each year, roads may become impassable during rainy seasons. This problem is also highlighted in many disaster situations as host countries tend to be in the developing world where infrastructure is poor and where climates are tropical or subtropical with alternating dry and rainy seasons and heavy rain a common feature.

When considering rail transport, Fawcett, McLeish and Ogden (1992) described four main advantages:

1 capacity;
2 speed;
3 safety and security;
4 reduced delays in bad weather.

The main advantage of using rail transport is rail's ability to carry large amounts of cargo cheaply over long distances. In most developing countries and within Eastern Europe, rail is cheaper because it is either subsidized or it has not seen large investment for many years. Rail is also often faster than road transport, especially over long distances, but over short distances any advantage gained in time is generally consumed by the transfer of the cargo from road to rail. Unfortunately, rail does not offer door-to-door service, and this means that a degree of road transport is almost always needed whenever rail is utilized.

Safety and security is normally an advantage of using rail transport because of the general nature of railway infrastructure, as it is less susceptible to pilferage or damage. However, relief or aid goods can suffer or disappear when stored in railway wagons or containers for long periods of time in remote yards and in humid conditions.

In contrast to road transport, rail is less affected by adverse weather conditions, making it a more attractive method of transportation in areas with dramatic changes in weather. The major disadvantages of rail transport are its fundamental inflexibility, its lack of gearing to commercial-level service needs and, in the case of many countries, a basic lack of railway infrastructure. Rail can also be susceptible to flooding and landslides; and even rail bridges can collapse in heavy rain.

In a crisis condition, and particularly in a humanitarian situation, the major factor in the choice of mode is availability, both of infrastructure and of trucks or railway wagons. The unfortunate situation is that the majority of humanitarian crises where aid is urgently needed often occur where roads are poor and rail is either unavailable or unusable.

Another problem for landlocked countries is the lack of, or conditions of, infrastructure in neighbouring countries (Beresford, 1999). Many humanitarian crises stem from war or civil conflict, where one of the aims of the warring parties is to destroy each other's transport infrastructure in an attempt to paralyse or immobilize enemy forces. In such circumstances, bandits often operate, making the transport of aid even more uncertain.

Many agencies adopt a 'convoy' system when transporting aid goods by road, but this means that aid is transported only when all the vehicles in the convoy are loaded and they have to travel at the speed of the slowest vehicle. It is also a major burden on human resources as soldiers tend to be diverted from other duties in order to protect the convoy. All these uncertainties, and the changeable nature of humanitarian situations, necessitates a considerable amount of contingency planning on the part of the aid agencies when designing their supply chains and transport networks.

Air transport

The most effective mode of transport in terms of speed and security for distributing aid goods is air transport. However, the cost of airfreight is far too high for most aid agencies to contemplate using it over a long period of time. Airfreight is generally used in the early stages of an emergency or when the humanitarian situation is in an area inaccessible by any other mode of transport. The most economical use of air transport for aid is the air-drop technique. This technique avoids the need for landing strips, which are often not available or poorly maintained or, if they are available, are short, thus restricting the size of aircraft that can carry the aid goods.

The goods will need to be packed in specially designed parcels that can withstand the shock of being dropped out of the back of a low-flying aircraft. The most suitable aircraft for this type of delivery is a relatively slow-moving propeller or turboprop aircraft such as the Hercules. However, due to the limited tonnage that can be carried in this manner, aid goods that are delivered must provide the maximum value to the affected area.

McClintock (1997) studied carrying capacities for respective aircraft types with, predictably, fuel consumption representing by far the biggest single operating cost. Airfreighters such as Hercules burn around 100,000 litres of aviation fuel per day on active service. During the relief operation in South Sudan in 1997 an estimated 500 flights per month were required.

The cost of chartering a civil aircraft for the distribution of aid goods is greatly increased as the payload is generally only being transported one way, ie there are no back-haul opportunities. Therefore, the cheapest option for an aid agency is often to utilize local aircraft, either military or civil, or aircraft from a donor country. In certain cases, the advantage gained through the speed of air transportation can be lost through bureaucratic delays. Although the procedures for the transport of aid goods by road and rail within a particular country are usually well established, authorization from the government of the host country to use aircraft can prove complicated, especially in a conflict situation.

This is the case with internally displaced refugees who often do not benefit from the same rights as those of externally displaced refugees. The international community does not automatically have the right to come to the aid of these people, therefore it can take just as long to gain the permission needed to fly aid in, as it does to ship it from the donor country. Even after permission has been granted it may be that aid goods must be delivered to the main airport on government instruction; this may be situated a considerable distance away from where the refugees are actually located.

The United Nations Children's Emergency Fund (UNICEF) frequently takes advantage of air transport for their emergency supplies. Approximately 25 per cent of UNICEF's aid goods, including articles other than food, are transported by air. Most of this aid is transported in the initial stages of an emergency, after which the aid is transported by sea. McClintock (1997) stressed how difficult the humanitarian supply chain management task becomes with uncertain truck arrival schedules, use of temporary warehouses and long distances from ports.

This situation was the case during the African refugee crisis in 1995–96, when UNICEF charted more than a dozen aircraft, each providing a capacity of 40 tonnes, in order to relieve pressure on the land supply routes that were up to 2,200 kilometres and taking anything up to 35 transit days (Beresford, 1998). The planes used were all donated for UNICEF's use by donor governments, although they did start by utilizing in-service military aircraft in 1995. The shipping officer and emergency co-ordinator of UNICEF during that period gave the following reply with regard to the use of military aircraft: 'Sometimes we use military aircraft of donor countries. They need flying hours to practise anyway. So they may as well lift our supplies at the same time.'

The selection of carrier and modes choices in humanitarian supply chains

The motivations of both aid agencies and carriers need to be understood as they affect carrier and mode choice selection. Humanitarian agencies sending aid goods are trying to maximize service and minimize cost for delivery when they offer a consignment of aid to an affected area. These agencies will look to do this by managing direct as well as indirect transport costs such as inventory costs that include in-transit, safety stocks and transaction costs, and the cost of service failure that includes the time specified for delivery, the lead time from order to receipt of goods and the condition of the goods on arrival.

Humanitarian organizations will also need to evaluate a number of shipping parameters to distinguish transport modes, which will vary by country and type of humanitarian crisis, including:

- the geographic coverage of the carrier (ie are they really worldwide?);
- the volume, weight, value and type of aid goods that the carrier can handle;
- any consignment, load and dimension limits;
- transit time from door to door;

- the carrier's reliability versus risk;
- the price for throughput, distance, time and the cost per 'unit' moved;
- the service frequency and schedule flexibility;
- the carrier's service range and choice, including the use of technology;
- any intermediate handling and/or alternative routings;
- any other environmental externalities.

On the other hand, carriers providing humanitarian services will have to try to balance their transport asset utilization versus the frequency of service provided to the humanitarian organization. In a humanitarian situation it might be difficult for carriers' goals to be achieved. These goals usually are to achieve a satisfactory return on investment (ROI) through the maximization of revenue and the minimization of costs by route or customer. Carriers will look to do this by managing fixed terminal costs, access or track costs, intermediate and terminal handling, maximizing load sizes through consolidation and return loading, and minimizing variable trip costs such as fuel, distance and labour (Grant, 2012).

In summary, how to decide on a mode of transport and carrier is multi-faceted. However, humanitarian organizations tend to purchase transport based on service parameters not modes or routes; these humanitarian organizations need to recognize that carriers have the local knowledge of infrastructure, routes and modes in affected areas. Humanitarian agencies also look for a 'one stop' provider and would like to base their decisions on cost, where the carrier can provide the reliability, transit time and efficiency desired at the lowest possible prices and where reliability equates to on-time and damage-free aid shipments. Such service parameters increasingly include the use of various forms of technology such as global positioning systems (GPS) and radio frequency identification (RFID) that enable track-and-trace capability in the humanitarian supply chain.

Third-party transportation

Humanitarian agencies can use third-party firms to arrange and manage their transport needs. Traditional types of third parties include freight forwarders, brokers and even shippers' associations. However, freight forwarders tend to be the most common type of third party used. Freight forwarders purchase transportation services from carriers and then sell on this capacity to shippers or, in this case, humanitarian organizations. Their role is to help design the logistics system needed for a developed humanitarian supply

chain through the use of their extensive network of agents and local providers in affected areas. Forwarders receive their remuneration in the form
of costs plus commission from humanitarian agencies and their traditional
services include:

- export/import documentation completion and compliance;
- planning and costing of 'through freight' movements;
- booking space from scheduled and charter carriers;
- consolidating payments to transport, ports, etc;
- presenting and arranging goods for customs clearance;
- advising humanitarian agencies on the current transport situation in the affected area;
- arranging for insurance.

The growth in global logistics since the 1970s has seen the service portfolio
of traditional third-party providers, such as freight forwarders, increase to
include:

- grouping small consignments, ie less-than-container load (LCL) or less-than-truckload (LTL) into regular scheduled services in their own name, using a shipping company's resources for all kinds of aid goods;
- providing their own collection of aid goods and delivery vehicles;
- providing their own warehouses to hold aid goods either in-bond or in standard domestic conditions based on pre-positioning requirements;
- preparing appropriate packing and labelling;
- co-ordinating multiple consignments into single movements;
- tracking and tracing of consignments;
- providing assured security compliance.

An example of a third party providing such aid is discussed in the case
example on UPS providing flu vaccines in Laos.

CASE EXAMPLE   UPS delivering flu vaccines to Laos

Flu vaccines bring better health to the people of Laos. The country is situated in
Southeast Asia, where waves of the virus can originate. Not only could a vaccine
help prevent cases of respiratory disease in Laos – it could potentially help prevent

influenza strains from spreading to other places. When the US retail pharmacy chain Walgreens donated 375,000 flu vaccine doses totalling more than US \$9 million to the Laos Ministry of Health, UPS was engaged to deliver these doses to Laos. The delivery involved various challenges: precise temperature control, travel through five countries, complex customs brokerage, detailed regulatory compliance and multiple contingency plans, all of which needed to be handled on an extremely tight time line.

Dimitri Zacharenko, a UPS manager of temperature and sensitive health-care solutions, noted that the UPS health-care group has a very engaged solutions team with the ability to look at a situation and think outside the box to come up with a solution. Planning was a round-the-clock effort by a large team thinking of every small detail and it included UPS specialists in health care, logistics, brokerage, freight forwarding and UPS Airlines. They collaborated to co-ordinate the 9,000-mile shipment, ensuring uninterrupted movement through UPS's international transportation network using a temperature-controlled cargo container, available through UPS.

The PharmaPort™ 360 is an environmentally friendly active container that maintains a constant internal temperature regardless of external conditions. Two of these units kept the vaccine within a critical range of 2°C to 8°C throughout the trip to Laos, even despite 40 degrees of outside temperature variation. By employing simple and easily accessible mobile phone technology the containers' locations and internal temperature could be tracked at all times. Early on, UPS discovered it could not fly directly into Vientiane, Laos due to infrastructure limitations and instead flew to Bangkok, Thailand.

Zacharenko noted that UPS transported the vaccine on the ground for the rest of the way, using Google Earth to get satellite shots of the roads from Bangkok to Vientiane to see if it was potentially possible to use them – UPS does not have normal transportation set-ups for trucking between those places.

Transportation entailed a 19-hour trek by truck over roads with sections left unpaved, and the UPS Asia/Pacific Solutions group was involved in orchestrating this delivery as well as helping to arrange customs clearance in Thailand and Laos. Work instructions were translated into multiple languages to ensure the shipment went smoothly. According to Kevin Etter, a product manager for UPS Health-Care Logistics Strategy Group, there were 47 people from 15 different departments on two different continents working on this project, and in less than seven days everyone was brought together to make it happen.

SOURCE: UPS (2015)

Outsourcing and third-party logistics service providers

The use of third-party logistics (3PL) service providers in humanitarian situations is related to the phenomena of outsourcing. Outsourcing has been an area of growing interest and activity in business since the early 1990s (Quinn and Hilmer, 1994). In the humanitarian context outsourcing is not new but is less structured than in commercial environments. Logistics outsourcing often involves many different logistics activities, including transportation, warehousing, forwarding, brokering, reverse logistics services and information technology. The reasons to outsource logistics activities include:

- an ability to concentrate on what Quinn and Hilmer (1994) refer to as 'core competencies';
- the avoidance of large capital investments in logistical assets or a release of existing capital;
- converting logistics activities from a capital to current expenditure;
- reducing labour costs;
- improving standards of logistics service level;
- enjoying a greater logistical expertise offered by a 3PL and their economies of scale in vehicle acquisition, fuel, etc;
- a need for wider geographical coverage than can be offered by a 3PL such as DHL;
- access to a network of local logistics experts and subcontractors who may provide the best feasible solution in a humanitarian situation.

However, several critical success factors must be taken into account by humanitarian agencies when outsourcing, including:

- ensuring there is a selective match of 3PLs to the need of the humanitarian agency;
- two-way information sharing between the humanitarian agency and the 3PL;
- proper role specifications for both sides;
- appropriate ground rules for engagement;
- an exit provision if the arrangement doesn't work out in a worst-case scenario.

An extension to a 3PL is the concept of a fourth-party logistics (4PL) service provider. The 4PL aims to establish a more comprehensive supply chain solution rather than simply improve the efficiency of the physical logistics operation – and thus becomes the architect of a humanitarian supply chain and network for an affected or crisis area.

The nature of a 4PL is similar to that of a lead logistics partner (LLP), which is a firm that organizes other 3PL partners in outsourcing of logistics functions. However, a 4PL combines a humanitarian organization's in-house resources and capabilities with those of outside agencies, and essentially controls the supply chain for the humanitarian organization. A 4PL can also take a lead role in creating value, for example undertaking the assembly of finished goods on behalf of aid agencies (Cabodi, 2004). A 4PL operates almost virtually, ie it typically does not need to own any assets like a 3PL, but does make very intense use of technology and software in managing the outsourced and supply chain processes.

A reference framework for transport in humanitarian supply chains

Although each humanitarian crisis is unique in its characteristics, most crises exhibit similar logistical elements. These elements allow transport in humanitarian supply chains to follow a structured response pattern when dealing with any humanitarian crisis. This response pattern is illustrated in the reference framework described in Figure 6.1.1.

The logistics of transporting aid to an actual humanitarian crisis situation is obviously far more complex than any model can portray. However, the model shown in Figure 6.1.1 does illustrate the key difficulties and decision nodes that can arise in a humanitarian crises and the possible thought processes that a humanitarian organization, a 3PL or a 4PL may use. Aid network charging, and if necessary recharging, is the key ongoing task once supply lines are established, and managing the aid network in constantly varying conditions is an ongoing process. Aid network charging means filling up the network, while recharging means that the supply lines are being refilled.

In order to establish the transport network for aid, the humanitarian organization, the 3PL or 4PL must first assess various attributes of the host country and, in the case of landlocked nations, the neighbouring countries as well. First, a suitable port needs to be chosen: this decision will depend largely on the handling, storage and efficiency of the port in question. Second, the infrastructure from the port to the final destination needs to

Figure 6.1.1 Humanitarian aid transport reference model

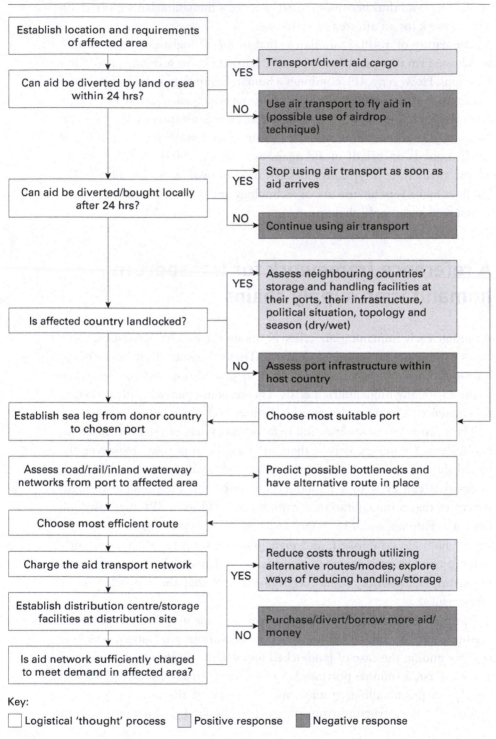

Key:

☐ Logistical 'thought' process ☐ Positive response ☐ Negative response

SOURCE: Adapted from Jennings, Beresford and Banomyong (2000)

be considered and assessed, as well as the political situation, topology and seasonal fluctuations of the weather. All these factors influence the choice of route and mode by which aid will be transported. Finally, a suitable storage site must be established at the distribution site, so as to ensure a constant supply in reserve at all times.

Once the port, route and storage facilities have been established and the aid network is sufficiently charged, alternative routes must be ascertained in case of bottlenecks and complications in the established aid network. It is of paramount importance throughout a humanitarian crisis to always deliver sufficient quantities of aid goods at regular intervals, as the livelihood of the affected area will depend on it. The Haiti earthquake in 2010 provides an interesting case on the transportation challenges involved in humanitarian supply chain management as faced by WFP.

CASE EXAMPLE
Logistical problems unfold as Haiti relief effort begins

In the wake of the devastating earthquake that struck Haiti on 12 January 2010, the UN World Food Programme (WFP) chartered ships to transport 90,000 tonnes of essential edibles over a period of three months, with the total relief effort possibly lasting up to a year. The shipping rule of thumb was to use smaller ships, capable of manoeuvring into really tight and hard-to-reach locations.

Stephen Cahill, head of operations at WFP's ocean transportation service, told Lloyd's List that WFP identified a need of US $800 million for food aid to Haiti for the duration of 2010. This amount included food as well as ocean transport. The first ship employed by the WFP for the Haitian relief mission was a US-flagged and US Coast Guard-controlled 6,200 dead-weight-ton (dwt) warehouse barge named *Crimson Clover*, which arrived in Port-au-Prince on 20 January with 123 containers bearing 2,200 tonnes of food aid.

The first ship specifically chartered by WFP for the Haitian relief effort was the 1979-built, 1,922 dwt roll-on roll-off *Inagua Espana*. Two more ships, the 1979-built, 3,000 dwt landing craft *Cristina Express* and the 1999-built, 205 twenty-foot-equivalent (TEU) container ship *Habib Express*, were scheduled to reach the Dominican Republic on 29 January. This duo loaded up in Miami in the week following the earthquake. *Habib Express* carried 1.5 million ready-to-eat meals. *Cristina Express* was time-chartered, while *Habib Express* was booked on a per voyage basis. The 1982-built, 1,195 gross tonnage, 224-berth passenger ship *Sea Voyager* was also engaged, and used to house WFP personnel and other relief workers. The WFP fixed this ship for three months, with one-month renewal options thereafter.

The tiny sizes and specifications of *Inagua Espana* and *Cristina Express* are a telling reminder of the ground realities in Haiti, which at that point were simply incapable of berthing large ships. Cahill noted that both these ships were designed as shallow-draught landing craft with the ability to roll right up onto a beach for unloading. The utter devastation of Haitian infrastructure wrought by the earthquake had made it necessary for the WFP to use multiple emergency bases for relief in order to reach the stricken country.

The WFP also performed a 'corridor analysis' and conducted other logistical reality checks, which led to a co-ordinated strategy. Altogether, five humanitarian corridors into Haiti were identified, two of which were airstrips – one in Port-au-Prince and the other in Barahonas (located in the Dominican Republic).

Seaports in the Dominican Republic, as well as the tiny port in Cap-Haitien and the possible revival down the track of Port-au-Prince sea port, were designated to bear the major portion of the food aid delivered over the six months after the earthquake. Rio Haina and Barahonas in the Dominican Republic served as the main hubs for arriving ships. Cap-Haitien in Haiti was capable of very limited operations as well, and had been earmarked for early direct voyages into Haiti. However, Cap-Haitien only had warehouse capacity of 7,000 tonnes. Cahill noted that the security situation in Haiti had made it necessary for WFP personnel to be judicial in the timing and quantity of food aid released for distribution, and this factor might have meant that the Cap-Haitien warehouse filled up quickly.

These factors posed unique challenges to the WFP ocean transportation service's projected goal of procuring and shipping supplies of 1,000 tonnes a day to Haiti over the first 90 days, which the WFP had to work around through common sense. The selection of the two Dominican Republic hubs, apart from the fact that they did not succumb to the earthquake, was driven by the fact that food, once it reaches these locations, could be sent into Haiti on lorries. Coasters such as *Inagua Espana* and *Cristina Express* were the WFP's workhorses as the relief mission unfolded. These ships allowed the WFP the flexibility to move cargo up and down the coast as the actual condition of Haitian terminals became clearer.

Some of the chartering activity, or lack thereof, would also depend on how quickly the donor governments moved. For instance, Thailand promised the WFP 20,000 tonnes of food aid, projected at 1,000 tonnes a week beginning in mid-February. That aid amounted to about 40 containers per week. The WFP, at any given time, has between 30 and 40 ships on the water, carrying food aid destined for donor nations. The standard model was that about 65 per cent of these were time-chartered ships, and the other 35 per cent were mostly fixed on a voyage-charter basis. When faced with emergencies that required food delivery to stricken locations as fast as possible, it was common for the WFP to divert some of these ships at short notice, always presuming that their original destination has sufficient food stocks.

In 2009 WFP formed a partnership with California-based technology company GT Nexus especially for this purpose, whereby GT Nexus's web-based platform allowed WFP to track all its containers so that the most suitable cargoes can be redirected. The Haiti earthquake posed a unique challenge as a diversion could not be conducted in the first two weeks because no ships were close enough. That made it necessary for WFP to concentrate on sourcing the food to be sent to Haiti primarily from the United States, and transporting it from the Gulf of Mexico. That kept transport times short and allowed WFP to co-ordinate its work more thoroughly, with the equally complicated logistical machinery set in motion by the US Agency for International Development. With no existing ships being redirected, the successful delivery of 90,000 tonnes over the first three months was totally dependent on the WFP finding, and the shipping industry providing, enough ships with which to accomplish the mission. The initial charters, *Inagua Espana*, *Cristina Express*, *Habib Express* and *Sea Voyager*, were therefore only the first sliver of WFP business that came the shipping industry's way in those lean times. When asked whether the WFP paid over the odds for the first four charters, which by necessity had to be fixed in a hurry, Cahill said: 'We did not get a bargain basement price, but we are happy that we got a fair price.'

SOURCE: Lloyd's List (2015)

Summary

The role of transportation in humanitarian aid is important not just from a logistics perspective but also as a key activity in humanitarian supply chain design in terms of providing goods in a timely and efficient manner. Humanitarian supply chains require that normal modes of road, rail, water and air become more integrated from both an intermodal and outsourcing perspective. In this chapter, the role of transportation in the humanitarian supply chain was explored. The basic transport modes were described, including intermodal combinations and the possible role of third-party and fourth-party providers.

The main aim in humanitarian supply chain management is to establish a transport network for aid goods that is tailored to fit a particular crisis and, which in the long run, must minimize costs. This is due to the fact that by minimizing the total cost of operations, more money will become available to purchase the much-needed aid.

Therefore, it is of paramount importance that humanitarian organizations embrace a flexible planning approach to allow for different transport scenarios in the design of their humanitarian supply chains. The transport reference framework proposed in this chapter clarifies the options available in supply chain planning for humanitarian situations and should assist managers in humanitarian agencies in doing so.

References

Beresford, A K C (1998) *Re-evaluation of the Transport Sector in Rwanda*, UNCTAD, Geneva, April, p 25

Beresford, A K C (1999) *Improvement of Transit Transport Systems in Africa, Asia and Latin America*, UNCTAD, Geneva, April, p 88

Cabodi, C (2004) The fourth way, *Supply Chain Standard* (formerly *Logistics Europe*) **12** (3), pp 24–28

Fawcett, P, McLeish, R E and Ogden, I (1992) *Logistics Management*, Pitman, London

Grant, D B (2012) *Logistics Management*, Pearson Education, Harlow UK

Jennings, E, Beresford, A K C and Banomyong, R (2000) Emergency Relief Logistics: A disaster response model, Occasional Paper No. 64, Department of Maritime Studies and International Transport, Cardiff University, ISSN 0967-5566

Lloyd's List (2015) [accessed 4 October 2015] Logistical Problems Unfold as Haiti Relief Effort Begins [Online] http://www.lloydslist.com/ll/sector/ship-operations/article9700.ece

McClintock, A (1997) The Rwandan refugee crisis 1994: the logistics of a third-world relief operation, in *Global Cases in Logistics and Supply Chain*, ed D Taylor, Thomson, London, Case 33, pp 356–71

Myat, T (1995) Keynote speech at the Conference on Planning and Conducting Large-Scale Emergency Operations, World Food Programme, Rome, 13–15 June

Quinn, J B and Hilmer, F G (1994) Strategic outsourcing, *Sloan Management Review*, **35** (4), pp 43–55

UPS (2015) [accessed 3 October 2015] Temperature-Controlled Shipping [Online] http://www.ups.com/content/us/en/bussol/browse/article/temperature-controlled-shipping-ups.html

WFP (1992) *Annual Report: Food aid review*, World Food Programme, Rome

Humanitarian aid supply corridors

6.2

Europe–Iraq

ANTHONY BERESFORD, STEPHEN PETTIT AND ZIAD AL HASHIMI

Cardiff Business School, Cardiff University, UK

Background

The key aim of this chapter is to explore and evaluate various multimodal transport corridors currently being used for both commercial trade and aid shipments from Europe to Iraq. By concentrating flows into particular corridors, the volume of cargo becomes higher, security is improved and optimum transport choices can be made. However, distances may be longer, several modes may be required and cargoes may be handled several times before reaching their final destination. Transport operators have some flexibility to design solutions within the respective corridors, however, enabling them to select the most appropriate modes and nodes and to create solutions with the maximum resilience.

The research presented in this chapter makes use of data and information obtained from interviews with shipping lines, port authorities, terminal operators and logistics service providers, as well as from United Nations (UN) bodies (Kormilitsyn, 2013; Denktas and Beresford, 2010; Al-Hashimi, 2010); the data is then moderated by means of comparing outcomes with those derived from secondary source information and with logistics solutions in standard operating conditions (Pettit and Beresford, 2009). Specifically, information covering pre-carriage services, costs, schedules and operating conditions for containerized cargo shipments from Europe to Iraq was collected. In addition, views of agents and shippers were obtained on the performance of principal routes, and on the main factors affecting modal choice, main loading ports and destination hubs.

In 2015 operating conditions in northern Iraq and adjacent regions of Syria were of an extremely fluid and volatile nature, further worsened by the activities of several warring factions – in particular the emergence of the extremist militant group ISIS. Due to this a number of the routes explored are either not currently practicable, or have been 'temporarily suspended'. In this study Corridor 4 is especially vulnerable, providing a route for Iraqi inbound freight and aid cargo via Homs and Palmyra. However, at the time the data was obtained, the main access routes were operational, allowing the research to explore the aid distribution options when conditions are stable or relatively stable.

The humanitarian crisis in Iraq

The UN estimates that, as of early summer 2015, Iraq had between 3.5 and 4.5 million displaced people due to 12 years or so of conflict following the fall of Saddam Hussein's regime in 2003. In recent years, at least in northern and central Iraq, the situation has become even more complex with the rise of ISIS, which has accelerated the instability in parts of the country as well as in neighbouring Syria. Even 'Camp Liberty', a major former United States military base in Baghdad, is now a refugee camp, which was itself attacked during 2013. Six new camps near to, or within Baghdad, have been constructed to accommodate internally displaced refugees from Anbar province and local and foreign non-government organizations (NGOs) are expanding existing camps in accordance with need. The camps act as focal points for aid cargo, and the established towns of Iraq form the base demand for conventional imported freight (UNHCR, 2015).

The humanitarian picture is extremely complex. Large numbers of people have been internally displaced once, but large numbers have also been repeatedly displaced, and some of these have been displaced internally before fleeing camps. The profile of refugee by type therefore covers people who have been displaced and multi-displaced, refugees who are local but stateless and refugees who are seeking asylum. The camps typically accommodate a mixture of these types, and the need for aid covers the full range of aid items (eg food, shelter, water, medicine, clothing and utensils) but in a different balance from camp to camp.

Although airlifts are employed for aid delivery to remote communities and to certain camps, surface transport is the mainstay of aid supply into Iraq. While some land routes into northern Iraq were established through Syria in late 2013, the uncertain security in the region and the expansion of ISIS-controlled areas means that these routes are particularly high risk.

Route choice and risk spreading

The concept of risk spreading in a trade context is not new (see for example Beresford and Zheng, 2010). It is also central to humanitarian logisticians' thinking, such that the delivery of most consignments is successful most of the time (Pettit and Beresford, 2009, 2012). In operational terms this translates into the use of multiple routes to a holding or distribution centre, each offering a different blend of qualities. Ideally, routes are cheap, fast, robust and flexible (Beresford, Pettit and Liu, 2011). In practice, in crisis conditions the most robust route is the preferred option; the cheapest route can often be the least reliable; and the most expensive route (eg airfreight) is a serious drain on resources and unsustainable in the long term.

Routes that are favoured in the long term, therefore, are typically surface, combining shipping with land-haul (normally truck); the route alternatives offer different proportions of sea–truck transport in accordance with risk minimization – something that does not necessarily stem from distance or time minimization on very challenging overland hauls. These principles were tested to their limits in other humanitarian crises, eg the recovery and rebuilding phases following the Rwanda genocide of 1994 (Choi *et al*, 2010). A typical response to fragile or dynamic conditions is route switching, which although resulting in higher costs in the short to medium term, ensures continuity of supply. Reverse rerouting (ie switching movements back to a first-choice route when conditions restabilize) is often possible, provided operating conditions on respective corridors are closely monitored.

Cost and transit time are the main performance measures for shipments from northern Europe to Iraq and five principal routes emerge as key to the import of both commercial freight and aid cargo into Iraq from northern Europe. Two of the case routes now discussed begin in Germany, and three begin in Spain, as detailed in the two sections following.

Multimodal corridors from Germany to Baghdad

Most consignments shipped from northern Europe to Iraq are mixed and include food, machinery and aid cargoes. A high proportion of shipments start from Germany, eg Munich. The routes are long and complex and they naturally lend themselves to multimodal solutions.

Corridor 1: Munich – Antwerp – Jeddah – Aqaba – Baghdad (Table 6.2.1)

Containers normally take one day to reach Antwerp port from Munich inland container depots (ICDs), using road transport only, since the railroad tends to be expensive and the network is not extensive. Two days are required to ship boxes through the port shipping-line interface. The transit time between Antwerp and Jeddah ports is 11 days, and from Jeddah the boxes are transhipped to Aqaba port within three days. At Aqaba port, containers take about two days to be cleared and loaded onto trucks, since no other modes are utilized for boxes for Iraq. Thereafter, the inland route starts from Aqaba port, reaching Turaibeel (Iraq border) and then containers are switched to Iraqi trucks, according to government instruction, to perform the final leg to Baghdad via Highway 10. In total, containers take 23 days to reach Baghdad from Munich, covering 10,504 kilometres.

Table 6.2.1 Corridor 1: Munich – Antwerp – Jeddah – Aqaba – Baghdad

Route Progress	Transit Time (day)	Cost ($US/TEU)	Mode	Distance (km)
Munich ICD	–	160	–	–
Antwerp Port	1	1,210	Trucking	620
Antwerp Port	2	200	Port Charges	–
Jeddah Port	11	1,423	Sea	7,400
Aqaba Port	3	0	Transhipment	1,062
Aqaba Port	2	200	Port Charges	–
Iraqi Border	2	1,500	Trucking	850
Baghdad	2	0	Trucking	572
Total	**23 Days**	**US $4,693**		**10,504 km**

The total cost, as detailed in Table 6.2.1, is US $4,693. This route has higher pre-carriage costs compared to other routes. However, some businesses, especially those shipping technology-based products, have been attracted to the route due to its shorter transit time, and because the Jordanian banks (used by some for Iraqi consignees) recommend using Aqaba port. The shipping leg of 7,400 kilometres (3,996 nautical miles) accounts for 81 per cent of the total corridor distance. However, although this is by far the largest part of the overall journey, it is not dominant in cost terms, representing only 30 per cent of door-to-door costs. Road charges, on the other hand, in aggregate form a higher proportion (58 per cent) of the overall cost. Furthermore, there are still some security problems along the inland route inside Iraq, and therefore some clients tend to use other safer corridors with more certain cargo delivery. Currently, the proportion of cargo on this route is still low, with about 12 per cent of major shipping lines' containers transported from northern Europe to Iraq, indicating that cost and safety factors are still predominant.

Corridor 2: Munich – Hamburg – Khorfakkan – Um Qasr – Baghdad (Table 6.2.2)

This route also begins at Munich, with the operation taking two days for rail haul to Hamburg and two days for vessel loading. Shipping on this route crosses the Red Sea towards the Arabian Sea and discharges containers at Khorfakkan port. The transit time for this leg is the longest at 18 days. Thereafter, containers are transferred to another local base port (Jebel Ali), and then containers are transhipped by feeders to Um Qasr port (Iraq), taking about eight days. At Um Qasr port, containers will be inspected and cleared in about two days. Finally, containers are trucked from Um Qasr via Basra, Amara and Kut and then to Baghdad, as rail is ill-equipped to carry containers, taking about one day to reach the delivery point and covering about 610 kilometres on Highway 6.

Costs are typically US $160 for container stuffing at the ICD, the pre-carriage and port charges from Munich to Hamburg port using rail are US $549 and US $250 respectively. From Hamburg to Um Qasr via Khorfakkan, the freight rate increases to US $2,321 per 20-foot container (TEU), covering the sea leg. At Um Qasr port, each TEU costs about US $655, covering customs clearance, handling, x-ray and delivery. Finally, the Um Qasr to Baghdad leg costs US $630 per TEU.

Table 6.2.2 Corridor 2: Munich – Hamburg – Khorfakkan – Um Qasr – Baghdad

Route Progress	Transit Time (day)	Cost ($US/TEU)	Mode	Distance (km)
Munich ICD	–	160	–	–
Hamburg Port	2	549	Railroad	610
Hamburg Port	2	250	Port Charges	–
Khorfakkan Port	18	2,321	Sea	11,610
Jebel Ali Port	2	–	Transhipment	322
Um Qasr Port	6	655	Port Charges	953
Baghdad	3	630	Trucking	610
Total	**33 Days**	**US $4,565**		**14,105 km**

This route is mainly used for capital goods and high-volume shipments, such as wheat or foodstuffs, for Iraqi ministry accounts. Some delays can occur, especially in Um Qasr port, where berth operations are inefficient. Such conditions have led to congestion in the port, which, in turn, creates vessel queues. Nevertheless, most shipments under contract with government parties are discharged at Um Qasr port, since there is a governmental instruction to all state companies to contribute to port business. Any delay that occurs at Um Qasr port would be covered by the governmental end users. This ultimately affects both mode and route choice as it encourages shippers who have signed contracts with the Iraqi Government to exploit the route via Um Qasr, and to focus on the transit time before discharging at Um Qasr. This leaves the government to bear the costs of any delay, especially where such contacts have high-volume cargoes and include several partial shipments – and any delay, if calculated, would incur high costs. About 70 per cent of major shipping lines' boxes from northern Europe are discharged at Um Qasr.

Multimodal corridors from west Mediterranean to Baghdad

These corridors typically begin in Spain, as regular shipments are made from this country to Iraq. Loads are transported mainly through letters of credit, which have been opened by Jordanian or Emirates banks. Cargoes include tiles, industrial ceramics, animal feed, paper and waste paper.

Regular services from Spain to the Middle East use Valencia port as a hub for western Mediterranean services linking Port Said, Jeddah and Khorfakkan directly. The following corridor analyses will focus on shipments of ceramics and rebuild cargo from Castellon (the biggest ceramic tiles production area in Spain, located in the south) to Baghdad. Trucking is the predominant mode used to transport containers to Valencia. As the export of ceramics is high volume, the flow forms an ideal base cargo onto which intermittent or spasmodic aid freight can 'piggyback', keeping down unit costs and enabling despatches to be reliable.

Corridor 3: Castellon – Valencia – Khorfakkan – Jebel Ali – Um Qasr – Baghdad (Table 6.2.3)

In Castellon, ceramic shipments are normally made in 20-foot containers, due to the cargoes' weight and volume. Each box is transported by a truck to Valencia port within one day, a distance of about 65 kilometres. In the port, container handling and loading operations require about two days before vessels depart. The shipping leg for this route runs from Valencia – Khorfakkan – Jebel Ali to Um Qasr, a distance of 9,443 kilometres within 20 days. At Um Qasr port, containers require two days, under normal circumstances, to be discharged, cleared and loaded onto trucks. Finally, the inland leg requires one day to reach Baghdad, crossing about 610 kilometres to the final destination, using Highway 6.

Table 6.2.3 Corridor 3: Castellon – Valencia – Khorfakkan – Jebel Ali – Um Qasr – Baghdad

Route Progress	Transit Time (day)	Cost ($US/TEU)	Mode	Distance (km)
Castellon	–	145	–	–
Valencia Port	1	326	Trucking	65
Valencia Port	2	196	Port Charges	–
Khorfakkan Port	12	1,441	Sea	8,168
Jebel Ali Port	2	–	Transhipment	322
Um Qasr Port	6	655	Port Charges	953
Baghdad	3	630	Trucking	610
Total	**26 Days**	**US $3,393**		**10,118 km**

Costs start at the Castellon shippers' premises with US $145 per TEU for loading. Trucking to Valencia port costs about US $326. In Valencia port, the total charges per TEU are US $196, and then the shipping leg from Valencia to Um Qasr costs around US $1,441, including all charges. At Um Qasr port, each container costs about US $655. In the final leg, the trucking mode costs US $630 per TEU to Baghdad. The private sector is the main user of this route importing ceramics to the Iraqi market but the Iraqi Government can exploit spare capacity for aid shipments. The consignees deem Um Qasr to be a reasonable gateway to Iraq, since the route to Baghdad is safer than other routes from Syria and Jordan, and the entire motorways used for the final trucking leg are well monitored and protected by the police and army.

Corridor 4: Castellon – Valencia – Port Said – Lattakia – Baghdad (Table 6.2.4)

The route begins at Castellon and containers take about one day to be trucked to Valencia port, a distance of 65 kilometres. Two days are then required for port operations until loading. The shipping leg runs from Valencia port to Lattakia, via Port Said, taking about nine days for 3,660 kilometres. At Lattakia port, each container needs about three days to be handled, checked and cleared. The inland route can only use the trucking mode from the port to the border with Iraq, since no railroad services are

Table 6.2.4 Corridor 4: Castellon – Valencia – Port Said – Lattakia – Baghdad

Route Progress	Transit Time (day)	Cost ($US/TEU)	Mode	Distance (km)
Castellon	–	145	–	–
Valencia Port	1	326	Trucking	65
Valencia Port	2	196	Port Charges	–
Port Said	7	795	Sea	3,088
Lattakia Port	2	260	Port Charges	572
Iraqi Border	4	250	Trucking	650
Baghdad	1	1,750	Trucking	446
Total	**17 Days**	**US $3,722**		**4,821 km**

available for container transport. This route runs from Lattakia via Tartous, Homs, Palmyra and Al Waleed border point, crossing about 650 kilometres within one day. At the border, if there is no delay, boxes can be cleared and switched to Iraqi trucks in one day, and it takes another day to travel 446 kilometres on Highway 1 to the final destination in Baghdad. The costs start accumulating as usual during cargo stuffing operations, which carry a charge of US $145, cargoes are US $326 for trucking to Valencia port and US $196 per TEU for the port's fees. The shipping to Lattakia thus costs US $795 in total. On the Syrian side, each box costs US $260 in the port, US $250 at the border and US $1,750 in total for trucking from the port to Baghdad. Lattakia port conditions are relatively poor and the main berths and handling equipment are mainly designated for break-bulk cargoes.

Further, the Syrian Government has its own influence on the port; applying some restrictions to control transhipments, limiting the number of containers crossing the port and posting high charges for each container. Accordingly, port competitiveness has been enormously affected and traders normally attempt to find other alternatives; however, the route is still viable for time-sensitive shipments, where shippers have to achieve shorter transit time to comply with their swift delivery commitments, and aid cargo often fits into this category. In terms of transport conditions inside Iraq, there are still some security concerns, and consignees tend to arrange for convoys to protect their shipments. Therefore, container movements on this route are relatively small as commercial clients have been influenced by safety concerns and cost, and some decide to find other safer and cheaper routes.

Corridor 5: Castellon – Valencia – Jeddah – Aqaba – Baghdad (Table 6.2.5)

On this route, containers are transported 65 kilometres by truck to Valencia port from Castellon in one day, and two days are required in the port before vessel departure. The sea leg requires nine days and crosses 4,422 kilometres to Jeddah port. In the second shipping phase, containers are transhipped to Aqaba port after three days, through third-party feeders, covering around 1,062 kilometres. At Aqaba port, each container requires two days for processing, and one day to get to the Iraqi border, where containers could be delayed for two days as a result of swapping trucks. The final road leg needs another two days to reach the final delivery point in Baghdad, covering about 1,422 kilometres in total on Highway 10.

Table 6.2.5 Corridor 5: Castellon – Valencia – Jeddah – Aqaba – Baghdad

Route Progress	Transit Time (day)	Cost ($US/TEU)	Mode	Distance (km)
Castellon	–	145	–	–
Valencia Port	1	326	Trucking	65
Valencia Port	2	196	Port Charges	–
Jeddah Port	9	1,066	Sea	4,422
Aqaba Port	3	0	Transhipment	1,062
Aqaba Port	2	200	Port Charges	–
Iraqi Border	2	1,500	Trucking	850
Baghdad	2	0	Trucking	572
Total	**21 days**	**US $3,433**		**6,971 km**

Container stuffing at Castellon costs US $145 per TEU and US $326 for the road leg to Valencia port. At the port, each TEU costs US $196 for handling and loading operations. For the shipping leg, all-inclusive charges from Valencia to Aqaba port, via Jeddah are about US $1,066. At Aqaba port, container handling and clearance charges are US $200 per box, and finally, US $1,500 is a typical total charge from Aqaba to Baghdad, including all charges for trucking and border crossings. This route is often chosen by Iraqi consignees who have a business presence in Jordan, making it easier for them to arrange payments through Jordanian banks. Furthermore, the Jordanian Government adopted some steps to facilitate cargo transit to Iraq via Aqaba to attract more businesses and to revive the bilateral agreement that had been signed with the former Iraqi regime. Therefore, a good proportion of shipments to Baghdad are routed this way, despite some ongoing security issues.

Summary and conclusions

This chapter has focused on some of the multimodal corridors initiated from north Europe and west Mediterranean zones to Iraq, based on major shipping liners' services. Several important points have been highlighted during the discussion, implying that modal choices could vary between shippers and consignees, based on differences between countries of origin and destination. In northern Europe, the cost factor still has a prominent influence on modal choice, and thus, on route selection. This can be seen from the two corridors starting from Munich, where shippers balance cost and transit time, usually preferring to use cheaper modes and a route with a longer transit time and distance, rather than a route with shorter transit time but with higher costs. On the Iraqi side, beside the cost factor, safety and security have a direct impact on modal and route choice, and the tendency is to divert containers to safer routes despite bearing higher costs and longer transit times. Thus, Iraqi consignees' key trade-offs are security or risk versus time, and security/risk versus cost.

Although Iraqi imports from Europe are not dominated by humanitarian cargoes, they are influenced by them as emergency relief and rebuild freight is often taken as make-up loads that contribute to ship-fill on the marine leg. Indirectly this has the effect of reducing cost per tonne of cargo. On the inland transport legs, where distribution is more dispersed, humanitarian freight is often pathed separately from normal trade cargo according to the logistical needs of, for example, the aid agencies.

Governmental policy also has some impact on modal choice, encouraging state companies and ministries to monitor and steer the flows to optimize both cost and reliability; solutions sometimes incur higher costs and longer transit times, but achieve greater reliability and certainty. The case of Iraqi corridors highlights that modal choice is also related to route choice. This can be found when Iraqi consignees tend to use routes via Um Qasr port, which have a longer shipping leg, rather than other routes that include a shorter shipping leg and longer inland mode, indicating that modal choice diversification does not necessarily include shifting to another mode, but could be as an extension of the same mode, which leads to the use of a particular corridor. The case study presented here highlights the importance of commercial considerations in variable and sometimes fragile operating conditions. A key message is that several routes are required in volatile conditions as a mechanism to broker risk, but the key parameters under consideration for all routes, and hence logistics solutions, remains distance, time, cost and an evaluation of risk. This suggests that, even when conditions become uncertain or volatile, service providers, cargo owners, shippers and agents still concern themselves with the same elements that are of primary concern during standard commercial operating conditions.

In summary, the multimodal transport concept is essential to transport cargoes from Europe to Iraq and several multimodal corridors are being used. Seaports located in neighbouring countries have become vital for linking transport legs in some of the multimodal corridors to Iraq. Nevertheless, the direct corridors to Iraq via its own seaports are still more attractive compared to other routes, as a result of safety and security concerns and government policy. The major shipping lines use several corridors to broker risk and to enable performance and process comparisons to be made.

Finally, an interesting finding of this study, emerging from the case study routes, is that there is a fairly strong inverse relationship between overall transport costs and speed. That is to say, for the movements originating in Munich, the slower route (Route 2) is significantly cheaper than the quicker route (Route 1). Although this comparison is dependent on a comparatively limited set of data, this inverse relationship is also visible with the shipments originating in Castellon: the three Castellon–Baghdad routes also show a clear inverse relationship between cost and speed. This opens opportunities for testing the time/cost sensitivity of unitized freight more rigorously in both unstable emergency and stable commercial environments.

References

Al-Hashimi, Z (2010) Multimodal Transport Corridors from Europe to Iraq Based on UASC Line Lifting and Services, unpublished MSc Dissertation, Cardiff University

Beresford, A K C, Pettit, S J and Liu Y (2011) Multimodal supply chains: iron ore from Australia to China, *Supply Chain Management: An international journal*, **16** (1), pp 32–42

Beresford, A K C and Zheng, C (2010) The multimodal transport of flowers between Taiwan and China, in *International Handbook of Maritime Business*, ed K Cullinane, pp 80–102, Edward Elgar, Cheltenham

Choi, K-Y, Beresford, A K C, Pettit, S J and Bayusuf, F (2010) Humanitarian aid distribution in East Africa: a study in supply chain volatility and fragility, *Supply Chain Forum: An international journal*, **11** (3), pp 20–31

Denktas, G and Beresford, A K C (2010) Achieving Competitiveness Through 'Leagile' Intermodal Transport Systems, Proceedings of International Symposium on Logistics, Kuala Lumpur, July

Kormilitsyn, F (2013) [accessed 25 April 2016] UNESCAP Time/Cost–Distance Methodology: A Tool to Identify Barriers and Monitor Performance, Policy Dialogue on Strengthening Transport Connectivity among the South and South-West Asian Countries, 26–27 June 2013, Dhaka, Bangladesh [Online] http://www.unescap.org/sites/default/files/4.4.Time-cost-distance-methodology-ESCAP.pdf

Pettit, S J and Beresford, A K C (2009) Critical success factors in humanitarian aid logistics, *International Journal of Physical Distribution and Logistics Management*, 39 (6), pp 450, 468

Pettit, S J and Beresford, A K C (2012) Humanitarian aid logistics: the Wenchuan and Haiti earthquakes compared, in *Relief Supply Chain Management for Disasters: Humanitarian, aid and emergency logistics*, eds G Kovács and K Spens, IGI Global, Hershey PA

UNHCR (2015) [accessed 25 April 2016] 2015 UNHCR Country Operations Profile – Iraq [Online] http://www.unhcr.org/pages/49e486426.html

PART SEVEN
Warehouse and inventory management

Warehousing in humanitarian logistics 7.1

ALAIN VAILLANCOURT

Jönköping International Business School, Centre of Logistics and Supply Chain Management, and HUMLOG Institute, Finland

Warehousing in supply chains

Supply chains often include some form of warehousing where items can be stored and managed. Humanitarian supply chains are no different and often will include some warehouses, either permanent (the United Nations Humanitarian Response Depot, for instance) or temporary during emergencies (mobile storage units, for example). Warehouses create a physical decoupling point in the supply chain where orders can be grouped or split, as well as a temporal decoupling point where items can be withheld to be used at a later date. Warehousing usually follows a basic set of inventory management processes that include receiving goods, storing goods, picking goods and shipping goods. Additionally, warehouses can also provide value-adding activities such as packing, kitting, quality control, labelling and returns management.

Warehouses can be classified by different type: first, one can classify them according to the ownership of the warehouse, with private warehouses, contracted (sole user) warehouses and public warehouses. Second, one can classify them based on the type of goods handled at a warehouse, where bulk warehouses (for example: grains, minerals, liquids or chemicals) or refrigerated warehouses have specific requirements in relation to their material handling and installations. Third, in the context of imports or special export zones (often called free trade zones) some warehouses can be duty exempt (often called bonded warehouses) under specific conditions. Fourth, warehouses can also be differentiated by the amount of time the goods stay at the location. In the case of cross-docking centres, goods are received from multiple sources and are almost immediately consolidated and shipped to multiple destinations, usually on the same day.

In the humanitarian context, there are two additional types of warehouses that might be used to accommodate the need for urgency. Quick-rotation warehouses are often set up during an emergency and store goods that move in and out on a daily basis to be distributed to affected populations. There are also temporary collection sites that can consist of any form of space available where items can be stockpiled before being sorted and sent to an appropriate warehouse. These two types of ad hoc solutions can be complemented with standard general-delivery warehouses. Other unique characteristics of humanitarian warehouses include high staff turnover, low funding and a large participation of volunteers.

When deciding what type of warehouse or warehouses are relevant for an organization's supply chain, the first thing to consider is the difference between decentralized and centralized warehousing. Centralized warehouses aim to store and ship high volume of goods to multiple clients. By regrouping the needs of multiple clients, centralized warehouses offer two main benefits. First, they enable pooling of safety stocks previously required because of multiple locations and, in turn, reducing the total required safety stock across a network. Second, the reduced number of locations offers the opportunity to focus on standardizing lead times. These benefits come with an increase of transport costs and an increase in distance travelled but with a reduction of total inventory holding costs and economies of scale through higher volume management (Wanke and Saliby, 2009). In contrast, decentralized warehouses allow the use of smaller warehouses closer to the clients in order to reduce transportation costs. However, this also implies bigger safety stocks across the entire network and thus bigger inventory holding costs, as well as less standardized lead times in between warehouses.

In general, the aim of warehouses in supply chains is to reduce total cost while addressing the trade-offs between a large number of smaller decentralized warehouses and a small number of large centralized warehouses. With a large number of decentralized warehouses, transportation costs for replenishments are higher but distribution transportation costs are lower; operation costs are also higher (as the number of warehousing processes required is multiplied by the number of warehouses operated). With a small number of centralized warehouses, cost-efficiencies in terms of operation – from the scale of operations and potential automation – are available although distribution transportation costs will increase. However, a decentralized warehouse network also helps organizations to be closer to their clients and a larger number of warehouses makes the organization less at risk in zones of potential disasters or conflicts. It is important to keep in mind these issues in the underlying trade-off between decentralized and centralized warehouses when considering how to design the network of warehouses required for a supply chain. Other considerations when choosing warehouses inside a supply chain include a good understanding of the demand in terms of quantity, timing and type of product. This will then have to be reflected in choosing the number, size and location of relevant warehouses. In the context of disaster response, the use of mobile storage units for warehouses allows the opportunity to focus on a shorter delivery time by being closer to the beneficiaries, it helps organizations to be flexible in their deployment to different disasters and, in some cases, mobile storage units can solve the issue of a lack of local warehouse capacity where needed.

When the issue of the number, size and location of each warehouse is resolved, organizations will often need to consider if they want to outsource their warehousing activities. Private warehousing gives better control over warehousing strategy and operations and lowers handling costs, while public warehousing results in higher handling costs but no upfront infrastructure costs, as well as more flexibility to adapt to infrequent warehousing needs. It is important to consider the throughput of material through the warehouses when taking the outsourcing decision. With a small/infrequent throughput, a public warehouse where goods are managed by a third party in a facility that stores the goods of multiple other organizations is the most appropriate. As the throughput increases, leasing a warehouse from a third party for only the goods of the organization might be more appropriate. The next step is owning a private warehouse entirely managed by the organization; at this point the throughput will help define if the warehouse should use manual or automated handling systems.

Once the choice of the type of warehouse is narrowed down, strategic, tactical and operational decisions need to be assessed. On a strategic level, the design of process flow and the choice of handling and storage systems are identified to help orient the proper investments to put in place and will be relevant on a long-term basis (around five years). These strategic choices will influence the tactical options on a mid-term basis (around two years) for relevant storage systems, layout designs, equipment and workforce capacity. Finally, operational short-term (on a weekly or monthly basis) decisions will have to be implemented, and will help determine activities such as dock assignments, storage plans and picking plans, as well as workforce assignment.

Assessing the warehouse needs

With a clear understanding of what role warehouses play inside an organization's supply chain, it is important to choose the appropriate warehouse at the right location, and predict the demand it will handle. Warehouse location needs to take into account the costs of operations, including asset acquisition, fiscal opportunities, taxes and the cost of inbound and outbound transportation. Other non-cost-related criteria are proximity to the beneficiary, availability of labour, available resources, and political and security issues. Warehouse locations can be optimized in terms of costs, using different quantitative methods such as the Weber, geometric median, p-median and p-centre problems. These models need basic data such as the number of warehouses, distances to users/customers, quantities, transportation costs and warehouse acquisition costs.

In practice, choosing the location of a regional warehouse might not require an extensive quantitative model as potential locations would be relatively constrained. Industrial zones, areas near ports and airports, as well as near main roads and highways are usually where warehouses are already present and may limit the potential locations of a warehouse. Other constraints might take into account municipal zoning laws, construction laws and the actual physical characteristics of the plot (load bearing, disaster risk, etc). There may be further limitations to consider as a result of a proper assessment of each warehouse, which can include capacity, management, facilities and handling as well as security and access considerations. Finally, warehouses for distribution in the field can face other related constraints of storage through temporary solutions (containers or tents) and proper location to install them.

One of the most important steps in determining a warehouse's requirements is determining demand. With a good understanding of demand it is possible to decide on outsourcing and take the appropriate strategic and tactical decisions to plan the proper warehouse size and material handling requirements. There are two basic approaches for demand planning, one qualitative and the other quantitative. Qualitative methods rely on personal judgement and interpretation from experts. The opinions of specialists in the field and a panel of experts offers the possibility to gauge what are the trends and to help in determining how demand will evolve over time. Quantitative methods require appropriate data in the first place, at the very least the date, quantity ordered and quantity dispatched are needed; additional information such as volume, weight, size, value, packaging type, item description and particular stocking requirements would also be necessary to plan appropriately. Quantitative methods make the assumption that future demand can be forecasted based on the past history of demand.

In the context of humanitarian supply chains, the demand is often unknown in terms of location, quantity and timing, especially when it comes to large, fast onset disasters. Even if demand is well known, there might also be limited funding to respond to an emergency. Nevertheless, trying to determine the demand will help in designing the proper warehouse and taking the proper subsequent decisions. Quantitative models might be useful for major regional warehouses, while local warehouses might benefit from qualitative approaches. Getting information from local experts in combination with a knowledge of ongoing and future programme activities, as well as the funding applied for and received, would give a better idea of potential requirements for warehousing management. This basic information should give an overall idea of the different stocks to be managed – the organization can then plan the different warehouse areas and material handling equipment.

Warehousing material handling equipment

In warehousing, material handling equipment usually consists of dynamic and static equipment. Dynamic equipment is equipment needed to handle and move material around the warehouse such as pallet movers or forklifts, while static equipment is used for storage of relevant items – it can range from simple bulk storing on pallets to complicated racking systems. Other material handling equipment includes unitizing equipment to regroup items together (eg pallets, cartons and roller cages), dock equipment (eg dock bumpers, levellers and cranes) and identifying equipment (eg barcode readers and radio-frequency identification (RFID) tags). The warehouse choice, the demand for storable items, as well as the funding available will influence the type of warehouse material handling equipment used. Other constraints can include a lack of spare parts/maintenance options, untrained staff and structural constraints (such as walls, ceilings and floor strength).

When considering static equipment, there is a trade-off to take into account between the density and access, that is, how compactly stock can be stored and how easily the stock can be accessed to pick the items. Choosing an option with high density will lead to a very high use of space and allow an increase in the overall warehouse capacity. However, as the density of items stored increases, the ease of accessing items in the warehouse decreases; this can be especially problematic when the type of items stored are items that require to be managed in a first-in first-out (FIFO) manner. Often the ad hoc nature of humanitarian activities will lead organizations to opt for storage on pallets. This is a high-density option that helps in reducing costs but is conditional to stacking constraints and will create issues with access. An alternative is pallet racks, which improves ease of access for picking but reduces density. There is a whole range of pallet racks available that can be divided into static pallet racks (fixed pallet racks single deep/double deep or drive-in/drive-thru racks) and dynamic pallet racks where pallets are moved through the racks as they arrive or are picked (either through a mobile system or with gravity and rollers). When evaluating which static system is more appropriate, the following should be taken into account:

- the required ease of access to items;
- the range of order sizes from the warehouse;
- the throughput and number of pallets/boxes expected per item;
- the investment costs;
- the floor/volume utilization;
- the ease of adjustment to the new system and procedures for stock management (FIFO, or first-expired first-out, FEFO).

In the case where items are ordered as cartons or by individual units, a different approach than pallet racks or bulk storing is required. In this case, the use of shelves would be more appropriate as it offers easier access to pick smaller items. Just as is the case with racks, there are different shelving options available, from the standard open-shelf option to shelves where cartons are moved via gravity (carton-flow) or moved mechanically in carrousels. In addition to shelves, modular cabinets might also be used for smaller items. The number of individual items or boxes picked every day, as well as the size of these items, would help define the best static equipment, from standard shelving for low pick-rates to actual pallet racking for high pick-rates.

Dynamic material handling equipment aims to be as efficient as possible and to reduce the travel time and distance for receiving, picking and packing at different workstations. Such material handling choices are related to both the actual layout of the warehouse in terms of aisle width and height, as well as to the choice of static storage used. Other considerations for material handling equipment include the weight and configuration of the items and environmental restrictions. Apart from the usual pallet movers and forklifts, there are a slew of different material handling options such as reach, double-reach and swing-reach trucks.

Another type of dynamic equipment for moving materials is automated systems. These types of systems can include a combination of conveyors, cranes, automated-guided vehicles and robots. These require both a large investment and planning effort and are reserved for warehouses with very high throughputs. The UNICEF Supply Division warehouse in Copenhagen is an example of a highly automated warehouse, with cranes and guided conveyors. If the funding is available and the throughput high enough for an automated warehouse, there are different aspects to take into account when evaluating the best automated option, such as performance measure (speed, capacity, accuracy, efficiency, repeatability), technical attributes (maintenance, convenience, compatibility with other systems, technology risk, safety), economic constraints (initial cost and operational cost) and strategic issues (flexibility of reconfiguration, reputation of manufacturer and future capacity plans).

Warehouse layouts

Once the role of the warehouse in the supply chain, the warehousing needs and the required material handling equipment have been identified, it is possible to look into organizing a relevant layout to handle and store goods inside the warehouse. The first step in determining how to establish a layout is assessing the amount of space required. This is based on the planned demand over a certain time horizon and can also include any seasonal variations throughout the year, month or week, as well as trends in high-demand and low-demand items, order mix and partial or full loads. In the context of an emergency, not only is the demand often unknown before proper assessments are completed but unsolicited in-kind donations might be delivered, which will complicate the calculation of space requirements. Warehousing space can be divided into different categories:

- Gross space: total warehouse space in square metres (found by multiplying length by width).
- Gross cubic metres: this takes into account the height to the gross space to obtain the total volume.
- Structural loss: space that cannot be used due to characteristics of the structure (overhead obstructions, pillars or walls, for example).
- Support space: space required for administrative offices, maintenance and other amenities such as storing equipment.

- Operational space: space required for receiving, picking in aisles, dispatching and any other activities such as packaging or kitting.

- Net square metres/net cubic metres: the space that is available for actually storing goods.

It is important to note that capacity can be modified in accordance with adaptations to the storage equipment. Indeed, a bulk warehouse where items are stacked on the ground could potentially increase its overall capacity by implementing a racking system. Storage systems will also interact with the type of handling equipment used and the required aisle space, thus modifying the operational space required.

Warehouse layouts are generally divided into four general areas: administrative, reception, storage and dispatch. The administrative area includes space for empty pallets, aisles, room for security, maintenance and other technical areas, offices and meeting rooms, bathrooms, showers as well as other special considerations (eg fuel tanks, generators, etc) or value-adding activities (eg kitting or labelling). The reception area contains the arrival docks, inflow control (for quantities, quality and management purposes), packing and repacking, and quarantine areas. The storage area is where static storage equipment is organized to store the different types of items throughout the warehouse. The dispatch area is where consolidation, packing, dispatch control and waiting for dispatch takes place.

When considering the layout of a warehouse the following objectives should be taken into consideration:

- Maximize the use of space.
- Facilitate the flow of goods to minimize costs and increase productivity.
- Protect items from damages.
- Offer a safe environment for workers.
- Use appropriate materials handling equipment.

Usually warehouse layouts follow a rectangular shape for the actual storage area in order to maximize the use of space. With this layout the shipping and receiving areas can be positioned in one of three configurations, as seen in Figure 7.1.1. When putting down racks there are a few general guidelines to follow:

- Do align the aisles so that they follow the length of the warehouse and are perpendicular to the shipping/reception areas.
- Do not put an aisle along the walls of the building – so as to ensure that aisles serve two sides.
- Do not put racks oriented in a different way in the same area.

Figure 7.1.1 Potential warehouse configurations

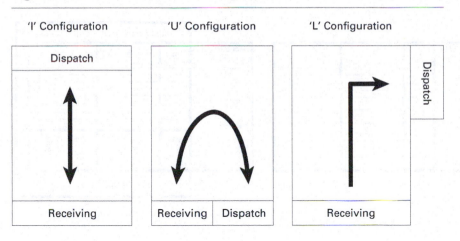

An important aspect of the layout planning is determining the assignment of items to the correct storage location. This planning activity can help to improve warehouse performance by reducing unnecessary movements and thus reducing the cost and time of material handling. Planning usually starts with assigning classes of goods to warehouse storage locations in relation to the receiving and shipping areas or specific considerations (eg cold storage, quarantine, valuable goods). Following this classification, items are then put into each class. Different principles can be observed when choosing which items go into which class; one common approach is to put high-demand items in the closest areas to shipping. Another approach is to disperse high-demand items across warehouse zones to reduce congestion in the aisles. Items can also be put close together if they are often ordered in tandem, or be put in zones further apart if there are safety hazards or a risk of contamination. The characteristics of the item (eg physical attributes, demand, value, dangerous goods) might also help determine if it is kept in a dedicated storage area or if it follows a randomized storage approach. Proper zone decision is important as it will affect the performance of put-away and picking activities. In addition to planning, the proper layout and choosing the location of each zone and item, it is also important to clearly mark the different layout characteristics inside the warehouse. Floor marking for aisles for pedestrians and trucks, as well as a clear address system on racks, can help as reminders of the layout during day-to-day operations.

Warehouse zones play an important role in managing warehouse activities, by dedicating certain areas for specific types of activities or storage.

Figure 7.1.2 Zone management example

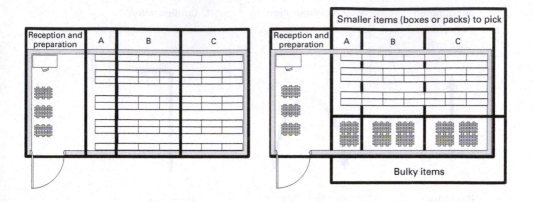

These dedicated zones are planned on the volume of activity required on the specific type of throughput and items used. Zones can be used to decide where to place items inside a warehouse. Figure 7.1.2 offers an example of zone management. In one case, the warehouse only uses shelves; in the other pallets are used for bulky items, and thus two zones are created for different item types that require different storage equipment. An additional use of zones is to classify items based on their turnover (in Figure 7.1.2 items 'A' have the highest turnover, followed by 'B' then 'C') and assign them to zones according to the proximity of the zone to the order preparation area.

Inventory management processes

Inventory management processes can be split into three general categories: receiving, monitoring and controlling goods, and dispatching. There are multiple types of stocks, such as general stocks, transit stocks, safety stocks, preparedness stocks and seasonal stocks. The point of these processes is to manage these stocks appropriately. There are different costs associated with stock management such as procurement costs (per unit and per order), storage costs (investment costs, warehouse space and insurance costs) as well as stock-out costs (in the commercial sector this is the cost of a missed sale, while in the humanitarian sector the stock-out cost is the inability to respond to the needs of the beneficiary and is much harder to estimate); these affect service levels – and in the humanitarian organization are hard to quantify.

Receiving

The receiving process usually starts with an order placement, which needs to take into account different factors such as the demand, the number of products, potential for delays, any potential discounts and the relevant costs. There are a number of different models and heuristics (near-optimal models) that can be used to calculate the best amount to order, as well as the proper time to order.

One of the simpler methods used for stock ordering is the economic order quantity (EOQ) model. This model determines a fixed order quantity under the condition of uncertainty. The model is based on the trade-off between inventory carrying costs and procurement costs, and determines the optimal quantity required to minimalize total costs. There are other similar approaches that help in establishing replenishment policies for stocks to address an unknown demand. One approach is to order a quantity that increases stock levels to a predefined point when stock levels dip below a certain threshold. Another approach is to order stock at predetermined time intervals to raise the stock level back up to a predefined point. Both approaches can be combined with stock-level checks at specific time intervals; if the stock levels reach a certain point, an order is made of a quantity that brings stock levels back up to a predefined point.

The receiving processes not only include the reception of replenishments to the warehouse but also include the management of incoming trucks, which require room for circulation, parking and accessing docks. Dock assignment policies might also be put forward if needed. Once in the receiving area some controls will be made on the deliveries. Some administrative control of documents related to a shipment is required to ensure that everything is in order. This is followed by a quantitative and qualitative control where the accuracy of quantities, weights and the absence of defects and broken items or packaging is confirmed through a physical examination. This control further helps in identifying any leaks, broken/rusty packages, evidence of rifling and torn labels. Further randomized controls might be required following appropriate testing protocols, but this will be dependent on the individual items and the specifications they need to meet. Following this, the items will be brought to their assigned location with the appropriate material handling equipment, or returned if they fail some of the controls. If necessary, items might need relabelling or repackaging before they are put away in the warehouse.

Monitoring and controlling

After goods reception comes monitoring and controlling of items in storage. One way to monitor stock is to organize physical counts, which are comprised of two general steps: checking physical stock against a stock report, and verifying that all records (eg receiving, dispatches, expiry dates and batches) support the documented balance. The physical count will help show that records are up to date; that all records are complete; that quantities are received, stored and dispatched correctly; that actual quantities respond to documented quantities; and that materials are in good condition and correctly stored.

Counts can be done through sporadic spot checks, cycle counts or full physical counts. Usually a full physical count is required at least once a year for accounting purposes. However, a full physical count requires a halt in warehousing operations as such; for a warehouse with a large amount of stocks, a rolling inventory count, where different sections of the warehouse are counted at different times, might be appropriate. Spot checks can be done at any time during the year and can be either random or directed towards items with high demand or high value. There are other aspects of control and monitoring relevant to inventory management. One aspect is to make sure the information about stock is recorded in the relevant system or ledger. Another aspect is the use of stock control cards, manual or electronic, available for each item in the warehouse and on which information on quantities, put-away and picking, the physical address of the goods inside the warehouse and any other information required (eg project, value, purchase order number) are kept up to date.

Monitoring and controlling of goods can help find any inaccuracies that need to be adjusted in the proper ledgers and systems. Monitoring and controlling can also lead to the discovery of expired or damaged goods held inside the warehouse. When this situation arises, it is important to quarantine the items. Depending on the type of items, the issue with them and following evaluation by a knowledgeable expert, different options are available to manage quarantined items. Items can be donated to a selected recipient, sold to a known buyer, reused in another programme according to donor requirements, returned to the supplier if appropriate, destroyed or recycled. If the material is to be disposed as waste it is important to follow proper guidelines and local laws, with the supervision of a specialist if necessary.

Dispatching

The dispatch process follows the receiving and inventory management processes. It is important to consider what and who triggers the process for the dispatch. When the items to be dispatched have expiry dates, the use of the first-in first-out (FIFO) or first-expired first-out (FEFO) approach is appropriate. Once the stock owner requests a stock release for programme activities, the next step is to plan the picking of items. This is the actual collection of items (from shelves or pallets) to fulfil an order; it can be prepared with a pick list that specifies information such as the name of the item, the batch and expiry date if applicable, the quantity to pick and its location in the warehouse. Picking is also linked to the layout: the different decisions taken on where to place items inside the warehouse during the layout planning will affect the efficiency of picking activities.

As picking requires handling and moving goods across the warehouse, proper planning of picking helps to reduce costs through the efficient use of labour and equipment. There are two general picking strategies: either picking across the whole warehouse or only picking in specified zones. When zones are used, the items are either consolidated after each zone is picked, or an order is passed on from zone to zone. Zone picking is especially useful for large warehouses as it helps prevent bottlenecks and can help pickers to become more knowledgeable about items held in inventory.

Once the picking strategy is chosen, further considerations must be given to evaluating the different picking options. The first step to selecting the most appropriate pick option is to determine if each order should be picked individually or if picking will be done for multiple orders, as well as whether the sorting of orders should take place immediately or at the end of the picking. The second step is to determine if items should be packed as they are picked, or if they will be packed after the picking process. To help determine which approach best suits a warehousing operation, the number of units per order line and the number of order lines per picking list should be considered. A high number of units per order line would require orders to be picked individually, while a low number of units per order line would require picking multiple orders at the same time. When it comes to a high number of order lines per picking list, picking then packing later would be preferable, while a small number of order lines per picking list allows orders to be picked and packed.

With the picking strategy and best picking options determined, the next step is to establish route picking policies. The objective of route picking is to sequence the items on a picking list in an efficient route through the warehouse. When it is impossible to calculate the optimal route, several different methods are available to organize pick routes. These include s-shape, returns, midpoint, largest gap and combined approaches:

- In the s-shape method the order picker enters only aisles where there is an item to pick and traverses it entirely. This approach is easy to organize and can be useful if picking is done with material handling equipment, which cannot easily turn around in the aisles.

- The return method aims to have the order picker enter and leave the aisles from the same end and is only efficient if the aisle is a dead end.

- The midpoint method splits the warehouse into two areas along the middle of each aisle; pickups in the front half are done from the front aisles and pickups from the back half are done from the back aisles, stopping at the middle. This approach is more efficient than the s-shape if the pick route averages one pick per aisle.

- The largest gap method is similar to the midpoint approach except that the order picker will enter the aisles as far as the largest gap between two adjacent picks, or a pick and the end of the aisle, with the largest gap not travelled.

- Composite methods include a combination of multiple methods, and require some dynamic programming to establish exactly the picking process.

Following the picking process, it is important to update inventory information, stock card and records. The material will then be prepared in the dispatch area for dispatch. At this point, some form of repackaging of the stock might be required in order to fit the mode of transport and to prevent damages. Before the items are loaded, an appropriate control of the item quality, quantity and accompanying paperwork must be done. Loading must be done with the appropriate material for the transportation mode in order to ensure that no items are damaged.

Warehouse management systems and performance improvement

In order to analyse the warehouse needs, identify the appropriate material handling, layout and processes, and monitor and control warehouse activities, data and the means to record it are required. Warehouse management systems

(WMSs) play an important part in collecting this data and processing it. Information systems in general, and WMSs when properly used, offer a range of benefits for humanitarian organizations by enhancing needs assessments, sharing lists of supply, communicating information to programme staff, giving accurate financial information, providing relevant reports, helping monitor stock and helping to measure the overhead of logistics costs.

WMSs can vary in complexity; the simplest WMS helps with stock control and location while an advanced WMS can help in planning resources and activities as well as analysis. A complex WMS can cover multiple warehouses and track items to optimize decision making according to multiple storage strategies, as well as interface with automated handling of materials. A WMS can also be a module inside an enterprise resource planning system and can share information with other modules, or be used as a standalone system. Depending on the complexity of the operations, a WMS can be standard or custom-made; standard WMSs require the organization to adapt its processes and structure to the functionalities of the WMS, while custom WMSs are tailored to the organization's needs. Custom WMSs are useful for highly complex warehouses; however, they are more costly due to their complicated requirements, which extends implementation times. A key issue with regard to WMSs in the humanitarian context is the lack of resource and infrastructure issues, as some WMSs require electricity and good internet access in order to be useful. The access to computer-trained staff who can actually use the WMS effectively might also be an issue.

A WMS helps in simplifying stock control as well as acting as a repository for relevant operational data, which can then be used for analysis either through standard reports or through manipulation of these reports. The benefits of a proper WMS and its standardized data depend on the quality of the data first put into the system. These benefits include but are not limited to:

- improve or optimize stock location, transit and movement, schedules of activities, packing, picking routes, layouts and resource use;
- improve tracking and tracing;
- reduce discrepancies in inventory counts;
- reduce errors in order preparation.

Another practical aspect of a WMS can be its ability to interface with data-capturing material. This can come in varied forms such as keyboards, magnetic bands, voice recognition, optical detection, barcodes and RFID.

The two most common systems are barcodes and RFID. Barcodes are ubiquitous and offer a simple way to encode data relevant to stocks and read it either through a handheld device or through an automatic reader. Barcodes follow specific international standards that might change depending on the region or industry. Warehouses also have the option to print their own barcodes to put on their stock to help in collecting relevant data. One of the issues with barcodes is the limited amount of information that can be encoded in them; however, the recent development of two-dimensional barcodes (such as QR codes) allows users to encode more data. RFID tags contain a certain amount of coded information that they communicate to receivers installed at crucial points of the process through the warehouse. RFID tags offer real-time dynamic data, can communicate without direct line of sight, have a long reading distance and multiple tags can be read at the same time. These characteristics make RFID exceptionally good at tracking and tracing goods, but RFID tags can be expensive, depending on their technical details, and there can be issues when used with metals and liquids.

With the data accumulated from a WMS it is possible to put in place warehouse performance improvement projects. Warehouse performance is important for the organization managing the warehouse as well as for the organization receiving the goods. Internal performance includes throughput time, storage costs, handling costs, age of stock, and safety and security. External performance includes delivery time, product quality, product cost and flexibility. In the humanitarian context, flexibility is one of the most important performance indicators and achieving it might come with some additional costs, but will improve a warehouse's capacity for disaster response. Warehouse performance improvement projects can be done either through re-engineering or continuous improvement. Re-engineering consists of rethinking management and process activities from scratch, while continuous improvement consists of small incremental changes to current activities. Improvement projects follow these steps:

- Identify the area to improve.
- Identify the problem.
- Find potential causes.
- Put forward solutions.
- Evaluate and choose solutions.
- Implement a plan to put in place the solution.
- Measure the results and correct any issues.
- Standardize and implement the solution throughout the organization.

To support the analysis of problems and improve warehouse performance, there are different tools available. If accurate and relevant data is present in the WMS, the data can be used in conjunction with quantitative tools such as sensitivity analysis, ABC analysis, linear programming and even simulations. If the data is inaccurate, non-existent or not relevant for the problem at hand, qualitative tools such as process maps, ishikawa (or fish bone) diagrams, sociograms and causal maps can be used instead.

One especially useful method in warehousing is the ABC analysis. The ABC analysis is based on the notion that 20 per cent of the items in stock will account for 80 per cent of the cumulative percentage of the scores for the criteria being investigated. However, this is an approximation and in reality these percentages will not be exact. Nevertheless, this analysis helps in narrowing down the items represented in the biggest weight across all items according to the criteria selected and helps focus the efforts on a limited set of items for a greater impact. This analysis can be used in order to categorize issues according to their importance and help focus attention on them.

The choice of different ranking criteria in the ABC analysis can lead to different results. For instance, an analysis that uses the volume of items as a criteria would help focus attention on the 20 per cent of items that represent around 80 per cent of the volume. This analysis would help in identifying storage needs for different item categories. An analysis of the turnaround of each item would identify the 20 per cent of items with the fastest turnaround. This analysis would help in deciding what items to place closest to the order preparation area to facilitate picking activities. An analysis of the age of stock would help in identifying the 20 per cent of items that account for the 80 per cent of age of stock. This analysis would help in identifying slow-moving items and help address any issues with the stock owner about distribution to the field. Of course it is important to understand the characteristics of the data, for instance in the last example of the age of stock, because if the warehouse has an important contingency stock for an emergency that has never occurred then this would skew the data.

Warehouse security and safety

The final important choice for warehousing is the level of security required. Security is an issue for every warehouse but especially for humanitarian warehouses that may be deployed in conflict or disaster areas where the security of the environment is problematic. Warehouse safety and security is made more complex due to the fact that rules or laws can differ from country to country and their in-country interpretation or application can be fraught with ambiguity, for example, the definition of an acceptable risk level and the availability of proper warehouse installations may vary. There are a multitude of potential risks present in warehouses. These risks are accentuated in the humanitarian context either by the lack of resources or by the unavailability of proper warehouse premises and the subsequent use of inadequate buildings. The main risks are:

- hits, collisions of mobile and fixed equipment;
- falls or collapses of racks;
- fire;
- explosions;
- floods;
- pollution of water, air and soil;
- vermin;
- theft.

There are different approaches to reducing warehouse risks. To address the risks of hits and fire, the following should be kept in mind:

- Hits, collision and falls/collapses:
  - Add bumpers to racking.
  - Build and assemble racking according to specifications.
  - Use the right material handling equipment with the racking.
  - Enforce rules for pedestrian and motorized aisles.
  - Enforce weight limits for stacks and equipment.
  - Ensure floor maintenance.
  - Ensure material-handling maintenance.
  - Use appropriate lighting.
- Fires:
  - Limit the amount of flammable material in the warehouse.
  - Do not store items together that might lead to a chemical reaction.
  - Enforce smoking bans.
  - Implement good electrical maintenance.

- Use caution with welding activities.
- Keep the warehouse clean.
- Use the proper containers and material-handling equipment for flammable goods.
- Establish clearly marked and accessible fire exits.
- Install smoke detectors.
- Install adequate firefighting equipment (eg sprinklers, fire extinguishers, water hose).
- Ensure appropriate distance of the warehouse from houses and roads/railways.

Certain items might be dangerous in their own right (for instance chlorine) while others might become dangerous when mixed (or when mixed with water during firefighting). As such, being knowledgeable of the different dangers and risks from each item is important. Another important issue when emergency strikes inside the warehouse is how critical the response time is. The steps required when an incident occurs are usually:

- triggering of the detection system;
- informing the response team;
- verifying the potential issue;
- recognizing the nature of the issue;
- transmitting the information to local emergency services;
- waiting for the arrival and deployment of emergency services.

For organizations working in humanitarian activities, there may not be any emergency services available, which makes the relevance of proper safety procedures, training and equipment even more important. Operating in a difficult environment with limited resources can create some issues when keeping stocks safe and secure, especially when considering pharmaceutical and nutrition items. Special consideration should be given to these classes of items; the most important is following FEFO as opposed to FIFO. Another issue is proper temperature control, as pharmaceutical items might lose efficacy and nutrition items can spoil or become rancid. This in turn increases costs when items are discarded or, worse, jeopardizes the health of users if they are distributed. Unfortunately, cold storage rooms are not always available in the field, which can preclude the storage of items such as vaccines. Nevertheless, items that should be stored below 30°C might be present in the warehouse. Here are some simple procedures to accommodate these items:

- Measure and record temperatures across the warehouse (both on the floor and at different heights up to the roof).
- Measure these at different times of the day and throughout the year.
- Document and create a diagram of temperature averages and variations in the warehouse.
- Place the items that have temperature guidelines in areas with cool and stable conditions.

Pharmaceutical and nutrition items should be kept cool and clean as well as be checked for spoilage or vermin. These items should be inspected, cleaned and, if required, appropriately discarded if the following are discovered:

- insects, spider webs, cocoons or faecal matter;
- water damage (mould, stains, discolouration);
- leaks or tears in packaging;
- bulging, rusting of tins or fermentation.

Conclusion

Warehousing in humanitarian logistics plays a key role for humanitarian organizations in both preparing and responding to sudden disasters. In the context of emergencies where there are issues of unknown demand levels and a lack of resources, proper warehouse management can benefit organizations. On a larger scale, regional warehouses offer the possibility to store contingency stock in advance of a crisis and put in place standard operation procedures to respond in an efficient manner to sudden emergencies. At the field level, warehouses play an important role for proper inventory management and safe distribution to the beneficiaries. For organizations that operate in a more stable environment and deal with issues related to development where programme activities and demand are well known, proper planning of warehousing needs in the network will lead to improvement in terms of cost and inventory management. The distinction between sudden disasters or volatile conflicts and development activities and protracted conflicts will lead organizations to make their strategic decisions for warehousing decisions, taking into account the trade-off between decentralized and centralized warehousing networks. Once the type of constraint is known, proper planning for either an unknown demand or a steady long-term approach can help define the underlying systems to be put in place in the warehouse.

Lessons learnt

The lessons that this chapter has tried to illustrate are as follows:

- Understand the role of the warehouse inside an organization.
- Understand the different decisions to make when designing layout and processes.
- Understand the basics of improving performance in a warehouse.
- Understand the basic issues for keeping the stock safe, secure and usable.

Reference

Wanke, P F and Saliby, E (2009) Consolidation effects: whether and how inventories should be pooled, *Transportation Research Part E*, **45**, pp 678–92

The ABC analysis

7.2

ALAIN VAILLANCOURT

Jönköping International Business School, Centre of Logistics and Supply Chain Management, and HUMLOG Institute, Finland

To support the analysis of problems and improve warehouse performance there are different tools available. One especially useful method in warehousing is the ABC analysis. This analysis can be used in order to rank in-stock items according to a specific criteria to organize them in different classes. These classes are based on a specific characteristic of the items, which needs to be assessed for potential improvement or for a particular management procedure. The choice of different ranking criteria can lead to different results. For instance, an analysis that uses the volume of items as a criteria would help focus attention on the 20 per cent of items that represent around 80 per cent of the volume of stock. This analysis would help in identifying storage needs for different item categories. An analysis of the turnaround of each item would identify the 20 per cent of items with the fastest turnaround. This analysis would help in deciding what items to place the closest to the order preparation area to facilitate picking activities. An analysis of the age of stock would help in identifying the 20 per cent of items that account for 80 per cent of age of stock. This analysis would help in identifying slow-moving items and help address any issues with the stock owner about distribution to the field.

Once an issue is identified for further improvement, and a basic stock classification is used to address this issue, it is important to decide which criteria is relevant and what it represents. It is also possible to combine multiple criteria together to create a macro criteria. Once the results are obtained they should be analysed and used to prepare and guide the proper course of action. Of course it is important to understand the characteristics and the context of the data. For instance, in the case of the age of stock, if the warehouse has an important contingency stock for an emergency that has never occurred then this would skew the data.

The steps of the ABC analysis are as follows:

- Step1: rank the items in descending order of importance according to the criteria, and sum the total of the criteria for all items.
- Step 2: calculate the per cent for each item in relation to the total of all items.
- Step 3: calculate the cumulative per cent of the total for each item (using the ranking done above).
- Step 4: identify the items that account for the most important weight of the criteria and their relevant categories: A are the top 20 per cent of items that account for 80 per cent of the criteria, B are the next 30 per cent of items that would account for another 15 per cent of the criteria, with the last 50 per cent, C, accounting for 5 per cent.

In the following example, an NGO running medical programmes has received funding for medication from the European Commission's Humanitarian Aid and Civil Protection (ECHO) department, with a contract stipulating that at the end of the project there needs to be only 5 per cent of value left in stock. At the beginning of the project an ABC analysis is done on the reception of items with their value in order to identify critical items for which consumption must be tracked and reported on frequently:

1 With a total stock value of US $11,357.48 and 488,310 items, identify which items would be A items, B items and C items.

2 How would this ABC analysis influence your warehouse reporting for programme activities?

3 How would this ABC analysis affect field distribution?

The list of items can be found in Table 7.2.1 and the ABC analysis classification can be found in Table 7.2.2.

Table 7.2.1 Item list for ECHO inventory

Item Name	In Stock	Value Per Unit of Item (US$)
ACETYLSALICYLIC ACID, 100 mg, tab.	1680	0.452
ADRENALINE (EPINEPHRINE), 1 mg/ml, 1 ml, amp.	16	0.015
ALBENDAZOLE, 200 mg, tab.	3279	0.008
ALBENDAZOLE, 400 mg, tab.	726	0.008
ALCOHOL-BASED HAND RUB SOLUTION, BOTTLE + DOSING PUMP	52	1.575
ALCOHOL-BASED HAND RUB SOLUTION, BOTTLE 500 ml	118	2.538
ALUMINIUM HYD. / MAGNESIUM HYD., 400/400 mg, tab.	1246	0.013
ALUMINIUM HYD. / MAGNESIUM HYD., 500 mg, tab.	6129	0.003
AMLODIPINE, 5 mg, tab.	5	0.005
AMOXICILLIN / CLAVULANIC ACID, 1 g/200 mg, pder for inj., vial	2227	0.154
AMOXICILLIN / CLAVULANIC ACID, 500/125 mg, tab.	444	0.081
AMOXICILLIN, 125 mg/5 ml, 100 ml susp.	175	0.154
AMOXICILLIN, 250 mg, tab.	37800	0.009
AMOXICILLIN, 500 mg, tab.	5182	0.023
AMOXICILLIN, Bottle, powder for oral susp., 125 mg/5 ml, 100 ml	752	0.278
AMPICILLIN, 1 g, powder, vial	28	0.188
AMPICILLIN, 500 mg, powder, vial	6162	0.074
BENZATHINE BENZYLPENICILLIN, 2.4 M IU, pder, vial	8	0.152
BENZYLE BENZOATE, 25% lotion	189	1.342
BENZYLPENICILLIN (peni G), 5 M IU, powder, vial	539	0.109
BETAMETHASONE, 0.1%, cream	3262	0.18
BIPERIDEN, 2 mg, tab.	385	0.035

Table 7.2.1 *Continued*

Item Name	In Stock	Value Per Unit of Item (US$)
CALAMINE, 15% lotion	20	1.259
CALCIUM GLUCONATE, 1 mg/ml, 10 ml, (2.23 mmol) amp.	382	0.073
CARBAMAZEPINE, 200 mg, tab.	1943	0.009
CEFTRIAXONE, 1 g, powder, vial	98	0.196
CHLORPHENAMINE, 4 mg, tab.	21416	0.001
CIPROFLOXACIN, 250 mg, tab.	33021	0.017
CLOTRIMAZOLE, 500 mg, vaginal tab.	554	0.102
CLOXACILLIN, 250 mg, cap.	28800	0.015
CLOXACILLIN, 500 mg, cap.	3454	0.003
CLOXACILLIN, 500 mg, powder, vial	630	0.095
COTRIMOXAZOLE, 200 mg/40 mg/5 ml, pdr for oral susp.	3390	0.297
COTRIMOXAZOLE, 400 mg/80 mg, tab.	525	0.01
COTRIMOXAZOLE, 800 mg/160 mg, tab.	140	0.009
DEXAMETHASONE SODIUM PHOSPHATE 5 mg/ml, 1 ml inj	123	0.069
DICLOFENAC, 25 mg, tab.	3147	0.004
DICLOFENAC, 50 mg, tab.	1054	0.005
DOXYCYCLINE, 100 mg, cap.	5562	0.007
ENALAPRIL, 5 mg, tab.	10401	0.0003
ERYTHROMYCIN, 125 mg/5 ml, 100 ml, pdr for oral susp.	24	1.102
ERYTHROMYCIN, 250 mg, tab.	752	0.02
ETHINYLESTRADIOL/LEVONORGESTREL, 0.03/0.15 mg, tab.	830	0.073
FERROUS FUMARATE 100 mg/5 ml oral suspension	66	0.556
FERROUS SULFATE/FOLIC ACID, 200 mg (65 mg iron)/0.4 mg, tab.	16261	0.002
FOLIC ACID, 5 mg, tab.	41730	0.003
FUROSEMIDE, 20 mg/ml, 2 ml, amp.	41	0.002
FUROSEMIDE, 40 mg, tab.	1969	0.002

Table 7.2.1 *Continued*

Item Name	In Stock	Value Per Unit of Item (US$)
GENTAMICIN, 20 mg/ml, amp.	902	0.037
GENTAMICIN, 80 mg/ml, amp.	203	0.079
GLIBENCLAMIDE, 5 mg, tab.	1387	0.004
HALOPERIDOL, 5 mg, tab.	1008	0.006
HYDROCHLOROTHIAZIDE, 50 mg, tab.	2344	0.001
HYDROCORTISONE ACETATE, 1%, ointment	17	0.265
HYDROCORTISONE, eq.100 mg base, powder, vial	4254	0.351
IBUPROFEN, 200 mg, tab.	15947	0.004
IBUPROFEN, 400 mg, tab.	474	0.008
ISOSORBIDE DINITRATE, 10 mg, tab.	138	0.013
LEVONORGESTREL, 0.75 mg, tab.	141	0.107
MEBENDAZOLE, 100 mg, tab.	1157	0.006
MEDROXYPROGESTERONE, 150 mg, 1 ml, vial	141	1.141
METFORMIN, 500 mg, tab.	17152	0.007
METFORMIN, 850 mg, tab.	10828	0.002
METHYLDOPA, 250 mg, tab.	368	0.021
METOCLOPRAMIDE, 10 mg, tab.	1992	0.0003
METRONIDAZOLE, 200 mg/5 ml, pder for oral susp.	144	0.626
METRONIDAZOLE, 250 mg, tab.	4022	0.001
METRONIDAZOLE, 500 mg, tab.	5008	0.009
METRONIDAZOLE, Bottle, 5 mg/ml, 100 ml, plastic bt. for infusion	203	0.579
MICONAZOL nitrate, 2%, cream	4749	0.004
MULTIVITAMINS, tab.	6710	0.005

Table 7.2.1 *Continued*

Item Name	In Stock	Value Per Unit of Item (US$)
NIFEDIPINE, 10 mg, immediate release cap.	1141	0.043
NIFEDIPINE, 20 mg, controlled release cap.	1681	0.012
NYSTATIN, 100.000 UI, vaginal tab.	1350	0.041
OMEPRAZOLE, 20 mg, cap.	818	0.011
ORAL REHYDRATION SALTS (ORS), 20.5 g/l, sachet	10621	0.029
PARACETAMOL, 100 mg, tab.	33450	0.001
PARACETAMOL, 500 mg, tab.	77600	0.003
PERMETHRIN, 1% lotion	201	1.463
POLYVIDONE IODINE, 10% solution	153	0.164
RANITIDINE, 150 mg, tab.	231	0.013
SALBUTAMOL, 0.1 mg/puff, 200 puff., aerosol	5	1.92
SALBUTAMOL, 2 mg, tab.	5600	0.001
SALBUTAMOL, 5 mg/ml, solution for NEBULIZER	159	0.112
SALBUTAMOL, bottle, 2 mg/5 ml	1589	0.525
SODIUM CHLORIDE, 0.9%, 250 ml, without set	1677	0.282
SPIRONOLACTONE, 25 mg, tab.	892	0.018
TETRACYCLINE, 1%, eye ointment	2160	0.127
VITAMIN A (RETINOL), 200,000 UI, cap.	94	0.015
VITAMIN A (RETINOL), 50,000 UI, cap.	2878	0.009
VITAMIN C (ASCORBIC acid), 250 mg, tab.	19611	0.006
WATER for inj., 10 ml, amp.	224	0.035
ZINC SULFATE, eq. 20 mg zinc mineral, tab.	149	0.004

Table 7.2.2 ABC analysis solution

Item Name	Step 1 Ranked Total Value	Step 2 %	Step 3 Cumulative %	Step 4 Item Class
HYDROCORTISONE, eq.100 mg base, powder, vial	$1,493.15	13.1469%	13.1469%	A
COTRIMOXAZOLE, 200 mg/ 40 mg/5 ml, pdr for oral susp.	$1,006.83	8.8649%	22.0118%	A
SALBUTAMOL, bottle, 2 mg/5 ml	$834.23	7.3452%	29.3570%	A
ACETYLSALICYLIC ACID, 100 mg, tab.	$759.36	6.6860%	36.0429%	A
BETAMETHASONE, 0.1%, cream	$587.16	5.1698%	41.2128%	A
CIPROFLOXACIN, 250 mg, tab.	$561.36	4.9426%	46.1554%	A
SODIUM CHLORIDE, 0.9%, 250 ml, without set	$472.91	4.1639%	50.3193%	A
AMPICILLIN, 500 mg, powder, vial	$455.99	4.0149%	54.3341%	A
CLOXACILLIN, 250 mg, cap.	$432.00	3.8037%	58.1378%	A
AMOXICILLIN / CLAVULANIC ACID, 1 g/200 mg, pder for inj., vial	$342.96	3.0197%	61.1575%	A
AMOXICILLIN, 250 mg, tab.	$340.20	2.9954%	64.1529%	A
ORAL REHYDRATION SALTS (ORS), 20.5 g/l, sachet	$308.01	2.7119%	66.8648%	A
ALCOHOL-BASED HAND RUB, BOTTLE 500 ml	$299.48	2.6369%	69.5017%	A
PERMETHRIN, 1% lotion	$294.06	2.5892%	72.0909%	A
TETRACYCLINE, 1%, eye ointment	$274.32	2.4153%	74.5062%	A
BENZYLE BENZOATE, 25% lotion	$253.64	2.2332%	76.7394%	A
PARACETAMOL, 500 mg, tab.	$232.80	2.0498%	78.7892%	A
AMOXICILLIN, bottle, powder for oral susp., 125 mg/5 ml, 100 ml	$209.06	1.8407%	80.6298%	B
MEDROXYPROGESTERONE, 150 mg, 1 ml, vial	$160.88	1.4165%	82.0464%	B
FOLIC ACID, 5 mg, tab.	$125.19	1.1023%	83.1486%	B
METFORMIN, 500 mg, tab.	$120.06	1.0571%	84.2058%	B

Table 7.2.2 *Continued*

Item Name	Step 1 Ranked Total Value	Step 2 %	Step 3 Cumulative %	Step 4 Item Class
AMOXICILLIN, 500mg, tab.	$119.19	1.0494%	85.2552%	B
VITAMIN C (ASCORBIC ACID), 250 mg, tab.	$117.67	1.0360%	86.2912%	B
METRONIDAZOLE, bottle, 5 mg/ml, 100 ml, plastic bt. for infusion	$117.54	1.0349%	87.3261%	B
METRONIDAZOLE, 200 mg/5 ml, pder for oral susp.	$90.14	0.7937%	88.1198%	B
ALCOHOL-BASED HAND RUB SOLUTION, BOTTLE + DOSING PUMP	$81.90	0.7211%	88.8409%	B
IBUPROFEN, 200 mg, tab.	$63.79	0.5616%	89.4025%	B
ETHINYLESTRADIOL/ LEVONORGESTREL, 0.03/0.15 mg, tab.	$60.59	0.5335%	89.9360%	B
CLOXACILLIN, 500 mg, powder, vial	$59.85	0.5270%	90.4630%	B
BENZYLPENICILLIN (peni G), 5 M IU, powder, vial	$58.75	0.5173%	90.9803%	B
CLOTRIMAZOLE, 500 mg, vaginal tab.	$56.51	0.4975%	91.4778%	B
NYSTATIN, 100,000 UI, vaginal tab.	$55.35	0.4873%	91.9652%	B
NIFEDIPINE, 10 mg, immediate release cap.	$49.06	0.4320%	92.3971%	B
METRONIDAZOLE, 500 mg, tab.	$45.07	0.3968%	92.7940%	B
DOXYCYCLINE, 100 mg, cap.	$38.93	0.3428%	93.1368%	B
FERROUS FUMARATE 100 mg/5 ml oral suspension	$36.70	0.3231%	93.4599%	B
AMOXICILLIN/CLAVULANIC ACID, 500/125 mg, tab.	$35.96	0.3167%	93.7766%	B
MULTIVITAMINS, tab.	$33.55	0.2954%	94.0720%	B
PARACETAMOL, 100 mg, tab.	$33.45	0.2945%	94.3665%	B
GENTAMICIN, 20 mg/ml, amp.	$33.37	0.2939%	94.6603%	B

Table 7.2.2 *Continued*

Item Name	Step 1 Ranked Total Value	Step 2 %	Step 3 Cumulative %	Step 4 Item Class
FERROUS SULFATE/FOLIC ACID, 200 mg (65 mg iron)/0.4 mg, tab.	$32.52	0.2863%	94.9467%	B
CALCIUM GLUCONATE, 1 mg/ml, 10 ml, (2.23 mmol) amp.	$27.89	0.2455%	95.1922%	C
AMOXICILLIN, 125 mg/5 ml, 100 ml susp.	$26.95	0.2373%	95.4295%	C
ERYTHROMYCIN, 125 mg/5 ml, 100 ml, pdr for oral susp.	$26.45	0.2329%	95.6624%	C
ALBENDAZOLE, 200 mg, tab.	$26.23	0.2310%	95.8933%	C
VITAMIN A (RETINOL), 50,000 UI, cap.	$25.90	0.2281%	96.1214%	C
CALAMINE, 15% lotion	$25.18	0.2217%	96.3431%	C
POLYVIDONE IODINE, 10% solution	$25.09	0.2209%	96.5640%	C
METFORMIN, 850 mg, tab.	$21.66	0.1907%	96.7547%	C
CHLORPHENAMINE, 4 mg, tab.	$21.42	0.1886%	96.9433%	C
NIFEDIPINE, 20 mg, controlled release cap.	$20.17	0.1776%	97.1209%	C
CEFTRIAXONE, 1 g, powder, vial	$19.21	0.1691%	97.2900%	C
MICONAZOL NITRATE, 2%, cream	$19.00	0.1673%	97.4572%	C
ALUMINIUM HYD. / MAGNESIUM HYD., 500 mg, tab.	$18.39	0.1619%	97.6191%	C
SALBUTAMOL, 5 mg/ml, solution for NEBULIZER	$17.81	0.1568%	97.7759%	C
CARBAMAZEPINE, 200 mg, tab.	$17.49	0.1540%	97.9299%	C
ALUMINIUM HYD. / MAGNESIUM HYD., 400 mg, tab.	$16.20	0.1426%	98.0725%	C
SPIRONOLACTONE, 25 mg, tab.	$16.06	0.1414%	98.2139%	C
GENTAMICIN, 80 mg/ml, amp.	$16.04	0.1412%	98.3551%	C
LEVONORGESTREL, 0.75 mg, tab.	$15.09	0.1328%	98.4879%	C
ERYTHROMYCIN, 250 mg, tab.	$15.04	0.1324%	98.6204%	C
BIPERIDEN, 2 mg, tab.	$13.48	0.1186%	98.7390%	C

Table 7.2.2 *Continued*

Item Name	Step 1 Ranked Total Value	Step 2 %	Step 3 Cumulative %	Step 4 Item Class
DICLOFENAC, 25 mg, tab.	$12.59	0.1108%	98.8498%	C
CLOXACILLIN, 500 mg, cap.	$10.36	0.0912%	98.9411%	C
SALBUTAMOL, 0.1 mg/puff, 200 puff., aerosol	$9.60	0.0845%	99.0256%	C
OMEPRAZOLE, 20 mg, cap.	$9.00	0.0792%	99.1048%	C
DEXAMETHASONE SODIUM PHOSPHATE 5 mg/ml, 1 ml inj.	$8.49	0.0747%	99.1795%	C
WATER for inj., 10 ml, amp.	$7.84	0.0690%	99.2486%	C
METHYLDOPA, 250 mg, tab.	$7.73	0.0680%	99.3166%	C
MEBENDAZOLE, 100 mg, tab.	$6.94	0.0611%	99.3777%	C
HALOPERIDOL, 5 mg, tab.	$6.05	0.0533%	99.4310%	C
ALBENDAZOLE, 400 mg, tab.	$5.81	0.0511%	99.4821%	C
SALBUTAMOL, 2 mg, tab.	$5.60	0.0493%	99.5314%	C
GLIBENCLAMIDE, 5 mg, tab.	$5.55	0.0488%	99.5803%	C
DICLOFENAC, 50 mg, tab.	$5.27	0.0464%	99.6267%	C
AMPICILLIN, 1 g, powder, vial	$5.26	0.0463%	99.6730%	C
COTRIMOXAZOLE, 400 mg/80 mg, tab.	$5.25	0.0462%	99.7193%	C
HYDROCORTISONE ACETATE, 1%, ointment	$4.51	0.0397%	99.7589%	C
METRONIDAZOLE, 250 mg, tab.	$4.02	0.0354%	99.7943%	C
FUROSEMIDE, 40 mg, tab.	$3.94	0.0347%	99.8290%	C
IBUPROFEN, 400 mg, tab.	$3.79	0.0334%	99.8624%	C
RANITIDINE, 150 mg, tab.	$3.00	0.0264%	99.8888%	C
ENALAPRIL, 5 mg, tab.	$3.00	0.0264%	99.9153%	C
HYDROCHLOROTHIAZIDE, 50 mg, tab.	$2.34	0.0206%	99.9359%	C
ISOSORBIDE DINITRATE, 10 mg, tab.	$1.79	0.0158%	99.9517%	C

Table 7.2.2 *Continued*

Item Name	Step 1 Ranked Total Value	Step 2 %	Step 3 Cumulative %	Step 4 Item Class
VITAMIN A (RETINOL), 200,000 UI, cap.	$1.41	0.0124%	99.9641%	C
COTRIMOXAZOLE, 800 mg/160 mg, tab.	$1.26	0.0111%	99.9752%	C
BENZATHINE BENZYLPENICILLIN, 2.4 M IU, pder, vial	$1.22	0.0107%	99.9859%	C
METOCLOPRAMIDE, 10 mg, tab.	$0.66	0.0058%	99.9917%	C
ZINC SULFATE, eq. 20 mg zinc mineral, tab.	$0.60	0.0052%	99.9969%	C
ADRENALINE (EPINEPHRINE), 1 mg/ml, 1 ml, amp.	$0.24	0.0021%	99.9991%	C
FUROSEMIDE, 20 mg/ml, 2 ml, amp.	$0.08	0.0007%	99.9998%	C
AMLODIPINE, 5 mg, tab.	$0.03	0.0002%	100.0000%	C

PART EIGHT
Information technology

Information systems for humanitarian logistics

8.1

Concepts and design principles

TINA COMES

Centre for Integrated Emergency Management,
University of Agder, Norway

BARTEL VAN DE WALLE

Policy Analysis Section, Department of Multi-Actor Systems,
Delft University of Technology, the Netherlands

Introduction

Disasters continue to topple our expectations: they are unpredictable, unexpected, unprecedented or unimaginable. One of the few certainties, however, is that humanitarians are dealing with an ever-growing number and increasing diversity of disasters. Paralleling these changes, information about disasters has continued to increase in volume, variety and velocity (Van de Walle and Comes, 2014; IFRC, 2013). In this chapter, we characterize specific challenges for information collection, sharing and processing in complex and sudden-onset disasters and map these to the information needs of humanitarian logisticians. Although information management (IM) principles, practices, tools and technologies are often viewed as different from logistics – as is demonstrated in their representation in different United Nations (UN) clusters – we will highlight how information technologies and IM can support the work of humanitarian logisticians in the field.

A key success factor in disaster management is to achieve and maintain situation awareness, ie to understand and interpret 'the current local and global situation and how this may evolve over time' (Endsley, 1995). The goal of any humanitarian logistics information system is therefore to help humanitarian logisticians to attain situation awareness, and provide decision support for the logistics decisions they face. This means that humanitarian logistics information systems need to be designed to collect timely, correct and relevant information about:

- The disaster: needs, gaps and humanitarian priorities; available resources and funding; state of infrastructures and access conditions.

- The supply chain: capacities; goods and delivery status; all actors within the supply chain (eg suppliers; transport and infrastructure providers; end users).

Such systems will support both supply chain operations and strategic planning by improving agile adaptations to the situation on the ground and strategic supply chain adaptation to changing conditions and needs. The challenges of humanitarian logistics have been listed by many (for a recent overview, see Kovács and Spens, 2011) and include a lack of predictability of demand (timing, location, type and volume), short lead times, high stakes associated with the timeliness of deliveries, or a lack of resources and capacities. Beyond those generic points that provide for the setting of our considerations, we here want to focus on challenges that have a specific link to IM and to information and communication technologies (ICT):

- The increasing privacy and security concerns related to both responders and end users that prevent information sharing (eg patient data in the Ebola response or the location of schools, camps, hospitals or bakeries in the Syria crisis).

- The complexity and novelty of supplies that are only partially standardized and pre-packaged (eg personal protective equipment in the case of Ebola), which require an ad hoc adaptation of logistics and monitoring processes.

- A shift from the provision of food and material assistance towards vouchers or cash transfer programmes (CTPs), for instance in the Philippines and Syria (GHA, 2015). Since CTPs rely on electronic transfers or e-commerce, they depend largely on functioning ICT and the private sector. Even in less developed countries, increasing technology adoption will accelerate the change from distribution of relief goods to cash transfers. While this shift locally enables self-organization in the affected communities, it challenges traditional schemes of logistics, (donor) accountability and control.

- New humanitarian actors, such as grass-roots non-government organizations (NGOs), or co-ordinating bodies such as the African Union or the Organisation of Islamic Cooperation (OIC); in 2013, Saudi Arabia and the United Arab Emirates (UAE) became the sixth and fifteenth largest government donors, respectively (GHA, 2015). All these actors bring their own information systems, logistics, management and decision processes, which only adds to the existing lack of interoperability, eg between military and civilian actors.

In the following, we first outline the specific challenges that disaster management information systems must address to achieve overall situation awareness and provide specific logistics decision support. Subsequently, we derive design requirements that will support the further improvement of the systems and tools used today. Beyond those generic points that provide for the setting of our considerations, we here want to focus on challenges that have a specific link to IM and Information and Communication Technologies (ICT); see Figure 8.1.1.

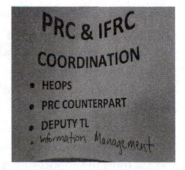

Figure 8.1.1 Humanitarian information management: field realities. Photo taken at the 2013 Haiyan response, Tacloban. IM is only an afterthought

Disaster management information systems

Information and communication technologies enable humanitarians, affected communities and volunteers to create, collect, share and use more information than ever before. Via Twitter, Facebook, blogs or directly through the dedicated websites of UN agencies and NGOs we can see pictures, maps or videos, and follow any ongoing humanitarian operation.

At the same time, retrieving reliable and relevant information that answers specific information needs has become like the proverbial attempt of '*drinking from a fire hose*' (Crowley and Chan, 2010). This environment creates a frantic pattern of constant information requests, surveys, questionnaires, reports and maps from headquarters to the field and back. The response to recent sudden onset disasters such as typhoon Haiyan in the Philippines in November 2013, the 2015 Nepal earthquake, the health disaster of Ebola and probably most prominently the ongoing crises in South Sudan, Central African Republic (CAR) or the Middle East, highlight that the potential of technology has not yet been (fully) transformed into more effective and efficient provision of aid. On the contrary: Twitter feeds, Facebook pages or micro blogs provide – by their very nature – subjective and conversational information that is a snapshot reflecting personal beliefs, attitudes and perceptions, which is in stark contrast with objectivity and neutrality. Yet, along with the rise of ICT there is the expectation that any type and granularity of information is available for anyone at any time. In the absence of agreed processes and procedures to handle, interpret and integrate social media or other primary data into standard reporting, assessment and logistics processes, logisticians and information managers alike are under increasing pressure to deliver granular data – but they are without the systematic means to do so.

Humanitarian logistics has emerged as a discipline relatively recently (Van Wassenhove, 2006). At the same time, information management (IM) is increasingly seen as a key activity in humanitarian response, and an enabler of more effective and efficient humanitarian operations (Van de Walle, Van Den Eede and Muhren, 2009). Less attention has been paid to the development of the link between logistics and the rapidly unfolding potential of new ICT, or the implications of IM for humanitarian logistics. In this section, we review the different IM tools that provide information to support the management functions of humanitarian logistics, as well as specific tools to support logistics processes and tracking.

Humanitarian information systems for situational awareness and supply chain management

Generally speaking, humanitarian information systems are dedicated to three main objectives:

1 assessments: providing an overview of humanitarian needs, the situation on the ground (access, security situation, resources, etc) and monitoring how they evolve;

2 co-ordination of all humanitarian activities to avoid gaps and overlaps;

3 humanitarian briefs and appeals towards donors.

While the third group of headquarters-driven products has important implications for humanitarian IM, we focus here on field-based IM and information systems dedicated to assessments (point 1, above) and co-ordination (point 2).

Assessments

The needs of affected communities can only be addressed if they are identified, assessed and translated adequately into products and services. In very general terms, needs assessments describe how humanitarian organizations identify and measure humanitarian needs in order to determine what assistance shall be provided to whom (ACAPS, 2014). Hence, needs assessments are the basis for accountability towards end users and donors.

For natural disasters, the response typically focuses on supporting the local and national efforts in restituting the situation prior to the disaster. Therefore, assessments typically start with assessing damages and the local and national response capacities. A typical example is the Needs Assessment Report for the tropical cyclone Pam that hit Vanuatu in March 2015.[1] From those damages, the subsequent needs of communities for shelter, food, water or medical care can be derived, and response gaps that need to be addressed by the international community can be determined.

However, in supplying free commodities or services such as housing, rice, water or medicine to meet these needs, local markets that are already affected by the disaster can be disrupted even more. Careful monitoring of market prices, combined with tracking of the goods that are bought in shops or via cash-programmes will help tailor the delivery of goods, and will allow aid agencies to balance the necessary provision of goods with longer-term development aims. In addition, logistics needs to address the loss of livelihoods.

Typhoon Haiyan in the Philippines in 2013, for instance, affected more than 25,000 fisher families who were unable to continue their activities due to damaged or lost boats (see Figure 8.1.2). While restoring the livelihoods of these families – by replacing or repairing the damaged boats – is not traditionally the focus of disaster response, such interventions are becoming increasingly important (GHA, 2015). As the distinction between

Figure 8.1.2 'We Need Food S.O.S.' from Tacloban, field research in the
Philippines in December 2013

disaster response and development becomes increasingly blurred, logistics information systems will need to support community resilience.

For protracted crises, incomplete and fragmented information is characteristic. One of the most prominent examples of such diverse quality of data is the Syria crisis. As of March 2016, ECHO counts 4.6 million Syrian refugees in neighbouring countries and the wider region. In addition, more and more refugees have embarked on the dangerous journey to Europe. The UN High Commissioner for Refugees (UNHCR) reports that since the beginning of the Syria crisis until November 2015, the total number of asylum applications from Syrians in Europe has reached more than 800,000 – the worst exodus since the Rwandan genocide in 1994. The majority of Syrian refugees are living in Jordan, Lebanon and Turkey. Probably the most well-known refugee camp is the Za'atari camp, currently home to approximately 81,500 Syrians, making it Jordan's fourth largest city. The formerly barren desert is crowded with acres of white tents; makeshift shops line the main road, rather ironically nicknamed the 'Champs-Elysées'. While the refugees in the camps and their needs can be relatively easily assessed, the situation within Syria is to a large extent unknown, and it is uncertain how the conflict will continue. Since summer 2014, four different 'Syrias' has emerged: a Syria under the control of the government in Damascus; another dominated by the Islamic State and its local allies; a third in the hands of a plethora of armed groups who call themselves part of the opposition; and a fourth under Kurdish militias. Also in 2014, the UN Security Council adopted a second resolution on humanitarian access to Syria (UN resolution 2165) effectively legalizing cross-border operations, leading to the establishment of a UN monitoring mission and a steadily increasing aid flow through Turkey and Jordan into opposition-controlled areas of Syria. However, the different efforts of the humanitarian response to Syria are still largely unconnected, making it difficult to assess the needs on the ground.

Beyond merely counting population numbers and damage figures, setting up systems to communicate with the local governments and the population requires overcoming barriers such as language/literacy problems, failing infrastructures, lack of knowledge about culture and norms, and difficulties of access. In a nutshell, engaging with the population and local or national governments and decision makers requires that information systems are interoperable, including the definition of common standards and interfaces.

Traditional assessments, such as the Multi-Cluster Rapid Needs Assessment (MIRA[2]), are designed to provide fundamental information on the needs of end users and to support the identification of strategic humanitarian priorities. While MIRA is comprehensive, and typically supported by all stakeholders in the field, it does take considerable time and effort until all data is collected, standardized, verified, approved and finally published. MIRA is an instrument for advocacy and is of limited use for operational purposes, given the time it requires until the report is published, and its lack of granularity and detail. New data-collection approaches that complement the traditional approaches are emerging, and are supported by data collection tools such as the KoboBox,[3] or survey tools that are tailored for a specific purpose, for instance the UNICEF Cholera Toolkit;[4] iMMAP's OASIS is an open-source mobile data collection system that provides a development environment for the production of mobile forms for Android.[5]

Whereas such tools are still relying on humanitarians that collect data on the ground, remote efforts have grown in importance since the Haiti earthquake in 2010. Since then, volunteer and technical communities (V&TCs) have emerged that contribute remotely to the response. Many of these communities or networks, such as Crisis Mappers,[6] Ushaidi,[7] the Standby Task Force,[8] or Humanitarian Open Street Map,[9] are organized under the umbrella of the Digital Humanitarian Network (DHN).[10] Aware of the potential significance of social media in disaster response, technology companies such as Twitter, Facebook and Google have launched specific 'disaster services'. Twitter Alert broadcasts and highlights critical information to the general public when authoritative accounts mark tweets as alerts. Facebook created the Safety Check, for people in a disaster area to check if they/their friends are safe. And Google, through the Crisis Map, displays geographic information, such as storm paths, shelter locations and power outages from a variety of sources, including official and user-generated content. These tools enable users around the globe to provide and share useful information. As such, they provide real-time snapshots and contribute to the situation awareness of responders. However, the link to the official realm of needs assessments is still unclear, and often ad hoc.

Co-ordination

Co-ordination is crucial to disaster response to ensure that humanitarian needs are addressed without duplication of efforts. To this end, co-ordination needs to align the interests of different actors, so that the limited resources and budgets available can be used most efficiently with respect to operational or strategic aims. Challenges to efficient co-ordination range from limited information, unpredictable developments, short time windows and high risks, to competition and conflicting aims. All these issues threaten the decision makers in their ability to make rapid and sound decisions. Efficient disaster co-ordination is mainly facilitated through: 1) organizational structures; 2) collaborative decision processes; 3) the contribution of advanced information systems, all of which are highly interdependent (Chen *et al*, 2008).

The very crux of any co-ordination problem during a crisis is that the exact actions to be taken cannot be predetermined; on the contrary, co-ordination relies on feedback on the prevalent situation (Turoff *et al*, 2004). Response and logistics plans are subject to constant change and updates as new information becomes available. In order to avoid 'threat rigidity' (ie people following predefined plans while not taking into account the reality of new threats in the crisis) logistics information systems need to be designed to embrace flexibility, enabling logisticians to act and adapt as new possibilities or constraints emerge. For instance, the distribution of aid depends on access to affected regions. The logistics infrastructure, however, may be affected by the crisis, either because it is damaged or destroyed, or is still intact but nevertheless cannot be used due to security concerns (Kovács and Spens, 2009). Such concerns are today not systematically integrated into the logistics planning, putting responders at risk and making it difficult to support populations in contested regions.

Knowing who is doing what, where and when, the so-called '4W', has long been among the most important tools for co-ordination, providing information important for the planning of humanitarian assistance. Overlaying 4W maps with information on access and movement of (armed) actors and internally displaced persons and refugees is an important co-ordination mechanism. Yet, the information necessary to populate the maps is often difficult to obtain, and it can take weeks until data is turned into a product, which is clearly problematic when the situation evolves dynamically. Most recently, tracking of humanitarian responders and automated updating of their location and responsibilities has been piloted for Nepal, Vanuatu and the Philippines. The Humanitarian ID provides a platform for decentralized updates of contact information, in which responders 'check in' and 'check out' via an app (Figure 8.1.3).[11]

Other designated disaster information platforms, such as Sahana Eden,[12] focus on the co-ordination and planning of humanitarian operations, providing tools for dedicated tasks such as missing persons registries or volunteer management. Although Sahana includes modules on request and inventory management, material and information flows are not captured completely by this system (Blecken and Hellingrath, 2008).

Figure 8.1.3 Humanitarian ID interface

Overall, co-ordination and needs assessment information systems do provide important background information for humanitarian logistics. To address the full complexity and detail of humanitarian supply chains, however, dedicated logistics information systems need to complement the generic humanitarian information systems.

Humanitarian logistics information systems

One of the key pillars of the Transformative Agenda is the activation of clusters, strengthening their role to inform strategic decision making (IASC, 2015). As such, much of the information regarding logistics is typically shared via the logistics cluster (see Figure 8.1.4). Information on major hubs and distribution lines as well as meeting minutes, contact lists, service request forms, or standard operating procedures (SOP) are publicly available on the global logistics cluster website,[13] and distributed via Reliefweb,[14] or Humanitarian Response.[15]

Many publicly available infographics, dashboards and humanitarian snapshots are designed to improve accountability. Indeed, reporting on activities and needs and measuring progress against the cluster strategy and agreed results are among the cluster core functions (IASC, 2015). Tools such as the UN-OCHA LogIK Tool provide information about which goods were delivered to which destination and enable donors to track and compare the flows of goods (see Figure 8.1.5).[16]

In contrast to such information-sharing platforms, tools developed for humanitarian logistics typically aim at improving efficiency of management and logistics processes. Often, these tools build upon technology that has been initially developed for the business sector. In essence, the aims of such systems are twofold: 1) improving visibility and accountability by providing documentation, monitoring and tracking functionalities; 2) providing specific decision and management-support functions, such as routing and navigation, inventory management, and facility location or distribution planning.

Visibility and tracking

Most well-known comprehensive humanitarian logistics information systems share the characteristics of enterprise resource planning (ERP) systems. These include Helios,[17] LSS/SUMA,[18] HLS by the Fritz Institute,[19] or OpenERP by MSF (Laguna Salvadó et al, 2015b). While these systems can be used for co-ordinating the response with respect to flows of goods, finances and

Figure 8.1.4 Logistics cluster map of the April 2015 Nepal earthquake (as of 4 May 2015)

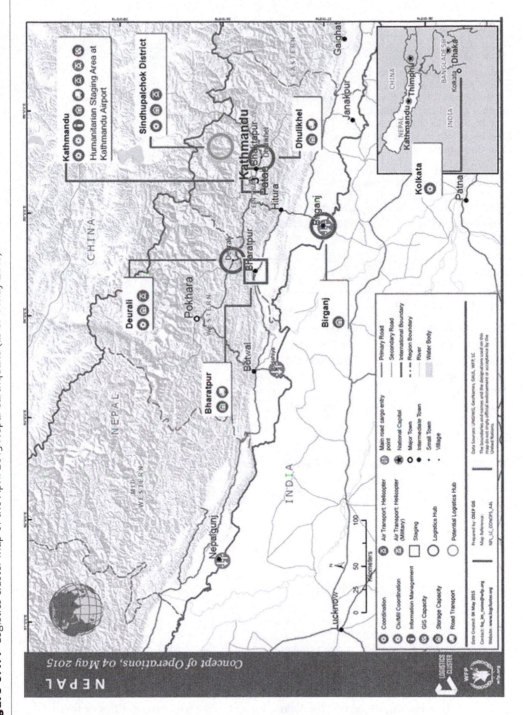

Figure 8.1.5 LogIK screenshot for the 2015 Nepal earthquake

Emergency: Nepal - Earthquake - Apr 2015
In-Kind relief aid as of 9/6/2015 1:27:31 AM
Compiled by OCHA on the basis of information provided by senders
Number of In-Kind Contributions: 77
Total IK value in USD: 29,986,279
Total IK weight in MT: 8,648.097
Total Contributions:

Top 5 Relief Item Categories in USD	
Plastic sheeting	5,106,000 USD
Tent (family tent)	895,296 USD
Hygiene kit	315,434 USD
Blanket	277,200 USD
Plastic roll	193,200 USD

Top 5 Relief Item Categories in Quantity	
High protein biscuit	150,000
Plastic sheeting	148,008
Water purification tablet	120,000
Tent (family tent)	105,971
Blanket	101,784

Top 5 Senders in USD	
Direct Relief International	14,800,000 USD
GlobalMedic	4,915,340 USD
China	3,300,000 USD
United States Office for Foreign Disaster Assistance	2,321,788 USD
Japanese Red Cross Society	918,421 USD

Beneficiaries by Relief Items	
Tent (family tent)	526,880
Kitchen set	128,420
Emergency Health Kit	109,500
Blanket	91,544
Hygiene kit	22,810

Transport:

Mode	Committed	Dispatched	Delivered	Total
Air	10	1	91	102
Road	1	0	133	134
Sea	0	0	0	0

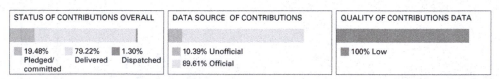

STATUS OF CONTRIBUTIONS OVERALL	DATA SOURCE OF CONTRIBUTIONS	QUALITY OF CONTRIBUTIONS DATA
19.48% Pledged/committed 79.22% Delivered 1.30% Dispatched	10.39% Unofficial 89.61% Official	100% Low

information, the task and activity components (including prioritization of needs) or the management of risks to the supply chain operations are not covered (Blecken and Hellingrath, 2008).

In addition, there are specific tracking systems for commodities or financial flows such as the International Rescue Committee's (IRC) Open Source

CTS,[20] or the World Food Programme's (WFP) OpsFeed[21] (both developed and piloted in response to the Syria crisis), or commercial fleet management and tracking systems such as HumaNav System,[22] which has been adopted by WFP, the International Committee of the Red Cross (ICRC) and the UN High Commissioner for Refugees (UNHCR). These systems provide dedicated information on the location and use of specific goods, often in near real-time, enabling analysis of patterns and detection of outliers or risks. The OpsFeed currently includes information on access conditions and movements of armed actors, goods delivered and end users reached, and allows responders and donors to receive real-time updates via personalized layers of information directly from the ground (see Figure 8.1.6).

However advanced these systems are, they nevertheless typically lack integration in the overall planning, logistics decision making and co-ordination processes as well as specific quality management and control functions. The examples of rotten rice distributed in the aftermath of the 2015 Nepal earthquake,[23] or the non-Ebola-proof donations of personal protective equipment in Accra (Van de Walle and Comes, 2015), highlight the need for better product control and management throughout procurement and distribution cycles.

Decision and planning support

Providing decision support requires that the aims of a logistics operation are clearly defined. Often, however, they are just vaguely described as the 'efficient and effective' provision of aid (Thomas, 2007). Yet, the aims of efficiency and effectiveness are often conflicting: covering vast regions and reaching all end users usually will result in higher cost and slower delivery times. How the strategic aims for an operation are translated into actual logistics decisions depends on the organizational mandate and the type and nature of the disasters to which the response has been deployed. In general, organizations will balance effective and timely delivery with reduction of cost. Since media attention, political interest and presence of non-governmental organizations largely steer the volume of disaster relief goods and assistance available (Olsen, Carstensen and Høyen, 2003), efficient distribution of goods is required, particularly when media attention fades or political interest is low. Examples range from the recovery process of sudden onset disasters in Haiti or the Philippines, to the struggles in the Democratic Republic of Congo.

The 2014 West African Ebola outbreak is an example of flipping between different regimes of operations. Initially, the response received little attention, funding and resources, and initial outbreak control measures came

Figure 8.1.6 Screenshot of the real-time WFP OpsFeed for the Syria crisis, providing information on end users in the region

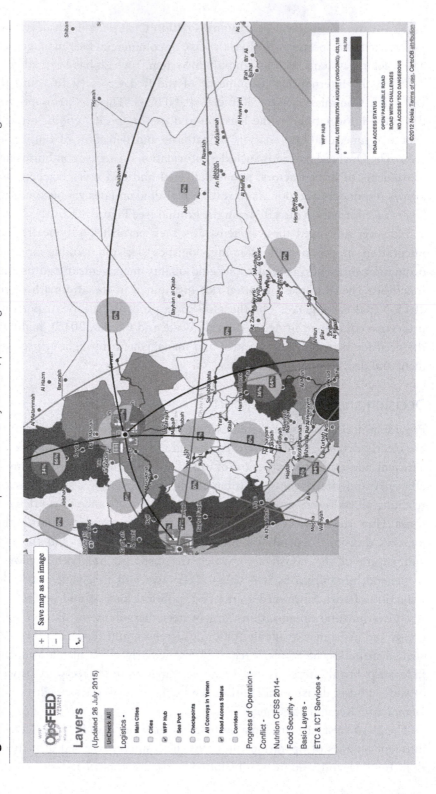

too late or were only half-heartedly implemented (Frieden *et al*, 2014). This implied that the operations of the few humanitarian organizations responding to Ebola at an early stage suffered from severe shortages in terms of staff, protective equipment, medicine, etc. In this regime, operations had to be highly efficient and focused – making most of the little there was. As the 'fight against Ebola' was finally recognized, funding was virtually unlimited, and a massive push-based operation was initiated that was based on effectiveness only (Laguna Salvadó, Lauras and Comes, 2015). Examples include thousands of smartphones and tablets from private donations, although the networks and coverage in the affected countries were unlikely to support their use.

There are a growing amount of simulations and modelling approaches that are designed to support logisticians in addressing facility location problems, distribution problems and inventory management problems (Galindo and Batta, 2013). While such models have improved, in particular, upstream supply chain processes (Van Wassenhove, Martinez and Alfonso, 2012), there is still a considerable gap in supporting operational decision makers in the immediate aftermath of a disaster (Holguín-Veras *et al*, 2012).

To improve efficiency and effectiveness in a humanitarian supply chain the material, information and financial flows need to be managed. To this end, the information systems, as described above, need to be extended and improved. In addition, the aims and priorities of a specific mission need to be communicated and embedded in information-sharing and planning procedures and policies. This also implies that the resources or people with appropriate skills and competences need to be available to conduct the planned tasks (Tomasini and Van Wassenhove, 2009) and that they need to be enabled to make decisions. Yet responders who collect and share information in the field state that feedback is often too late, and too little (Comes, Vybornova and Van de Walle, 2015). Moreover, they often do not perceive themselves as decision makers, although it has been argued that, in disasters, the power to make decisions should shift towards those who are closest to where decisions are made (Turoff *et al*, 2004). Starting from these considerations, we continue this chapter with considerations about the design of humanitarian logistics information systems.

Designing humanitarian logistics information systems

Challenges

The previous sections have provided an overview of information systems and ICT to support humanitarian logistics. Indeed, novel technologies are increasingly often described as a way to improve humanitarian operations in general (Meier, 2014; IFRC, 2013) or logistics in particular (Pettit *et al*, 2009; Kabra and Ramesh, 2015). Still, many logisticians on the ground rely on paper-based lists, white boards, face-to-face meetings and other low- or no-tech options (Altay and Labonte, 2014; Comes *et al*, 2015). Sometimes, even simple tools and checklists are reinvented because organizational infrastructures, co-ordination mechanisms, reporting and decision processes are unclear, as has been documented for instance for the Ebola response (Landgren, 2015). In part, this is due to the destruction or lack of infrastructures such as telecommunication networks, making it impossible to send out short text messages or to download files from the internet (Chan and Comes, 2014). Funding constraints, different organizational cultures or simply the wide gaps between tool developers, information managers and logisticians have so far impeded the development of systems that are tailored to the needs of humanitarians.

In addition, the delays between information collection/reporting and the creation of the final information product, and the limited operational usefulness of such products, conflict with the required 'information focus' of humanitarian information systems (Turoff *et al*, 2004): humanitarians work 14- to 18-hour shifts per day and have little tolerance or time for things unrelated to their immediate dealing with a crisis. This leads to considerable frustration and friction between the co-ordination structures and the field. Operational information sharing still happens ad hoc, often face-to-face, relying on bilateral and personal networks. Technology solutions that do not fit the emerging workflows are at times bypassed or, in many cases, completely abandoned.

The most successful tools for information sharing that fit the needs of field operations include systems such as Skype chat groups, Dropbox folders and also, recently, Whatsapp groups. Those tools support data tracking and exchange logs, enabling users to 'catch up' when connectivity improves while maintaining information-sharing environments with collaborative user groups. Nevertheless, responders continue to rely on direct and bilateral exchange in trusted and highly efficient low-technology environments that often also bypass official channels.

Decision support and analyses that do not adequately take into account the dynamics of the situation can be perceived as unreliable. In the case of Ebola, for instance, the initial assessments by the Centers for Disease Control and Prevention (CDC) communicated a potential 1.4 million cases in September 2014.[24] This number was widely reported without any error margins or uncertainties – and indeed attention increased and funding started to flow. However, the gap between CDC's prediction and the considerably lower number of cases that materialized in reality led to a deep resistance against any predictions and forecasting tools. Consequent planning was based on past and localized information from a few trusted sources – leading to a misallocation of goods, empty Ebola treatment units in parts of the region, untreated patients in others, and high cost (Bartsch, Gorham and Lee, 2014).

The management and co-ordination side of logistics are not explicitly supported by any of the tools described previously. Thus, the organizational challenges of information sharing; the management of relations to donors, partners and suppliers; or the development of security policies, risk assessments and (joint) contingency planning are left to the logisticians in the field. This gap implies that technology is currently used for only a limited share of logistics functions and tasks.

Another challenge is the need for contextualized information. During the rainy season, non-paved roads may become muddy and impassable; an earthquake may trigger landslides. Beyond just raw data on deliveries and transportation networks, the demography and socioeconomic trends, governmental decisions and infrastructure status may also need to be considered (Kovács and Spens, 2011). Maps and reports can hardly cover such complex and quickly evolving factors, and new ways of representing and working with information are needed.

Design principles and recommendations

As Turoff et al (2004) stated in their seminal paper on dynamic emergency response management systems (DERMIS), the unpredictable nature of a crisis implies that the exact actions and responsibilities of geographically dispersed individuals and teams cannot be predetermined. Therefore, a humanitarian logistics information system should be able to support assigning decision power to the most operational level, as well as allowing the reverse flow of accountability and status information upward and sideways throughout any responding organization. Frustration with tools will lead logisticians to revert back to the simplest possible means of communication instead of using interfaces and dedicated forms, particularly in the immediate response. Rather than changing this behaviour, the design of logistics information systems must take into account how orders are placed in the field and develop mechanisms for automated completion or remote support, rather than striving to change patterns that are deeply rooted in organizational and behavioural structures. In Table 8.1.1 we summarize the most important DERMIS design principles, describe the current status of humanitarian logistics information systems, and derive design implications.

Table 8.1.1 Humanitarian logistics information systems – design principles

DERMIS Principle	Humanitarian Logistics Information Systems	Design Implication
Premise 1 – system training and simulation: a system that is not used on a regular basis *before* an emergency will never be of use in an actual emergency.	Training for logisticians is still fragmented, and has been described as insufficient (Thomas and Mizushima, 2005; Kabra and Ramesh, 2015). While software for the upstream logistics processes is run on a continuous basis, there is a lack of familiarity by field staff with processes and tools, also highlighted by the often multiple roles in cluster systems that people take on.	Owing to the high staff turnover, skills need to be further developed across the humanitarian domain, including standard logistics processes, and specialized skill sets for complex and sudden-onset disasters.
Premise 2 – information focus: data and information needs to relate to the users dealing with the disaster.	Most information streams are currently dominated by advocacy and strategic considerations. Operational information requests are most often answered within networks of peers. In some of the ongoing conflicts, even basic information on population data, humanitarian needs, 3Ws or 4Ws – overviews on *W*ho does *W*hat, *W*here, (*W*)hen – are not available or very incomplete.	Information systems need to include operationally relevant information. This information needs to be easily retrieved and represented in a useful format. This includes interactive approaches and dynamic maps, in which users can customize the information they see. Information source and reliability need to be well documented.

Table 8.1.1 *Continued*

DERMIS Principle	Humanitarian Logistics Information Systems	Design Implication
Premise 3 – crisis memory: learning and understanding what actually happened before, during and after the crisis is extremely important for the improvement of the response process.	The humanitarian system is currently stretched to its very limits. There have been several reform processes, such as the 2016 World Humanitarian Summit.[1] There are too few reflections and lessons learned, due to the rapid cycles of humanitarian deployment, interventions and new functions of staff.	A culture of continuous learning oriented towards becoming a high-reliability organization should be implemented. This includes a culture of collective mindfulness and the willingness to learn from past failures (Weick, Sutcliffe and Obstfeld, 1999). While geographic and logistics information systems are very useful for map or chart making, their true strength is in analysis – yet we rarely see any significant analytical products that aim at forecasting and planning.
Premise 4 – exceptions as norms: almost everything in a crisis is an exception to the norm.	Humanitarian information systems rely on standardized products and tools, resulting in the (relatively) rapid and predictable production of, for example, maps, reports, 4Ws, cluster contact lists. Information tailored to the specific context of a disaster, however, is typically not produced, and only available by direct requests.	Downstream logistics information systems in particular need to become flexible and agile to adapt to the respective context, in terms of language; coverage and network; key issues and humanitarian needs in the crisis; expertise, skills and time available of the user. Uncertainties, unexpected developments and risks need to be highlighted and communicated.

Table 8.1.1 *Continued*

DERMIS Principle	Humanitarian Logistics Information Systems	Design Implication
Premise 5 – scope and nature of crisis: people, authority and resources need to be brought together at a specific period of time for a specific purpose.	Information and communication technologies enable contributions from remotely working experts and volunteers. However, with the increasing intervention of people not familiar with the context, the control and 'ownership' of a crisis may shift towards remote levels. Particularly, when organizational information is represented as a 'product' that is easier to share, it can be viewed as property owned by the organization (Yang and Maxwell, 2011), thus hampering the local response. While ICTs are increasingly used to support communication between headquarters and the field, there is little evidence of improved co-ordination on the ground.	The use of ICTs and the role of information management units or centres should be clearly linked to improvements in the effectiveness of aid delivery. These centres should effectively co-ordinate data collection and sharing. Despite discussions on interoperability and joint efforts, NGOs and agencies alike are still being asked to fill in different data collection forms. Multiple assessments take place in some areas and no assessments in others; data is collected in different formats by different agencies; and information is not being shared effectively. After typhoon Haiyan, projects such as the Internews Project Radyo Bakdaw ('rise'),[2] and self-organized community activities such as 'paglig on'[3] in Cebu highlight the need to support communication between the local population and governance structures in such IM centres.
Premise 6 – role transferability: it is impossible to predict who will undertake what role. The actions and privileges of the role need to be defined in the software, and people must be trained for the possibility of assuming multiple or changing roles.	Most current software systems support the definition of user profiles and specific user groups. This is particularly relevant in the context of sharing sensitive information. However, given the strength of bilateral personal networks, such role definitions embedded in software and tools alone are not sufficient.	Processes and procedures need to be established that give authority to collect and process information to specific roles. Particularly tacit privileges, norms and codes of conduct need to be made transparent through better training and good governance, bringing together tools and practices.

Table 8.1.1 *Continued*

DERMIS Principle	Humanitarian Logistics Information Systems	Design Implication
Premise 7 – information validity and timeliness: establishing and supporting confidence in a decision by supplying the best possible up-to-date information is critical to those whose actions may risk lives and resources.	In natural disasters, standardized products are available in a relatively short time, though sometimes at the cost of not fulfilling specific information requests. In conflicts, it typically takes a long time to collect, compare and process information, leading to long time delays. In addition, protection of sources hampers verifiability and required careful cross-checking, which may lead to unfounded rumours, and thus adding to a general atmosphere of mistrust.	Information cycles need to become predictable and transparent, such that decision makers can deliberate if the information is sufficiently reliable to make a decision, or if it is worthwhile to wait for more. This requires that data about the time of the information collection, and its inherent uncertainty, as well as potential implications in terms of humanitarian needs is clearly represented and communicated.
Premise 8 – free exchange of information: crises involve the necessity for hundreds of individuals from different organizations to freely exchange information, delegate authority and conduct oversight, without the side-effect of information overload.	Shifting formats and the use of different languages hamper access to information, particularly for local actors and emerging actors. Some of those novel actors, for instance charities from the Gulf states, follow their own norms and rules (Cotterrell and Harmer, 2005). In conflicts, information is often not shared, not even with partners or within the same organization. This is due to sensitivity, high pressure and the notion of ownership of information, and can result in parallel efforts across government agencies and international NGOs (Ebener, Castro and Dimailig, 2014).	Standardization and interoperability of tools and platforms need to be improved, enabling easy access and offline modes of work. Common operational data sets (CODs) and other basic information need to be made commonly available and continuously updated. Clear protocols and procedures for sharing sensitive information need to be established.

Table 8.1.1 *Continued*

DERMIS Principle	Humanitarian Logistics Information Systems	Design Implication
Premise 9 – co-ordination: the crux of the co-ordination is that the exact actions and responsibilities of the individuals cannot be predetermined.	Information systems do not replace management. In the past decade, all disasters have similar problems of information fragmentation, created by the need to function in rapidly changing environments, with multiple sources of information and many demands made upon staff for information from headquarters or outside the organization. The current practices of situation reporting and co-ordination meetings might actually be contributing to this fragmentation rather than mitigating it.	Research has shown that decisions for disaster co-ordination are mainly facilitated through organizational structures, collaborative decision processes, and the contribution of advanced information and decision-support systems, all of which are highly interdependent (Chen *et al*, 2010). While exact actions cannot be predetermined, co-ordination relies on feedback on the prevalent situation. Logistics plans are therefore subject to constant change and updates as new information becomes available. Policies that will be developed here will therefore take into account this flexibility, in order to avoid 'threat rigidity', ie people following predefined, rigid responses while not taking into account the reality of new threats in the crisis situation.

[1] For a reflection on the logistics innovation for the 2016 WHS by humanitarian practitioners, see
https://www.worldhumanitariansummit.org/node/504266.
[2] See http://www.comminit.com/media-development/content/radyo-bakdaw-rise.
[3] See http://www.cebu.gov.ph/typhoon-yolanda-updates/.

Conclusions

While it is commonly understood that information must be as relevant, accurate and timely as possible, the ever-growing complexity of disaster response has shown that many challenges remain. The evolution of ICT has opened up whole new possibilities for information collection, sharing and analysis. Although expectations are high, and there is a widespread belief in the transformative power of technology, the need for better humanitarian information systems is as urgent as ever before.

Since efficient logistics processes rely on information about gaps, capacities, resources or access, there is a strong link between information management and logistics that needs to be further developed, particularly when it comes to analyses and planning. By forecasting and tracking changes of needs over time, more efficient logistics can be provided. Naturally, uncertainties in disaster-struck areas are of a greater magnitude than in 'normal' conditions. Therefore, planning needs to focus on agile and flexible supply chains that can be adapted as the situation evolves, and as a better understanding of the needs emerges. This requires also that monitoring and measuring approaches be tailored to understand operational needs and emerging risks.

Logistics information systems need to pursue the same targets as the underlying logistics processes: they should enable that the right (information) products are delivered to the appropriate actors at the right time and in the right format. This implies that any information collected, processed and shared should be purposeful, ie contribute to situational awareness for specific logistics decisions. To reflect the complexity and the context of a disaster situation, each piece of information collected should be linked to other data serving as preconditions, triggers, being part of, used in, linked to, influencing, informing or referring to the given information, thus enriching a knowledge base of linked open data. This means that information products need to address specific organizations, formal or informal information systems, decision makers, problems and timescales to ensure that the information they convey finds its intended use.

Notes

1 http://www.ilo.org/wcmsp5/groups/public/--ed_emp/documents/publication/wcms_397678.pdf

2 https://docs.unocha.org/sites/dms/Documents/mira_final_version2012.pdf

3 http://hhi.harvard.edu/research/kobotoolbox

4 http://www.unicef.org/cholera/Cholera-Toolkit-2013.pdf

5 http://immap.org/?page_id=120#Software_Solutions

6 http://crisismappers.net/

7 http://www.ushahidi.com/

8 http://blog.standbytaskforce.com/

9 http://hotosm.org/

10 http://digitalhumanitarians.com/

11 http://humanitarian.id/

12 http://eden.sahanafoundation.org/

13 http://www.logcluster.org/

14 http://reliefweb.int/

15 https://www.humanitarianresponse.info/

16 http://logik.unocha.org/SitePages/SummaryReport.aspx

17 http://www.helios-foundation.org/

18 https://www.fmsinc.com/consulting/portfolio/logistics-support-system.aspx

19 http://www.fritzinstitute.org/prsrm-HLS.htm

20 http://www.rescue.org/press-releases/international-rescue-committee-open-sources-first-its-kind-humanitarian-digital-tool-

21 http://54.225.218.247/wfp/OpsFeed/OpsFeedRegional/OpsFeedRegional.html

22 http://www.novacom-services.com/en/humanav

23 http://www.asianewsnet.net/WFP-gives-rotten-rice-to-Nepal-earthquake-survivor-76830.html

24 http://www.cdc.gov/vhf/ebola/outbreaks/2014-west-africa/qa-mmwr-estimating-future-cases.html

References

ACAPS (2014) *Humanitarian Needs Assessment: The good enough guide*, Practical Action Publishing, Rugby

Altay, N and Labonte, M (2014) Challenges in humanitarian information management and exchange: evidence from Haiti, *Disasters*, 38, Suppl. 1, pp S50–72

Balcik, B and Beamon, B (2008) Facility location in humanitarian relief, *International Journal of Logistics: Research and application*, 11, pp 101–21

Bartsch, S M, Gorham, K and Lee, B Y (2014) The cost of an Ebola case, *Pathogens and Global Health*, 109 (1), pp 4–9

Blecken, A and Hellingrath, B (2008) Supply chain management software for humanitarian operations: review and assessment of current tools, in Proceedings of the 5th Annual ISCRAM Conference, Washington, pp 342–51

Chan, J and Comes, T (2014) Innovative research design: a journey into the information Typhoon, *Procedia Engineering*, 78, pp 52–58

Chen, R, *et al* (2008) Coordination in emergency response management, *Communications of the ACM*, 51 (5), pp 66–73

Chen, R, Rao, H R, Sharman, R, Upadhyaya, S J and Kim, J (2010) An empirical examination of IT-enabled emergency response: the cases of hurricane Katrina and hurricane Rita, *Communications of the Association for Information Systems*, 26 (1), p 8

Comes, T, Vybornova, O and Van de Walle, B (2015) Bringing Structure to the Disaster Data Typhoon: An Analysis of Decision-Makers Information Needs in the Response to Haiyan, 2015 AAAI Spring Symposium, pp 7–11

Cotterrell, L and Harmer, A (2005) [accessed 25 April 2016] Diversity in Donorship: The Changing Landscape of Official Humanitarian Aid, *Humanitarian Policy Group* [Online] https://www.odi.org/sites/odi.org.uk/files/odi-assets/publications-opinion-files/275.pdf

Crowley, J and Chan, J (2010) [accessed 25 April 2015] Disaster Relief 2.0: The Future of Information Sharing in Humanitarian Emergencies [Online] http://www.unfoundation.org/assets/pdf/disaster-relief-20-report.pdf

Ebener, S, Castro, F and Dimailig, L A (2014) [accessed 25 April 2016] Increasing Availability, Quality, and Accessibility of Common and Fundamental Operational Datasets to Support Disaster Risk Reduction and Emergency Management in the Philippines [Online] http://www.gaia-geosystems.org/PROJECTS/SIIEM/PHL/Green_Paper_DSWD-SIIEM_305014.pdf

Endsley, M R (1995) Toward a theory of situation awareness in dynamic systems, *Human Factors*, 37 (1), pp 32–64

Frieden, T R, *et al* (2014) Ebola 2014: new challenges, new global response and responsibility, *The New England Journal of Medicine*, 371, pp 1177–80

Galindo, G and Batta, R (2013) Review of recent developments in OR/MS research in disaster operations management, *European Journal of Operational Research*, 230 (2), pp 201–11

GHA (2015) Global Humanitarian Assistance Report, Somerset, UK

Holguín-Veras, J *et al* (2012) On the unique features of post-disaster humanitarian logistics, *Journal of Operations Management*, 30 (7–8), pp 494–506

IASC (2015) Reference Module for Cluster Coordination at the Country Level, New York and Geneva

IFRC (2013) World Disaster Report Technology and the Future of Humanitarian Action, Geneva

Kabra, G and Ramesh, A (2015) Analyzing ICT issues in humanitarian supply chain management: a SAP-LAP linkages framework, *Global Journal of Flexible Systems Management*, 16 (2), pp 157–71

Kovács, G and Spens, K (2009) Identifying challenges in humanitarian logistics, *International Journal of Physical Distribution & Logistics Management*, 39 (2), pp 506–28

Kovács, G and Spens, K M (2011) Trends and developments in humanitarian logistics – a gap analysis, *International Journal of Physical Distribution & Logistics Management*, 41 (1), pp 32–45

Laguna Salvadó, L, Lauras, M and Comes, T (2015) Humanitarian value stream mapping: application to the EBOLA outbreak, in *ISCRAM Kristiansand*, ed L Palen *et al*, Norway, pp 178–86

Laguna Salvadó, L, Lauras, M, Comes, T and Van de Walle, B (2015b) Towards More Relevant Research on Humanitarian Disaster Management Co-ordination, in: ISCRAM 2015, Kristiansand

Landgren, J (2015) Insights from an ethnographic study of a foreign response team during the EBOLA Outbreak in Liberia, in *ISCRAM Kristiansand*, ed L Palen *et al*, Norway, pp 114–19

Meier, P (2014) Next generation humanitarian computing, in *Proceedings of the 17th ACM Conference on Computer Supported Cooperative Work & Social Computing – CSCW 14*, pp 1573, ACM Press, New York

Olsen, G R, Carstensen, N and Høyen, K (2003) Humanitarian crises: what determines the level of emergency assistance? Media coverage, donor interests and the aid business, *Disasters*, 27 (2), pp 109–26

Pettit, S *et al* (2009) Disaster prevention and management: towards a humanitarian logistics knowledge management system, *International Journal of Physical Distribution & Logistics Management*, 20 (6), pp 6–26

Thomas, A (2007) *Humanitarian Logistics: Enabling disaster response*, The Fritz Institute, San Francisco

Thomas, A and Mizushima, M (2005) Logistics training: necessity or luxury?, *Forced Migration Review*, 22, pp 60–61

Tomasini, R M and Van Wassenhove, L N (2009) From preparedness to partnerships: case study research on humanitarian logistics, *International Transactions in Operational Research*, 16 (5), pp 549–59

Turoff, M *et al* (2004) The design of a dynamic emergency response management information system, *Journal of Information Technology Theory and Applications*, 5 (4), pp 1–36

Van de Walle, B and Comes, T (2014) Risk accelerators in disasters: insights from the typhoon Haiyan response on humanitarian information management and decision support, in *CAiSE2014*, ed M Jarke, J Mylopoulos and C Quix, pp 12–23, Springer, Berlin/Heidelberg

Van de Walle, B and Comes, T (2015) [accessed 25 April 2016] Running the Ebola Response: The Triple Helix of Information, Logistics and Coordination, Brussels [Online] http://reliefweb.int/report/ghana/running-ebola-response-triple-helix-information-logistics-and-coordination

Van de Walle, B, Van Den Eede, G and Muhren, W (2009) Humanitarian information management and systems, in *LNCS*, ed J Loeffler and M Klann, pp 12–21, Springer, Berlin

Van Wassenhove, L N (2006) Humanitarian aid logistics: supply chain management in high gear, *Journal of the Operational Research Society*, 57, pp 475–89

Van Wassenhove, L Martinez, P and Alfonso, J (2012) Using OR to adapt supply chain management best practices to humanitarian logistics, *International Transactions in Operational Research*, 19 (1–2), pp 307–22

Weick, K, Sutcliffe, K and Obstfeld, D (1999) Organizing for high reliability: processes of collective mindfulness, *Research in Organizational Behavior*, 21, pp 23–81

Yang, T M and Maxwell, T A (2011) Information-sharing in public organizations: a literature review of interpersonal, intra-organizational and inter-organizational success factors, *Government Information Quarterly*, 28, pp 164–75

GDACSmobile 8.2

An IT tool supporting assessments for humanitarian logistics

DANIEL LINK

Chair for Information Systems and Supply Chain Management,
Westfälische Wilhelms-Universität Münster, Germany

BERND HELLINGRATH

Chair for Information Systems and Supply Chain Management,
Westfälische Wilhelms-Universität Münster, Germany

Introduction

Since humanitarian organizations often operate in countries with poor infrastructure and low levels of data preparedness, and because disasters can frequently and drastically change the environment, assessments play an important role in gathering sufficiently timely and accurate information about the current needs of a population and the operational environment – for example its capabilities and restraints in terms of infrastructure and resources. This information serves as a decision base for other functional areas, like humanitarian logistics.

Humanitarian logistics plays a central role in disaster relief operations of humanitarian organizations, where it helps to meet beneficiaries' needs by procuring, storing and transporting goods that are either distributed directly to the affected population or used to support the provision of vital services, such as medical care.

According to the Assessment Capacities Project (ACAPS), assessments usually begin with collecting and analysing secondary data, ie data that has been available from before the disaster, in order to estimate the needs of the affected population as well as operational constraints. Secondary data exists in many forms, such as generic country overviews (see, for example, the CIA World Fact Book) that give an overview of demographics and other aspects, or specialized data sets (eg the Logistics Cluster's Logistics Capacity Assessments) that describe a country's logistics infrastructure and resources. In order to close information gaps and update existing information, primary data needs to be collected from the affected area via remote sensing, exploratory teams or other methods. Primary and secondary data together form the decision basis for decision making, in particular for planning operations.

During on-site assessments, professionals heavily rely on the use of paper forms, which are simple, easy to use and robust, low-tech tools. However, paper forms have several limitations in terms of processing speed, error rate and the ability to capture rich data such as geo-located images. This is one reason why humanitarian organizations increasingly look at mobile devices such as smartphones and tablets to support data collection, despite such devices having their own drawbacks, such as their dependence on electric power or access to telecommunication networks. Another emerging technology that can supply complementary data while possibly involving the affected population is crowdsourcing, eg collecting and analysing data from online social media. When developing a tool that makes effective use of both mobile and crowdsourcing technologies, and that targets both professional responders and the affected population as end users, one needs to be mindful of the primary functions of the application to ensure that it doesn't miss its purpose or attempt to over-exceed its capabilities.

The Global Disaster Alert and Coordination System (GDACS, www.gdacs.org) is a co-operation framework under the United Nations umbrella that aims at filling the information and co-ordination gap in the first phase after major disasters. To provide more ground truth to GDACS, the Joint Research Centre of the European Commission (JRC) had developed iGDACS as an app for Apple's iPhone that allowed users to submit a photo and a text description. In 2012, based on the iGDACS concept, the University of Münster collaborated with JRC and an emergency management expert to develop the online platform 'GDACSmobile' that aims to support the acquisition and dissemination of primary data in the first four weeks following a major sudden-onset disaster; for example about needs, issues of access, infrastructure damage and other cross-cutting operational issues. In contrast to similar tools, like KoBoToolbox, the platform simultaneously targets both the general public and professional responders as end users, which closes the information cycle between disaster managers and the affected population. The platform consists of an app for smart mobile devices, like Android phones, and a server side application that features a web front end and can harvest posts from the online social network Twitter. The GDACSmobile app can be used to share observations from the ground and to view all published observations, giving professionals and the affected population access to information valuable for their decision making. Data can be shared publicly with all users and in spaces called 'private missions' that are accessible only to selected users. This allows organizations to limit the visibility of their data while giving co-ordinating bodies, such as the United Nations Office for the Coordination of Humanitarian Affairs (OCHA), access to a bigger pool of information for co-ordination purposes. To ensure the quality of the disseminated information, professional analysts engage in a content moderation workflow, which determines the visibility of incoming observations. Feedback on the initial GDACSmobile concept and implementation was gathered from researchers and practitioners during workshops and live demonstrations. Following this, in 2014, OCHA joined the University of Münster and JRC to further refine GDACSmobile in terms of usability, interoperability and the communication between moderators and users. The set of new features includes a template system for the rapid set-up of public and private missions as well as observation-centred messaging that enables moderators to request additional information from the authors of observations.

In this chapter, we examine the design of GDACSmobile as an information system supporting assessments that provide information to humanitarian logistics operations. Furthermore, we present the solution's main stakeholder groups and information flows. Subsequently we illustrate its use through an application case structured into preparation phase (highlighting a possible stakeholder configuration) and rapid assessment phase (describing supported interactions). Eventually we draw a conclusion, giving an outlook on the future development of GDACSmobile.

Main stakeholder groups

The main stakeholders of GDACSmobile fall into four groups, as displayed in Figure 8.2.1. The groups are not intended to be mutually exclusive, as some professional responders and digital volunteers may belong to the

Figure 8.2.1 Main stakeholders of GDACSmobile

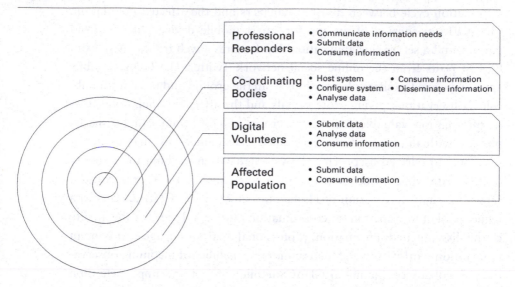

Professional Responders	• Communicate information needs • Submit data • Consume information	
Co-ordinating Bodies	• Host system • Configure system • Analyse data	• Consume information • Disseminate information
Digital Volunteers	• Submit data • Analyse data • Consume information	
Affected Population	• Submit data • Consume information	

affected population, and the employees of co-ordinating bodies are pro-fessionals who may be responding to a crisis:

- *Professional responders*: GDACSmobile seeks to enhance the decision making of professional responders by providing relevant and sufficiently timely, accurate and reliable information. They are arguably the most important source of ground truth from an affected region due to their education, training and experience.

- *Co-ordinating bodies*: co-ordinating bodies are, for example, OCHA, including the UN Disaster Assessment and Coordination (UNDAC) teams, and the Logistics Cluster (LogCluster). These bodies provide services such as information management and overviews of the operational environment to the humanitarian community via dedicated platforms or websites.

- *Digital volunteers*: in recent years, volunteer and technical communities (VTCs) such as the Stand-by Task Force (SBTF) or the Humanitarian OpenStreetMap Team (HOT) have demonstrated the capability to process data with the aim of supporting disaster response. Since the number of digital volunteer communities has grown quickly and the collaboration between VTCs and formal disaster management organizations has arisen, the Digital Humanitarian Network (DHN) was formed as a 'network of networks' that provides a single interface between formal disaster management organizations and VTCs.

- *Affected population*: the affected population does not only take a primary role in humanitarian response as beneficiaries, but local citizens often act as first responders (eg saving neighbours trapped under rubble), possess relevant knowledge of the area (eg about local suppliers) and can provide information about their needs and the operational environment (eg about the state of the road network or the security situation).

Information flows

Prior to information flowing in the system, the system has to be configured, ie an administrator needs to create a public or private mission for the relevant disaster. During mission set-up, the administrator defines hierarchical information categories, such as 'infrastructure/road network'. For each category, the administrator defines data input forms that range from a simple text field to complex form structures combining elements such as photo collections, checkboxes or numeric fields. The administrator can accelerate the form-building process by using templates based on previous disasters. In a public mission, observations of sufficient quality are visible to all users. The administrator may also specify organizations that are going to use the system and create private missions for these organizations, wherein content is only shared with users having access to the private mission. This is necessary for numerous reasons, such as to protect possibly harmful data in armed conflicts and to secure the competitive advantage that aid organizations need to maintain in the struggle for greater individual visibility and funding. Once the initial configuration is complete, information may start flowing, as illustrated in Figure 8.2.2.

The information flow begins with users submitting observations to a public or private mission they have access to. There are three types of users that can make observations: non-moderated app users, moderated app users and moderated Twitter users. The distinction between moderated and non-moderated users goes back to the assumption that some users (eg professional responders) will likely make relevant, timely, accurate and reliable observations, while others (eg the general affected population) are not familiar enough with assessment methodologies and humanitarian aid to provide information that is likely to directly benefit decision making.

If a non-moderated user submits an observation via the app, it bypasses moderation and will be published according to the initial configuration (eg only within a private mission space). Whether or not to place a user in the non-moderated group lies at the discretion of the administrator, which

Figure 8.2.2 GDACSmobile information flows

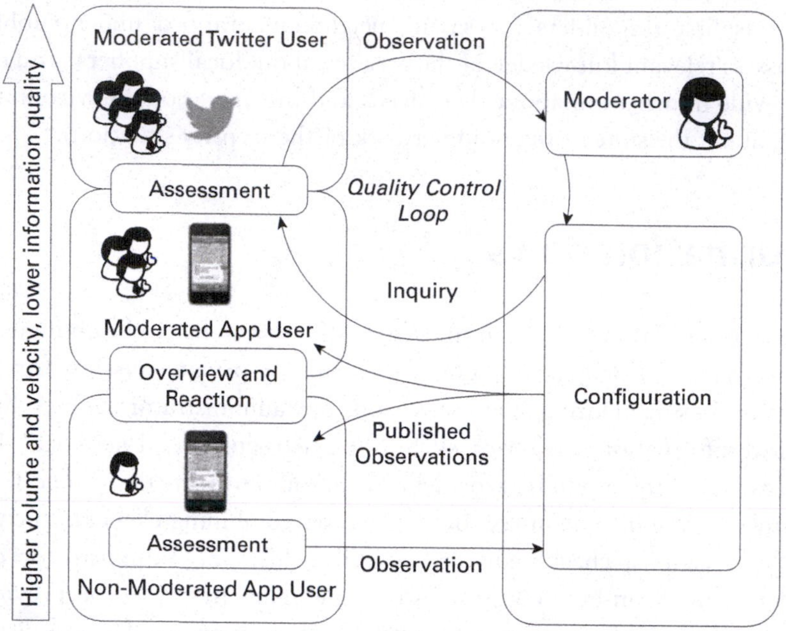

allows to distinguish between different levels of competency. This is particularly important when working with volunteers who underwent only very limited training.

If a moderated user submits an observation via Twitter or the app, it will enter a quality control loop. Therein, a moderator reviews the observation, possibly draws conclusions affecting the set-up of categories and data input forms (eg by adding a question) and, if needed, requests further information from the observation's author (eg to clarify ambiguous phrasing or ask for more details). Once a moderated observation shows a satisfying quality, it can be published according to the current configuration (eg to all users in the public mission of a disaster or to a limited user group in a private mission space).

Application case

The following fictitious case description is based on the 2015 Nepal earthquake response, informed by various published situation reports as well as a number of interviews with humanitarian aid professionals, especially logisticians.

Preparedness phase

OCHA's Disaster Assessment and Coordination (UNDAC) teams became a provider of the GDACSmobile solution, which entails much more than putting up a server and offering the client an app for download. It required work in the areas of promotion, preparation of information analysis, adoption and training. Promotion was necessary to make stakeholders aware of the existence, benefits and appropriate use of the platform. The preparation of information analysis included co-creating suitable policies and procedures that govern the collaboration and information exchange between stakeholders, working with data consumers such as logisticians to build catalogues of information needs, and ensuring systems interoperability (eg with the Virtual On-Site Operations Coordination Centre, Virtual OSOCC). The user base had to learn about the tool; perceive its benefits; decide on its specific usefulness for existing data collection, information analysis and decision-making processes; and commit to its use. Last but not least, it was essential to incorporate the solution into training, such as large-scale field simulation exercises, not only for the additional benefit of further promotion and simplified adoption in field deployments, but to make sure that the developed policies and procedures were well enough understood to allow the system to perform under the difficult circumstances of an emergency. Training sessions also helped identify potential areas for further improvement.

Furthermore, UNDAC decided to utilize their roster of assessment experts to guide overall assessment efforts and perform information analysis, including quality control for incoming observations.

In addition, UNDAC made collaboration agreements with:

- the Global Logistics Cluster Support Cell (GLCSC) to facilitate the specification of logistics-related information needs, analyse information and disseminate valuable findings to logisticians in the humanitarian community;

- the search-and-rescue (SAR) community, especially via the International Search and Rescue Advisory Group (INSARAG), to have SAR teams submit focused observations through the GDACSmobile app for rapid assessments, as SAR teams are often the first international responders to arrive in an affected area;

- the Virtual OSOCC providers to notify their users of GDACSmobile deployments and to support the dissemination of information, especially to the headquarters of responding organizations;

- the Digital Humanitarian Network (DHN) to serve as the primary interface to digital volunteer communities;
- the Standby Task Force (SBTF) and the Humanitarian OpenStreetMap Team (HOT) to assist the UNDAC teams in information analysis and mapping;
- international aid organizations such as Save the Children, to participate in joint assessments via private mission spaces;
- Nepalese aid organizations such as the Nepal Red Cross Society, to make observations in case of a disaster, especially contributing local knowledge, to be readily aware of GDACSmobile as a new source of information, and to advocate the solutions' use among the local population.

While preparing training, UNDAC already set up several organizations in the system, assigned respective users and granted adequate rights, eg to administrate an organization or to control the quality of incoming observations. Users created data input forms that match the methodologies of their organization or for joint assessments.

Rapid assessment phase

In April 2015, a 7.8 magnitude earthquake struck Nepal, triggering several avalanches and aftershocks in different parts of the country. The situation worsened when another earthquake of 7.3 magnitude struck the country only a few weeks later. OCHA estimated 8,700 fatalities, thousands of injured people and almost 800,000 buildings affected. Neighbouring communities in India, China and Bangladesh were affected as well, although with lower intensity. When the government requested international aid and assistance, aid organizations from different countries initiated the delivery of various goods (eg medicine, equipment and vehicles), financial support and staff to Nepal – intended to provide relief services such as search-and-rescue and medical assistance.

Once the magnitude of the disaster had become clear and Nepal had requested international assistance, UNDAC decided to deploy GDACSmobile. An UNDAC administrator created a public mission to which all interested users could submit observations and could access a publicly visible overview of the situation. The administrator also set up a private mission space for a joint assessment, using an existing earthquake template to rapidly configure data input forms. See Figure 8.2.3 for a screenshot of the form builder. The forms guided the first professional responders arriving in the area, especially SAR teams, by asking key questions.

Figure 8.2.3 Defining categories with the GDACSmobile form builder (screenshot)

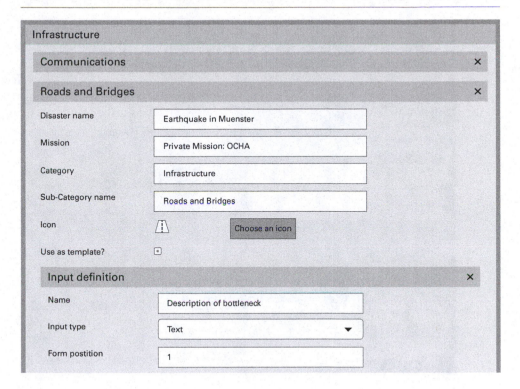

UNDAC utilized the International Search and Rescue Advisory Group network and the Virtual OSOCC system to notify search-and-rescue teams. Several team members were already familiar with the GDACSmobile app from previous training sessions, and had already been affiliated with their organization in the system, which further sped up configuration. Prior to their flight to Nepal team members logged into the app online. The app downloaded the private mission space with its category structure and data collection forms. The team members reviewed the categories and forms on the flight in order to know where they should direct their attention. After landing in Nepal, team members used the app to record their first observations about the airport and road infrastructure. See Figure 8.2.4 for a screenshot of the app while creating an observation. Once their smartphones were connected to the internet, the app submitted saved observations. Since the system considered the team members trusted observers, their observations did not have to enter the quality control loop but could bypass content moderation and were immediately visible to all members of the private mission space, which could be downloaded for offline access.

Figure 8.2.4 Creating a new observation using the mobile app (screenshot)

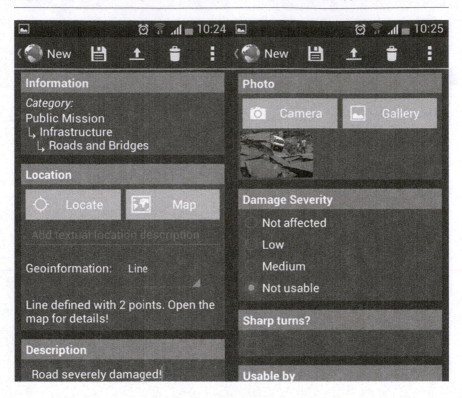

The private mission space was accessed by UNDAC information analysts and a GLCSC information manager, who studied the submitted observations and used these to help create first situation reports. A previous logistics capacity assessment (LCA) was also updated with new information, as many logisticians would refer to it for their planning.

Logisticians viewed published observations in the Web browser (see Figure 8.2.5) and thus learned that there were too many aircraft targeting Kathmandu airport and that it was becoming a bottleneck, also because its previously suboptimal condition worsened after the earthquake to a degree where it seemed like the weight of incoming aircraft would have to be restricted. This information directed logisticians' attention to other airfields in the country that had, or may have had, unused capacity. It also led to the consideration of smaller airplanes for transportation. As an additional way of circumventing the emerging issue of airport access, logisticians considered alternative points of entry, such as road transportation from Delhi to Kathmandu. Where possible, responders on those alternative routes used the GDACSmobile app to take pictures and enter

Figure 8.2.5 Filtered observation displayed on a map in the browser (screenshot)

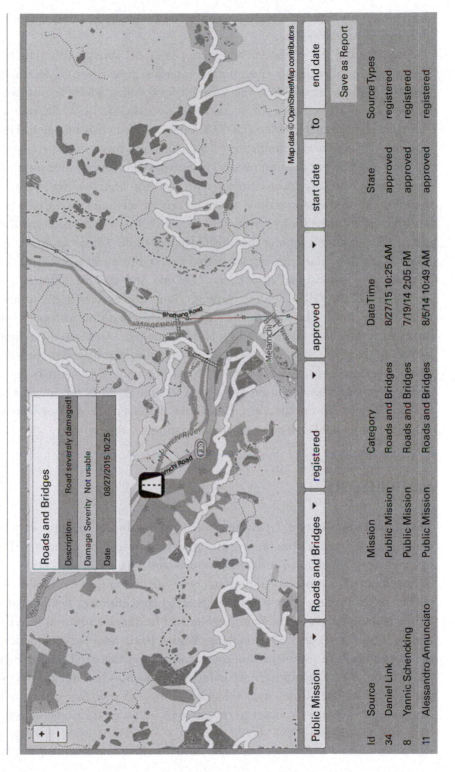

Map data © OpenStreetMap contributors

Public Mission ▾	Roads and Bridges ▾	registered ▾	approved ▾	start date	to	end date
						Save as Report

Roads and Bridges

Description	Road severely damaged!
Damage Severity	Not usable
Date	08/27/2015 10:25

Id	Source	Mission	Category	DateTime	State	Source Types
34	Daniel Link	Public Mission	Roads and Bridges	8/27/15 10:25 AM	approved	registered
8	Yannic Schencking	Public Mission	Roads and Bridges	7/19/14 2:05 PM	approved	registered
11	Alessandro Annunciato	Public Mission	Roads and Bridges	8/5/14 10:49 AM	approved	registered

short descriptions of constraints, such as road blockages and customs clearance at border crossings.

After creating the public mission space, UNDAC activated the Digital Humanitarian Network as the primary interface towards volunteer and technical communities such as the Standby Task Force, which in this case focused on the processing of social media messages. In addition, the Humanitarian OpenStreetMap (HOT) team supported crisis mapping. The engaged VTCs reviewed the defined data collection forms to learn about the most pressing information needs. They reviewed incoming observations from users (especially local citizens) that had not been assigned to any organization (and so not granted access to private mission spaces), or who had submitted observations via Twitter. Moreover, the VTCs promoted the use of GDACSmobile among the affected population. Where appropriate, VTCs asked users clarifying questions and marked promising observations as visible for professional responders. UNDAC and GLCSC information analysts used the GDACSmobile browser interface to selectively review these observations. This shed further light on the condition of local road infrastructure, which was utilized by HOT to update OpenStreetMap and by GLCSC to revise their maps of the area. In addition, it helped to identify empty warehouse spaces known to the local population, which may have still been in sufficient condition to serve as storage facilities for aid organizations. Where appropriate, the professional analysts marked observations as visible to the public, in order to raise situation awareness.

Conclusion

The information system GDACSmobile was developed to support the collection of primary data during the first four weeks of a disaster. Its browser interface gives co-ordinating bodies and VTCs access to observations submitted by professional responders or citizens via the GDACSmobile client app or Twitter. Users benefit from rapid configuration, flexible data inputs and a quality control featuring bilateral feedback loops that heavily rely on observation-centred messaging. Before being adopted in practice, the system needs to see further improvements. For instance, GDACSmobile needs to be able to incorporate secondary data, such as text documents or websites, which are already available when a disaster suddenly strikes and can serve as a baseline. In order to reduce the load on moderators, the content moderation workflow should be partly automated using advanced computer science techniques (eg supervised machine learning), especially for the filtering and categorization of incoming observations. Envisioning a future integration with third-party decision support systems, eg for planning systems to automatically retrieve and consider operational constraints, it is necessary to adapt the underlying data model and open interfaces. When these and further adjustments are made, there is reason to believe that the current positive feedback and interest from researchers and practitioners will further advance towards wider spread adoption of GDACSmobile, and positively impact humanitarian action.

Acknowledgements

We want to thank the following students at the Research Group on Information Systems and Supply Chain Management for their contribution: Anton Becker, Carsten Bubbich, Friedrich Chasin, Jonathan Dölle, Jonas Juchim, Sven Kronimus, Ferdinand Knoll, Magdalena Lang, Stefan Laube, Marius Pilgrim, Philipp Saalmann, Mohamed Junaid Shaikh, Yannic Schencking, Martin Vanauer and Patrick Vogel. The first design cycle owes heavily to the involvement of Adam Widera. For sharing their views in many discussions during design and development, we also want to thank practitioners Minu Limbu (UNICEF Kenya), Gintare Eidimtaite and Thomas Peter (both UN OCHA) as well as researchers Tom de Groeve, Alessandro Annunziato and Ioannis Andredakis (all JRC) and various members of the Humanitarian Logistics Association (HLA). The research leading to these results has partly received funding from the European Community's Seventh Framework Programme (FP7/2007–13) under Grant Agreement 607798.

PART NINE

Sustainability, performance measurement, monitoring/ evaluation and exit strategy

Logistics competency for humanitarian relief

The case of Médecins Sans Frontières

DIEGO VEGA

NEOMA Business School, France

- The complexity and scale of humanitarian relief appeals for a professionalization of humanitarian logistics.
- The rise of a great number of humanitarian organizations is turning this context into a highly competitive environment.
- In order to ensure economic sustainability, humanitarian organizations need to find ways to create a sustained competitive advantage.

Médecins Sans Frontières (MSF) is an international medical humanitarian organization that, since 1971, has provided assistance to populations in distress, to victims of natural or man-made disasters and to victims of armed conflict. Today, MSF provides aid in nearly 60 countries to people whose survival is threatened by violence, negligence or catastrophe, primarily due to armed conflict, epidemics, malnutrition and exclusion from health care or natural disasters. MSF is composed of five operational centres (Amsterdam, Barcelona, Brussels, Geneva and Paris) and 21 offices (Australia, Austria, Belgium, Brazil, Canada, Denmark, France, Germany, Greece, Holland, Hong Kong, Italy, Japan, Luxembourg, Norway, South Africa, Spain, Sweden, Switzerland, the United Kingdom and the United States).

In addition to this, MSF has three supply centres: MSF Logistique (France), MSF Supply (Belgium) and the Amsterdam Procurement Unit-APU (Netherlands), which offer logistical support to the different sections of the MSF movement and other non-governmental organizations (NGOs) such as Médecins du Monde and the International Committee of the Red Cross.

In 2015, MSF was appointed as the number one NGO worldwide, considered as 'the reference book for NGOs' by Global_Geneva's 2015 top 500 NGOs ranking. This recognition is the result of MSF's effort in achieving its objective, to respond to emergencies and to mitigate the suffering of populations at risk through proper medical action, an objective that has been reinforced by appropriate logistics (MSF, 2014a). Nevertheless, this objective cannot be achieved without the help of other areas of expertise. In addition to logistics and medical know-how, the organization's experience in responding simultaneously to multiple emergencies is perceived as one of MSF's strengths. Not surprisingly, logistics appears as one of the pillars to achieve this capacity.

From *l'intendance* to logistics

Cambodia, January 1979: the Cambodian genocide ends after four years of the Khmer Rouge regime. In October, after months of wandering, 30,000 refugees cross the border in a catastrophic state. This is where Jacques Pinel, a pharmacist and future inventor of MSF's logistics, meets for the first time Médecins Sans Frontières, discovers an '*organization without organization*', and realizes the logistical requirements needed to allow a medical team to do its job. In his own words:

> There were refugees everywhere; everyone was overwhelmed by the situation. In a corner of the MSF tents, there were plenty of boxes under a tarpaulin to protect them from the rain. Everyone had to use, search, see what there was. You had to go with the flow! For me it was the design of '*intendance*' – we did not call it logistics at the time... So I got in through the 'drugs' side, and then it was the overall organization that I started to develop. There was a part of administration and another one of basic *intendance*: be sure that the cars run, that leases are renewed, that drivers are paid, that there is money on hand, etc. And as it worked well, two years after my arrival, the leaders of the time asked me to come to Paris to do somewhat the same thing for the rest of the world.[1]

It was in the 1980s that MSF decided that, in order to bring relief to people affected by a crisis, it is imperative to have a good logistics tool.

In 1986, the French section of MSF created a purchasing centre, linked to its department of medical and logistical support, in order to respond quickly to needs while keeping full control of the supply chain. In 1992 the purchasing centre, MSF Logistique, was set up in Merignac near Bordeaux, with an initial surface of 36,000 square metres of which 2,700 square metres were for warehousing, providing medical (eg drugs, medical and surgical equipment) and non-medical (eg vehicles, water, food containers) supplies to missions of all sections, with high reliability and quality (MSF, 2014a), as well as organizing special cold chains and the transport of dangerous goods. It is recognized by the French Government as a public utility pharmaceutical establishment, a bounded warehouse, and is validated as a humanitarian procurement centre by ECHO (the humanitarian agency of the European Union).

For its part, the Belgian office of MSF created in 1989 its own supply centre, MSF Supply, in Merchtem near Brussels. This purchasing centre is responsible for the delivery of medical equipment and drugs to the field, as well as the packaging and clearance of goods for different offices of MSF, and for other NGOs. In its warehouse, MSF Supply offers different services including inventory management, supply of emergency kits and manufacturing. Concurrently with this the Dutch section created a purchasing office, Amsterdam Procurement Unit (APU), based in Amsterdam. Unlike MSF Logistique and MSF Supply, APU only performs the purchasing of goods based on the demand from the field, while other activities such as reception, storage and distribution of such goods are outsourced to freight forwarders and most products are purchased from distributors. MSF Logistique and MSF Supply buy batches directly from manufacturers and constitute the main APU suppliers of kits and the management of emergency stocks.

Logistics competency at MSF

MSF's logistics mission is to ensure the supply of MSF programmes (from purchasing to last-mile distribution) on material and medical equipment for both emergency response and development programmes. In order to achieve its mission the organization has developed the capacity to master a highly efficient supply chain made up of a series of links (purchasing, inventory, quality assurance and shipment, among others), all of them crucial, through their different supply centres, which provide the field with high-quality supplies, whether for emergency situations or normal operations (MSF, 2014a). This talent to operate such a performing logistics system is considered by its members as a logistics competency, which has led the organization to gain international recognition in this area, at the same level as that of their medical expertise. As stated by MSF Logistique's warehouse operations manager: 'For MSF, logistics is the first point that will lead to the success of a good response to an emergency... We could even deliver the material without having a medical team in the field and give this to other doctors different from MSF.'[2]

The importance and success of logistics at MSF is further attested by significant growth of activity in this area. For instance, from 2003 to 2014, MSF Logistique almost doubled the number of delivered parcels from 131,259 in 2003 to 253,771 in 2014. This was the result of a strategic decision to expand its warehousing capacity from 5,000 to 10,000 square metres and to develop three decentralized warehouses (Dubai, Nairobi and Panama) to ensure the flow management from the different sections (MSF, 2011). This allowed the organization to increase its medical and logistics stocks, and improved MSF's capacity to respond to multiple crises in different parts of the world at the same time.

For instance, during the emergency response to the 2010 Haiti earthquake, 17 planes chartered by MSF helped deliver equipment required for the assembly of an inflatable hospital within the first six days. At the end of the first month, the hospital consisted of 40 tents, of which 13 were inflatable, and included a triage room, an emergency room, an observation room, three operating rooms – including one reserved for osteosynthesis and clean surgeries – a sterilization section, a recovery room, an intensive care unit, several rooms of hospitalization, and a follow-up care and rehabilitation section. A specific burn treatment centre with its dedicated operating room was established in the third month of the intervention (MSF, 2010). In the words of the head of supply chain: 'We cannot be an emergency medical NGO with the level that we have without logistics... if we hadn't built this (MSFLog), we couldn't have responded to Haiti, it's impossible!'[3]

Another activity performed by the organization is the design and production of medical and non-medical kits, which are an important asset for the rapid deployment of resources when responding to humanitarian crises. These kits are produced by MSF mainly for their own missions but, thanks to their quality and usefulness, MSF produces emergency kits for other NGOs (eg the International Committee of the Red Cross and Médecins du Monde, among others), and MSF is responsible for the management of the 'emergency stock' for these NGOs and MSF's own sections. Furthermore, MSF also provides logistics training through their Logistics Training Centre (CEFORLOG) for future expatriates, field logisticians, doctors and nurses. From 2000 to 2010, a total of 731 logisticians and 1,158 interns were trained in different areas such as water, sanitation and hygiene (WASH), hospital management, vehicle maintenance, electronics, communications and emergency logistics, among others (CEFORLOG, 2010).

For MSF, logistics is considered the decisive factor that allows the organization to respond to humanitarian crises. It enables them to assist populations suffering humanitarian crises by supplying the required material, even if MSF's medical teams are not present in the field.

This is possible due to MSF's deep understanding of the logistical processes, and their transformation of this understanding into capabilities and competencies.

Competing through capabilities and competencies

A competency is considered as those functional areas, critical activities or organizational processes that lead organizations to perform better than others. In today's humanitarian context this notion is more important than ever, as most international NGOs raise funds that are later used for their projects and so they often compete with each other for donations. In order to remain competitive, humanitarian organizations attempt to differentiate themselves from one to another, for example by varying the type of goods or services they provide to crisis-hit populations. However, most of the largest NGOs have expanded their programme portfolios from initial emergency aid deliveries to long-term, anti-poverty activities throughout the developing world and this has made it more difficult to differentiate between organizations, as all provide similar types of assistance. Nevertheless, some international NGOs have found the means to achieve their goals and, at the same time, perform their activities better than others: through logistics capabilities and related competencies.

MSF's logistics is considered as one of the pillars for the success of their operations, and as essential for the medical activity. However, the organization's logistics effectiveness stands on an important number of competencies and capabilities, as set out below.

Technical capabilities

Technical capabilities are the foundation on which MSF's logistical competence is built. As such, MSF has worked hard to ensure that all activities within the supply chain are run and managed to a high professional standard. Technical capabilities include purchasing and procurement, supplier management, stock management, transportation management, warehouse management, order processing, operational flexibility, delivery and information management, among others.

Throughout its history, MSF has expanded its logistics system with the functions required to ensure good medical practice. Today, the organization benefits from an important internal cohesion of logistics activities that go even beyond the borders of the organization. For instance, in the late 2000s the technical department of MSF Logistique found an important number of cold-chain ruptures due to packaging. They searched new suppliers that could respond to the organization's specifications, but with no luck. Their solution was to co-design new packaging with their old supplier and, as a result, the product loss dropped from €100,000 in 2008 to less than €200 in 2010.

Integration competence

Logistics integration is crucial for the good unwinding of the operations. In order to ensure the delivery of the relief items requested by the teams on the field, without errors and within a limited period of time, MSF relies on a set of capabilities that, combined, create a successful integration of logistical functions. It all begins with the identification of the need expressed by the teams in the field. Good-quality information allows the purchasers and supply officers to find the specific products that respond to those needs, while freight and warehouse operators prepare what is needed to smooth the transit between the supplier and the field. In order to do so, capabilities such as accuracy of information, structural adaptation, standardization, information sharing and collaborative planning are particularly underlined by the organization.

MSF's operational structure, composed of three teams of the same specialists (medical, administrative and logistics) at three levels (field, capital city and headquarters) in addition to the different logistics facilities, enables downstream integration (to some extent) with the organization's first customers, ie the teams in the field, while good supplier management enables upstream external integration.

Adaptability competence

In 2013, MSF's operational portfolio was composed of 70 to 90 projects across 30 to 35 countries (MSF, 2014b). In some cases, a country's situation (eg the Saudi-led blockade in the 2015 Yemen crisis) can lead to constraints that make it difficult (or even impossible) to access and supply humanitarian teams in operation. In other cases, the nature and scale of the emergency (eg the 2008 Sichuan earthquake) can make it difficult to deliver aid. To deal with these factors MSF has, by necessity, developed the ability to adapt quickly to different contexts and emergencies, all of which can require very different logistical choices.

Upstream, the supply of products from the supplier can also result in constraints to which MSF's logistics must constantly adapt. Product quality is the first criterion for the choice of a supplier, while delivery time is also very important. In addition to this, and despite the fact that MSF is an international organization recognized worldwide, when seen as clients they represent a very small percentage of a supplier's market and, thus, the logistics team must be able to perform its activity by adapting to the constraints imposed by its suppliers.

Downstream, medical teams in the field often require specific items, which also results in an adaptation effort from logistics to supply what is needed. To provide high-quality medical assistance to affected populations is the organization's main goal. This involves medical equipment (eg biomedical) and medicines (eg temperature-controlled vaccines) that in some cases are difficult to manage. Logistics thus adapts to integrate the medical requirements into their standard processes and ensure an almost perfect environment for the medical activity to be performed.

MSF's adaptability competence consequently appears multidimensional: the first fixed dimension is the humanitarian context to which MSF has adapted; a second dynamic dimension relates to the constraints of countries in terms of clearance times and possibly access; a third dynamic dimension is linked to the complexity of the field – that is to say, the emergency being responded to; a fourth dynamic dimension is as a result of medical claims; and, finally, a dynamic dimension upstream with the suppliers.

Responsiveness competence

Since its creation, MSF has been present at most of the largest humanitarian crises in history, bringing assistance to affected populations. Emergency response, specifically to natural disasters, has been at the core of MSF's work from the beginning.

MSF Logistique's goal is to ensure a provision of the articles for shipment within four weeks to confirmation date for regular projects and within 24 hours for emergency response, lead times that can be seen as short, considering the environment in which the activity is performed. From 2005 to 2010, for instance, the French supply centre reduced their lead times from less than 10 per cent of orders delivered within five days and nearly 70 per cent within four weeks, to almost 20 per cent within five days and above 80 per cent within four weeks. This capacity to rapidly respond, considered by Rony Brauman, former president of MSF, as the 'culture' or 'know-how' of the emergency, is seen as the responsiveness competence within the organization, an ability to respond quickly to any type of humanitarian crisis around the world, deploying different types of resources (physical and human) belonging to different professions (medical, logistics, water and sanitation, nutrition, construction), by its own means, and without having too much impact on the course of other programmes and projects run by the organization in different countries. From natural disasters with high media coverage to silent crises, from armed conflicts to nutritional crises, MSF has shown that, even with very limited access, it is able to act and achieve its goal: to provide medical assistance to populations whose life or health is threatened. This capacity is achieved thanks to the responsiveness of the logistics system, which appears as the most important logistics competence within the organization. This responsiveness competence is due mainly to the capacity developed by the organization to prioritize emergencies.

Ensuring performance through logistics

Throughout its history, MSF has evolved from a medical emergency humanitarian organization to explore new areas (eg neglected diseases, slums, street children) that fit appropriately into the organization's operational choices. This expansion of MSF's activity has led the logisticians to rethink their strategy and develop new areas (such as construction, biomedical or information technologies) in order to respond to an increased scale and complexity of the organization's fields of medical and operational activity, and ensure MSF's performance of their operations. Therefore, the organization has adopted an holistic approach to logistics, seeking to build on the existing know-how and develop the capacity to innovate and react to the evolution of humanitarian relief.

The MSF approach to logistics shows that, in today's competitive humanitarian context, logistics can be considered as an organizational competence and can benefit the overall performance of these organizations. Currently, strategic decisions in most international NGOs are taken by the executive board, composed of doctors, economists and political specialists, among others, leaving little or no possibility for logistics to directly contribute to the establishment of the organizational strategy but rather following directions, probably because of its demonstrated capacity to adapt. However, recent developments on this topic point towards a strategic decision that would impact the current logistics structure of humanitarian organizations.

For instance, during the 2004 Asian tsunami response, and due to inadequacy of the quality of the products distributed to the victims, the logistics department proposed the creation of a stock of non-food items (NFIs) and tents in Dubai. Although questioned at some point, this strategy was acknowledged as appropriate following the acquisition and distribution of poor-quality tents during the 2010 Haiti earthquake response. The MSF case supports the idea of 'taking advantage' of the logistics competencies developed by any humanitarian organization, highlighting the central role that logistics can play in ensuring the performance of operations.

Strategizing logistics of humanitarian organizations

Logistics for humanitarian relief has gained increasing importance due to its capacity to ensure the good development of an operation. The evolution of the context has led logistics to constantly expand the scope to include other activities. The evidence from MSF shows that logisticians can be seen as a source for strategy rather than as a tool. When taken into account as a part of the strategy of an organization, logistics can contribute to the organization remaining competitive in a highly changing environment. This represents an opportunity for the development of logistics as a source for strategy and the achievement of the organization's goals, as is the case for many firms in the commercial sector. Integrating logistics in the overall strategy of humanitarian organizations represents a cornerstone for building sustained competitive advantage. Logistics competency can be thus considered as:

- a factor of differentiation between humanitarian organizations;
- a source for diversification of the activities performed and the assistance provided;
- a new profession for the humanitarian organization, offering logistics services to other organizations.

Notes

1 Interview with Jacques Pinel on 5 April 2011 (http://www.msf.fr/).
2 Interview with Olivier Laboucheix, November 2010, Mérignac, France.
3 Interview with Philippe Cachet, December 2010, Mérignac, France.

References

CEFORLOG (2010) *Activité du CEFORLOG 2001–2009*, Médecins Sans Frontières, Merignac, France
MSF (2010) *Réponse d'urgence après le séisme en haiti: choix opérationnels, obstacles, activités et finances*, Médecins Sans Frontières, Paris, France
MSF (2011) *Rapport annuel 2010/2011*, Médecins Sans Frontières, Paris, France
MSF (2014a) *Gestion harmonieuse des ressources humaines de l'administration et de la logistique – GHRHAL*, Médecins Sans Frontières, Paris, France
MSF (2014b) *Rapport annuel 2013/2014*, Médecins Sans Frontières, Paris, France

Community-managed rural water supply in Ethiopia

9.2

LINDA ANNALA

HUMLOG Institute, Finland

ARTO SUOMINEN

Community-managed Accelerated WaSH in Ethiopia (COWASH) project

Trade-offs

The following trade-offs are present in the case of community-managed rural water supply in Ethiopia, emphasis being given to issues that affect the overall supply chain design of rural water supply services:

- Short-term costs on training supply chain members versus long-term benefits of utilizing local resources.
- Decentralized versus centralized procurement.
- Operations and maintenance of small-scale simple technologies versus large-scale complicated technologies.

Water and sanitation are considered key elements in fostering development and reducing poverty around the world. The 2015 WHO/UNICEF Joint Monitoring Programme report indicates that 663 million people do not have access to an improved drinking-water source. Adding to the health benefits associated with clean drinking water, improved access to water reduces the time spent collecting and carrying water, improves school attendance, enhances food production and generates positive changes to livelihoods. The sustainability of water and sanitation services, however, remains a challenge: the Rural Water Supply Network estimated in 2010 that only two out of three hand pumps are working at any given time (RWSN, 2010).

The sustainability of rural water supplies has been well studied but there seems to be no simple solution to the problem. In the 1980s it became widely recognized among sector professionals that many rural water supply programmes in the Global South were performing poorly, regardless of the type of technology used. Communities lacked the sense of ownership in their water supply projects and were not satisfied with the projects implemented by donors and national governments. As a result, water supply systems were not repaired and maintained, and revenues from user tariffs were often insufficient to pay for even operation and maintenance, and much less for capital costs. The concept of community-managed water supplies grew from the first International Drinking Water Supply and Sanitation Decade of the 1980s. During the decade, water points were installed, but governments lacked the human capacity and financial resources to manage and maintain them. The solution was to encourage community ownership of water points, including their long-term maintenance.

In this chapter we focus on the context of Ethiopia, where the implementation and overall management of rural water points has been traditionally carried out by governmental bodies and donors. Such centralized top-down approaches, however, have failed to recognize the under-utilized local resources that could accelerate the implementation of water points. In line with the global trend of community-managed water supplies, Ethiopia has included a community-managed approach into its national water implementation policy. This community-managed project (CMP) approach uses a participatory framework where the community invests labour, cash and in-kind contributions during the implementation process. The philosophy of the CMP approach is to involve the community in the project implementation and financial management, from inception to post-construction, thus facilitating the formation of 'community ownership'.

Shifting responsibilities to communities has implications for the supply chains that are required for the material and financial flows of the initial implementation, and for long-term maintenance of water supply systems. First, material and financial flows need to be coupled with necessary training activities: community-managed water technologies require certain skills that can only be attained through capacity development activities. Here capacity development is defined as the process by which people, organizations and society systematically stimulate and develop their capability over time to achieve social and economic goals, including through improvement of knowledge, skills, systems and institutions. Governmental staff need to take the role of facilitator instead of technical implementer; community water committees require a multitude of new skills ranging from financial and contract management, to technical skills on operations and maintenance; local community members must also become trained as professional artisans. They receive an intensive training in masonry and water-pump installation, after which they are qualified for constructing water points throughout the rural districts based on contractual agreements with communities. Furthermore, continuous technical assistance and refresher training are required from local governmental agencies in order to sustain the required skills. All these training activities naturally incur additional costs, but the inherent long-term benefits and decreased workload of overburdened governmental agencies are very much worth considering.

Second, decentralized community-managed procurement of pumps and spare parts calls for functioning local markets and the availability of materials. Communities may require additional support from, for example, governmental actors in terms of receiving information about technical details, and about prices if private actors hold a monopolistic position in the market. Private suppliers may take advantage of communities' lack of knowledge on the prices of various spare parts, or it might happen that professional expertise is required to identify the spare part that needs replacement in the first place.

Third, local small-scale technologies require consideration on where the capacity for operations and maintenance should be located – whether in centralized or decentralized locations. Small-scale translates into multiple, scattered technologies that require manpower and skills for operations and maintenance. Whether these skills should be pooled from centralized sources, or from within decentralized communities, becomes a crucial decision. In the case of simple small-scale technologies, the necessary skills are not too difficult to obtain and sustain, thus making community management a viable option. For large-scale complex technologies the case would become very different. Furthermore, whether such maintenance activities should be undertaken by private or governmental professionals, or by trained community members, has crucial implications for the supply chains of spare parts. In the rest of this chapter, the implications of a community-managed approach are further discussed.

Performance

The CMP approach aims to do things more efficiently by harnessing new and under-utilized capacities. The fund flows are organized through the use of micro-finance institutions that can easily route funds to the communities.

The involvement of communities to plan and construct their own water points, with products and services being procured by communities from the expanded private sector, means that government officials can focus on the vital facilitation, training and technical support activities. Despite the complexity of the supply chains that enable the construction and maintenance of water points, with all these capacities being co-ordinated more can be achieved and faster. In fact, the CMP approach has led to a fivefold increase in the construction rate of new water points in the Amhara region of Ethiopia – from an average of 200 water points per year between 1994 and 2003, increasing steadily to over 1,500 water points per year in 2014 (COWASH, 2014a). Monitoring and evaluation data shows that, over the same period, the implementation costs per water point have been halved.

Sustainability

In Ethiopia it has become evident that project-based, one-off and stand-alone implementation of water points should be replaced with sustainable, large-scale approaches that actualize the philosophy of decentralized service delivery. Moreover, the approach should preferably be embedded in the permanent governmental structures to guarantee long-term support for the communities. Large-scale approaches further contribute to the harmonization of monitoring and evaluation systems, when reporting is conducted in a uniform manner.

Sustainability in the context of rural water supply mainly deals with questions related to the long-term usage of the water point. Accordingly, operations and maintenance, availability of spare parts, as well as community management become crucial factors in determining sustainability of a water point in a rural, remote area. Functionality rates for water points implemented with the CMP approach reach 93 per cent (COWASH, 2014b), which is above the national average of 77 per cent for water points constructed with traditional approaches (according to data obtained from the National Water, Sanitation and Hygiene Inventory for Ethiopia for 2013). This means that at the time of monitoring, 93 per cent of water points were operating and in use. CMP water points have been found to be better maintained, at least partly due to the training of community water committees and pump attendants/caretakers. Furthermore, the roles of governmental authorities need to be clear in order to provide the necessary support to communities.

At present, there is no clear system for supporting communities in the maintenance and operations of water points, and no organized spare parts supply. However, a few solutions are currently being tested, ranging from the training of technical maintenance and operations persons at the village level, to establishing a spare parts supply system where a regional revolving fund office procures spare parts in bulk and delivers them to the district governmental offices. Another issue jeopardizing the sustainability of CMP water points may be technology choice. The CMP approach in Ethiopia is intended mainly for low-level technologies such as hand-dug wells and spring protections, and therefore the hydrogeological conditions need to be taken into account. It can be questioned, though, whether such small-scale technologies are sustainable in the long run, as the design period of hand pumps usually ranges from 10 to 15 years. After the design period, new investments are required from the government and from the donors to implement new water points. Time will show whether more complicated piped supply systems or household self-supply rope pumps will be found more appropriate in the future. To conclude, CMP shows promising results in terms of sustainability, but issues related to spare parts and technology choice still remain unsolved and require careful consideration between the trade-offs involved.

Community

The community is at the centre of the CMP approach. Communities organize themselves through selecting a representative water committee that includes both female and male members. This committee then submits an application to the district governmental office, which demonstrates the need for the water point. Due to this procedure, and the community contributions embedded in the process, CMP is called a demand-driven approach. The major innovation of the CMP approach, however, is to transfer funds for physical construction directly to the community. With support from the governmental agencies, communities are then responsible for the full development process, through planning, implementation (including procurement) and maintenance. The community contracts an artisan to conduct the cement works of the water point, and engages in the supervision of the construction process. In most cases community members also take part in the digging of the well, and contribute a minimum of 15 per cent in cash or in kind for the construction of the water point. Additional cash is posited in the micro-finance institution's savings account for future operations and maintenance expenses. Other future financial contributions include payments for the spare parts, and salary of the guard of the water point. The role of the guard is in monitoring the proper use of the water point, and making sure that community members collect water only during the 'opening hours' of the water point. In some instances, the community members have to travel a long way to another city to procure spare parts if they are not available locally.

As opposed to traditional top-down approaches, the CMP approach avoids any 'handing over' of water points and thus contributes to community ownership. This is turn builds a strong foundation for future long-term sustainability of the water point. The success of CMP is helping to dispel the myth that communities cannot manage funds for such development processes. In fact, communities make the processes more efficient and thus contribute to accelerating the water supply coverage in Ethiopia.

Collaboration

Community-managed water supplies create new supply chains and novel relationships between the members of the supply chains. In traditional, centralized service delivery, pumps and spare parts are procured in bulk and routed to the districts with relatively simple procedures. In such an approach, the governmental agencies remain in control of the material and financial flows and this adds to the workload of the government. In the CMP approach, pumps and spare parts need to be locally available, and the local private sector has an important role to play. In most cases, the local suppliers procure pumps and spare parts from importers and transport them to the remote areas. Moreover, technical support and training are required at multiple levels. Building relationships for the implementation and usage of a new technology calls for additional information and new practices.

The CMP approach is helping local government to achieve more by drawing on the additional capacity of communities, micro-finance institutions and the private sector. These new supply chains, however, require collaboration between the governmental agencies, communities, local suppliers, micro-finance institutions as well as the importers of the pumps and spare parts. Moreover, governmental agencies are required to change their role and to allow for other actors to step in. Naturally, the communities need to be willing to accept the new responsibilities for the CMP approach in order to be successful. This involves financial contributions and management responsibilities, against which the benefits of communal water supply need to be justified.

Hints for practitioners

- Decentralized procurement may lead to complex supply chains, but it fosters growth of local markets and flexible utilization of local resources.
- Analyse whether the sustainability aspects of the chosen technology (such as durability, easy to operate, spare parts available) have been considered adequately, and whether funds have been reserved for adequate training for the members of the supply chain.
- Alignment with government structures will ensure long-term government support to communities.

References

COWASH (2014a) Community-Led Accelerated Water, Sanitation and Hygiene project, 2007 EFY Performance Report

COWASH (2014b) Community-Led Accelerated Water, Sanitation and Hygiene project, Annual Report, 2014

RWSN (2010) RWSN Executive Steering Committee, Myths of the Rural Water Supply Sector, RWSN Perspective No 4 , RWSN, St Gallen, Switzerland

Managing supply chain sustainability risks

9.3

ALEXANDER BLECKEN, ANNA GAARDE AND NIVES COSTA

United Nations Office for Project Services (UNOPS), Denmark

Highlights

- For our case study organization looked at in this chapter, the United Nations Office for Project Services (UNOPS), integrating sustainability into the core of its operations has become a key priority. As procurement and supply chain processes contribute around 75 per cent of overall delivery, these processes inherit a particular significance when assessing and managing sustainability risks.

- At UNOPS, we developed a methodology that can effectively assess supply chain and procurement sustainability risks and lead to action plans with which these risks can be mitigated. This methodology leads to robust results, focuses on the most important areas where action is required, is easily applied by practitioners and is relevant even in some of the most difficult environments.

- Our sustainability risk assessment is based on a mapping of the organization's spend as well as category risks and leverage profile. We have used the methodology in the UNOPS office in South Sudan where a collaborative one-day workshop led to a specific action plan for the office.

- Managing sustainability risks in procurement is possible even in difficult environments and markets. It is important to focus on the most relevant areas and make the process easily applicable (without oversimplifying matters) such that colleagues working in country offices accept and apply the methodology and implement the recommended actions.

- Continuous follow-up and reporting on implementation progress is required to ensure successful implementation.

UNOPS is an operational arm of the United Nations (UN), supporting the successful implementation of its partners' peace-building, humanitarian and development projects around the world. UNOPS does this by providing project management, procurement and infrastructure services. In particular, 'UNOPS provides sustainable project management services in peace-building, humanitarian and development environments.' 'UNOPS manages the construction of infrastructure projects that promote sustainable development for people in need.' 'UNOPS is a central procurement resource in the UN, working towards including sustainability considerations in all its procurement.' These excerpts, taken from the UNOPS website's homepage (www.unops.org), indicate that integrating sustainability into the core of its operations has become strategically important for the organization. Out of an overall delivery of around US $1.1 billion, procurement constitutes US $669 million and thus a significant fraction through which sustainability can be promoted; to do so effectively, supply chain sustainability risks need to be managed.

A significant part of an organization's sustainability risks and impacts are clustered in its supply chain. Nonetheless, the supply chain remains the 'soft spot' of many sustainable procurement approaches. When we approached this problem in UNOPS, we were first faced with the challenge of identifying the materiality and the scope of such risks in our global operations. Second, as in every risk management framework, we needed a robust approach to guide and prioritize our action. These two components were both essential to ensure that due diligence was applied to our supply chains, in line with our ambition of achieving excellence in our corporate, social and environmental responsibility. In order to effectively manage supply chain sustainability risks, we needed to come up with a methodology and a tool that could take into account the UNOPS specific operating environment. UNOPS delivers over 1,000 projects a year in more than 80 countries. Procurement is highly decentralized at UNOPS, with more than 80 per cent of the annual spend procured through country offices, and so is the community of procurement and supply chain specialists in the organization. High turnover in personnel, a general reluctance to embrace initiatives that are perceived as top-down impositions from headquarters, and high workload at country offices pose further challenges to promoting sustainable procurement and managing sustainability risks in the organization's supply chain.

Therefore, we needed to come up with a methodology that was easy to understand and apply by procurement practitioners; that could produce results quickly but robustly; and that involved the country offices in a way that promoted their buy-in and would lead to implementable action plans, ultimately leading to changing how a specific country office would manage its supply chain sustainability risks.

Our methodology is based on an integrated approach that combines expert activities carried out by sustainability specialists prior to assessing a specific country office's sustainability risk profile, and an in-country one-day workshop that serves to create buy-in from country personnel who are responsible for the daily implementation of sustainable procurement. The risk assessment is then further refined and developed into an implementable action plan. Our methodology comprises four key steps: mapping the procurement spend; evaluating sustainability category risks; evaluating leverage with suppliers for each category; and prioritization of actions and the implementation of the action plan. The first two of these steps can largely be carried out from a central location and expert team (in our case by the sustainability team in the headquarters' procurement department), while the latter two are crucial to be carried out together with the country office team. The need to perform the last two steps of the process at local level is because crucial intelligence on local markets, suppliers, circumstances and procedures is almost exclusively available in country offices. Figure 9.3.1 provides an overview of the risk assessment and prioritization process. The circle represents key process steps, while the squares highlight key stakeholders to consult. The arrows in the centre indicate that it is a continuous process that should be reviewed and updated on a regular basis.

Figure 9.3.1 Risk assessment and prioritization workshop

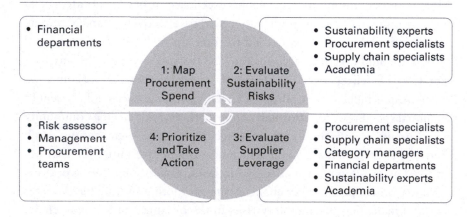

Map procurement spend

Creating a category-based spend overview is a critical step in the process of gaining overview of aggregated impact and the associated sustainability risks. We used our enterprise resource planning (ERP) system to obtain the necessary data and paid particular attention to cleaning up the data, in particular attributing purchase orders to the right categories. From our experience, cleaning up data stemming from central ERP systems is important, as automatic or standard classification often yields incorrect category spend information. While this step can be carried out in advance of an in-country workshop, it is important to analyse the spend profile together with the country office in order to see if any irregular, one-off or otherwise non-repetitive purchases need to be offset. Naturally, any backwards-looking spend profile will only provide historic data, while sustainability risks need to be managed looking forward. Therefore, the in-country workshop also includes a discussion on future programmes and procurement plans of the country office. The result of this step is a procurement spend profile for the country office that describes the key procurement categories at a reasonable granularity, and brings financial transparency to the country office in terms of the most important spend categories.

Evaluate sustainability risks

Once a category-based spend overview has been created, the sustainability risks that are connected to each of the categories can be evaluated. The sustainability risk depends on the types of products or services that the categories consist of and how they are typically produced or provided. In order to avoid blind spots in the assessment, all high-level categories need to be reviewed and the sustainability risks in their respective subcategories considered. This is important, as the high-level categories may consist of a broad range of products or services. Scores are set for the categories based on their respective risks. In this assessment, it is important to consider the whole life-cycle impacts of products and services in order to gain a full understanding of their sustainability risks and to avoid a limited focus on the usage phase. As this may require specific local or sectoral knowledge, for this exercise we used input from a number of experts, including representatives from the sustainability team, procurement officers, academics and supply chain specialists.

We assessed category sustainability risks through three factors. First, the level of material environmental risks associated with the products or services in the category, including air emissions, waste-water discharge, waste generation, use of non-renewable or vulnerable renewable resources, management of hazardous materials, fossil fuel and water consumption, impact on ecosystems, and transport and logistics. Second, the level of socioeconomic risks associated with the products or services in the category, including human rights risks, limitations to freedom of association, risks of forced or child labour, risks of discrimination or unfair remuneration, risk of corruption, risks to occupational health and safety, negative community impact or limited local participation. Third, the complexity of the supply chain for the products or services – including consideration of the number of tiers in the supply chain, level of knowledge of subsuppliers, level of control of subsuppliers, known challenges to law enforcement in the countries of the supply chain, and risks of unfair trade practices in the supply chain. This latter supply chain complexity factor is one that can amplify the sustainability risk score for complex supply chains in challenging geographical contexts. We chose to assign a score of 1–5 for each of these three components, where a score of 5 indicates very high risks and a score of 1 indicates very low risks. Once individual scores for the three factors are set, a final value can be determined, resulting in a fair overall risk value that considers all the individual factors contributing to the sustainability risks.

Similar to the first step, this activity can be largely carried out prior to an in-country workshop. Yet, while some category risks are universal, the accuracy of the assessment benefits greatly from being tailored to the specific market and supply chain conditions of a country. Therefore, and in order to strengthen buy-in of the country office, it is important that the sustainability risks are reviewed and verified together with the country office team during an in-country workshop.

Evaluate supplier leverage

The next step in the sustainability risk assessment is to map the leverage that a specific country office has over key suppliers in the respective categories. If a country office has no leverage over certain suppliers, it is not likely to be able to positively influence such suppliers to change business practices. Hence, leverage over suppliers is important to help set priorities, ie shape the action plan such that it has the biggest impact.

At the minimum, two factors influence leverage: overall procurement spend in a specific category and scope to influence suppliers in that category. To improve applicability and in order to avoid excessive complexity of the methodology, we evaluated procurement spend relative to total procurement spend of the country office. Based upon this largely automatic calculation, we assigned scores of 1–5 according to the percentage of the total procurement that the category represents. High spend is an indicator of high potential for generating change.

Spend alone will not determine, however, in which categories a country office has scope to influence suppliers. This also very much depends on its operational environment, the market and the position of suppliers. Therefore, setting the right values for the country office's ability to influence suppliers is a key component of the in-country workshop. Representatives of the country office, together with the workshop facilitator, agree on a score for the scope of influence in each category. A number of indicators can be considered for this purpose. These include market share of the country office for the specific supplier, ie if a country office's procurement typically represents a significant part of the supplier's turnover within the category. This will indicate if a country office holds a strong position vis-à-vis other customers of the supplier in the category. Another indicator is reputation with suppliers, ie do suppliers have other reasons to be eager to maintain a good relation with the country office (eg for reputational reasons, reliability or is there a long-standing relationship with the country office and business continuity)? An external factor that can also be considered when assessing leverage within the categories is to explore whether there are already initiatives in place to address sustainability risks in the specific category. If there are such initiatives, a country office can potentially capitalize on these existing avenues of action. This also means that suppliers in the category may be sensitized to addressing sustainability issues, which will make it easier to work with these suppliers.

Scores from 1 to 5 are set for the scope of influence in the categories, where a score of 5 represents the strongest level of influence. Once individual scores for spend level and scope of influence are set, a final single score can be determined for each category in order to identify the overall leverage score.

In order to facilitate and support the sustainability risk-assessment process, we have developed an Excel-based tool that guides a country office through the first three steps of the process. Spend data can be filled in (or within UNOPS we pre-fill that data), standard category sustainability risks are already determined together with a group of experts, and leverage scores can be easily inserted. Based on this data, a number of graphs are automatically created, which can be used in the in-country workshop to determine and prioritize actions. Copies of these documents remain with the country office after the workshop in order to serve as a measure to monitor progress against the implementation plan.

Prioritize and take action

While UNOPS has committed to have sustainability as an integral part of its procurement and supply chain processes, we do not mistake this for doing everything at once. Considering time and resource constraints, our approach promotes a clear prioritization of actions that help manage supply chain sustainability risks. In order to create an implementable action plan, it is important to focus both on actions within certain categories of spends, as well as actions in relation to certain suppliers.

To prioritize actions within spend categories, we plot sustainability risk scores against leverage scores. Figure 9.3.2 provides an overview over the four quadrants that can be established, roughly separating between high/low sustainability risks and high/low leverage. Figure 9.3.2 also includes suggestions for the type of actions that can be taken to address the sustainability risks according to the categories' scores. Categories are grouped into 'critical', 'easy-win', 'challenging' and 'latent', depending on their distribution in the four quadrants of the matrix. Naturally, most attention should be paid to the critical categories, which are prone to a high degree of sustainability risk, and which an office has a high degree of leverage over. These are categories where the biggest impact can be achieved and action is most critical. The easy-win categories are those with a low level of sustainability risk, but where an office has a significant degree of leverage. Therefore, sustainability measures can fairly easily be introduced and categories from this quadrant could be next as they represent easy wins. Continued successes and improvements in the sustainability footprint can help maintain momentum and convince senior management to continuously commit to the programme. The challenging categories are those with high sustainability risks but where an office only has a limited degree of leverage. The categories that fall within the field of low level of sustainability risks and low level of leverage can be categorized as latent categories. There may be some important sustainability measures to be taken within these categories but, in relation to the other categories, these are deprioritized. Figure 9.3.2 suggests a range of appropriate actions at the category level for each of the four quadrants.

Figure 9.3.2 Suggested actions to address sustainability risks in procurement categories, according to positioning on the sustainability risk/leverage matrix

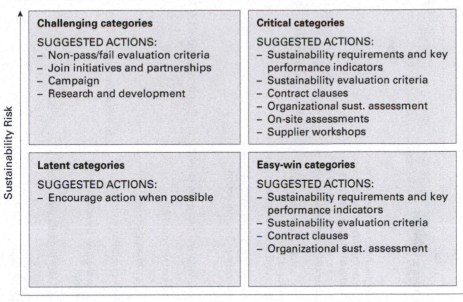

Another important perspective is achieved by ranking all suppliers according to their spend with the office and clustering them according to a standard ABC analysis. Assigning a score based on their spend with the office and combining this score with the category risk score will yield a ranked and prioritized list of suppliers for a country office. Depending on the resource availability within the country office, a threshold base limit can be set. Only suppliers above this threshold will be included in the organization's supply chain sustainability programme, and the country office will work closely with these suppliers to measure their sustainability impact and manage their sustainability risks. In our case, we decided to define some further criteria that will determine whether or not suppliers will be included in the sustainability programme, eg the existence of a long-term supply agreement. From our experience, it is important to keep these criteria simple such that they can be easily applied and understood and still yield a robust selection.

Pilot workshop

We piloted the in-country workshop to assess and manage supply chain sustainability risks with the UNOPS office in South Sudan. After general

Figure 9.3.3 Action plan developed at UNOPS South Sudan country office

Our Sustainable Procurement Priorities and Targets

Priority categories	Action commitment	Target
Construction Services	– Based on the project context and location and wherever found to be feasible we shall include an evaluation criteria in ITBs (Pass/Fail) to companies to include upon signing the contract documentation proof that at least 50% of manual labours is carried out by local employees and 10% are female. – All bidders must confirm on applying UNOPS environmental management system / guidelines for any work to be carried for UNOPS. – All bidders must confirm on applying UNOPS health and safety procedure and guidelines for employees under any work to be carried for UNOPS. – In line with the UN Global Compact – all bidders must submit documentation that they respect ILO core conventions. – The contractor must submit documentation that they respect ILO core conventions. – SOW to include the requirements to obtain natural resources and construction materials from the local community whenever feasible.	In all contracts above US $50,000
Vehicles	• SSOC will use the exiting LTA through UNWebbuy at HQ who will place the call-off order. • Use the online Life-Cycle Costing Tool to guide the procurement decision	In all contracts above US $50,000
Furniture	• Procurement official should consult the furniture UN SP product guideline and background report • Emphasize where possible to include in the specification of furniture the point of using recycled materials, textile, metal and wood. • The supplier has to follow an environmentally friendly packaging by considering the cardboard packaging consists of 80% recycled material	In all contracts above US $50,000
IT	• Procurement official should consult the IT Equipment UN SP product guideline and background report • Conduct life cycle costing with consultation with Sustainability team at HQ • The supplier has to follow an environmentally friendly packaging by considering the cardboard packaging consists of 80% recycled material	In all contracts above US $30,000

training on sustainable public procurement, which was attended by more than 20 participants, we ran a one-day in-country sustainability risk assessment workshop with eight participants. The participants, who mainly came from the procurement unit but also included the head of Support Services, developed the specific spend and sustainability risk profile of the UNOPS South Sudan country office, based on the preparatory work carried out by the sustainability team at UNOPS headquarters. The methodology proved to be relevant and applicable even in a market as challenging and unique as South Sudan. A high-level overview of the commitment of the office to sustainable procurement, and the action plan developed during the course of the workshop, can be seen in Figure 9.3.3.

The participants of the risk assessment workshop evaluated the workshop highly favourably across the board, namely: high satisfaction with the quality of the workshop (averaged 4.63 over a maximum score 5.00); the workshop helped participants to gain a better understanding of their organization's spend composition and procurement sustainability risks (4.38); after the workshop the participants felt better equipped to identify procurement sustainability risks and to prioritize action to address risks in the most effective manner (4.38); and participants ranked it highly likely that they would apply some of what they had learned (4.43). All participants stated that they would recommend the workshop to colleagues.

Conclusions

Through the pilot workshop and sustainability initiative undertaken together with UNOPS country offices, we found that the developed methodology is a very good way to facilitate discussion on sustainability and sustainable procurement in each local and regional context. We found that the methodology serves as an effective way to operationalize sustainable procurement and ensure that learning from training can be translated into action. We also found that some concepts in sustainable procurement are complex for colleagues who have so far not often been exposed to the topic. Therefore, our approach to keep the methodology simple, while providing central expert support, proved to be the right one. In a decentralized set-up such as at UNOPS, local management commitment to the developed action plan is of utmost importance. Sustainability risk assessments need to become a part of the early stages of the procurement process, eg procurement planning. In this way, country offices will be able to anticipate and mitigate sustainability risks continuously and in advance of their procurements.

Most importantly, only if country office management continues to commit time to follow up, monitor and request reporting on progress made against the action plan, will change be made and sustainability risks effectively managed. Yet, with the significant impact that procurement can have in shaping sustainable development, we believe that more and more local procurement units will adopt an effective way to manage their sustainability risks.

Hints for practitioners

- Supply chain sustainability assessments work and are relevant even in very difficult environments.
- Keep sustainability assessments simple but don't oversimplify matters.
- Analyse your supply chain data and develop results and action plans always together with the colleagues who will be responsible for implementation.
- Regularly follow up and monitor implementation progress.
- Contact any of the authors if you would like to discuss if supply chain sustainability assessments can be used to improve your organization's footprint and impact.

Using three-dimensional printing in a humanitarian context

9.4

Challenges and solutions

PETER TATHAM

Department of International Business and Asian Studies,
Griffith University, Australia

JENNIFER LOY

Queensland College of Art, Griffith University, Australia

Introduction

In any humanitarian context, be it the aftermath of a natural disaster or complex emergency or in a development operation, there is almost always a requirement for improved water, sanitation and hygiene (WASH) facilities. Unfortunately, however, the physical environment in which humanitarian logisticians operate frequently presents multiple challenges such as broken roads, destroyed bridges and sometimes a less than totally supportive response from national customs authorities. Thus, for example, the lead time to replace a broken item of equipment that is not available locally can stretch into weeks or even months. However, the emergence of three-dimensional printing (3DP) technology has the potential to mitigate these challenges by enabling the manufacture of a particular item of equipment such as a spare part or component at a location that is close to the area where it is needed.

Since the early 2000s, the ways in which 3DP is being employed in a commercial context have expanded considerably but, to date, there has been relatively limited consideration of its application within a not-for-profit/humanitarian context. This chapter describes how the potential for the use of 3DP was investigated with the assistance of the staff of a major international non-governmental organization (Oxfam GB), and the resulting management and organizational lessons that were identified are presented.

Key logistic trade-offs of 3DP

- The most important trade-off is between the desire for a swift provision of a component to meet an identified need, and ensuring that the printed item is truly 'fit for purpose'.

- From a logistic perspective, 3DP offers the potential to reduce the transport and warehousing burden and, thereby, reduce the logistic lead time, but the overall cost/component may well rise.

- Circumventing the traditional supply chain avoids some of the complicating factors that can arise when importing products to unstable regions, but this approach is likely to increase the workload and responsibilities for field staff.

- Although 3DP has the potential to enable individuals or businesses within a region to undertake local production, such a strategy relies on the existence of resilient communication and power systems.

- Whilst the geometry of existing products is easily available and accessible, products need to be redesigned for 3DP production to ensure that they are compatible with, and optimize the capabilities of, the technology. This, in turn, requires appropriate skills at the field operator level, as well as the ability to collect and communicate accurate and appropriate information.

3D printing

Three-dimensional printing (3DP) – otherwise known as additive manufacturing, rapid prototyping or rapid manufacturing – builds an item or component layer by layer without the need for a mould or cutting tool. Thus, 3DP can be distinguished from traditional production methods that, typically, involve the removal of material from an initial large block or the use of injection moulding techniques (Kreiger *et al*, 2014). Although 3DP has been in existence since the early 1990s (Campbell, Bourell and Gibson, 2012), the development of new and improved technical approaches is changing what is possible to be created as well as the economics of the process.

However, notwithstanding the massive growth in the ways in which the printers operate, as well as the materials that are used, the underpinning principles, benefits and challenges remain the same whatever physical mechanism and medium is used to produce the required item of equipment. Thus, whilst multiple 3DP technologies exist, this chapter discusses the use of 'fused deposition modelling' (FDM) as this technology is ideal for printers that are mobile, low cost, easy to operate and can utilize a range of source materials. As a result, it is well suited for a role in supporting humanitarian logistic operations.

Within this family of printers, most basic-level FDM machines operate by heating a single filament of material, such as an engineering grade polymer called acrylonitrile butadiene styrene (ABS), which is a strong, stable polymer suitable for end-use applications. The filament is then extruded in a continuous feed (like a glue gun), and at the same time the bed of the machine moves slowly downwards thereby allowing an object to build. As can be seen in Figure 9.4.1, such machines start at around the size of a desktop printer, and are easily transported. They are also relatively inexpensive, with entry-level machines priced at less than US $800 and, reflecting 'Moore's Law', the capability of such machines is growing at a fast rate, whilst at the same time the cost for a given capability is reducing. Furthermore, FDM machines are now available that can use multiple raw materials at the same time, and there is also an increasing range of such materials that are available for different applications.

Single-filament FDMs are also the least problematic of current printers to operate as they do not require a sealed print environment and can even be used outdoors if necessary – although wind strength, dust and changes in humidity will affect them. They are not expensive to run, with the filament costing around $40 per kilogramme and, as the workings are readily accessed,

Figure 9.4.1 Photograph of a portable FDM printer in use in a pilot trial location

they are also the easiest printers to maintain, to adjust on site, and/or to repair if damaged in transit.

This relatively simple system can build complex objects such as pipes and connectors that can then be used in a WASH context in order to, for example, replace a broken component. This can be achieved using designs that are based, in the first instance, on an assessment of the requirements and workload of the part that is needed. Importantly, the printing technology enables the basic design to be adjusted as necessary, without the loss of structural integrity. For example, whilst a standard water-pipe bend might be 90 degrees, a site-specific layout may call for a pipe with an angle of 75 or 120 degrees. In this case, the standard design held on the computer can be manipulated to achieve the required dimensions, and an appropriately redesigned model printed off in a relatively short time.

In an ideal world the printer should be supported by an uninterrupted power supply, as a component must be printed in one continuous process, and this can take as long as 12 hours for a large or complex item of equipment. Thus, in a humanitarian context, it may be necessary to provide either a dedicated mini-generator or a battery back-up in the case of power failures. Such facilities already exist in many field locations, but in any event, this issue also supports the use of a desktop FDM in that any interruption to the power supply will cause the print to fail but not compromise the machine itself.

From a theoretical perspective, the use of 3DP has multiple advantages that include:

- The use of a single raw material from which multiple items can be created to meet an identified need. This reflects the concept of logistic postponement (Christopher, 2011) and avoids the 'just in case' requirement to transport items into, and warehouse them within, the field location.

- The reels of raw material require limited packaging and have a high mass-to-volume ratio compared to finished goods. This makes them more efficient to transport (Macharis *et al*, 2014).

- Given the often remote and/or challenging location of a humanitarian operation, the logistic lead time for the provision of spare parts can be lengthy, with Durgavitch (2009) suggesting that delays of up to six months for some countries have been encountered. In addition, 70 per cent of respondents in a recent Organization for Economic Co-operation and Development/World Trade Organization (OECD/WTO) survey reported that there were delays in customs clearance when importing goods (Shepherd, 2013). Thus, whilst a print time of up to 12 hours may sound lengthy, it is clearly a significant improvement over the lead time needed for a component to be sourced outside the country in which the field operation is being conducted.

- Overcoming incompatibilities between the equipment supplied by different NGOs. This is, according to de Leeuw, Kopczak and Blansjaar (2010), a particular challenge where WASH equipment is involved as, unfortunately, the items provided by one organization may not be compatible with that provided by another – for example, through the presence of different pipe bore sizes and/or screw thread arrangements. Thus, 3DP is potentially able to produce a suitable item of equipment that can overcome such incompatibility challenges that are difficult to forecast and, hence, allow advanced pre-positioning of suitable interchange items.

- The use of 3DP also allows for the design of components that are not constrained by the limitations of mass production techniques. For example, it is relatively simple to incorporate in-line filtration into a printed part when using an FDM machine, whereas this is difficult to achieve if injection moulding is used as the production method.

In summary, from a review of the literature, there appear to be no reasons in principle why the benefits of 3DP should not be transferable from the 'for profit' to the 'not for profit' environment.

Moving from theory to practice

Based on the above outline of the potential benefits (and some challenges) for the use of 3DP in a humanitarian context, the first stage of the case study was to interview 13 senior logisticians based in the UK, Africa, Southeast

Asia and Australia in order to obtain their perspectives on the potential for using this technology. Without exception, there was considerable interest in the proposal to trial the technology and, at the same time, there was a clear understanding of the potential it offered to improve logistic efficiency/effectiveness. Furthermore, these key informants were able to confirm that, to the best of their knowledge, 3DP technology was not being currently used by any of the major aid agencies.

As a result, and with financial support from a number of sources – the major funding ones being the Humanitarian Innovation Fund, RedR Australia, HK Logistics and various departments within Griffith University – a researcher and a 3D printer (similar to that shown in Figure 9.4.1) were deployed for two separate 30-day periods to the headquarters of Oxfam GB in Nairobi. During the first research period the 3DP process was demonstrated to some 150 individuals, ranging from the head of Oxfam's team to the office cleaners, as well as to the members of the regional WASH cluster. During this period, multiple items of WASH-related fixtures and fittings were printed (see examples in Figures 9.4.2a and b).

The response of those to whom the 3DP process was demonstrated was very similar on each occasion, and can be summarized as follows:

- Initially, considerable cynicism regarding the benefits of the technology.

- Subsequent amazement at its capability, which was amplified when the robustness of the printed products was demonstrated.

- A resulting 'light bulb moment' when the potential and implications of the use of 3D printing was appreciated by the audience.

Figure 9.4.2a and b Examples of WASH fittings produced by 3D printing at Oxfam GB headquarters in Nairobi

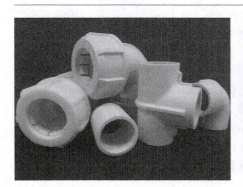 

In summary, whilst the trial achieved its aim of confirming the findings of both the desk study and subsequent key informant interviews that the advantages of 3DP (as described above) are applicable in a humanitarian context, however it also underlined a number of potential technical challenges. For example, WASH equipment typically comes in one of three standard diameters: 32 millimetres, 63 millimetres and 90 millimetres. The printer used for the trial was entirely capable of replicating parts in the 32 millimetre series, but was not big enough to support printing of items in the larger sizes.

Second, because the filament is extruded at a thickness of only 0.2 millimetres, some complex or thick-walled items can take as long as 12 hours to print, even if they have a small overall build size. Whilst this is not a short time period, it should be compared with the one to three months that Oxfam staff indicated is the typical lead time for resupply from their UK warehouse. Nevertheless, particularly in a field location, such a lengthy print duration is likely to coincide with a downtime in the local power generation systems that, typically, need to be changed over every six to eight hours. Thus it is clear that either the 3D printer needs to have its own power generator or that some form of battery must be provided to cover the power outage. Without ensuring that there will be continuous power during the planned print time, there is a danger that the print will fail and the partially built component will need to be scrapped and a reprint commenced.

Management of 3DP in a humanitarian context

In addition to the challenges (such as ensuring an uninterrupted power supply) discussed above, it became abundantly apparent during the research that a key issue was that of ensuring that the printed component was 'fit for purpose'. In other words that it was, for example, of sufficient structural robustness to accommodate the working pressures to which it would be subjected whilst operating.

This key concern can be overcome in one of two generic ways:

- Provide field staff with the necessary knowledge and skills to ensure that they are able to modify and/or print components with the appropriate design and/or structure to ensure safe operation. This approach implies a requirement for the appropriate computer-based specifications of a range of items to be pre-loaded or readily available from an external source. In addition, in order to ensure that field staff are able to operate the modelling software and printers in a safe way, and to avoid the trap of equipment malfunctions at the hands of 'enthusiastic amateurs', a significant and ongoing training commitment would also be necessary.

- Developing and operating a hub-and-spoke organizational construct. This approach would see the design and testing of components being undertaken centrally by trained staff with 'design for process' expertise and access to the necessary testing equipment. This is important as, given the different constraints and opportunities of using this technology, components need to be specifically designed for 3DP (Loy, 2014). The resulting prototypes of the designs also need to be validated for performance under workload and environmental pressures. Once it has been confirmed in the hub (ie laboratory) environment that a particular printed item is fit for purpose, it can be transmitted to the field location (the spoke) and subsequently printed out. The printed component would then be subject to further (limited) testing to ensure that the printer had operated correctly.

The second alternative (ie the hub-and-spoke model) is currently perceived to be the most appropriate, given the relative novelty of 3DP. For this approach to be successful it is clearly essential to understand the training/ education needs and ongoing support requirements of the operators at the spoke.

Summary

In summary, 3DP is perceived to have major potential in a humanitarian environment, and especially in the major area of WASH operations. The case outlined above clearly supports this perception and, indeed, the use of 3D printing could be further enhanced by the parallel use of 3D scanning. Combining these technologies would enable the field operator to identify and document their specific requirements swiftly and accurately, thereby simplifying the work of the design team in the proposed hub-and-spoke model.

From a financial perspective, both the initial capital cost, as well as that of the raw material, is relatively small (and reducing). However, it is also clear that the safe use of a 3DP system, as well as the maximization of its capability, would require a significant investment in the training and education of staff – particularly at the spoke end of the organizational model. It would also require investment in the development of the necessary parametric models and of the performance testing and standards compliance regimes.

A further aspect that will need to be considered is the optimal location for a printer facility as well as the factors that would influence this decision. On the one hand, positioning a printer as far downstream as is practicable would maximize the logistic and postponement benefits described above. On the other hand, adopting such a strategy would lead to an increased burden in training and equipment purchases/maintenance.

Hints for practitioners

- Whilst all the evidence to date would indicate that 3DP will become an important item in the toolkit of the humanitarian logistician, it is strongly recommended that the use of this technology be adopted with caution and in a measured way.

- To be successful and to ensure the production of 'fit for purpose' components, it is recommended that the use of 3DP be managed and overseen by appropriately qualified designers and engineers rather than operated by unqualified staff.

- It is argued that this balance between capturing the logistic benefits of the technology and avoiding malfunctions that might lead to injury, or worse, is best achieved through a hub-and-spoke organizational model.

- If a 3DP system is to be employed, it will be necessary to consider the optimum location that will reflect the trade-off between obtaining the maximum logistic benefit and the associated management, training and education burden.

References

Campbell, I, Bourell, D and Gibson, I (2012) Additive manufacturing: rapid prototyping comes of age, *Rapid Prototyping Journal*, **18** (4), pp 255–58

Christopher, M G (2011) *Logistics & Supply Chain Management*, 4th edn, Prentice Hall, Harlow, UK

de Leeuw, S, Kopczak, L and Blansjaar, M (2010) What really matters in locating shared humanitarian stockpiles: evidence from the WASH Cluster, *PRO-VE 2010*, pp 166–72

Durgavich, J (2009) [accessed 7 June 2015] Customs Clearance Issues Related to the Import of Goods for Public Health Programs, *US AID* [Online] http://deliver.jsi.com/dlvr_content/resources/allpubs/policypapers/CustClearIssu.pdf

Kreiger, M, Mulder, M L, Glover, A G, and Pearce, J M (2014) Life cycle analysis of distributed recycling of post-consumer high density polyethylene for 3-D printing filament, *Journal of Cleaner Production*, 70, pp. 90–96

Loy, J (2014) eLearning and eMaking: 3D printing blurring the digital and the physical, *Education Sciences*, 4 (1), pp 108–21

Macharis, C, Melo, S, Woxenius, J, and Van Lier, T (2014) The 4 A's of sustainable logistics, in *Sustainable Logistics (Transport and Sustainability, Volume 6)*, ed C Macharis, S Melo, J Woxenius and T Van Lier, pp xv–xxviii, Emerald Group Publishing Limited, Bingley

Shepherd, B (2013) [accessed 7 June 2015] Aid for Trade and Value Chains in Transport and Logistics, *WTO/OECD* [Online] http://www.wto.org/english/tratop_e/devel_e/a4t_e/global_review13prog_e/transport_and_logistics_28june.pdf

Making performance measurement work in humanitarian logistics

The case of an IT-supported balanced scorecard

9.5

ADAM WIDERA

Chair for Information Systems and Supply Chain Management, Westfälische Wilhelms-Universität Münster, Germany

BERND HELLINGRATH

Chair for Information Systems and Supply Chain Management, Westfälische Wilhelms-Universität Münster, Germany

Introduction

'*You can't manage what you don't measure*' answered a logistician with several years of working experience in non-governmental organizations (NGOs) and United Nations (UN) organizations when asked what his understanding is of the term *performance measurement*. The question was part of a survey that was conducted by the authors between the years

2012 and 2014 across selected practitioner networks such as the Global Logistics Cluster meetings. We have observed that such a positive attitude regarding performance measurement is exceptional within the humanitarian domain. There are many reasons why this is the case, but in this chapter we examine mainly the issue of appropriateness of performance measurement systems (PMS) for the logistics domain in the humanitarian context. To anticipate the need of a performance measurement system for humanitarian logistics: it is not that logisticians in humanitarian organizations do not want to measure their performance, but the existing performance measurement approaches do not offer the required fittingness and functionality to unfold the intended positive effects on logistics management.

In the past, only few authors dealt with practitioner realities when investigating the topic of performance measurement in the humanitarian domain. A good example for how important the role of the end user is can be found in Schulz and Heigh (2009), who presented their experiences with the development of a performance measurement tool for the International Federation of Red Cross and Red Crescent Societies (IFRC). In contrast to such a practice-oriented procedure, many approaches emphasized a rather universal understanding of how logistics performance in a humanitarian context should be measured and analysed. The *acceptance* of the researched performance indicators and the performance measurement approaches within the (often business) logistics communities played a bigger role than their applicability, appropriateness and sustainability in humanitarian organizations. By doing so, practitioner realities in planning, monitoring, analysing and learning have been neglected. In consequence, humanitarian organizations have limited capabilities to develop an organization-specific PMS that is able to utilize the existing knowledge base from the humanitarian logistics domain. Hence, it was not surprising to discover in our survey that the large majority of the interviewees agreed that, in general, performance measurement of humanitarian logistics is feasible – however, more than 63 per cent of them denied that performance is measured sufficiently in their organizations.

The objective of our research was to develop an IT-supported PMS applicable to very different types of humanitarian organizations. This was done by building on a common knowledge base as well as leaving the PMS open and modular in order to being adjustable to organization- and operation-specific settings. The research was conducted with practitioner involvement from interviews and workshops in the very beginning, up to the implementation of the PMS within a humanitarian organization. A very close and recurring collaboration between practitioners and the research team led to a trustful environment, and resulted in both groups contributing to, and benefitting from, each other's work. In order to give an insight on how the developed PMS works, we focus here on the basic idea and the fundamental functionality of the PMS, both from a conceptual and technical point of view. The aim of this chapter is to present an IT-supported balanced scorecard dashboard application (HumLogBSC) for supporting humanitarian logistics in their performance measurement and monitoring tasks. By using such an application, humanitarian organizations are able to analyse their tasks and processes in order to identify optimization possibilities. Through its application, effectiveness and efficiency can be improved resulting from eliminating weaknesses in the supply chain and saving logistics-related costs. A broad overview of the research process can be found in Widera and Hellingrath (2013a). In this chapter we first briefly give an overview of the process-orientation of the PMS. The second part of the chapter will deal with the IT-supported PMS dashboard and its implementation in different organizations. We will close with some lessons learnt and an outlook of the research process.

What to measure – the balanced scorecard approach

As mentioned in the introduction, respecting practitioner realities has to be the first step for the development of a sustainable performance measurement approach. The project fails if you do not include the user from both the top and the bottom organizational levels. Therefore, a closer look at the humanitarian logistics processes was our starting point to ensure that the real performance drivers receive adequate consideration.

Process-orientation

To ensure a *process-driven* understanding of the application domain we decided to use so-called *reference models* to identify the relevant key performance indicators (KPIs) and appropriate PMS. Reference models contain universal patterns of certain domains or objects and so they can be utilized to generate specific ones. A good comparison are the LEGO® model kits: having, for example, a generic hospital model at hand, the planner got all the relevant elements required to build a specific construction. Such a construction might be suggested or *referenced* by the LEGO® designer, but it can also be modified according to certain settings and preferences of the planner. In any case, the user will be aware of crucial elements such as the reception area, operating theatres or a cafeteria. The reasons for not building a cafeteria, for example, might be intended in terms of not being needed, but it also can be a simple mistake. The reference model supports the planner in distinguishing those two cases. Besides these advantages of generality, reusability and adaptability we can highlight also the modularity and simplicity of reference models as beneficial when it comes to providing as comprehensive as possible a view of the humanitarian supply chain within an appropriate amount of time. Of course, 'from scratch' approaches promise to provide more detailed and specific pictures of a certain scenario, but the disadvantages are time-consuming process mapping, a relatively higher error-prone and also a limited transferability within the humanitarian domain.

In this chapter we have identified the Reference Task Model (RTM) for Humanitarian Supply Chains (Blecken *et al*, 2009; Blecken, 2010) to be the option best able to meet the application domain and performance measurement requirements. The RTM, developed with more than 30 humanitarian organizations, supports the visualization, understanding and communication of humanitarian logistics processes structured according to the logistics functions along all the planning horizons. In order to make use of the RTM for the development of a PMS, we have extended the model in terms of KPIs, best practices and logistics software support. The research process has been executed in co-operation with three humanitarian organizations, covering the IFRC, governmental (GO) and NGO sectors. One of them, the NGO, can be described as a main research partner where not only the RTM and PMS have been applied but an actual organizational change has been implemented (see next paragraph for how the implementation has been executed). The IFRC and GO have been involved in a rather artificial environment such as workshops, interviews or simulations. By these means, we could evaluate the applicability and correctness of the RTM being the fundament for the overall approach (see also Widera and Hellingrath 2011a, 2013b). In Figure 9.5.1 we have depicted how the RTM supports a process-driven visualization of logistics tasks and how the performance dimension has been added to the RTM.

Figure 9.5.1 depicts an exemplary cut out of warehousing tasks on an operational level. At the very top the tasks are listed as they are stored in the RTM. In the middle box these tasks are displayed in a *logical* structure ensuring an ideal flow of the sequence, eg the shipment information should

Figure 9.5.1 From reference tasks to assignment of KPIs

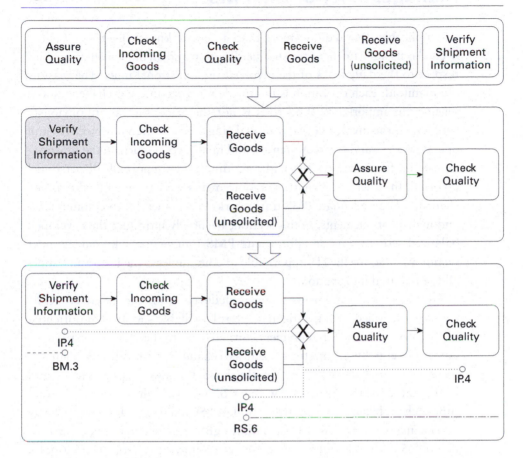

be verified (grey box marking the starting event) before the delivery gets accepted. The lines tagged IP.4, BM.3 and RS.6 in the lowest box represent how measuring points are assigned to the processes. Assuming that a KPI such as 'Mean quality inspection costs per incoming goods item' (IP.4) is an important performance driver in humanitarian logistics, an organization applying the PMS would automatically identify this importance plus the necessity to collect and analyse the data between the measuring start and end points during the process mapping.

By the means of the research approach we were able to identify a set of relevant KPIs covering the whole logistics chain on all planning horizons. In result, the extended RTM can be understood as an information repository for the design, planning, monitoring and analysis of logistics processes of humanitarian organizations.

Manageability of the PMS

An applicable PMS requires more than a generic knowledge base. What is needed is its adjustment to the specific situation and an implementation with respect to the daily tasks of the involved organizational units. The reasons are manifold: each operation is unique, leading to different challenges and set-ups; the importance of all KPIs is not the same, several are obviously conflicting; the involved organizational stages have different objectives and operate under varying circumstances; and finally, yet important, the functioning of the PMS requires the understanding and support of all personnel involved. In order to tackle these requirements we have identified two key elements: 1) an adequate PMS framework; 2) the method to communicate and manage its elements. In this section, we briefly introduce the developed balanced scorecard as an appropriate PMS framework, while in the next section we describe the IT support able to communicate the PMS and handle all the required information.

Following a requirements analysis deduced from the extended RTM we have identified and investigated several available supply chain-oriented PMSs. An additional requirement turned out to be that a relation to domain-overarching objectives, such as reliability or bottleneck management, have to be ensured within the PMS framework (see Widera and Hellingrath, 2011b). As a result we have designed a dedicated humanitarian supply chain balanced scorecard (HumLogBSC), illustrated in Figure 9.5.2.

The main advantages of the HumLogBSC, depicted in the centre of Figure 9.5.2, can be seen in supporting the following criteria: 1) multi-level assessment model; 2) high application flexibility; 3) low application complexity; 4) mix of financial and non-financial metrics. Three of the perspectives – financial, process, and learning and growth – are well known from the classical balanced scorecard approach. The network emphasizes the performance of the collaboration with external actors of the supply chain. One specific adjustment for the humanitarian context is the replacement of the 'customer perspective' by the 'beneficiary and donor perspective' (other examples can be found in Samii, 2010; de Leeuw, 2010). The reason here is that it is hardly possible to transfer the concept of a customer to the humanitarian context (see Widera and Hellingrath, 2013a). We addressed this issue by integrating all beneficiary- and donor-related KPIs – partly conflicting, partly conforming – in one perspective. Thus, the organization applying the PMS is incumbent to adjust the targeted balance between beneficiaries and donors' interests. Besides, we identified 10 generic objectives,

Figure 9.5.2 Balanced scorecard for humanitarian logistics

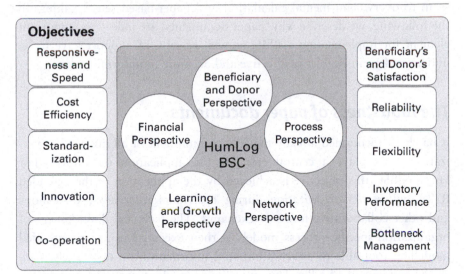

illustrated within the left- and right-sided boxes in Figure 9.5.2, containing the identified KPIs and structured along the five perspectives. Taking into account that a decentralized organization structure is frequent practice, at least divided into headquarters and field offices, the different HumLogBSC perspectives allow a role-based monitoring both in terms of functions and data aggregation levels. Hence, management staff will be served with the required information of budgets available for the ongoing missions while the field offices gets an overview for their current operation. By doing so, the performances reached for the different perspectives are able to be *balanced* with regards to the organization- and operation-specific objectives. At the same time, the monitoring results do not remain unchangeable values but evolve as management capability because of its grounding and relation to the actual logistics tasks and processes.

How to measure – the IT supported dashboard approach

If you google PMS you will find more than one software advertisement in addition to the regular hits on the first results page. We can conclude two aspects from this observation: first, PMS is widely recognized as a technical issue; second, the requirements towards the amount and analysis of data seem to overwhelm mental calculation and paper-based sense making. In the following, we describe why 'paper documents' are indeed an important element for implementing a PMS, as well as why IT support have to be understood as an enabler of effective and accurate monitoring tasks.

The robustness of paper documents

It has been mentioned already that the commitment of all involved organization units plays a central role for the application of a PMS. For HumLogBSC this objective is achieved by the application of the extended RTM *within the organization* during individual interviews, workshops and other collaborative forms of exchange. The technical development of organization-specific process models is then executed using an extended modelling tool able to attach additional information on task levels, such as the assignment of KPIs. This modelling tool does not only contain the RTM (such as task descriptions or reference processes), but it also offers an analysis and a reporting function. While the application of the developed modelling tool plays a supporting role for the modeller, the personnel from humanitarian organizations are mainly working with its main output, being the 'Humanitarian Logistics Handbook'. Figure 9.5.3 illustrates the logic.

The actual front end of the modelling tool is depicted on the left side of Figure 9.5.3. Here we can find the generated process models, including all the relevant information such as relevant KPIs, possible best practices or existing software solutions supporting particular tasks. Those two categories, best practices and software support, have been added to the process models in order to enable the managerial components of the PMS. The main *product* of the modelling tool is a Word document containing all the process models, its explanations and additional information, such as KPIs or best practices. In Figure 9.5.3 we have depicted again the task 'Verify shipment information'; its report output is displayed in the box at the top-right of the figure. Hence, the user of HumLogBSC concerned with this task is able to learn *how* the process should be conducted, *which* impact it has on the relevant *KPIs* and *what* could be done in order to improve the performance. These three main modules represent the functionality of the HumLogBSC, which are applicable even without dashboard software. Even more, the expression of the PMS within the handbook ensures its sustainability as the involved personnel is – by definition of the development process – co-author of the current state as well as the designer of tomorrow's set-up at the humanitarian organization. The end user becomes the designer and owner of the tool.

Figure 9.5.3 Humanitarian Logistics Handbook

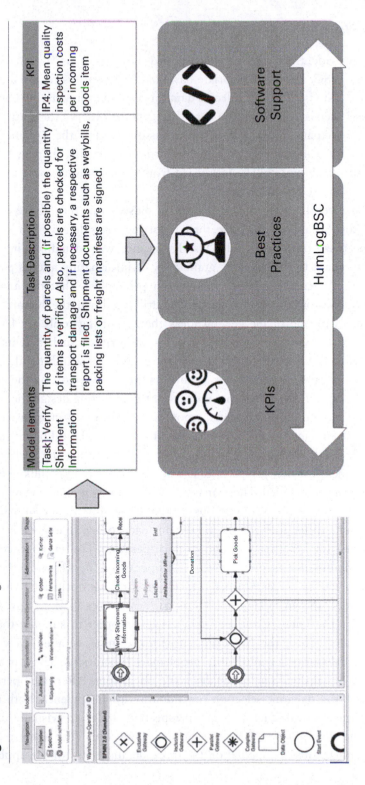

Model elements	Task Description	KPI
[Task]: Verify Shipment Information	The quantity of parcels and (if possible) the quantity of items is verified. Also, parcels are checked for transport damage and if necessary, a respective report is filed. Shipment documents such as waybills, packing lists or freight manifests are signed.	IP:4: Mean quality inspection costs per incoming goods item

KPIs

Best Practices

Software Support

HumLogBSC

The HumLogBSC dashboard

We have identified the above-described handbook as a key result of HumLogBSC, but an appropriate dashboard software is required to store, analyse and visualize the collected data. In combination with the handbook, the end user is able to set the agreed targets, to observe the status as well as to anticipate and communicate measures within the organization in case of not being satisfied with the performances. In this chapter, we briefly describe the HumLogBSC dashboard front end, without going into detail in terms of used technologies.

The overall reporting structure is based on the above-described HumLogBSC approach. Hence, three reporting levels do exist in a hierarchy: perspectives, objectives and KPIs. Each part was visualized in another way, to adapt to the changing granularity of information and its particular purpose. A general applied visualization principle is that the amount of displayed information increases when drilling down the hierarchy. This originates in one of the general ideas that reporting tools are based on: the question whether the organization is performing such that its targets will be achieved or not. Subsequently, it initiates the search for the issue in case the organization does not achieve its targets. Supporting the end user in that search is the factor that influenced the reporting design the most.

The first and most aggregated report view is the perspective visualization illustrated in Figure 9.5.4. The left side consists of the HumLogBSC perspectives. A traffic light is assigned to each circle indicating the current target achievement for that perspective. The perspectives are hyperlinked to views that are more detailed. The management and domain expert view includes data sets for multiple operations at the same time. Since humanitarian operations differ most of the time from each other, it might be possible that one issue just applies to one specific operation. The bar chart combines the two dimensions perspectives and operations by showing the target achievement as percentage per perspective for each operation. The choice of colours (shown in Figure 9.5.4 as patterned tints/shades of grey etc) is based on the same colour set as the circles in order to simplify the visual connection. Thus, the bar chart provides a more detailed view of the perspectives in order to identify problematic operations. There is also the option for selecting one of the displayed operations. After one operation is selected, the dynamic selection functionality applies. Hence, both the bar chart and the traffic lights in the perspective circles are visually updated, showing the data that is in the current scope only. The same principles and mechanisms are applied on the more detailed level of the application.

Figure 9.5.4 HumLogBSC management overview

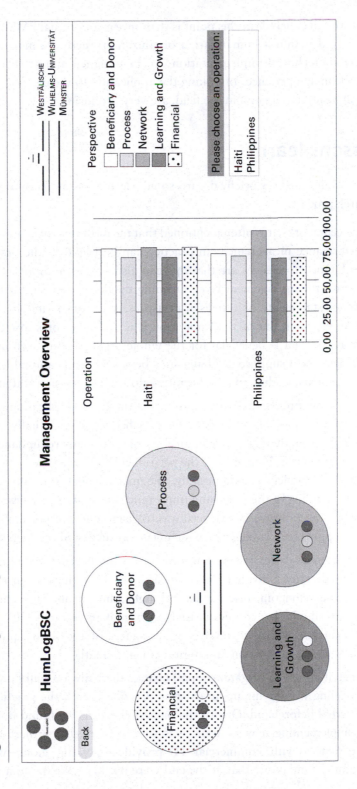

What we can conclude at this point is that once a conceptual PMS approach is deployed within a humanitarian organization, there are many ways as to how its technical implementation can be designed and applied. In our case, the first experiences of linking the application to the existing IT tools, both at headquarters and in the field, are very promising.

Lessons learnt

In this section we very briefly discuss some selected lessons learnt during our research process:

- In recent works, it is often mentioned that the most fervent critics towards performance measurement in practice can be found at the operational level. Our experiences are that this can also – or even more so – be the case for the management level. Opening the discussion on, for example, mission statements, objectives or measures, is sort of sharing the decision-making power. But at the same time it is a sharing of knowledge and awareness that is beneficial for the whole organization. Even more, the dialogue itself supports bridging silos between organizational levels and departments, leading to a better internalization of mission statements.

- During the process mapping sessions, ie the RTM application, we have discovered that the understanding of what logistics actually is differs widely within the organization. In consequence, many redundancies have been found and eliminated by the personnel before even the as-is scenario has been modelled. Additionally, the management staff got a better understanding of the range and importance of logistics processes. One of the first reactions we experienced was to define a new responsibility called the 'supply chain manager' – which was not suggested by the researcher!

- The internal discussion and agreement on the process mapping results required many individual checks and internal meetings. Even more, we still observe ongoing discussions and slight adjustments. The actual result is and should be communicated as a moving target. The involved personnel recognize themselves as designers of the status quo, which offers a huge innovation and improvement potential.

- When it comes to (organizational) change there always will be someone struggling with giving up an existing practice, even if the practices were criticized beforehand. One of the biggest concerns we found in the area of implementing new IT tools was that our project partners had bad experiences with commercial IT providers coming along with big promises (and costs) that at the end were not kept. We found a way out of this dilemma by letting the potential user and decision maker experience new tools in an artificial or safe environment. Such a simulated working space decreases objections and supports the acceptance of new habits. In our case, the practitioners even forgot the new IT environment by playful testing of the effects of certain decisions, eg visualized on a bar chart or a speedometer. Hence, the discovery of the developed IT-supported PMS is about to be internalized as a practitioner reality through a virtual one.

Outlook

We have presented our results on the action/research-based development of an IT-supported balanced scorecard (HumLogBSC) for supporting human-itarian logistics in their performance measurement and monitoring tasks. Our main research partner has already implemented the HumLogBSC approach in their organization and is currently deploying the dashboard software. As at the time of writing, the tool is being tested within an artificial environment of a broader crisis management demonstration project in order to run further analysis regarding the understanding of decision-making processes and the impact of the PMS on the actual performances. Based on our experiences we can summarize the following hints for pract-itioners interested in setting up PMS within their organizations:

- All organizational levels should be aware of the benefits of a PMS. You can't *manage* what you don't measure.

- Ensure a common understanding of what logistics processes are and who is doing what.

- Take care of a continuous communication supporting bridging silos, not only within your organization.

- Don't be afraid of new practices and technology. In case something is not working (better), you still can revise your decision.

- Haste makes waste. Plan enough time for each step, especially at the very beginning.

References

Blecken, Alexander (2010) *Humanitarian Logistics: Modelling supply chain processes of humanitarian organisations*, 1. Aufl. Bern, Haupt, Schriftenreihe Logistik der Kühne-Stiftung, 18

Blecken, Alexander, Hellingrath, B, Dangelmaier, Wilhelm and Schulz, Sabine F (2009) A humanitarian supply chain process reference model, *International Journal of Services Technology and Management*, **12** (4), pp 391–413

de Leeuw, Sander (2010) Towards a reference mission map for performance measurement in humanitarian supply chains, in *Collaborative Networks for a Sustainable World, Proceedings of the 11th IFIP WG 5.5 Working Conference on Virtual Enterprises*, St Etienne, France, 11–13 October, ed L M Camarinha-Matos, X Boucher and H Afsarmanesh, pp 181–88, Springer

Samii, Ramina (2010) *Leveraging Logistics Partnerships: Lessons from Humanitarian Organizations*, VDM Verlag Dr. Müller, Saarbrücken

Schulz, Sabine F and Heigh, Ian (2009) Logistics performance management in action within a humanitarian organization, *Management Research News*, **32** (11), pp 1038–49

Widera, Adam and Hellingrath, Bernd (2011a) Improving humanitarian logistics: towards a tool-based process modeling approach, in *Logistikmanagement: Herausforderungen, Chancen und Lösungen*, ed Björn Asdecker, Alexander Dobhan, Sabine Haas, Jonas Wiese and Eric Sucky, pp 273–95, University of Bamberg Press, Bamberg

Widera, Adam and Hellingrath, Bernd (2011b) Performance measurement systems for humanitarian logistics, in *Proceedings of the 23rd Annual NOFOMA Conference: Logistics and Supply Chain Management in a High North perspective, 23rd Annual NOFOMA Conference*, pp 1327–42, Harstad, Norway, 9–10 June, Nordic Logistics Research Network (NOFOMA)

Widera, Adam and Hellingrath, B (2013a) From process analysis to performance management in humanitarian logistics, in *Managing Humanitarian Supply Chains: Strategies, practices and research*, ed Bernd Hellingrath, Daniel Link and Adam Widera, pp 244–64, DVV Media Group (Literature series: economics and logistics), Hamburg

Widera, Adam and Hellingrath, Bernd (2013b) Understanding humanitarian supply chains: developing an integrated process analysis toolkit, in ISCRAM2013 Academic Papers, 10th International Conference on Information Systems for Crisis Response and Management, ed T Comes, pp 210–19, Baden-Baden

Acknowledgements

We would like to thank our project partners for their time, patience, and trust in our work. Parts of the project have received funding from the European Union's Seventh Framework Programme for research, technological development and demonstration under grant agreement no 607798.

Boko Haram 9.6

The security and supply chain management challenges of providing relief

RICHARD OLORUNTOBA

University of Newcastle, Australia

Introduction and background

This chapter is concerned with the current status of internally displaced persons (IDPs) and refugees arising from the insurgent activities of Boko Haram, an Islamic terror organization operating mostly at the north-eastern tip of Nigeria. The chapter begins with an overview summary of major religious and political conflict in Nigeria. It describes Boko Haram as an organization, and describes its insurgent activities that have resulted in displacement of significant numbers of people, and attendant large-scale socioeconomic disruption. The chapter then provides an analysis of the proportion, gender and status of IDPs and refugees, as well as the complex challenges of providing appropriate and timely relief assistance to the displaced. The chapter further highlights what needs to be done, and the tasks that must be completed in order to provide timely, adequate and appropriate assistance to the IDPs and refugees. It outlines existing relief actors, relief supply chains and associated security concerns in the execution of those relief supply chains. The chapter concludes by outlining a framework of how humanitarian relief organizations can mitigate security challenges in enacting and managing their relief operations and associated relief supply chains.

Nigeria: sociopolitical

The area of West Africa around 20 degrees of latitude north of the equator down to the West African coast, and eastward to 15 degrees of longitude, has a long and illustrious history before colonization by European powers (Armstrong, 1964). The more populous region of West Africa, which used to be referred to as the 'Niger area' by British colonialists, is today known as Nigeria (Armstrong, 1964). Post-colonial Nigeria is a highly complex geographically and ethnically diverse country (Jerome, 2015).

Nigeria has a landed area of about 923,768 square kilometres (356,669 square miles), an area that is the size of France, Britain and the Netherlands combined (Arnold, 2004). It has a diverse climate and terrain, ranging from the equatorial climate of the southern lowlands, through the tropical central hills and plateaus of central Nigeria to the arid northern plains of Nigeria that mark the southernmost boundaries of the Sahara Desert (see Figure 9.6.2 in the Appendix at the end of this chapter for a map of Nigeria showing the major cities). The country has over 400 ethnic groups. The Nigerian population was estimated at 178.5 million people in 2014, with Christianity and Islam practised by almost the entirety of the population and split at approximately 50 per cent each.

However, the country also has many who embrace traditional religions (Jerome, 2015). Nigeria's diversity is often daily played out in the fissures along the lines of language, culture, ethnicity, regional identity and religion. There are enormous territorial, population and economic disparities between the country's 36 states and over 200 nationalities, a legacy of British colonial rule, and the Berlin Conference of 1884 where the then European powers drew national boundaries, and signed the treaty of Berlin to partition Africa for colonization. The 1914 amalgamation of Southern and Northern Nigeria by Britain seems to have also contributed to these enduring national fissures.

Also, endemic corruption, bad governance and political instability have resulted in significant parts of the population failing to benefit from the country's strong economic growth and its enormous oil, gas and other mineral resources. Nigeria has experienced a recurrence of large and extremely violent ethnic, religious and communal conflicts before and since independence from Britain in 1960 (Salawu, 2010). For example, the Nigerian–Biafran war, a civil war that lasted from 1967 to 1970 was estimated to have resulted in 1 million to 3 million deaths (Akresh *et al*, 2012). One of the most prominent religious conflicts pitching Muslims against Christians was the Maitatsine uprising in Kano in December 1980, in which an estimated

4,177 Nigerians were killed (Abdullahi, 2015; Isichei, 1987). There are scores of other significant communal clashes and religious flare-ups that are beyond the scope of this chapter.

Boko Haram

It has been estimated that about 40 per cent of all large violent conflicts have taken place since Nigeria's return to democratic civilian rule in 1999 (Salawu, 2010). The latest among these large, violent and decimating sectarian conflicts is the Boko Haram Islamic insurgency. Boko Haram is officially called Wiliāyat Gharb Ifrīqīyyah and formerly called Jamā'at Ahl as-Sunnah lid-Da'wah wa'l-Jihād, meaning 'group of the people of sunnah for preaching and jihad'. Boko Haram is an Islamic extremist terror group based in north-eastern Nigeria, but it is also active in the neighbouring countries of Niger Republic, Chad and northern Cameroon (US Bureau of Counterterrorism, 2013).

Boko Haram is led by Sheikh Abubakar Shekau, and estimates of the group's fighting membership ranges between 7,000 and 10,000 fighters (US Bureau of Counterterrorism, 2013). Boko Haram initially had links to al-Qaeda, but in 2014 it openly expressed support for the Islamic State of Iraq and the Levant (ISIL) also known as the Islamic State of Iraq and Syria (ISIS), and went on in March 2015 to pledge formal allegiance to ISIL (Celso, 2015; BBC, 2015a; BBC, 2015b; Al Arabiya, 2014; The Telegraph, 2014).

Sustained campaign of violence

Boko Haram has attacked police personnel and police stations as well as military bases. It has bombed or attacked schools, religious buildings, public institutions, media offices, markets, bars and cafes – with more than 15,000 civilians killed, including rival Islamic clerics and politicians. The insurgent activities of Boko Haram have included: a suicide attack on a United Nations (UN) building in Abuja; the bombing of the Nigerian national police headquarters in June 2011; and the destruction of a major Nigerian Air Force base in Maiduguri in December 2013. There are innumerable other attacks that have burnt and devastated villages, and destroyed infrastructure (Jerome, 2015). Thousands of people have been killed, including hundreds of students (Jerome, 2015). Boko Haram's April 2014 abduction of 276 schoolgirls from Chibok attracted extensive international attention (Byman, 2016; Jerome, 2015).

Thousands of insurgents and, according to rumours, foreign fighters, have in recent times aggressively and directly challenged the Nigerian Army and Nigerian Air Force through direct confrontation in open and sustained battles. Boko Haram has used armoured vehicles, including tanks, and other heavy weapons (Jerome, 2015). It has erected flags over the territories, villages and towns it has seized. It is forcing any remaining residents to follow its version of sharia or be killed, mostly through beheadings – just like its Sunni masters, ISIS, in Iraq and Syria. More than 16,000 civilians are estimated to have been killed in Boko Haram-related insurgency since 2009 (Okeke-Uzodike and Onapajo, 2015). In fact, a report by the Global Terrorism Index published by the Institute for Economics and Peace in 2015, indicated that Boko Haram was responsible for 6,664 deaths in 2014 alone, more than any other terrorist group in the world, including the Islamic State (ISIS), which in comparison killed 6,073 people in 2014. Furthermore, the amount of military deaths is unconfirmed but it is not insignificant.

Thus, the Boko Haram crisis may be classified as a complex emergency. A complex emergence arises when the capacity of an individual or a population to sustain livelihood and life is threatened primarily by political and/or religious factors and, in particular, by high levels of violence (Burkle Jr, 1999). Such complexity refers to the multifaceted responses initiated by international organizations such as the UN, and is further complicated by the lack of protection normally provided by international covenants and treaties, and the UN Charter during conventional inter-state warfare.

Internally displaced persons and refugees

Attacks by Islamist Boko Haram insurgents increased dramatically from mid-2014, causing an unprecedented protection crisis in north-eastern Nigeria (Internal Displacement Monitoring Centre, 2014). Violent clashes between government forces and Boko Haram in the north of Nigeria triggered large waves of displacement. UN and Nigerian officials report that over 6 million Nigerians have been affected by the conflict between Boko Haram and Nigerian state authorities (Jerome, 2015; United Nations High Commission for Refugees, 2015). Other estimates indicate that more than 1.65 million people had fled the war zone as of August 2015, an increase of 800,000 since May 2014 (Jerome, 2015; IPI Global Observatory, 2015; US Agency for International Development, 2015). These figures make Boko Haram the deadliest Islamic terrorist group in the world (Jerome, 2015; IPI Global Observatory, 2015; US Agency for International Development, 2015).

According to Boko Haram Victims Relief (BHVR), a Canadian not-for-profit corporation, registered federally in Canada in January 2015, and operating under the informal name 'Secours aux Sinistrés de Boko Haram', in the three most distressed Nigerian states alone, some 13 million people have been directly or indirectly affected by Boko Haram and, given the destruction of crops and thefts of livestock and foodstuffs, famine and epidemic disease appear inevitable unless drastic relief action is taken (BHVR, 2015).

Although the majority of IDPs and refugees are not in official camps, according to the US Agency for International Development (2015) and the International Organization for Migration (2015), it seems clear that, as at the time of writing, over 1.5 million Nigerians have fled their homes in response to the insurgency, while more than half a million civilians have crossed borders into Chad, Cameron and Niger and, as a result, become refugees (International Organization for Migration, 2015; United Nations High Commission for Refugees, 2015).

The International Organization for Migration (IOM) collaborates with the National Emergency Management Agency (NEMA) in the Displacement Tracking Matrix (DTM) programme, with the objective of providing accurate and up-to-date information regarding the movements of IDPs in Nigeria for the purpose of providing relief. The DTM programme is funded by the United States Agency for International Development (USAID) and the European Commission's Humanitarian Aid and Civil Protection department (ECHO). The aim of the DTM programme is to support the Nigerian Red Cross Society (NRCS) and States Emergency Management Agency (SEMA), and other partners in the field, to establish a comprehensive system to collect and disseminate data on IDPs. The data collected through the DTM aims at establishing a comprehensive profile of the IDPs in Nigeria, and to inform the humanitarian community accordingly.

According to the International Organization for Migration (2015): the population of IDPs is composed of 52 per cent female and 48 per cent male; over 57 per cent of the IDP population are children, 28 per cent of whom are under five years old, while over 94 per cent of IDPs were displaced as a direct result of the insurgency and associated violence. A significant proportion of the current IDP population (65 per cent) has been displaced since 2014 (International Organization for Migration, 2015).

The IDPs come mainly from the north-eastern Nigerian states of Borno (68 per cent), Adamawa (15 per cent) and Yobe (11 per cent) (International Organization for Migration, 2015). More positively, 90 per cent of IDPs are being hosted informally within extended families and by friends, relatives and well-wishers, while 10.1 per cent live in formal IDP camps or camp-like sites within the boundaries of Nigeria (International Organization for Migration, 2015). The UN High Commission for Refugees (UNHCR) (2015) estimated the number of Nigerian refugees who fled outside Nigerian borders in Cameron and Chad at 90,921. Neighbouring Niger Republic is hosting more than 100,000 other Nigerian refugees who have fled Boko Haram (Daily News, 2015).

As of April 2015, 147,285 individuals have been estimated to be in three categories of IDP sites comprising: 1) camps made of open-air settlements, usually made up of tents, where IDPs find accommodation; 2) collective centres, made up of various pre-existing buildings and structures, routinely utilized for collective and communal settlements of the displaced population; and 3) transitional centres, which provide short term/temporary accommodation for the displaced population. Of the IDP population in the three categories, 61.7 per cent of IDP sites are female while 38.3 per cent are male; 54.3 per cent of the total number of individuals residing in sites are children under 18 years old, while children under five years old constitute 28 per cent of the total number of individuals (International Organization for Migration, 2015).

Relief challenges: shortage of funds, nature of affected demographics and absorption

The army of displaced Nigerians has been left mostly to fend for itself to find shelter, food and water. The Nigerian Government has been limited in its response, and members of the international community such as the European Union (EU) have only made pledges of funds. With the recent exception of the Red Cross/Red Crescent, no major international charities have mounted special appeal campaigns or solicited funds earmarked for those harmed by the insurgency. A limited amount of aid is being provided by the kin of IDPs affected, and by Nigerian non-government organizations (NGOs) such as the Nigerian Red Cross and Red Crescent Society. Likewise, some aid is being provided to refugees outside Nigerian borders by the UNHCR as well as international NGOs such as Médecins sans Frontières (BHVR, 2015).

The main issue is that many of the displaced persons and refugees are vulnerable women and children, and not all are receiving aid. The US Agency for International Development (2015) identified over 190,000 displaced households, accounting for nearly 1.5 million people, in northern Nigeria's

Adamawa, Bauchi, Borno, Gombe, Taraba and Yobe states. An estimated 90 per cent of these IDPs are not receiving any formal relief assistance because they are wandering, and not residing in IDP camps. The US Agency for International Development (2015) reports that some other IDPs are attempting to integrate into host communities. This has further complicated issues of access as Nigeria's response agency, the Nigerian Emergency Management Agency (NEMA), finds it more challenging to find people who have integrated into host communities in order to provide assistance to them.

Furthermore, the mass movement of IDPs has often aggravated social tensions in north-eastern Nigeria and in foreign host communities in countries such as Chad, Niger and Cameroon (IPI Global Observatory, 2015). Clashes between displaced communities and their hosts have often occurred when displaced people are viewed as a drain on limited resources, or as unfairly benefitting from charity or government support (IPI Global Observatory, 2015).

Also, existing IDP sites across Nigeria's north-east have limited facilities, a shortage of supplies and are overcrowded. The increasing influx of displaced people worsens an already fragile situation, and the lack of sanitation poses a major public health challenge as regards the threat of cholera, measles and other diseases. Many IDPs and refugees are also traumatized by the violence, and are afraid to return, and many whose homes have been destroyed by conflict have nowhere to go back to. Hence, there is a need for trauma and psychological counselling services in addition to basic relief.

The immediate response task

Caring for those who have been displaced by Boko Haram is challenging, and immediate humanitarian assistance should be complemented by longer-term integration and livelihood-generating programmes. Unfortunately, there appears to be less international will to provide support for these humanitarian efforts, other than to lend a military hand to the Nigerian authorities. It appears that the overarching attitude of those who should be responsible for caring for these IDPs and refugees is that the IDP and refugee condition is only 'temporary' pending the complete military defeat of Boko Haram, a belief shared by many of the displaced themselves. However, such a comprehensive defeat of Boko Haram is yet to manifest despite seven years of fighting. Likewise, it seems that the attitude of the Nigerian government led by the immediate past president Dr Goodluck

Jonathan, and newly elected government's president, Mohammadu Buhari, is that the Boko Haram crisis is temporary, and both presidents have consistently assured Nigerians and the world that terrorism and insurgency will be brought under control 'soon'.

The mindset of completely defeating Boko Haram before addressing the problem of disaster relief is further compounded by the absence of a humanitarian law and policy framework in Nigeria that clearly defines the roles and responsibilities of humanitarian agencies. Such a situation hampers the co-ordination of various humanitarian and relief efforts. The lack of systematic data collection in Nigeria by Nigerian agencies poses significant challenges to the estimation of the exact number of displaced people in need (Global IDP Project, 2014).

The International Displacement Monitoring Centre reports that 90 per cent of the IDPs that the organization works with around the world have been displaced for 10 years or more. This means that longer-term (re)integration and rehabilitation strategies are necessary. However, there is no evidence of a longer-term recovery plan for IDPs and refugees. Failing to promote school enrolment or educational assistance to displaced refugee children from Nigeria may produce a lost generation of children who may not be able to get back into education as their displacement becomes prolonged; failing to promote employment and productive engagement for adult refugees will similarly render these persons unable to reintegrate into communities, making such communities even more vulnerable to the next round of crises.

Logistical distribution challenges: scale and dispersion

It is difficult and expensive to support refugees who are dispersed over a large geographical area the size of Belgium (BHVR, 2015). It is also difficult to provide relief to those scattered, and in devastated homes and communities, in order to begin the process of rebuilding their lives and communities. Similarly, major IDP camps are scattered over an enormous geographical area and there is limited access to rural 'peripheral' areas by the various humanitarian agencies, due to volatility. It is less challenging, however, to provide the necessities of life to the same number of refugees if they are congregated in a few concentrations of refugee camps, camps for IDPs or living with kin in major urban centres.

Security challenges to relief supply chains

Regardless of the supply of relief to IDPs and associated supply chains, pro-vision of relief and social protection face severe security challenges, poor funding and poor co-ordination at the federal and state government levels. Security of the relief supply chains and security of relief workers in undertaking field relief activities, as well as the last-mile distribution of relief goods is a most important challenge and barrier to effective distribution of relief. No social protection intervention can reach IDPs, let alone be effective when there is pervading news of insecurity such as beheadings, bomb explosions, improvised explosive devices (IEDs), suicide bombings and IED booby traps, risk of land mines, truck bombings and Boko Haram firearm attacks. The Nigerian Government as well as several other agencies and organizations appear to be having a very difficult time confronting persistent security issues that adversely impact upon the supply chain logistics of providing relief to IDPs within Nigeria. In September 2015, a bomb blast rocked an IDP camp in Yola (north-eastern Nigeria), Maikohi Camp – one of Nigeria's largest IDP camps – leaving at least seven people dead and 20 injured (Premium Times, 2015). The aim of the bombing was to scare off humanitarian organizations, their relief workers and others who want to provide relief to IDPs. Within the period November 2015 to February 2016, over 70 people, including IDPs, were killed within supposedly safe IDP camps in north-eastern Nigeria by Boko Haram female suicide bombers (Aljazeera Online, 2016).

The insecurity and total breakdown of authority resulting from the Boko Haram violence requires a relief response that goes beyond the capacity of any single agency and/or the ongoing UNHCR country programme (IASC). The insecurity is characterized by extensive violence and loss of life; dis-placements of populations – the largest in Africa, and one of the largest in the world. Other features include: widespread damage to housing, infrastructure, societies and economies; the need for large-scale, multifaceted humanitarian relief assistance; the hindrance, or prevention of humanitarian relief assist-ance by government and military constraints such as large areas containing IDPs being declared 'do not go' areas of ongoing military operations which poses significant security risks for humanitarian relief workers. As earlier indicated, Boko Haram violence, and associated insecurity, often involves warlike encounters with the Nigerian Army, and such outbreaks of war triggers displacements that pose large-scale health/medical problems to the population, and further exacerbate the problem of security.

As a result, access by relief responders is constrained due to continu-ing insecurity and damaged infrastructure. Much of Borno and parts of

Adamawa and Yobe states of Nigeria cannot be reached by humanitarian actors as a result of security and other challenges that disrupt relief supply chains. This is despite the 2015 establishment of a joint border patrol command with Chad, Niger and Cameroon to address the increasing security challenges attributed to the insurgency (Emmanuela, 2015). Continuing unmet needs include shelter, livelihood, protection, health, food, nutrition and education for school-age children.

Challenges of finding reliable persons and organizations, and inadequate media coverage

A continuing problem for international non-profits and charities dispensing relief in the north-eastern part of Nigeria is the identification and recruitment of local persons, groups and organizations with integrity, who are capable of reliably receiving and managing relief-related assistance with a high level of probity and accountability. Many potential donors and their financial institutions are discouraged by Nigeria's reputation for corruption and scams. Furthermore, global news coverage of the plight of those impacted by Boko Haram has been sparse, while media focus has tended to focus on the military and human rights failures of, until recently, one of Africa's most respected and most professional armies. As a result of such media coverage, many potential donors are ignorant of the ways of life in north-eastern Nigeria and the constraints of the environment; neither are they aware of the enormity of killings, kidnappings and village burnings.

Existing relief operations and supply chains

Humanitarian organizations currently providing relief may be categorized into five groups: 1) multilateral UN organizations (eg UNHCR); 2) Nigerian government agencies responsible to two of the three tiers of Nigerian government, ie the federal government of Nigeria (eg National Emergency Management Agency [NEMA]) and the state governments responsible for each of the affected states (eg the State Emergency Management Agency for each state); 3) large international humanitarian organizations (eg International Rescue Committee, Médecins sans Frontières (MSF) and International Red Cross/Red Crescent); 4) Nigerian humanitarian NGOs and charities (eg Nigerian Red Cross); and 5) a range of private organizations and donors, international and Nigerian, such as the American University of Nigeria in Yola, Adamawa Peace Initiative and Kinjir Foundation:

- The UNHCR provides protection and assistance for Nigerian refugees (not IDPs) fleeing Boko Haram attacks in Cameroon, Chad and Niger. For example, there are more than 30,000 Nigerian refugees at Minawao camp in the northern region of Cameroon.

- The Nigerian Federal Government recently announced a three-pronged national emergency relief programme for the IDPs and others impacted by the activities of Boko Haram. The initiative involves an emergency relief window, a reconstruction and rehabilitation window and a safe-schools window, all of which are still in the infancy stage (Tade, 2015).

- The state governments of Borno, Yobe and Adamawa through their state emergency management agency (SEMA) set up committees that co-ordinate relief activities and supply chains at the campsites for IDPs (Tade, 2015). The SEMAs distribute relief materials from state government funds from time to time. There is also the Victim of Terrorism Committee of Borno State (VTC), which co-ordinates and consults with the governor of Borno State on those in need of special assistance for approval. This is not without its bottlenecks (Tade, 2015).

- Médecins sans Frontières (MSF) has been active in north-east Nigeria for several years, and operates in the Maiduguri area, the capital city of Borno State and epicentre of the crisis. MSF is also working in the refugee camps in the neighbouring countries of Cameroon, Chad and Niger.

- The International Rescue Committee (IRC) provides emergency support in refugee camps in Niger and IDP sites in Nigeria for those impacted by the activities of Boko Haram. IRC is currently supporting thousands of refugees fleeing ongoing violence in the north-east that has plagued the region. It is working with local primary health-care facilities to reduce malnutrition and improve water, sanitation and hygiene in conflict-affected areas for more than 300,000 people.

- The Nigerian Red Cross and Red Crescent Society, an affiliate of the International Red Cross and Red Crescent Society, provides first aid, evacuation of the injured, restoration of family links, economic assistance to widows and psycho-social support (Tade, 2015).

- The American University of Nigeria (AUN) in Yola, the capital city of the state of Adamawa, a state under emergency rule due to the Boko Haram insurgency. AUN is a private university with some focus on development. In 2012, AUN partnered with local Christian, Muslim and other community leaders and groups to form the Adamawa Peace Initiative (API). The AUN and API have been sourcing, organizing and distributing humanitarian aid to IDPs (BBC, 2015c).

- The Kinjir Foundation, Yola is a private foundation founded in 2005, and incorporated with the Nigerian Corporate Affairs Commission. The Kinjir Foundation formed a National Relief Committee that includes representatives of various nationalities from the north-eastern part of Nigeria. The group has been distributing relief assistance to IDPs for several years.

Framework for mitigating security challenges in relief operations and associated relief supply chains

This section outlines a framework of how humanitarian relief organizations can mitigate security challenges (Figure 9.6.1) in enacting and managing their relief operations and associated relief supply chains. The framework is drawn from the empirical details of the Boko Haram crisis, and it comprises three broad components: 1) seeking and obtaining community acceptance; 2) humanitarian–military co-operation and protection; 3) deterring would-be attackers.

Figure 9.6.1 Framework of how relief actors can mitigate security challenges

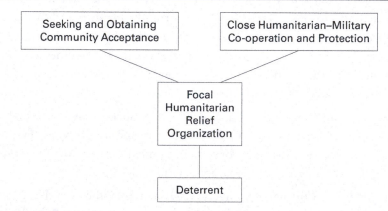

SOURCE: Richard Oloruntoba

Seeking and obtaining community acceptance

Humanitarian organizations seeking to provide relief need first to seek and obtain community support. This includes securing approval from the Nigerian Government and Nigerian military authorities before deploying. Securing community acceptance helps protect the relief supply chain by softening the threat of violence against it. Acceptance is understood to be when the community in which a humanitarian organization is working accepts and supports the presence of that humanitarian organization, and its relief supply chains and activities. Acceptance often translates to security. Some acceptance strategies may be to reach out to Boko Haram and seek consent for humanitarian relief activities if at all possible. Also, another strategy may be to ensure that the community in which IDPs are hosted has a stake in the relief operation and relief supply chain, as well as participating and benefitting actively from it. IDPs and host communities may be involved in the assessment and design of the relief supply chain and relief programme, and activities broadly communicated, and perceived as impartial – all of which must be accomplished in a culturally and politically sensitive manner. This will increase security of relief supply chain activities such as road transport, field warehousing, delivery and distribution.

Relief operations should reflect a willingness to invest the time and effort to involve the community in every facet of the humanitarian and relief project. In relief scenarios such as in the Boko Haram crisis, the pressure to rapidly start distributing relief is a hurdle that may limit the ability of humanitarian relief organizations to thoroughly involve the local community. It is crucial that a limited vision of the mission must not obscure this key element in the framework of how to mitigate security challenges in enacting and managing their relief operations and supply chains. Another hurdle, as in the case of Boko Haram, is that acceptance by beneficiary communities may seem to have been significantly overshadowed by the hostility and intransigence of Boko Haram, which as a result makes it necessary for humanitarian and relief organizations to build strong security protection and deterrence strategies, as discussed in the next section.

Humanitarian–military co-operation and protection

If acceptance cannot be obtained from one of the protagonists, strong protection and deterrence strategies need to be implemented. The Nigerian Government and Nigerian Army should be requested to provide more effective protection and security for relief operations in IDP camps and for associated relief supply chains. The Nigerian Government and the Nigerian Army should be persuaded to realize that Boko Haram, IDP and refugees are long-term issues that need to be addressed as such. Therefore, the government should change its seeming short-term mindset and provide effective security to relief workers, relief supply chains and IDP camps. Bombs should not be exploding in supposedly 'safe' IDP camps. Security forces need to be provided with clear mission statements, effective intelligence and robust rules of engagement. This will make humanitarian and relief operations more effective in complex emergencies. It will also make associated relief supply chains more resilient and robust, as well as afford a protected and secure relief supply chain.

Furthermore, to succeed the Nigerian military and humanitarian relief organizations may need to train together as field squads in order to know and trust each other better, and to ensure security and relief to IDPs without a compromise of agencies' autonomy and neutrality. The Nigerian Government may need to co-ordinate with the existing humanitarian architecture already in place in order to ensure continuity of relief supply chains. Violence caused by Boko Haram terrorists may be managed via a joint process that marries governmental decision makers, trained relief workers, tactical-level scientists and the military with self-sufficient and tailored operational-level task forces. An integrated education and training on relief and relief supply chains may be beneficial.

Furthermore, the quality of situational awareness and personal protective equipment deployed is an important component of this framework. Organizations providing relief must be aware of situational developments, perhaps, through their close liaison with government and security/military authorities. Such situational awareness includes an accurate understanding of risks, more insightful briefings and guidelines, as well as provision of personal protective equipment such as helmets and protective jackets, where appropriate. To more comprehensively understand the risks of Boko Haram attacks and the potential for prevention, a comprehensive and prospective approach to data collection, analysis and monitoring is required. Much stands to be learned from such databases as a repository of valuable planning and decision-making data.

Likewise, threat assessment and response should follow initial relief assessment, and be undertaken continuously through relief operations. Security threat assessments should include a range of inputs from the Regional Joint Military Command, Nigerian Government and Nigerian Army, the UNHCR and other NGOs, local government, community leaders and individuals in the affected community. What security threats to relief supply chains and relief operations are of the highest probability and greatest consequence? Once identified, relief organizations need to prioritize and customize resources to these threats accordingly.

Other strategies for mitigating security challenges in enacting and managing the relief supply chains in humanitarian–military co-operation and protection might include the following: humanitarian and relief organizations must implement strict but clear vehicle operations policies and strict discipline regarding vehicle/transport and warehousing operations, as well as enforce searches, curfews and no-go zones, where appropriate. For instance, in the case of Boko Haram, in IDP camps it is necessary to prevent bombings and use of other improvised explosive devices by Boko Haram. Furthermore, enhanced communications protocols, training and disciplined radio usage – as well as detailed security orientation for incoming staff, including personal security training – should be provided.

Deterrence

Humanitarian relief organizations may implement deterrent strategies to ensure the security of their relief supply chains and operations. Deterrence strategies are for keeping away a protagonist group that is a threat to relief supply chains as a result of their fear of retaliation if they carry out a violent act against the relief supply chain and the operations of a humanitarian organization. Often deterrence strategies can be based on relationships that have been built by large national, regional or international humanitarian organizations with powerful foreign governments. Elements of such strategies may comprise the deployment of diplomatic pressure from powerful foreign governments on protagonists that are threats to relief supply chains. Such diplomatic pressure may be deployed by humanitarian organizations to influence local actors and authorities, and actors who pose security threats or who are well placed to promote the security of humanitarian relief supply chains. Such a deterrent will depend on the quality of relationship with key embassies such as the United States, associated diplomats and the quality of the relationship between the humanitarian relief organization and the UN. In the case of the Boko Haram crisis, whoever has an influence on ISIS probably will be able to influence its Nigerian affiliate Boko Haram, since Boko Haram pledged allegiance to ISIS. This is a crucial component in order to mitigate security challenges in enacting and managing their relief supply chains.

Summary and conclusions

This chapter has provided a brief overview summary and trajectory of the evolution of violent political and religious conflict in Nigeria since the 1960s until the current Boko Haram crisis, which seems to have an international dimension to it. The chapter has also described the Boko Haram terror organization, the main protagonist of the current conflict, and resulting displacement of the most vulnerable segments of Nigerian society. An analysis and profile of the displaced IDPs and refugees, including their status and demographics, was also provided. The challenges and complexities of providing timely and appropriate assistance to the IDPs and refugees was discussed, while the immediate assistance tasks that are required to be undertaken are highlighted. The chapter concludes by outlining a framework of how humanitarian relief organizations can mitigate security challenges in designing and managing their relief operations and associated relief supply chains.

Key considerations for practitioners

- Provision of relief in emergencies and disasters such as the Boko Haram crisis require acceptance by the community and the protagonists to enact effective relief supply chains.
- Provision of relief in large, diverse, multi-ethnic countries differs significantly from small monolithic and homogeneous countries as a result of the need to negotiate multiple acceptances with various groups; the need to negotiate geographical challenges; and the unique, non-conventional nature of the violence.
- Provision of relief in geostrategic countries is more complex than in countries with minimal geopolitical forces at work.
- Displaced IDPs and refugees are often women and children, hence gender- and children-tailored assistance is required for these special groups.
- Close co-operation with host communities and other stakeholders such as the military is required to reduce security challenges to relief supply chains.

References

Abdullahi, S A (2015) Ethnicity and Ethnic Relations in Nigeria: The case of religious conflict in Kano, in *Regional and Ethnic Conflicts: Perspectives from the front lines*, eds J Carter, G Irani and V D Volkan, Routledge, Taylor & Francis Group, London and New York, p 292

Akresh, R, Bhalotra, S, Leone, M and Osili, U O (2012) War and stature: growing up during the Nigerian Civil War, *The American Economic Review*, 102 (3), pp 273–77

Al Arabiya (2014) [accessed 3 January 2015] Boko Haram Voices Support for ISIS, *Baghdadi Al Arabiya*, 13 July 2014 [Online] http://english.alarabiya.net/en/News/africa/2014/07/13/Boko-Haram-voices-support-for-ISIS-Baghdadi.html

Aljazeera Online (2016) [accessed 10 June 2016] Boko Haram: Nigerian Refugee Camp hit by Twin Suicide Bombings [Online] http://www.aljazeera.com/news/2016/02/suicide-bombers-hit-nigerian-displaced-persons-camp-160210184351280.html

Armstrong, R G (1964) *The Study of West African Languages*, University of Ibadan Press, Ibadan

Arnold, G (2004) *The Resources of the Third World*, Fitzroy Publishers, Dearborn, p. 123

BBC (2015a) [accessed 25 April 2015] Analysis: Islamic State Strengthens Ties with Boko Haram, *BBC News*, 24 April 2015 [Online] http://www.bbc.com/news/world-africa-32435614

BBC (2015b) [accessed 7 March 2015] Boko Haram Pledges Baya to the Islamic State, *BBC News*, 7 March 2015 [Online] http://www.bbc.com/news/world-africa-31784538

BBC (2015c) [accessed 3 September 2015] University Feeds, 270,000 People Taking Refuge from Boko Haram, *BBC News* [Online] http://www.bbc.com/news/business-31663910

BHVR (2015) [accessed 3 September 2015] Boko Haram Victims Relief (BHVR) (2015) [Online] http://www.bokoharamvictimsrelief.org/

Burkle Jr, F M (1999) Fortnightly review: lessons learnt and future expectations of complex emergencies, *British Medical Journal*, 319 (7207) p 422

Byman, D (2016) ISIS goes global: fight the Islamic State by targeting its affiliates, *Foreign Affairs*, 95, p 76

Celso, A N (2015) The Islamic State and Boko Haram: fifth wave jihadist terror groups, *Orbis*, 59 (2), pp 249–68

Daily News (2015) [accessed 12 August 2015] Niger Troops Deport 3,000 Nigerians Who Fled From Boko Haram [Online] http://www.nydailynews.com/news/world/niger-deports-3-000-nigerian-refugees-fled-boko-haram-article-1.2212514

Emmanuelar, I (2015) Insurgency and humanitarian crises in northern Nigeria: the case of Boko Haram, *African Journal of Political Science and International Relations*, 9 (7), pp 284–96

Global IDP Project (GIP) 9 May 2014 [accessed 10 December 2015] Training Workshop on the United Nations Guiding Principles on Internal Displacement, Borno, Nigeria 17–19 February 2003: Workshop Report [Online] http://www.ifrc.org/Docs/idrl/I266EN.pdf

Internal Displacement Monitoring Centre (2014) [accessed 12 August 2015] Nigeria: Multiple Displacement Crises Overshadowed by Boko Haram [Online] http://www.internal-displacement.org/sub-saharan- africa/nigeria/2014/nigeria-multiple-displacement-crises-overshadowed-by-boko-haram

International Organization for Migration (2015) Displacement Tracking Matrix Round III Report – April 2015

IPI Global Observatory (2015) [accessed 11 August 2015] Responses Fall Short as Violence Displaces More Nigerians, Written by H Matfess, 11 June [Online] http://theglobalobservatory.org/2015/06/minawao-nigeria-refugees-buhari/

Isichei, E (1987) The Maitatsine risings in Nigeria 1980–85: a revolt of the disinherited, *Journal of Religion in Africa*, **17** (3) pp 194–208

Jerome, A (2015) Lessons from Colombia for curtailing the Boko Haram insurgency in Nigeria, *Prism: A journal of the Center for Complex Operations*, **5** (2), p 94

Okeke-Uzodike, U and Onapajo, H (2015) The rage of insurgency: why Boko Haram may remain untamed, *African Renaissance*, ISSN: 1744-2532, **12** (2)

Premium Times (2015) [accessed 24 November 2015] 7 Killed in Yola IDP Camp Bomb Blast [Online] http://www.premiumtimesng.com/news/headlines/189822-7-killed-in-yola-idp-camp- bomb-blast.html

Salawu, B (2010) Ethno-religious conflicts in Nigeria: causal analysis and proposals for new management strategies, *European Journal of Social Sciences*, **13** (3), pp 345–53

Tade, O (2015) [accessed 3 September 2015] Boko Haram Victims and the Dilemma of Human Security [Online] http://www.thenigerianvoice.com/news/165646/1/boko-haram-victims-and-the-dilemma-of- human-securi.html

The Telegraph (2014) [accessed 1 September 2014] Al-Qaeda map: Isis, Boko Haram and other affiliates' strongholds across Africa and Asia, 12 June [Online] http://www.telegraph.co.uk/news/worldnews/al-qaeda/10893889/Al-Qaeda-map-Isis-Boko-Haram-and-other-affiliates-strongholds-across-Africa-and-Asia.html

United Nations High Commission for Refugees (2015) [accessed 12 August 2015] UNHCR Sub-Regional Operations Profile – West Africa [Online] http://www.unhcr.org/pages/49e484f76.html

United States Agency for International Development (USAID) (2015) [accessed Jan–May 2016] Displacement Tracking Matrix Round III Report – April [Online] https://nigeria.iom.int/sites/default/files/dtm/01_IOM%20DTM%20Nigeria_Round%20III%20Report_20150429.pdf

US Bureau of Counter Terrorism (2013) [accessed 7 September 2014] Country Reports on Terrorism 2013, *U.S. Department of State* [Online] http://www.state.gov/j/ct/rls/crt/2013/

Appendix

Figure 9.6.2 Map of Nigeria showing major cities

Measuring the supply chain performance of humanitarian organizations

9.7

The case of Thai Red Cross in Chiangmai

RUTH BANOMYONG

Centre for Logistics Research, Thammasat Business School,
Thammasat University, Thailand

PAITOON VARADEJSATITWONG

TU-Kuehne HUMLOG Team, Thammasat Business School,
Thammasat University, Thailand

Introduction

The issue of performance measurement has been widely researched in humanitarian logistics and supply chain management (Pujawan, Kurniati and Wessiani, 2009). However, it was observed that there is a lack of standard assessment toolkit to measure the supply chain performance of humanitarian organizations. The purpose of this chapter is therefore to propose a standard methodology to assess the supply chain performance of humanitarian organizations.

It is necessary to be able to assess humanitarian organizations' supply chain performance as it is a reflection of their capabilities when providing humanitarian aid. Even though each humanitarian disaster is different there is still a need to assess the initial supply chain response capability of humanitarian organizations involved in the response phase. Understanding current supply chain performance will allow assessed humanitarian organizations to improve on identified supply chain weaknesses, especially in terms of responses to humanitarian situations.

The proposed assessment methodology is known as the quick scan audit methodology (QSAM) and has mostly been used in a business context across countries (Childerhouse *et al*, 2011). In this chapter, the Chiangmai Red Cross station in Thailand was selected to illustrate how the assessment of a humanitarian organization could be made with QSAM and what the findings mean for the organization being assessed. It is hoped that this proposed assessment methodology could become a reference toolkit when assessing the supply chain performance of humanitarian organizations.

Quick scan audit methodology (QSAM)

QSAM is a diagnostic approach designed to perform the health check of a given supply chain (Naim *et al*, 2002). It has been specifically developed to enable logistics and supply chain researchers to obtain accurate performance and operational assessments while minimizing disturbance to the organization. In theory, QSAM could also be used in the assessment of humanitarian organizations and could prove a useful tool for humanitarian supply chain management.

Typically it takes four researchers one man-week each to fully audit the supply chain of a medium-sized organization, during which period around half of the time is spent on-site disrupting managers' time. In the case of humanitarian supply chains it is important not to disrupt the assessed humanitarian organization during an emergency response phase with data collection. QSAM should be used when assessing the initial preparedness capability of humanitarian organizations or after response has been delivered. It is important to note that QSAM is a team-based approach that includes 'players' from the host humanitarian organization so that both sides contribute considerably to the assessment programme.

In many ways QSAM is an overall framework that has been developed to allow researchers with a range of expertise to work together and build a consensus view of real-world supply chains. To this end, a battery of tools and checklists are used that ensure comparability and standardization. For instance, process mapping follows a standard approach to aid the transfer of best practice. Similarly, a database of good, bad and indifferent practice is augmented each time QSAM is conducted. Cross-referencing this archive helps to develop improvement opportunities for the current supply chain being audited. There are a range of quantitative and attitudinal questionnaires that facilitate cross-comparisons and triangulation of subjective data sources. A set of standard interview protocols and semi-structured questions for each managerial role within the supply chain is also utilized. To summarize, the key QSAM elements that will result in a successful supply chain audit are:

- A team of at least four researchers ensures investigator triangulation.

- The use of four data collection approaches – namely interviews, attitudinal questionnaires, process mapping and archival data – provides methodology triangulation.

- Direct involvement of practitioners during the data collection and analysis, coupled with the verification during a feedback presentation, greatly enhances the reliability of the audit.

- The buy-in obtained during the preliminary presentation, based around the targeted win-win situation of the identification of improvement opportunities, provides open access to research data and practitioner participation.

- The application of a refined, systematic and hence holistic methodology makes it feasible to conduct a comprehensive assessment of a complex phenomenon.

Figure 9.7.1 illustrates the scope of QSAM while Figure 9.7.2 describes the process involved when conducting QSAM. The scope of QSAM is based on the understand, document, simplify and optimize (UDSO) framework – and it should be understood that QSAM is not a miracle tool that can address all supply chain problems or even humanitarian supply chain problems.

It can be seen that QSAM primarily focuses on the first two stages: understand and document. Although any identified high-impact, quick-hit opportunities tend to be tackled early in the simplification stage in order to demonstrate in-house capability and an early return on the QSAM effort, nevertheless the ultimate aim of QSAM is to identify the types of soundly underpinned and customized supply chain recommendations that tend to require persistent implementation effort and longer-term organization commitment.

Figure 9.7.1 Scope of QSAM in the UDSO model

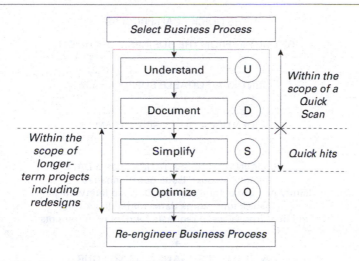

SOURCE: Childerhouse, Disney and Naim (1999)

QSAM team members frequently take on a steering group role for such endeavours. By closing the gap between researcher and subject, QSAM yields consistent results and provides close, customized supply chain integration support to practising supply chain professionals. In essence, it helps managers to identify the root cause of operational issues (Tillman *et al*, 2008a). The QSAM is akin to being diagnosed initially by a generalist medical doctor, and if specific symptoms require expert advice then referrals can be made to the most appropriate specialist.

Another core objective of QSAM is the measurement of uncertainty as a key performance metric. This is based on assessing the uncertainty of four discrete points linking up with system interfaces. Hence the sources of uncertainty are: 1) our process; 2) supply side; 3) demand side; 4) control side. By coding these uncertainties on a four-point Likert scale by reference to specific observed phenomena, every supply chain in a QSAM may be allocated an uncertainty score. It has already been shown elsewhere (Childerhouse, Disney and Towill, 2004) that such scores are reliable indicators of bottom-line performance in real-world scenarios.

The concept of uncertainty is prevalent in humanitarian supply chain management. Many authors have identified the need to minimize and remove uncertainties in order to increase control and co-ordination, and improve decision-making effectiveness. Supply chain uncertainty has been classified into four general types in order that root causes and methods for minimization can be developed, namely process uncertainties, supply uncertainties, demand

Figure 9.7.2 The quick scan audit methodology (QSAM) process

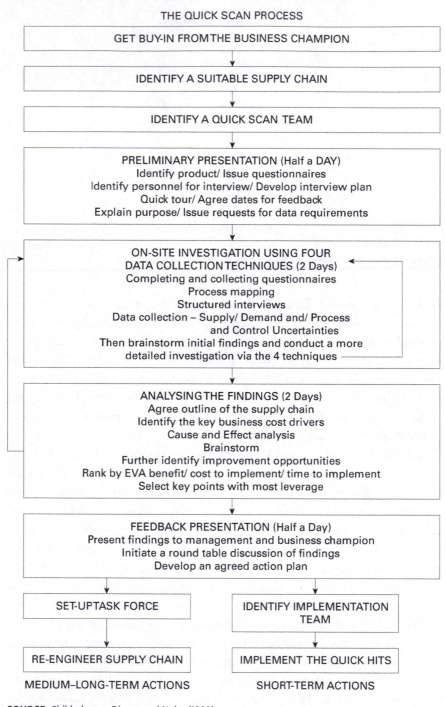

THE QUICK SCAN PROCESS

GET BUY-IN FROM THE BUSINESS CHAMPION

IDENTIFY A SUITABLE SUPPLY CHAIN

IDENTIFY A QUICK SCAN TEAM

PRELIMINARY PRESENTATION (Half a DAY)
Identify product/ Issue questionnaires
Identify personnel for interview/ Develop interview plan
Quick tour/ Agree dates for feedback
Explain purpose/ Issue requests for data requirements

ON-SITE INVESTIGATION USING FOUR
DATA COLLECTION TECHNIQUES (2 Days)
Completing and collecting questionnaires
Process mapping
Structured interviews
Data collection – Supply/ Demand and/ Process
and Control Uncertainties
Then brainstorm initial findings and conduct a more
detailed investigation via the 4 techniques

ANALYSING THE FINDINGS (2 Days)
Agree outline of the supply chain
Identify the key business cost drivers
Cause and Effect analysis
Brainstorm
Further identify improvement opportunities
Rank by EVA benefit/ cost to implement/ time to implement
Select key points with most leverage

FEEDBACK PRESENTATION (Half a Day)
Present findings to management and business champion
Initiate a round table discussion of findings
Develop an agreed action plan

SET-UP TASK FORCE

IDENTIFY IMPLEMENTATION
TEAM

RE-ENGINEER SUPPLY CHAIN

IMPLEMENT THE QUICK HITS

MEDIUM–LONG-TERM ACTIONS

SHORT-TERM ACTIONS

SOURCE: Childerhouse, Disney and Naim (1999)

uncertainties and control uncertainties, in what Mason-Jones and Towill (1997) termed the 'uncertainty circle':

- *Supply uncertainty* results from an inability of an organization to order raw material efficiently and can be evaluated by looking at supplier delivery performance, time series of orders placed, call-offs, deliveries from customers, lead times, supplier quality reports and raw material stock-time series. This is an important aspect that affects humanitarian supply chain performance.

- *Demand uncertainty* is associated with a specific customer in relation to schedule variability and can be visualized as the difference between the end-customer demand and real orders placed by your customer, and is also an indication of how well you meet your customer requirements. Developing a time series of customer orders, call-offs, deliveries and forecasts identifies this uncertainty. This is probably the most challenging aspect of humanitarian supply chain, as demand is something that is very difficult or almost impossible to predict in the case of a natural disaster. The customers are the affected populations and their needs will differ depending on the type of humanitarian situation.

- *Process uncertainty* affects an organization's ability to meet service or delivery targets. Understanding yield ratios and lead-time estimates in the operations of each business process identifies this uncertainty. Also, if the value stream is competing against others for resources, then the interaction between these value streams must be identified. Processes in humanitarian organizations needs to be standardized for optimal response.

- *Control uncertainty* affects an organization's ability to manage its activities and to transform humanitarian aid requests into production, delivery targets and supplier material requests; it can be investigated via the time series of humanitarian aid requirements and supplier requests to deliver. Additionally, a time series of service targets is required, as well as a thorough understanding of the decisions or control systems that are used to transfer the aid requirements into service targets and supplier raw material requests.

Figure 9.7.3 provides a conceptual illustration of the 'uncertainty circle' and its relationship with supply chain uncertainty.

Each of these uncertainties creates a drag on operational performance, and supply chain professionals often are so busy dealing with the fallout that they do not have time to attack the root causes of the problem (Tillman *et al*, 2008b). If managers could just understand which of the four areas was causing the greatest uncertainty, they could prioritize resources when embarking on a supply chain improvement programme. In the humanitarian

Figure 9.7.3 The 'uncertainty circle'

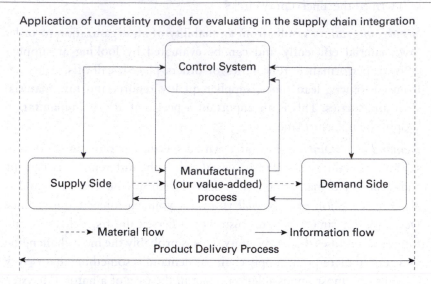

SOURCE: Mason-Jones and Towill (1997)

context, the challenges in managing an efficient and effective supply chain requires a thorough and holistic understanding of one's own supply chain capability and uncertainties.

The unit of analysis for QSAM is a value stream, which was popularized by Womack and Jones (1996). In many respects 'supply chain' and 'value stream' are synonymous; a practical interpretation is that a supply chain consists of a bundle of value streams. During a typical QSAM, material and information flows are process mapped; key managers are interviewed; company archive information is evaluated; and attitudinal questionnaires are completed concerning the interfaces of each value stream. The QSAM adopts the most common supply chain perspective: that of a focal organization and its integration into the wider supply chain.

CASE STUDY   Thai Red Cross Chiangmai Office

A QSAM was conducted at the Thai Red Cross Chiangmai office to test whether the audit tool was able to assess the supply chain performance of this particular humanitarian organization station in north Thailand. The scope of the supply chain reflects a basic or direct supply chain with three levels: the disaster victims, the Thai Red Cross and the suppliers. Figure 9.7.4 describes the scope of the supply chain under study.

Figure 9.7.4 Thai Red Cross supply chain scope

In order to refine the unit of analysis, the case study was developed to reflect the information and physical flow that occurs within the Thai Red Cross supply chain. Figure 9.7.5 describes the flows moving within the supply chain. The information flow starts from the request for aid by the victims, while the physical flow in the supply chain under study starts from the suppliers. It must not be forgotten that the humanitarian information flow also has to inform the local Red Cross association and the director of the relief and community health bureau for the aid approval.

Figure 9.7.5 Information and physical flow in Thai Red Cross supply chain

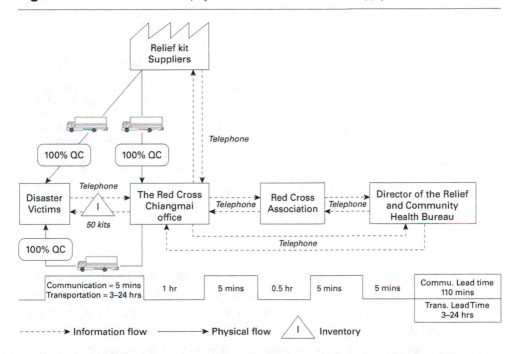

An input/output diagram can be helpful to view how information and physical flow within the organization flows from function to function. It was found that there are eight related functions within this humanitarian supply chain: disaster victims, the

Thai Red Cross Chiangmai office, the local Red Cross Association, response team, nurses, drivers, supplier and the director of the relief and community health bureau – as shown in Figure 9.7.6. This shows that the Thai Red Cross Chiangmai office is the focal point for either information or physical flow.

Figure 9.7.6 Input and output analysis of the Thai Red Cross

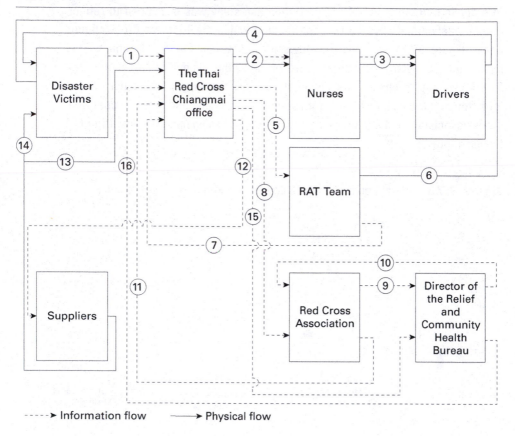

--------▶ Information flow   ──────▶ Physical flow

A value stream analysis was further conducted to identify activities in the supply chain processes that were either value added or non-value added, as per the lean paradigm. This value stream analysis was done on a Thai Red Cross supply chain. Table 9.7.1 describes the value stream from the disaster victims to the Thai Red Cross to the relief kit suppliers. Value-added activities only represent 17 per cent of all activities and 12 per cent of total time related to the transportation and distribution of relief kits to the victims.

Table 9.7.1 Value stream analysis on Thai Red Cross supply chain

	Activity	Time (minutes)
Value added (VA)	17%	12%
Non-value added (NVA)	44%	3%
Non-valued added but necessary (NNVA)	39%	85%
Total	100%	100%

The number of non-value added (NVA) and non-value added but necessary (NNVA) has a higher portion than the value added (VA) activities. That is for both numbers of activities and time consumption, which accounts for more than 80 per cent. The NVA activities relates to quantity and quality check and approval process, while the NNVA activities relates to the relief kits preparation from both suppliers and the staff at the Thai Red Cross office. The most common NVA and NNVA activities relate to the waiting time for approval, transportation and relief kits preparation, and if the Thai Red Cross is able to reduce the overall waiting time this could help reduce not only its response time but also increase the ratio of value-added activities in the relief process.

The capability to reduce or eliminate non-value-added activities in humanitarian supply chains is not sufficient. It is important for humanitarian supply chains when managed to be the subject of minimum uncertainty. The rationale behind such a statement is derived from Tillman *et al* (2008b), as low levels of uncertainty have shown to correlate directly with best-in-class practice in which supply chains are highly integrated. Humanitarian supply chains need to be integrated in order to improve relief responsiveness.

The Thai Red Cross supply chain 'uncertainty' cycle highlighted that its process uncertainty impacted the supply chain under study. In many instances, there was a lack of procedures for collaboration between the Thai Red Cross and 13 other local agencies. In order to increase collaboration it is necessary to enhance the quality and accountability of humanitarian programmes by providing stakeholders with thorough knowledge of the humanitarian sector and issues at stake. Collaboration can be an organization's source of competitive advantage because it does not occur naturally – far from it. Indeed, several barriers impede collaboration within complex multi-unit organizations, as each humanitarian organization will have different objectives and purposes. In order to overcome those barriers, organizations will have to develop distinct organizing capabilities that cannot be easily imitated. Figure 9.7.7 summarizes the supply chain uncertainty circle in the Thai Red Cross supply chain under study.

Figure 9.7.7 Thai Red Cross uncertainty circle

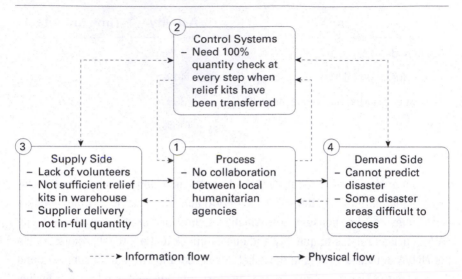

---- Information flow   → Physical flow

Control uncertainty was ranked the second-highest uncertainty to impact the Thai Red Cross supply chain, followed by supply and demand uncertainty. However, it is interesting to note that the uncertainty that impacts the Thai Red Cross supply chain the most is in fact internal rather than external uncertainty.

Based on QSAM, a number of questionnaires are then used to help reflect challenges in the management of the Thai Red Cross supply chain under study. The first three questionnaires look into the organization structure and lean indicators of the humanitarian organization. They explore the perception of the humanitarian organization related to continuous improvement and decision-making capability. The results show that the internal structure within the organization provides a high level of decision making to each individual unit when dealing with humanitarian situations. The Thai Red Cross also encourages continuous improvements. The result is displayed in Figure 9.7.8.

Figure 9.7.9 presents the perceptions of performance in terms of cost, quality, service level and lead times within its own area of responsibility, internal customers and internal suppliers. It is not surprising that the head of the local Red Cross office will evaluate their own performance better than that of their staff. The staff evaluated their own performance lower than their chief. This does make sense as the chief is the only one who can make a decision, while the staff must ask and get the approval from the chief before performing any actions. It is also interesting to note that the drivers evaluated their performance lower than the chief and the nurses, which may be because transporting the relief kits to the disaster area is, in their perception, a supporting activity. The results are not surprising if seen within the context of Thai culture, where the person in charge has strong authority and is less likely to be challenged due to the hierarchical nature of the society.

Figure 9.7.8 Organization structure and lean indicators

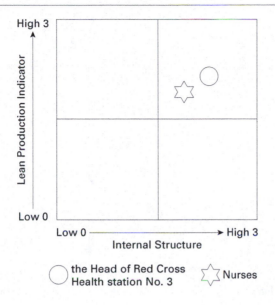

the Head of Red Cross Health station No. 3   Nurses

Figure 9.7.9 Attitudes towards control procedures

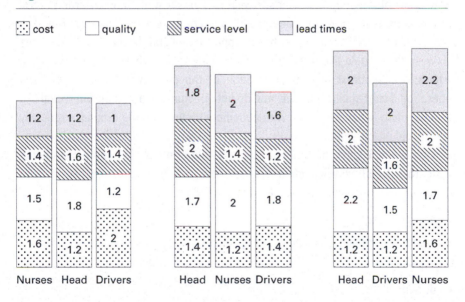

The next issue to consider is the attitudes towards control procedures in the organization. If there is a low score then that means there is a strong positive attitude towards control procedures, while if the scores are relatively high, the attitude is generally negative. Figure 9.7.10 shows that the head of the local

Figure 9.7.10 Attitudes towards control procedures

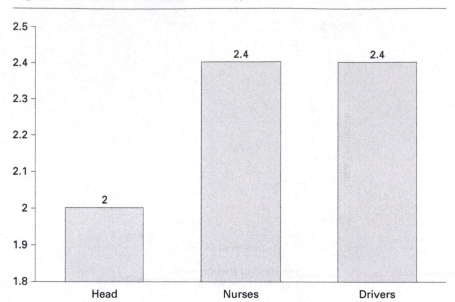

Red Cross office under study has a relatively positive attitude towards control procedures, as the processes developed by the Red Cross head office in Bangkok are sufficiently clear and robust but the operational staff have a less favourable view as they would like to have more flexibility when providing relief services, which is in contrast to their perception of the performance dimension. The operational staff accept authority and do not question the protocols but would like to have more flexibility to deal with specific situations on the ground, especially in terms of procurement issues.

Last but not least, humanitarian supply chain integration key performance indicators (KPIs) were identified to reflect the level of external integration with suppliers and customers. These KPIs are related to:

- contract length;
- joint research and development programme;
- trust;
- dependence;
- commitment;
- communication;
- information sharing;
- cost transparency.

Figure 9.7.11 reflects the level of relationship between the Thai Red Cross Office with suppliers and victims. There is no contract between supply chain members, while it seems that the Thai Red Cross is more integrated with its victims than its suppliers, which is not surprising. This is reflected in Figure 9.7.11 in the level of joint research and development, commitment and communication. This means that the collaboration effort is much stronger with victims than with suppliers.

Figure 9.7.11 Integration with suppliers and victims

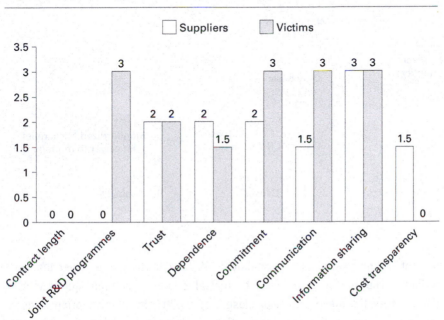

The last analytical technique used is the causal loop diagram described in Figure 9.7.12. The main problem is the long response lead time caused by both internal and external uncertainty, as discussed above. This problem has four main root causes as follows:

- no collaboration among local humanitarian agencies;
- financial hierarchical approval system;
- suppliers cannot always deliver in-full quantity;
- victims' requirements are varied.

The main symptom of this humanitarian supply chain is the long lead time to respond to a humanitarian situation. It is important to segregate the symptoms from the root causes. In order to find the root causes it is often useful to ask 'why'

Figure 9.7.12 Causes and effects in the Thai Red Cross supply chain

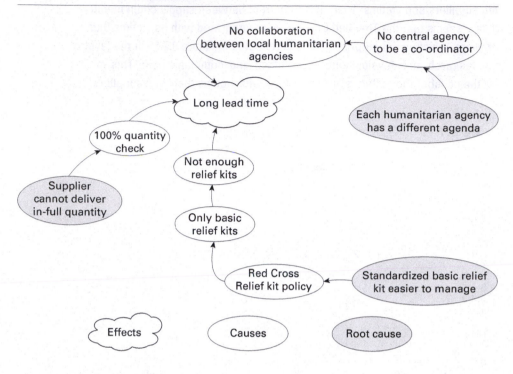

at least five times. This is a commonly used heuristic to help uncover the real problems. The advantage of using the causal loop diagram technique is that it also enables the identification of close loops within the humanitarian system under study. The identification of these close loops is critical and needs to be dealt with as a priority, as their impact is to self-reinforce the observed symptoms. In this particular case the lack of collaboration framework between agencies is a key root cause.

Case study summary

Based on the obtained results, as presented here, the team that audited the humanitarian supply chain was able to provide a number of short-term and medium to long-term suggested improvements for the Thai Red Cross Chiangmai office to implement. In the short term, the focus should be on providing in-house workshops on humanitarian logistics and supply chain as well as to educate other related local agencies on how to work as key humanitarian supply chain members. In the medium to long-term improvement actions, the focus should be on developing a collaboration framework with existing local relief agencies.

References

Childerhouse, P, Deakins, E, Böhme, T, Towill, D R, Disney, S M and Banomyong, R (2011) Supply chain integration: an international comparison of maturity, *Asia Pacific Journal of Marketing & Logistics*, **23** (4), pp 531–52

Childerhouse, P, Disney, S M and Naim, M M (1999) A Quick Scan Method for Supply Chain Diagnostics, Proceedings of the 4th International Symposium on Logistics, Florence, July, pp 755–60

Childerhouse, P, Disney, S M and Towill D R (2004) Tailored toolkit to enable seamless supply chains, *International Journal of Production Research*, **42** (17), pp 3627–46

Mason-Jones, R and Towill, D R (1997) Information enrichment: designing the supply chain for competitive advantage, *Supply Chain Management: An international journal*, **2** (4), pp 137–48

Naim, M M, Childerhouse, P, Disney, S M and Towill, D R (2002) A supply chain diagnostic methodology: determining the vector of change, *Computers and Industrial Engineering*, **43**, pp 135–57

Pujawan, I, Kurniati, N and Wessiani, N (2009) Supply chain management for disaster relief operations: principles and case studies, *International Journal of Logistics Systems and Management*, **5** (6), pp 679–92

Tillman, B, Childerhouse, P, Deakins, E, Potter, A and Towill, D (2008a) Supply chain diagnosis, *Operations Management*, **2**, pp 12–17

Tillman, B, Childerhouse, P, Deakins, E, Potter, A and Towill, D R (2008b) Why diagnosis supply chain uncertainty?, *Operations Management*, **3**, pp 19–23

Womack, J P and Jones, D T (1996) *Lean Logistics*, Simon and Schuster, New York

INDEX

Note: The index is filed in alphabetical, word-by-word order. Within main headings, numbers are filed as spelt out in full. Acronyms are filed as presented. Page locators in *italics* denote information contained within a Figure or Table.

Wake Tech Community College Libraries
RTP Campus
10908 Chapel Hill Road
Morrisville, NC 27560

DATE DUE

GAYLORD		PRINTED IN U.S.A.

CPSIA information can be obtained
at www.ICGtesting.com
Printed in the USA
LVOW13s2009070518

576285LV00022B/247/P

9 780749 474683